SMALL PLACES, LARGE ISSUES

Anthropology, Culture and Society

Series Editors:
Professor Vered Amit, Concordia University
and
Dr Jon P. Mitchell, University of Sussex

Published titles include:

SMALL PLACES, LARGE ISSUES

An Introduction to
Social and Cultural Anthropology

THIRD EDITION

THOMAS HYLLAND ERIKSEN

PlutoPress
www.plutobooks.com

First published 1995.
This edition published 2010 by Pluto Press
345 Archway Road, London N6 5AA and
175 Fifth Avenue, New York, NY 10010

www.plutobooks.com

Distributed in the United States of America exclusively by
Palgrave Macmillan, a division of St. Martin's Press LLC,
175 Fifth Avenue, New York, NY 10010

British Library Cataloguing in Publication Data
A catalogue record for this book is available from the British Library

ISBN   978 0 7453 3050 1   Hardback
ISBN   978 0 7453 3049 5   Paperback

Library of Congress Cataloging in Publication Data applied for

This book is printed on paper suitable for recycling and made from fully managed
and sustained forest sources. Logging, pulping and manufacturing processes are
expected to conform to the environmental standards of the country of origin.

10   9   8   7   6   5   4   3   2   1

Designed and produced for Pluto Press by
Chase Publishing Services Ltd, 33 Livonia Road, Sidmouth, EX10 9JB, England
Typeset from disk by Stanford DTP Services, Northampton, England
Printed and bound in the European Union by
CPI Antony Rowe, Chippenham and Eastbourne

CONTENTS

SERIES PREFACE

Anthropology is a discipline based upon in-depth ethnographic works that deal with wider theoretical issues in the context of particular, local conditions – to paraphrase an important volume from the series: *large issues* explored in *small places*. The series has a particular mission: to publish work that moves away from old-style descriptive ethnography – that is strongly area-studies oriented – and offer genuine theoretical arguments that are of interest to a much wider readership but which are nevertheless located and grounded in solid ethnographic research. If anthropology is to argue itself a place in the contemporary intellectual world then it must surely be through such research.

We start from the question: 'What can this ethnographic material tell us about the bigger theoretical issues that concern the social sciences?', rather than 'What can these theoretical ideas tell us about the ethnographic context?' Put this way round, such work becomes *about* large issues, *set in* a (relatively) small place, rather than detailed description of a small place for its own sake. As Clifford Geertz once said: 'anthropologists don't study villages; they study *in* villages'.

By place we mean not only geographical locale, but also other types of 'place' – within political, economic, religious or other social systems. We therefore publish work based on ethnography within political and religious movements, occupational or class groups, youth, development agencies, nationalists; but also work that is more thematically based – on kinship, landscape, the state, violence, corruption, the self. The series publishes four kinds of volume – ethnographic monographs; comparative texts; edited collections; and shorter, polemic essays.

We publish work from all traditions of anthropology, and all parts of the world, which combines theoretical debate with empirical evidence to demonstrate anthropology's unique position in contemporary scholarship and the contemporary world.

Professor Vered Amit
Dr Jon P. Mitchell

PREFACE TO THE THIRD EDITION

This book, now in its third, revised and updated edition, is a rather conventional introduction to social and cultural anthropology. As the chapter titles indicate, the book does not represent an attempt to 'reinvent' or revolutionise the subject, but simply, and in a straightforward way, introduces the main tools of the craft, the theoretical discussions, the subject-areas and some of the main empirical fields studied by anthropologists. By 'conventional', incidentally, I do not necessarily mean 'boring'. (Innovation is not always a good thing. Who wants to go to an innovative dentist? Or to fly with an innovative and creative pilot?)

Today, anthropology is a global discipline, but it is unevenly distributed across the globe. English is the dominant language of anthropological discourse, indeed more so today than before, but important research is also being carried out in other languages, from Russian and Japanese to French and Spanish. It is beyond my abilities to do justice to all these national traditions of anthropology, but I have made some feeble attempts. It remains a fact, though, that this book is written from a vantage-point in Anglophone anthropology. For many years, it was common to distinguish between a British 'social' and an American 'cultural' anthropology. Today, this boundary is blurred, and although the distinction is sometimes highlighted in the text, the book is deliberately subtitled with 'social and cultural anthropology' in a bid to overcome an unproductive boundary.

The most controversial aspect of this book may be the prominence given to 'classic' anthropological research in several of the chapters. In my view, it is not only a great advantage to be familiar with the classic studies in order to understand later trends and debates, but I also remain convinced that a sound grasp of classic modern (mid-twentieth-century) anthropology is essential for doing good research in the twenty-first century. Since many students no longer read classic monographs and articles, the capsule reviews provided here may also give an understanding of the context of contemporary research – its intellectual origins and theoretical debates on which it elaborates. I do not want to give the impression that contemporary anthropologists are dwarfs standing on the shoulders of giants, but they do stand on the shoulders of anthropologists of considerable achievement, and their work needs to be known, even if superficially, in order to understand properly what anthropological researchers are doing now. Some of these people were actually quite impressive.

The general development of this book, both at the theoretical and at the empirical level, moves from simple to increasingly complex models and sociocultural environments – from the social person to the global ecumene. The book is intended as a companion volume to ethnographic monographs, which remain an indispensable part of an anthropologist's training notwithstanding the summaries a textbook is capable of providing.

This book introduces both the subject-matter of social anthropology and an anthropological way of thinking. It is my conviction that the comparative study of society and culture is a fundamental intellectual activity with important implications for other forms of engagement with the world. Through the study of different societies, we learn something essential not only about other people's worlds, but also about ourselves. In a sense, anthropologists excel in making the familiar exotic and the exotic familiar through comparison and the use of comparative concepts. For this reason, comparisons with modern urban societies are implicit throughout, even when the topic is Melanesian gift-giving, Malagasy ritual or Nuer politics. In fact, the whole book may, perhaps, be read as an exercise in comparative thinking.

In this third edition, I have kept the structure and chapter titles nearly unchanged, but both ethnographic examples and theoretical discussions have been updated and modified. Some new areas of research are introduced, but scarcely any of the older ones have been deleted. The increased interdependence of human worlds (often described under the headings of globalisation, transnationalism, etc.), described already in the first edition and elaborated further in the second edition, now pervades the text throughout. Just as no man is an island, one can no longer speak of isolated societies.

Also, the strengths of social and cultural anthropology as ways of knowing are emphasised more explicitly in this (and the second, 2001) edition than in the 1995 book. In recent years, anthropology has increasingly been challenged by alternative, highly articulate and publicly visible ways of accounting for the unity and diversity of humanity. One the one hand, humanistic disciplines (sometimes lumped together as 'cultural studies') and, on the other hand, approaches based on natural science (evolutionary psychology, or second-generation sociobiology, being the most powerful one), propose answers to some of the questions typically raised in social anthropology – concerning, for example, the nature of society, the predicaments of ethnic complexity, kinship, ritual and so on. In this situation, neither antagonistic competition nor the merging of disciplines into a 'super-discipline' of sociocultural science appear as attractive options; instead, I advocate openness, dialogue and interdisciplinarity when feasible. Owing to the prevalence of competing claims, however, I try to state explicitly what it is that the methods, theory and body of research in anthropology have to offer in studies of the contemporary world. I argue that credible accounts of culture and society should have an ethnographic component, and that proper knowledge of traditional or otherwise 'remote' societies greatly enhances the understanding of phenomena such as tourism, ethnic violence or migration. If social anthropology does have a bright future, it is not in spite of, but because of global change.

In a certain sense, this is the fifth version of this book. The first edition, *Små steder, store spørsmål* in Norwegian, was originally published in 1993. Subsequently, Anne Beech at Pluto Press invited me to make an English version, but it would have to be substantially shorter than the original, which was a large, expensive and lavishly illustrated book. I kept the basic structure and chapter titles, but compressed and adjusted the content to make it suitable for a non-Scandinavian readership. In 1998, a revised and updated version of the Norwegian original was published, and in 2001, the second edition of *Small Places*, similarly revised, appeared.

When Anne Beech suggested a third edition, I had already been contacted by Universitetsforlaget, my Norwegian academic publisher, about the book. The editor, Per Robstad, wanted an updated *Små steder, store spørsmål*, but he held, doubtless correctly, that the 1998 edition was too bulky to fit the current structure of academic teaching in Norway, which is now based (as in the English-speaking world) on smaller, more clearly focused courses than had been the case before the Bologna reforms of 2003. Our conclusion was that making a Norwegian translation of the English edition might solve the problem. So in a sense I have come full circle with this textbook, ending this revision by translating the third edition of the English version into Norwegian (with, as always, a number of minor adjustments). Obviously, when I began drafting the first chapters in 1992, a reasonably happy young man just having emerged from his PhD rite of passage, it would never have occurred to me that I should still be working on the book 18 years on. Perhaps it is exactly the rather conventional structure of the book that has passed the test of time; whatever the case may be, it is a privilege to be allowed once more to develop, and not least to revise, my vision of anthropology through a fairly comprehensive text like this.

Over the years, I have received many suggestions and comments on the earlier editions of the books from people all over the world, and for this I am grateful. I see the production and dissemination of knowledge as an essentially collective endeavour, as a gift economy of the kind described especially in Chapter 12. This, then, is my belated return gift to my teachers – Harald Eidheim, Eduardo Archetti, Fredrik Barth, Axel Sommerfelt, Arne Martin Klausen and others – to my students, colleagues, translators and everybody who has cared to read the book and send me their comments and questions. Finally, I owe a special debt of gratitude to Anne Beech at Pluto Press for her encouragement and a regular sprinkling of positive energy over quite a few years now.

Oslo, January 2010

1   ANTHROPOLOGY: COMPARISON AND CONTEXT

[Anthropology] is less a subject matter than a bond between subject matters. It is in part history, part literature; in part natural science, part social science; it strives to study men both from within and without; it represents both a manner of looking at man and a vision of man—the most scientific of the humanities, the most humanist of sciences.
— *Eric Wolf*

Studying anthropology is like embarking on a journey which turns out to be much longer than one had initially planned, possibly because the plans were somewhat open-ended to begin with and the terrain turned out to be bumpier and more diverse than the map suggested. Fortunately, like many journeys which take an unexpected turn, this one also has numerous unexpected rewards in store (as well as, it is only fair to concede, a few frustrations en route). This journey brings the traveller from the damp rainforests of the Amazon to the cold semi-desert of the Arctic; from the streets of north London to mud huts in the Sahel; from Indonesian paddies to African cities. The aim of this book is dual: to provide useful maps, and to indicate some of the main sights (as well as a few less visited sites).

In spite of the dizzying geography of this trip, it is chiefly in a different sense that this is a long journey. Social and cultural anthropology has the whole of human society as its area of interest, and tries to understand the ways in which human lives are unique, but also the sense in which we are all similar. When, for example, we study the traditional economic system of the Tiv of central Nigeria, an essential part of the exploration consists in understanding how their economy is connected with other aspects of their society. If this dimension is absent, Tiv economy becomes incomprehensible to anthropologists. If we do not know that the Tiv traditionally could not buy and sell land, and that they have customarily not used money as a means of payment, it will be plainly impossible to understand how they themselves interpret their situation and how they responded to the economic changes imposed on their society during colonialism in the twentieth century.

Anthropology tries to account for the social and cultural variation in the world, but a crucial part of the anthropological project also consists in conceptualising and understanding similarities between social systems and human relationships. As one of the foremost anthropologists of the twentieth century, Claude Lévi-Strauss (1908–2009), has expressed it: 'Anthropology

1

has humanity as its object of research, but unlike the other human sciences, it tries to grasp its object through its most diverse manifestations' (1983, p. 49). Differently phrased: anthropology is about how different people can be, but it also tries to find out in what sense it can be said that all humans have something in common.

Another prominent anthropologist, Clifford Geertz (1926–2008), expresses a similar view in an essay which essentially deals with the differences between humans and animals:

If we want to discover what man amounts to, we can only find it in what men are: and what men are, above all other things, is various. It is in understanding that variousness – its range, its nature, its basis, and its implications – that we shall come to construct a concept of human nature that, more than a statistical shadow and less than a primitivist dream, has both substance and truth. (Geertz 1973, p. 52)

Although anthropologists have wide-ranging and frequently highly specialised interests, they share a common concern in trying to understand both connections *within* societies and connections *between* societies. As will become clearer as we proceed on this journey through the subject-matter and theories of social and cultural anthropology, there is a multitude of ways in which to approach these problems. Whether one is interested in understanding why and in what sense the Azande of Central Africa believe in witches (and why most Europeans have ceased doing so), why there is greater social inequality in Brazil than in Sweden, how the inhabitants of the densely populated, ethnically complex island of Mauritius avoid violent ethnic conflict, or what has happened to the traditional ways of life of the Inuit (Eskimos) in recent years, in most cases one or several anthropologists would have carried out research and written on the issue. Whether one is interested in the study of religion, child-raising, political power, economic life or the relationship between men and women, one may go to the anthropological literature for inspiration and knowledge.

Anthropologists are also concerned with accounting for the interrelation-ships between different aspects of human existence, and usually investigate these interrelationships taking as their point of departure a detailed study of local life in a particular society or a more or less delineated social environment. One may therefore say that anthropology asks large questions, while at the same time it draws its most important insights from small places.

For many years, it was common to see its traditional focus on small-scale non-industrial societies as a distinguishing feature of anthropology, compared with other subjects dealing with culture and society. However, owing to changes in the world and in the discipline itself, this is no longer an accurate description. Practically any social system can be studied anthropologically and contemporary anthropological research displays an enormous range, empirically as well as theoretically. Some study witchcraft in contemporary South Africa, others study diplomacy. Some travel to Melanesia for fieldwork, while others take the bus to the other side of town. Some analyse the economic adaptations of migrants, others write about the new social networks on the Internet.

AN OUTLINE OF THE SUBJECT

What, then, is anthropology? Let us begin with the etymology of the concept. It is a compound of two ancient Greek words, 'anthropos' and 'logos', which can be translated as 'human' and 'reason', respectively. So anthropology means 'reason about humans' or, rather, 'knowledge about humans'. Social anthropology would then mean knowledge about humans in societies. Such a definition would, of course, cover the other social sciences as well as anthropology, but it may still be useful as a beginning.

The word 'culture', which is also central to the discipline, originates from the Latin *'colere'*, which means to cultivate. (The word 'colony' has the same origin.) Cultural anthropology thus means 'knowledge about cultivated humans'; that is, knowledge about those aspects of humanity which are not natural, but which are related to that which is acquired.

'Culture' has famously been described as one of the two or three most complicated words in the English language (Williams 1981, p. 87). In the early 1950s, Clyde Kluckhohn and Alfred Kroeber (1952 [1917]) presented 161 different definitions of culture. It would not be possible to consider the majority of these definitions here; besides, many of them were – fortunately – quite similar. Let us therefore, as a preliminary conceptualisation of culture, define it as those abilities, notions and forms of behaviour persons have acquired as members of society. A definition of this kind, which is indebted to both the Victorian anthropologist E.B. Tylor (1832–1917) and to Geertz (although the latter emphasises meaning rather than behaviour), is the most common one among anthropologists.

Culture nevertheless carries with it a basic ambiguity. On the one hand, every human is equally cultural; in this sense, the term refers to a basic *similarity* within humanity distinguishing us from other animals including the higher primates. On the other hand, people have acquired different abilities, notions, etc., and are thereby *different* because of culture. Culture can, in other words, refer both to basic similarities and to systematic differences between humans.

If this sounds slightly complex, some more complexity is required at this point. As a matter of fact, the concept of culture has been contested in anthropology for decades. The influential Geertzian concept of culture, which had been elaborated through a series of erudite and elegant essays written in the 1960s and 1970s (Geertz 1973, 1983), depicted a culture both as an integrated whole, as a puzzle where all the pieces were at hand, and as a system of meanings that was largely shared by a population. Culture thus appeared as integrated, shared within the group, and sharply bounded. But what of variations within the group, and what about similarities or mutual contacts with neighbouring groups – and what to make of, say, the technologically and economically driven processes of globalisation, which ensure that nearly every nook and cranny in the world are to varying degrees exposed to news about football world cups, to wagework and the concept of human rights? In many cases, it could indeed be said that a national or local culture is neither shared by all or most of the inhabitants, nor bounded – I have myself explored this myth regarding my native Norway, a country usually considered 'culturally homogeneous' (Eriksen 1993a; cf. Gullestad 1992, 2006). Many began to criticise the overly neat and tidy picture suggested in the dominant concept of culture, from a variety of viewpoints, some of which will be discussed in later chapters. Alternative ways of conceptualising culture were proposed (e.g. as unbounded 'cultural flows' or as 'fields of discourse', or as 'traditions of knowledge'), and some even wanted to get rid of the concept altogether (for some of the debates, see Clifford and Marcus 1986, James et al. 1997, Ortner 1999). As I shall indicate later, the concept of society has been subjected to similar critiques, but problematic as they may be, both concepts still seem to form part of the conceptual backbone of anthropology. In his magisterial, deeply ambivalent review of the culture concept in American cultural anthropology, Adam Kuper (1999, p. 226) notes that '[t]hese days, anthropologists get remarkably nervous when they discuss culture – which is surprising, on the face of it, since the anthropology of culture is something of a success story'. The reason for this 'nervousness' is not just the contested meaning of the term 'culture', but also the fact that culture concepts that are close kin to the classic anthropological one are being exploited politically, in identity politics (see Chapters 17–19).

The relationship between culture and society can be described in the following way. Culture refers to the acquired, cognitive and symbolic aspects of existence, whereas society refers to the social organisation of human life, patterns of interaction and power relationships. The significant implications of this analytical distinction, which may seem bewildering or irrelevant, will eventually be evident.

A short definition of anthropology may read like this: 'Anthropology is the comparative study of cultural and social life. Its most important method is participant observation, which consists in lengthy fieldwork in a specific social setting.' In other words, anthropology compares aspects of different societies, and continuously searches for interesting dimensions for comparison. If, say, one chooses to write a monograph about a people in the New Guinea highlands, an anthropologist will always describe it with at least some concepts (such as kinship, gender and power) that render it comparable with aspects of other societies.

Further, the discipline emphasises the importance of ethnographic fieldwork, which is a thorough close-up study of a particular social and cultural environment, where the researcher is normally required to spend around a year. Many do shorter fieldwork, but many also return to the field several times, often spanning decades altogether.

Anthropology has many features in common with the other social sciences and humanities that were developed between the late eighteenth century and the late nineteenth century. Indeed, a difficult question consists in deciding whether it is a science, narrowly defined, or one of the humanities. Do we search for general laws, as the natural scientists do, or do we instead try to understand and interpret different societies? E.E. Evans-Pritchard in Britain and Alfred Kroeber in the USA, leading anthropologists in their day, both argued around 1950 that anthropology had more in common with history than with the natural sciences. Although their view, considered something of a heresy at the time, has become commonplace since, there are still anthropologists who feel that the subject should aim at a degree of scientific rigour similar to that of the natural sciences.

Some of the implications of this divergence in views will be discussed in later chapters. A few important defining features of anthropology are nevertheless common to all practitioners of the subject: it is comparative and empirical; its most important method of data collection is fieldwork; and it has a truly global focus in that it does not single out one region, or one kind of society, as being more important than others. Unlike sociology proper, anthropology does not concentrate its attention on the industrialised world; unlike philosophy, it stresses the importance of empirical research; unlike history, it studies society as it is being enacted; and unlike linguistics, it stresses the social and cultural context of speech when looking at language. Definitely, there are great overlaps with other sciences and disciplines, and there is a lot to be learnt from them, yet anthropology has its distinctive character as an intellectual discipline, based on ethnographic fieldwork, which tries simultaneously to account for actual cultural variation in the world and to develop a theoretical perspective on culture and society.

THE UNIVERSAL AND THE PARTICULAR

'If each discipline can be said to have a central problem,' writes Michael Carrithers (1992, p. 2), 'then the central problem of anthropology is the diversity of human social life.' Put differently, one could say that anthropological research and theory tries to strike a balance between similarities and differences, and theoretical questions have often revolved around the issue of universality versus relativism: to what extent do all humans, cultures or societies have something in common, and to what extent is each of them unique? Since we employ comparative concepts, that is supposedly culturally neutral terms like kinship system, gender role, system of inheritance, etc., it is implicitly acknowledged that all or nearly all societies have several features in common. However, many anthropologists challenge this view, and claim the uniqueness of each culture or society. A strong universalist programme is found in Donald Brown's book *Human Universals* (1991), where the author claims that anthropologists have for generations exaggerated the differences between societies, neglecting the very substantial commonalities that hold humanity together. In this controversial book, Brown draws extensively on an earlier study of 'human universals', which included:

age-grading, athletic sports, bodily adornment, calendar, cleanliness training, community organization, cooking, cooperative labor, cosmology, courtship, dancing, decorative art, divination, division of labor, dream interpretation, education, eschatology, ethics, ethnobotany, etiquette, faith healing, family, feasting, fire making, folklore, food taboos, funeral rites, games, gestures, gift giving, government, greetings ... (Murdock 1945, p. 124, quoted in Brown 1991, p. 70)

And this was just the a-to-g segment of an alphabetical 'partial list'.

Several arguments could be invoked against this kind of list: that it is trivial and that what matters is to comprehend the unique expressions of such 'universals'; that phenomena such as 'family' have totally different meanings in different societies, and thus cannot be said to be 'the same' everywhere; and that this piecemeal approach to society and culture removes the very hallmark of good anthropology, namely the ability to see isolated phenomena (like age-grading or food taboos) in a broad context. An institution such as arranged marriage means something fundamentally different in the Punjabi countryside than among the French upper class. Is it still the same institution? Yes – and no. Brown is right in accusing anthropologists of having been inclined to emphasise the exotic and unique at the expense of neglecting cross-cultural similarities (and, I would add, mutual influence between societies), but this does not mean that his approach is the only possible way of bridging the gap between societies. In later chapters, several other alternatives will be discussed, including structural-functionalism (all societies operate according to the same general principles), structuralism (the human mind has a common architecture expressed through myth, kinship and other cultural phenomena), transactionalism (the logic of human action is the same everywhere) and materialist approaches (culture and society are determined by ecological and/or technological factors).

The tension between the universal and the particular has been immensely productive in anthropology, and it remains an important one. One common way of framing it, inside and outside anthropology, is through the concept of ethnocentrism.

THE PROBLEM OF ETHNOCENTRISM

A society or a culture, it was remarked above, must be understood on its own terms. In saying this, we warn against the application of a shared, universal scale to be used in the evaluation of every society. Such a scale, which is often used, could be defined as longevity, gross domestic product (GDP), democratic rights, literacy rates, etc. Until quite recently, it was common in European society to rank non-Europeans according to the ratio of their population which was admitted into the Christian church. Such a ranking of peoples is utterly irrelevant to anthropology. In order to pass judgement on the quality of life in a foreign society, we must first try to understand that society from the inside; otherwise our judgement has a very limited intellectual interest. What is conceived of as 'the good life' in the society in which we live may not appear attractive at all if it is seen from a different vantage-point. In order to understand people's lives, it is therefore necessary to try to grasp the totality of their experiential world; and in order to succeed in this project, it is inadequate to look at selected, isolated 'variables'. Obviously, a typical statistical criterion such as 'annual income' is meaningless in a society where neither money nor wagework is common.

This kind of argument may be read as a warning against ethnocentrism. This term (from Greek '*ethnos*', meaning 'a people') means evaluating other

---

Anthropology and the Good Life

'Anthropologists', claims Neil Thin, 'have been far more interested in pathologies and oddities than in normality' (2008, p. 23). Although Malinowski in his day saw happiness and the pursuit of the good life as worthy topics of comparative research, very few have followed his cue. According to Thin, basing his conclusion on a comprehensive database search, anthropologists appear to have been more interested in basket-weaving than in happiness! Thousands of academic articles have appeared on the topic of health, but they always concentrate on disease (Thin 2005). (Peace research, similarly, rarely studies peace, but war and violence.) Giving short shrift to the usually brief, often superficial and romantic (either Hobbesian or Rousseauian) depictions of 'the good life' that appear in anthropological monographs, Thin concludes, in a slightly exasperated vein, that 'the cold-shouldering of well-being by anthropologists is itself a bizarre feature of the culture of academic anthropology, one that begs to be analyzed' (2008, p. 26).

Moving on to propose a research programme for the anthropological study of happiness, or subjective well-being – a topic which has received massive interest in other social sciences, including psychology, recently – Thin argues that every society has notions about what it is to feel good as opposed to feeling bad, and that every society has significant distinctions between 'feeling well' and 'living a good life'. He then introduces a number of distinctions facilitating comparisons between 'happiness regimes', such as the contrast between this-worldly and other-worldly notions of the good life, short-term versus long-term orientations, and so on. An emergent anthropology of happiness is documented in a couple of recent edited volumes, Mathews and Izquierdo (2008) and Jiménez (2008), and both books showcase the superiority of anthropological field methods over questionnaire surveys in studying well-being and ideas of the good life. It goes without saying that more work is waiting to be done in this field.

people from one's own vantage-point and describing them in one's own terms. One's own '*ethnos*', including one's cultural values, is literally placed at the centre. Other peoples would, within this frame of thought, necessarily appear as inferior imitations of oneself. If the Nuer of the Sudan are unable to acquire a mortgage to buy a house, they thus appear to have a less perfect society than ourselves. If the Kwakiutl of the west coast of North America lack electricity, they seem to have a less fulfilling life than we do. If the Kachin of upper Burma reject conversion to Christianity, they are less civilised than we are, and if the Bushmen of the Kalahari are illiterate, they appear less intelligent than us. Such points of view express an ethnocentric attitude which fails to allow other peoples to be different from ourselves on their own terms, and can be a serious obstacle to understanding. Rather than comparing strangers with our own society and placing ourselves on top of an imaginary pyramid, anthropology calls for an understanding of different societies as they appear *from the inside*. Anthropology cannot provide an answer to a question about which societies are better than others, simply because the discipline does not ask such questions. If asked what is the good life, the anthropologist will have to answer that every society has its own definition(s) of it.

Moreover, an ethnocentric bias, which may be less easy to detect than moralistic judgements, may shape the very concepts we use in describing and classifying the world. For example, it has been argued that it may be inappropriate to speak of politics and kinship when referring to societies which themselves lack concepts of 'politics' and 'kinship'. Politics, perhaps, belongs to the ethnographer's society and not to the society under study. To this fundamental problem I shall return later.

Cultural relativism is sometimes posited as the opposite of ethnocentrism. This is the doctrine that societies or cultures are qualitatively different and have their own unique inner logic, and that it is therefore scientifically absurd to rank them on a scale. If one places a Bushman group, say, at the bottom of a ladder where the variables are, say, literacy and annual income, this ladder is irrelevant to them if it turns out that the Bushmen do not place a high priority on money and books. It should also be evident that one cannot, within a cultural relativist framework, argue that a society with many cars is 'better' than one with fewer, or that the ratio of cinemas to population is a useful indicator of the quality of life. (By the way, the Bushmen are sometimes spoken of as the San, since the term Bushmen is by some considered vaguely racist. However, since 'San' is a pejorative term used by the neighbouring Khoikhoi, the term Bushmen is again in common use; see Barnard 2007.)

Cultural relativism is an indispensable and unquestionable theoretical premise and methodological rule-of-thumb in our attempts to understand other societies in an as unprejudiced way as possible. As an ethical principle, however, it is probably impossible in practice (and most would say undesirable), since it seems to indicate that everything is as good as everything else, provided it makes sense in a particular society. Taken to its extreme, it would ultimately lead to nihilism. For this reason, it may be timely to stress that many anthropologists are impeccable cultural relativists in their daily work, while they may perfectly well have definite, frequently dogmatic notions about right and wrong in their private lives. In Western societies and elsewhere, current debates over minority rights and multiculturalism indicate both the need for anthropological knowledge and the impossibility of defining a simple, scientific solution to these complex problems, which are of a political nature.

Cultural relativism cannot be posited simply as the opposite of ethnocentrism, the simple reason being that it does not in itself contain a moral principle. The principle of cultural relativism in anthropology is a methodological one – it is indispensable for the investigation and comparison of societies without relating them to a usually irrelevant developmental scale; but this does not imply that there is no difference between right and wrong. Finally, we should be aware that many anthropologists wish to discover general, shared aspects of humanity or human societies. There is no necessary contradiction between a project of this kind and a cultural relativist approach, even if universalism – doctrines emphasising the similarities between humans – is frequently seen as the opposite of cultural relativism. One may well be a relativist at the level of method and description, yet simultaneously argue, at the level of analysis, that a particular underlying pattern is common to all societies or persons. Many would indeed claim that this is what anthropology is about: to discover both the uniqueness of each social and cultural setting *and* the ways in which humanity is one.

SUGGESTIONS FOR FURTHER READING

E.E. Evans-Pritchard: *Social Anthropology*. Glencoe, IL: Free Press 1951.
Clifford Geertz: *Available Light: Anthropological Reflections on Philosophical Topics*. Princeton, NJ: Princeton University Press 2000.
Adam Kuper: *Anthropology and Anthropologists: The Modern British School*, 3rd edn. London: Routledge 1996.

2   A BRIEF HISTORY OF ANTHROPOLOGY

I have spent over 8 months in one village in the Trobriand and this proved to me, how even a poor observer like myself can get a certain amount of reliable information, if he puts himself into the proper conditions for observation.
— *Bronislaw Malinowski (letter to A.C. Haddon, May 1916)*

Like the other social sciences, anthropology has fairly recent origins. It developed as an academic discipline during the late nineteenth and early twentieth century, but it has important forerunners in the historiography, geography, travel writing, philosophy and jurisprudence of earlier times. There are many ways of writing the history of anthropology, just as there may exist, in any given society, competing versions of national history or origin myths, promoted by groups or individuals with diverging interests. History is not primarily a product of the past itself, but is rather shaped by the concerns of the present. As these concerns change, past events and persons shift between foreground and background, and will be understood and evaluated in new ways. In a review of the state of the art in (chiefly) American cultural anthropology, Bruce Knauft (1996) distinguishes between at least four 'genealogies of the present' – four different ways of accounting for the present situation. Another fourfold division is apparent in a book entitled *One Discipline, Four Ways* (Barth et al. 2005), which describes the differences between the trajectories of American, British, French and German anthropology, revealing that the present can have many alternative origins. This ambiguity of the past not only has a bearing on the writing of intellectual history but is also itself a subject of anthropological inquiry to be dealt with later.

In other words there can be no totally objective, neutral history of anthropology (or of anything), but this chapter nonetheless amounts to an attempt to provide a brief and – as far as possible – relatively uncontroversial description of the development of the subject.

PROTO-ANTHROPOLOGY

If anthropology is the study of cultural variation, its roots may be traced as far back in history as the ancient Greeks. The historian Herodotos (fifth century BC) wrote detailed accounts of 'barbarian' peoples to the east and north of the Greek peninsula, comparing their customs and beliefs to those of

10

Athens, and the group of philosophers known as the Sophists were perhaps the first philosophical relativists, arguing (as many twentieth-century anthropologists have done) that there can be no absolute truth because, as we would put it today, truth is context-bound. Yet their interest in human variation and differing cultural values fell short of being scientific, chiefly because Herodotos lacked theory while the Sophists lacked empirical material.

A more credible ancestor is the Tunisian intellectual Ibn Khaldun (1332–1406), a remarkable genius who anticipated the social sciences by several centuries. His main work, the *Muqaddimah* ('An introduction to history'), was written in the years following 1375, and contains a wealth of observations on law, education, politics and the economy. Khaldun's main achievement nevertheless lies in his non-religious, theoretical framework, where he stresses differing forms of *social cohesion* as a key variable in accounting for historical change and the rise of new groups to power.

In Europe, scholarly interest in cultural variation and human nature re-emerged in the following century as a consequence of the new intellectual freedom of the Renaissance and, perhaps even more importantly, increasing European explorations and conquests of distant lands. Illustrious intellectuals such as Michel de Montaigne (sixteenth century), Thomas Hobbes (seventeenth century) and Giambattista Vico (eighteenth century) belonged to the first generations of European thinkers who tried to account for cultural variability and global cultural history as well as, in the case of Montaigne, taking on the challenge from relativism. Philosophers in the eighteenth century developed theories of human nature, moral philosophies and social theories, taking into account an awareness of deep cultural differences dividing humanity. David Hume (1711–76), along with Adam Smith the most important thinker of the Scottish Enlightenment, argued that experience was the only trustworthy source of valid knowledge. Hume's empiricist philosophy almost immediately became a source of inspiration for early social scientists, whose pioneers did not trust thought and pure speculation, but would rather travel into the social world itself in order to obtain first-hand experience through the senses (empirical means, literally, 'based on experience').

Many other eighteenth-century philosophers also made important contributions to the beginnings of a systematic, comparative study of culture. The most famous is perhaps Jean-Jacques Rousseau (1712–78), who saw the social conditions of 'savages' as a utopian ideal; but of equal interest is Baron de Montesquieu (1689–1755), whose *Lettres Persanes* ('Persian letters', 1722) was an early, fictional attempt to describe Europe as seen through the eyes of non-Europeans. Further, the great French *Encyclopédie* (1751–72), edited by Denis Diderot (1713–84) with Jean d'Alembert (1717–83), contained many articles on the customs and beliefs of other peoples. One of its youngest contributors, the Marquis de Condorcet (1743–94), who died in a Jacobin jail, tried to combine mathematics and empirical facts to produce general laws of society.

In Germany, different but no less important developments took place in the same period. Johann Gottlieb von Herder (1744–1803), a founder of the *Sturm und Drang* movement that soon evolved into Romanticism, challenged French Enlightenment philosophy, in particular Voltaire's universalist view that there existed a single, universal, global civilization. Herder argued that each people (*Volk*) had its own *Geist* or 'soul' and therefore a right to retain its own unique values and customs, in a manner reminiscent of later cultural relativism. Indeed, by the end of the eighteenth century, several of the theoretical questions still raised by anthropologists had already been formulated: universalism versus relativism (what is common to humanity; what is culturally specific), ethnocentrism versus cultural relativism (moral judgements versus neutral descriptions of other peoples), and humanity versus (the rest of) the animal kingdom (culture versus nature). Twenty-first-century anthropology teaches that these and other essentially philosophical problems are best investigated through the rigorous and detailed study of actual living people in existing societies, and by applying carefully devised methods of comparison to the bewildering variety of 'customs and beliefs'. Following Montesquieu's comparative musings about Persia and France, it would take several generations until anthropology achieved this mark of scientific rigour.

VICTORIAN ANTHROPOLOGY

A characteristic of the anthropology of the nineteenth century was the belief in social evolution – the idea that human societies developed in a particular direction – and the related notion that European societies were the end-product of a long developmental chain which began with 'savagery'. This idea was typical of the Victorian age, dominated by an optimistic belief in technological progress and, simultaneously, European colonialism, which was frequently justified with reference to what Kipling famously wrote of as 'the white man's burden'; the alleged duty of the European to 'civilise the savages'. The first general theories of cultural variation to enjoy a lasting influence were arguably those of two men trained as lawyers; Henry Maine (1822–88) in Britain and Lewis Henry Morgan (1818–82) in the United States. True to the spirit of the times, both presented evolutionist models of variation and change, where West European societies were seen as the pinnacle of human development. In his *Ancient Law* (1861), Maine distinguished between *status* and *contract* societies, a divide which corresponds roughly to later dichotomies between traditional and modern societies, or, in the late nineteenth-century German sociologist Ferdinand Tönnies' (1855–1936) terminology, *Gemeinschaft* (community) and *Gesellschaft* (society). Status societies are assumed to operate on the basis of kinship and myth, while individual merit and achievement are decisive in contract societies. Although simple contrasts of this kind have been severely criticised, they continue to exert a certain influence on anthropological thinking.

Morgan's contributions to anthropology were wide-ranging and, among many other things, he wrote an ethnography of the Iroquois. His evolutionary scheme, presented in *Ancient Society* (1877), distinguished between seven stages (from lower savagery to civilization), and the typology was mainly based on technological achievements. His materialist account of cultural change immediately attracted Karl Marx (1818–83) and, in particular, Friedrich Engels (1820–95), whose later writings on non- (or pre-) capitalist societies were strongly influenced by Morgan. Among Morgan's other achievements, his concern with kinship must be mentioned. Dividing human kinship systems into a limited number of types, and seeing kinship terminology as a key to understanding society, he is widely credited with making the study of kinship a central preoccupation of anthropology, which it has indeed remained to this day. Writing in the same period, the historian of religion William Robertson Smith (1846–94) and the lawyer J.J. Bachofen (1815–87), respectively, offered theories of monotheistic religion and of the (wrongly) assumed historical evolution from matriliny to patriliny.

An untypical scholar in the otherwise evolutionist Victorian era, the German ethnologist Adolf Bastian (1826–1905) reacted against what he saw as simplistic typological schemata. Drawing inspiration from both Herderian Romanticism and the humanistic tradition in German academia, Bastian wrote prolifically on cultural history, taking great care to avoid unwarranted generalisations, yet he held that all humans have the same pattern of thinking based on 'elementary ideas' (*Elementärgedanken*). This idea would later be developed independently, with great sophistication, in Claude Lévi-Strauss's structuralism.

The leading British anthropologist of the late Victorian era was Edward Tylor (1832–1917), who influenced Darwin's thinking about culture, and whose voluminous writings include the famous definition of culture mentioned in the first chapter:

Culture or Civilization, taken in its widest ethnographic sense, is that complex whole which includes knowledge, belief, art, morals, custom, and any other capabilities and habits acquired by man as a member of society. (Tylor 1968 [1871], p. 1)

This definition is still seen as useful by many anthropologists. Tylor's student James Frazer (1854–1941), who would eclipse his teacher in terms of fame and who held the first Chair in Social Anthropology in Britain, wrote the massive *Golden Bough* (1890, rev. edn 1911–15), an ambitious comparative study of myth and religion. Both Tylor and Frazer were evolutionists, and Frazer's main theoretical project consisted in demonstrating how thought had developed from the magical via the religious to the scientific.

Neither Tylor nor Frazer carried out detailed field studies, although Tylor spent several years in Mexico and wrote a book there. A famous anecdote tells of a dinner party where William James, the pragmatist philosopher, asked Frazer whether he had ever become acquainted with any of those savages he wrote so much about. Frazer allegedly replied, in a shocked tone of voice, 'Heaven forbid!' (Evans-Pritchard 1951, p. 72).

Important intellectual developments outside of anthropology in the second half of the nineteenth century also had a powerful impact on the field. Darwin's theory of natural selection, first presented in his *Origin of Species* from 1859, would be seen both as a condition for anthropology (positing, as it did, that all humans are closely related) and, later, as a threat to the discipline (arguing, as it seemed to do, the primacy of the biological over the cultural; see Ingold 1986). The emergence of classic sociological theory in the works of Comte, Marx and Tönnies, and later Durkheim, Weber, Pareto and Simmel, provided anthropologists with general theories of society, although their applicability to non-European societies continues to be disputed.

The quality of the ethnographic data used by the early anthropologists was variable. Most of the scholars mentioned above relied on the written sources that were available, ranging from missionaries' accounts to travelogues of varying accuracy. The need for more reliable data began to make itself felt. Expeditions and systematic surveys – among the most famous were the British Torres Straits expedition led by W.H.R. Rivers and the large-scale American explorations of the Indian cultures of the north-western coast – provided researchers around the turn of the last century with an improved understanding of the compass of cultural variation, which would eventually lead to the downfall of the ambitious theories of unilineal evolution characteristic of nineteenth-century anthropology.

An Austro-German speciality, proposed both as an alternative and a complement to evolutionist thinking, was diffusionism, the doctrine of the historical diffusion of cultural traits. Never a part of the mainstream outside of the German-speaking world (but counting important supporters in the English-speaking world, including Rivers), elaborate theories of cultural diffusion continued to thrive, particularly in Berlin and Vienna, until after the Second World War. Nobody denied that diffusion took place, but there were serious problems of verification associated with the theory. Within anthropology, diffusionism went out of fashion when, around the time of the First World War, researchers began to study single societies in great detail without trying to speculate on their historical development. However, a theoretical direction with elements of diffusionism returned in the 1990s, under the label of globalisation theory (see especially Chapter 19), attempting to understand and account for the ways in which modern mass communications, migration, capitalism and other 'global' phenomena interact with local conditions.

Notwithstanding these and other theoretical developments and methodological refinements, the emergence of modern anthropology is usually associated with four outstanding scholars working in three countries in the early decades of the twentieth century: Franz Boas in the USA, A.R. Radcliffe-Brown and Bronislaw Malinowski in the UK, and Marcel Mauss in France.

BOAS AND CULTURAL RELATIVISM

Boas (1858–1942), a German immigrant to the United States who had briefly studied anthropology with Bastian at Heidelberg, carried out important research among Inuit and Kwakiutl Indians in the 1890s. In his teaching and professional leadership, which spanned four decades, he strengthened the 'four-field approach' in American anthropology, which still sets it apart from European anthropology, as it encompasses not only cultural and social anthropology, but also physical anthropology, archaeology and linguistics. In spite of this achievement, Boas is chiefly remembered for his ideas. Although cultural relativism had been introduced in incipient form more than a century before, it was Boas who made it a central premise for anthropological research. Reacting against the grand evolutionary schemes of Tylor, Morgan and others, Boas took an early stance in favour of a more particularist approach. He argued that each culture had to be understood on its own terms and that it would be scientifically misleading to judge and rank other cultures according to a Western, ethnocentric typology gauging 'levels of development'. Accordingly, Boas also promoted *historical particularism*, the view that all societies or cultures had their own, unique history that could not be reduced to a category in some universalist scheme of development. On related grounds, Boas argued against the unfounded claims of racist pseudoscience, which were supported by most of the leading biologists of the time. Boas's insistence on the meticulous collection of empirical data was a result not only of his scientific views but also the realisation that cultural change appeared to obliterate what he saw as unique cultures, particularly in North America. Already in *The Mind of Primitive Man* (1911), Boas argued that anthropology ought to be politically engaged on behalf of threatened indigenous populations.

Perhaps because of his particularism, Boas never systematised his ideas in a theoretical treatise. Several of his students and associates nevertheless did develop general theories of culture, notably Ruth Benedict, Alfred Kroeber and Robert Lowie. His most famous student, however, was Margaret Mead (1901–78). Although her bestselling books from various Pacific societies have been criticised for being ethnographically superficial (see Chapter 4), they skilfully used material from non-Western societies to raise questions about gender relations, socialisation and politics in the West. Mead's work shows, probably better than that of any other anthropologist, the potential of cultural criticism inherent in the discipline (cf. Marcus and Fischer 1986).

One of Boas's most remarkable associates, the linguist Edward Sapir (1884–1939), formulated, with his student Benjamin Lee Whorf, the so-called *Sapir–Whorf hypothesis*, which posits that language determines cognition, and that the world's languages differ profoundly in this respect (see Chapter 15). Consistent with a radical cultural relativism, the hypothesis implies that, for example, Hopi Indians see and perceive the world in a fundamentally different way from Westerners, due to differences in the structure of their respective languages.

Due to Boas's influence, the materialist tradition from Morgan moved into the background in the USA during the first half of the twentieth century. After the Second World War, it re-emerged as cultural ecology and neo-evolutionism, and Morgan's legacy would later also be acknowledged by many Marxist anthropologists. But for now, Morgan's evolutionism was firmly sidelined, as was any direct influence from Darwin's theory of evolution.

THE TWO BRITISH SCHOOLS

While modern American anthropology had been shaped, on the one hand by the Boasians and their relativist concerns, and on the other hand by the perceived need to record native cultures before their feared disappearance, the situation in the major colonial power, Great Britain, was very different. The degree of complicity between colonial agencies and anthropologists working in the colonies is debatable (Kuklick 1991; Goody 1995), but the very fact of imperialism gave an inescapable, if usually implicit, context for British social anthropology in its first decades. While American anthropologists studying Indians concentrated on symbolic culture, as the original social organisation of the groups in question had usually been transformed, British anthropologists developed a strong interest in local politics among peoples often subjected to indirect rule from the Colonial Office.

The man who is often hailed as the founder of modern British social anthropology was a Polish immigrant, Bronislaw Malinowski (1884–1942), whose nearly two years of fieldwork in the Trobriand Islands (between 1914 and 1918) set a standard for ethnographic data collection that is still largely unchallenged. Malinowski stressed the need to learn the local language properly and to engage in everyday life in the society under scrutiny, in order to learn its categories 'from within', and to understand the often subtle interconnections between the various social institutions and cultural notions. Malinowski also placed an unusual emphasis on the acting individual, seeing social structure not as a determinant of but as a framework for action, and he wrote about a wide range of topics, ranging from garden magic, economics, technology and sex to the puzzling *kula* trade (see Chapter 12), often introducing new issues. Although he dealt with many topics of general concern, he nearly always took his point of departure in his Trobriand ethnography, demonstrating a method of generalisation very different from that of the previous generation with its more piecemeal local knowledge and grand comparative ambitions. Malinowski regarded all institutions of a society as intrinsically linked to each other, and stressed that every social or cultural phenomenon ought to be studied in its full context. He also held that inborn human needs were the driving force in the development of social institutions, and his brand of functionalism is often described as 'biopsychological functionalism'.

Fieldwork before Malinowski

By common consent, certainly in twentieth-century British social anthropology, modern fieldwork – time-consuming, strenuous, systematic, carried out in the local vernacular – was introduced by Malinowski, whose Trobriand fieldwork served as a model for later generations of ethnographers. However, ethnographic work had been carried out by others before Malinowski, often in systematic and thorough ways. A few examples follow.

In the United States, Lewis Henry Morgan did extensive field research among the Iroquois in the late 1840s, leading to an ethnographic study of their political system. However, Morgan – unlike Malinowski – depended on an interpreter and translator, the Iroquois lawyer Ely S. Parker. Later, however, Frank Hamilton Cushing did long-term fieldwork (1879–84) among the Zuñi of New Mexico, and may have been the first participant-observer, decades before Malinowski.

Russian ethnographers were active in the field around the same time as Morgan (Kuznetsov 2008). Working among ethnic minorities in Russia, but also overseas – the expedition to New Guinea led by Nikolai Mikluho-Maklai in the 1870s deserves mentioning – many Russian ethnographers were familiar with the languages of the people they studied.

In the Netherlands, according to Vermeulen (2008), ethnography was actively pursued in the Dutch colonies already in the 1770s, and was institutionalised from the 1830s. However, anthropology and ethnography were for a long time part of the training programmes for colonial civil servants, and thus had an applied bent; academic sociocultural anthropology nevertheless can be dated back to 1877, when the first chair in the subject was founded in Leiden.

Finally, the work of the French priest and ethnogapher Maurice Leenhardt deserves mentioning. Living in New Caledonia (Melanesia) from 1902 to 1927, Leenhardt carried out meticulous studies of Kanak culture and society, eventually published in a series of books which initially attracted little attention, but which are now recognised as exemplars of anthropological work, foremost among them Do Kamo (Leenhardt 1947).

What is left, then, of the 'Malinowskian revolution', given that he was not the first to do ethnographic fieldwork? Well, first, Malinowski described the requirements for ethnographic fieldwork systematically in *Argonauts*. Second, he insisted on participant observation, which was a new concept requiring the ethnographer to take active part in everyday life. Third, Malinowski insisted on moving beyond mere ethnography and providing theoretical and comparative analyses, thereby transcending the division between armchair anthropology (big questions) and ethnography (small facts).

The other leading light in inter-war British social anthropology, A.R. Radcliffe-Brown (1881–1955), had a stronger short-term influence than his rival, although it faded after the Second World War. An admirer of Emile Durkheim's sociology, Radcliffe-Brown did relatively little fieldwork himself, but aimed at the development of a 'natural science of society' – in the spirit of the Encyclopedists and of sociologists such as Auguste Comte – where the universal laws of social integration could be formulated. His theory, known as structural-functionalism, saw the acting individual as analytically unimportant, emphasising instead the social institutions (including kinship, norms, politics, etc.) and their interrelationships. According to this view, most tangible social and cultural phenomena could be seen as functional in the sense that they contributed to the maintenance of the overall social structure. Some of Radcliffe-Brown's most important essays are collected in *Structure and Function in Primitive Society* (1952), where he shows how societies, in his view, are integrated, and how social institutions reinforce each other and contribute to the maintenance of society.

Radcliffe-Brown's scientific ideals were taken from natural science, and he hoped to develop 'general laws of society' comparable in precision to those of physics and chemistry. This programme has been abandoned by most anthropologists – like structural-functionalism in its pure form – but many of the questions raised by contemporary anthropologists were originally framed by Radcliffe-Brown.

Despite their differences in emphasis, both British schools had a sociological concern in common (which they did not share with most Americans), and tended to see social institutions as functional. Both distanced themselves from the wide-ranging claims of diffusionism and evolutionism, and by the next generation of scholars, the influences of the two founding fathers may be said to have merged (Kuper 1996), although the tension between structural explanations and actor-centred accounts remains strong and productive in anthropology even today (see Chapter 6).

Malinowski's students at the London School of Economics included several anthropologists who would later rise to fame, such as Raymond Firth, Audrey Richards and Isaac Schapera, while Radcliffe-Brown, in addition to enlisting E.E. Evans-Pritchard and Meyer Fortes – possibly the most powerful British anthropologists in the 1950s – to his newly founded Institute of Social and Cultural Anthropology at Oxford, spent many years abroad and introduced his brand of social anthropology to the universities of Cape Town, Sydney and Chicago. British anthropology, as typified by the first generation after Malinowski and Radcliffe-Brown, was characteristically oriented towards kinship, politics and economics, with Evans-Pritchard's *The Nuer* (1940) demonstrating, perhaps better than any other monograph of the period, the intellectual power of a discipline combining detailed ethnography, comparison and elegant models. (Later, his models would be criticised for being too elegant to fit the facts on the ground – a very Malinowskian objection to be discussed in Chapter 11.)

MAUSS

Although anthropology and ethnology were still important subjects in the German-speaking region, they were set back seriously after the Second World War, as many leading anthropologists had supported Nazism (Gingrich 2005). Regarding France, the situation is different and, along with the UK and the USA, France was as a major centre of anthropological thought and research throughout the twentieth century. Already in 1903, Durkheim had published, with his nephew Marcel Mauss (1872–1950), an important treatise on knowledge systems, *Primitive Classification* (Durkheim and Mauss 1963). In 1909, Arnold van Gennep published *Les Rites de passage*, a strikingly original analysis of initiation rituals (a topic which was to become a staple in the discipline; see Chapter 14), and the philosopher Lucien Lévy-Bruhl developed a theory, which was later to be challenged by Evans-Pritchard, Mauss and others, on the 'primitive mind', which he held to be 'pre-logical'. A major expedition from Dakar to Djibouti (1922–23), led by the young ethnographer Marcel Griaule, and the sensitive and detailed writings of the missionary-turned-ethnographer Maurice Leenhardt on the natives of New Caledonia, furnished the French with much fresh empirical material.

Less methodologically purist than the emerging British traditions and more philosophically adventurous than the Americans, inter-war French anthropology, under the leadership of Marcel Mauss, developed a distinctive Continental flavour, witnessed in the pages of the influential journal *L'Année Sociologique*, founded by Durkheim and edited by Mauss after Durkheim's death in 1917. Drawing on his vast knowledge of languages, cultural history and ethnographic research, Mauss, who never did fieldwork himself, wrote a series of learned, original, compact essays on topics ranging from gift exchange to the nation, the body, sacrifice and the concept of the person. This exceptional body of work has regularly been rediscovered and praised in the English-speaking world ever since.

Mauss's theoretical position was complex. He believed strongly in systematic comparison and in the existence of recurrent patterns in social life at all times and in all places, and yet he often ends on a relativist note in his reasoning about similarities and differences between societies. Like Radcliffe-Brown, Mauss was inspired by Durkheim, but in a very different way. Rather than developing 'a natural science of society' complete with 'laws', his project consisted in describing and classifying greatly different societies in order to look for structural similarities. In this way, he hoped to develop an understanding of general dimensions of social life. Mauss never actually published a book in his own name, and his famous *The Gift* (1954 [1923–24]) originally appeared in issues of the journal *L'Année Sociologique*.

The Gift is seen by some as the single most important text in twentieth-century anthropology, and Mauss's shorter studies also continue to be read and admired. Ironically, recalls Dumont (1986), Mauss, who never did fieldwork himself, spent many of his weekly seminars giving detailed instructions in techniques of observation (see also Parkin 2005). He also spent considerable time completing unfinished work left by colleagues who died in the First World War, such as Robert Hertz.

The transition from evolutionist theory and grand syntheses to more specific, detailed and empirically founded work, which in different ways took place in the UK, the USA and France during the first decades of the twentieth century, amounted to nothing short of an intellectual revolution. In the space of a few years, the work of Tylor, Morgan and even Frazer had been relegated to the mists of history, and the discipline had in reality been taken over by small groups of scholars who saw intensive fieldwork, cultural relativist method, the study of single, small-scale societies and rigorous comparison as the essence of the new discipline. It can in fact be argued that even today, the academic institutions, the conferences and the learned journals of anthropology build on a view of the discipline that came into its own with Boas, Malinowski, Radcliffe-Brown and Mauss. This is, to a greater or lesser extent, also true of the anthropological traditions of other countries (see Vermeulen and Roldán 1995; Boskovic 2008), including India, Australia, Japan, Mexico, Argentina, the Netherlands, Spain, Scandinavia and, partly, the German-speaking world. Soviet/Russian and East European anthropologies have followed different itineraries, and have retained a connection with the older German *Volkskunde* tradition, which is more descriptive, as well as developing their own analytical instruments.

Later developments in anthropology, to which we now turn briefly, reveal both continuity with and reactions against the foundations that were laid before the Second World War.

THE SECOND HALF OF THE TWENTIETH CENTURY

The numbers of professional anthropologists and institutions devoted to teaching and research in the field grew rapidly after the Second World War. The discipline also diversified, partly because of 'population pressure' within the subject. New specialisations such as psychological anthropology, political anthropology and the anthropology of ritual emerged, and the geographical foci of the discipline multiplied: Whereas the Pacific had been the most fertile area for new theoretical developments in the 1920s and Africa had played a similar part for British and French anthropologists in the 1930s and 1940s, and the American preoccupation with North American Indians had been stable throughout, the 1950s saw a growing interest in the 'creole' (or '*mestizo*') societies of Latin America and the Caribbean as well as the anthropology of India and South-East Asia, while the New Guinean highlands became similarly important in the 1960s. Such shifts in geographical emphasis could be consequential in theoretical developments, as each region raises its own peculiar problems.

From the 1950s onwards, the end of colonialism has also affected anthropology, both in a banal sense – it has become more difficult to obtain research permits in Third World countries – and more profoundly, as the relationship between the observer and the observed has become problematic since the traditionally 'observed' peoples increasingly have their own intellectuals and spokespersons who frequently object to Western interpretations of their way of life. Anthropology has grown not only in size but in intellectual and academic importance, but the current situation also poses its own peculiar challenges.

STRUCTURALISM

The first major theory to emerge after the Second World War was Claude Lévi-Strauss's structuralism. An admirer of Mauss and, like him, not a major fieldworker, Lévi-Strauss (1908–2009) developed an original theory of the human mind, based on inspiration from structural linguistics, Mauss's theory of exchange and Lévy-Bruhl's theory of the primitive mind (which Lévi-Strauss rejected). His first major work, *Les Structures élémentaires de la parenté* (*The Elementary Structures of Kinship*, 1969 [1949]), introduced a formal way of thinking about kinship, with particular reference to systems of marriage (described by Lévi-Strauss as the exchange of women between groups). Lévi-Strauss later expanded his theory to cover totemism, myth and art. Never uncontroversial, structuralism had an enormous impact on French intellectual life far beyond the confines of anthropology, and many leading contemporary French anthropologists have been students of Lévi-Strauss. In the English-speaking world, the reception of structuralism was delayed, as Lévi-Strauss's major works were not translated until the 1960s, but they had both major admirers and detractors from the beginning. Structuralism was criticised for being untestable, positing as it did certain unprovable and unfalsifiable properties of the human mind (most famously the propensity to think in terms of contrasts or binary oppositions), but many saw Lévi-Strauss's work, always committed to human universals, as a significant source of inspiration in the study of symbolic systems such as knowledge and myth.

A rather different brand of structuralism was developed by another follower of Mauss, namely Louis Dumont (1911–99), an Indianist and Sanskrit scholar who did fieldwork both in the Aryan north and the Dravidian south. Dumont, closer to Durkheim's teachings on social cohesion than Lévi-Strauss, argued in his major work on the Indian caste system, *Homo Hierarchicus* (1980 [1969]), for a holistic perspective (as opposed to an individualistic one), claiming that Indians (and by extension, many non-modern peoples) saw themselves not as 'free individuals' but as actors irretrievably enmeshed in a web of commitments and social relations, which in the Indian case was clearly hierarchical.

Most major French anthropologists of later generations have been associated with either Lévi-Strauss, Dumont or Georges Balandier (b. 1920), the Africanist whose work in political anthropology simultaneously bridged gaps between France and the Anglo-Saxon world and inspired both neo-Marxist research and applied anthropology devoted to development.

REACTIONS TO STRUCTURAL-FUNCTIONALISM

In Britain and the colonies, the structural-functionalism now associated chiefly with Evans-Pritchard and Fortes was under increased pressure after the war. Indeed, Evans-Pritchard himself repudiated his former views in the 1950s, arguing that the search for 'natural laws of society' had been shown to be futile and that anthropology should fashion itself as a humanities discipline rather than a natural science. Retrospectively, this shift has often been quoted as marking a shift 'from function to meaning' in the discipline's priorities, and a leading American anthropologist of the period, Alfred Kroeber, expressed similar views in the US. Others found their own paths away from what was increasingly seen as a conceptual straitjacket, for example Malinowski's student Edmund R. Leach (1910–89), whose *Political Systems of Highland Burma* (1954) suggested a departure from certain orthodoxies, notably Radcliffe-Brown's dictum that social systems tend to be in equilibrium and Malinowski's view of myths as integrating 'social charters'. Later, Leach, always a controversial and creative thinker, would be a main promoter and critic of structuralism in Britain, an ambivalent but staunch admirer of Lévi-Strauss.

A few years earlier, Leach's contemporary Raymond Firth (1901–2002) had proposed a distinction between social structure (the sets of statuses in society) and social organisation (Firth 1951), which he saw as the actual process of social life, where choice and individual whims were seen in a dynamic relationship to structural constraints. Later in the 1950s and 1960s, several younger social anthropologists, notably F.G. Bailey and Fredrik Barth, followed Firth's lead as well as the theory of games (a recent development in economics and evolutionary theory) in refining an actor-centred perspective on social life, where the formerly paramount level of norms and social institutions were re-framed as contextual variables (or even, as in a programmatic statement by Barth, as unintended consequences of intentional action). Following a different itinerary, Max Gluckman (1911–75), a former pupil of Radcliffe-Brown and a close associate of Evans-Pritchard, also increasingly abandoned the strong holist programme of the structural-functionalists, reconceptualising social structure as a rather loose set of constraints, while emphasising the importance of individual actors. Gluckman's colleagues included a number of important Africanists, such as A.L. Epstein, J. Clyde Mitchell, Victor Turner and Elizabeth Colson. Working in Southern Africa, this group pioneered both urban anthropology and the study of ethnicity in the 1950s and 1960s (see Chapters 16–17).

NEO-EVOLUTIONISM, CULTURAL ECOLOGY AND NEO-MARXISM

The number of practising anthropologists has always been larger in the United States than anywhere else and, accordingly, the discipline has been very diverse there. In 2003, the Association of Social Anthropologists in the

UK had a membership of slightly over 500, while the American Anthropological Association had nearly 12,000 members (Mills 2003: 13). Although the population of the USA is only six times that of Britain, there are 24 times as many anthropologists who are members of the main professional organisation. Although the influence from the Boasian cultural relativist school remains strong in US anthropology to this day, other groups of scholars have also made their mark. From the late 1940s onwards, a resurgent interest in Morgan's evolutionism as well as Marxism led to the formulation of several non-Boasian, evolutionist and materialist research programmes. Julian Steward (1902–72), a student of Robert Redfield at Chicago (who had himself been a student of Radcliffe-Brown), proposed a theory of cultural dynamics where he distinguished between 'the cultural core' (basic institutions such as the division of labour) and 'the rest of culture' in a way strongly reminiscent of Marx, an influence which could not be acknowledged openly at the time, however, because of the persecution of 'Communists' in the USA of the 1950s. Steward directed research projects and supervised work among Latin American peasants as well as North American Indians, and encouraged a renewed focus on the relationship between culture, technology and the environment. His contemporary Leslie White (1900–75) held views that were more deterministic than Steward's (who allowed for major local variations), but also – perhaps oddly – saw symbolic culture as a largely autonomous realm (cf. Sahlins 1976; see also Chapter 13). Among the major scholars influenced by White, Marvin Harris retained the materialist determinism in his own theory, called cultural materialism (Harris 1979), while Marshall Sahlins in the 1960s made the move from a kind of neo-evolutionism to a symbolic anthropology influenced by structuralism (Sahlins 1976).

Cultural ecology, largely a North American speciality, sprang from the teachings of Steward and White, and led to some rare collaborations between anthropology and biology. Especially in the 1960s, many such studies were carried out; the most famous is doubtless Roy Rappaport's *Pigs for the Ancestors* (1968), an attempt to account for a recurrent ritual in the New Guinean highlands in ecological terms. However, the upsurge of Marxist peasant research, especially in Latin America, in the 1970s, was clearly also indebted to Steward.

The advent of radical student politics in the late 1960s, which continued to have an impact on academia until the early 1980s, had a strong, if passing, influence on anthropology virtually everywhere. Of the more lasting contributions, apart from the string of peasant studies initiated by Steward and furthered by Eric Wolf, Sidney Mintz and others, the French attempt at synthesising Lévi-Straussian structuralism, Althusserian Marxism and anthropological relativism must be mentioned here. Emmanuel Terray, Claude Meillassoux and, probably most importantly, Maurice Godelier were among those who tried to combine a concern with local conditions and a universalist, ultimately evolutionist theory of society. Although both Marxism and structuralism eventually became unfashionable, scholars –

particularly those engaged in applied work – continue to draw inspiration from Marxist thought.

SYMBOLIC AND COGNITIVE ANTHROPOLOGY

More true to the tenor of the Boasian legacy than the materialist approaches, studies of cognition and symbolic systems have developed and diversified enormously in the decades after the Second World War. A leading theorist was Clifford Geertz, who wrote a string of influential essays advocating hermeneutics (interpretive method) in the 1960s and 1970s. While his originality as a theorist can be questioned (possible precursors include the philosopher Paul Ricœur, whose influence Geertz acknowledges, as well as Evans-Pritchard and Malinowski himself), his originality as a writer is beyond doubt, and Geertz ranks among the finest writers in contemporary anthropology. His contemporary Sahlins is, along with Geertz (who died in 2006), the foremost proponent of cultural relativism in the early twenty-first century, and his work includes studies of Mauss's theory of exchange, a critique of sociobiology and an examination of the cultural circumstances surrounding the death of Captain Cook; see Chapter 15), consistently stressing the autonomy of the symbolic realm, thus arguing that cultural variation cannot be explained by recourse to material conditions or inborn biological properties of humans.

In British anthropology, too, interest in meaning, symbols and cognition grew perceptibly after the war, especially from the 1960s (partly due to the belated discovery of Lévi-Strauss). British social anthropology had until then been strongly sociological, and two scholars who fused the legacy from structural-functionalism with the study of symbols and meaning in outstanding ways, were Mary Douglas (1921–2007) and Victor Turner (1920–83). Taking his cue from van Gennep, Turner, a former associate of Gluckman, developed a complex analysis of initiation rituals among the Ndembu of Zambia, showing both their functionally integrating aspects, their meaningful aspects for the participants and their deeper symbolic significance. Douglas, a student of Evans-Pritchard and famous for her *Purity and Danger* (1966), analysed the human preoccupation with dirt and impurities as an indirect way of thinking about the boundaries of society and the nature/culture divide, thus joining the structuralism of Lévi-Strauss with that of Radcliffe-Brown, so to speak. Prolific and original, Douglas was for years the most consistent defender of a reformed structural-functionalism (Douglas 1987; see also Chapter 6).

Against all of these (and other) perspectives regarding how 'cultures' or 'societies' perceive the world, anthropologists stressing the actor's point of view have argued that no two individuals see the world in the same way and that it is therefore preposterous to generalise about entire societies. The impact of feminism has been decisive here. Since the 1970s, feminist anthropologists have identified often profound differences between male and female world-views, showing how classic accounts of 'societies' really refer to male perspectives on them as both the anthropologist and the main informants tended to be male (Ardener 1977). In a different vein, Fredrik Barth, who had earlier criticised structural-functionalism from a methodological individualist perspective, developed analyses of knowledge systems in New Guinea and Bali (Barth 1975, 1993; see Chapter 6) which revealed considerable variations within societies, even very small ones. A more radical critique came from the United States, especially following the publication of the influential volume *Writing Culture* (Clifford and Marcus 1986), where most of the contributors argued that notions of cultural wholes and integrated societies were anthropological fictions, claiming that the real world was much more complex and ambiguous than anthropological writings would tend to suggest. These and other publications contributed to a sense of crisis in the discipline in the 1980s and early 1990s, as some of its central concepts, including that of culture, were under severe strain.

Although symbolic anthropology often emphasises the culturally unique and thereby defends a relativist position, this sometimes conceals a deeper universalism. The most influential theory in linguistics during the latter half of the twentieth century was Noam Chomsky's generative grammar, which stressed the similarities between all languages. Even strong relativist positions need a notion of the universal in order to make comparisons. This universal is ultimately located to the human mind in structuralism and many varieties of cognitive anthropology (see D'Andrade 1995), and from this perspective, it can even be said that the relativity of cultures is merely a surface phenomenon since the mind works in the same way everywhere.

* * *

Anthropology in the twenty-first century is a sprawling and varied discipline with an academic foothold in all continents, although its intellectual centres remain in the English- and French-speaking parts of the world. It is still possible to discern differences between American cultural anthropology, British social anthropology and French *ethnologie*, but the discipline is more unified than ever before — not in its views, perhaps, but in its approaches (Eriksen and Nielsen 2001). Hardly a part of the world has not now been studied intensively by scholars engaging in ethnographic fieldwork, but since the world changes, new research is always called for. Specialisations proliferate, ranging from studies of ethnomedicine and the body to urban consumer culture, advertising and cyberspace. Although the grand theories of the nineteenth and twentieth centuries – from unilinear evolutionism to structuralism – have by and large been abandoned, new theories claiming to provide a unified view of humanity are being proposed; for example, new advances in evolutionary theory and cognitive science offer ambitious general accounts of social life and the human mind, respectively. The puzzles and problems confronting earlier generations of anthropologists, regarding, for example, the nature of social organisation, of knowledge, of kinship, of myth and ritual, remain central to the discipline, although they are explored in new empirical settings by scholars who are more specialised than their predecessors.

SUGGESTIONS FOR FURTHER READING

Alan Barnard: *History and Theory in Anthropology*. Cambridge: Cambridge University Press 2000.

Fredrik Barth, Andre Gingrich, Robert Parkin and Sydel Silverman: *One Discipline, Four Ways: British, German, French, and American Anthropology*. Chicago: University of Chicago Press 2005.

Aleksandar Boskovic, ed.: *Other People's Anthropologies*. Oxford: Berghahn 2008.

3 FIELDWORK AND ETHNOGRAPHY

Theory without data is empty, but data without theory are blind.

— *C. Wright Mills*

FIELDWORK

Anthropology distinguishes itself from the other social sciences through the great emphasis placed on ethnographic fieldwork as the most important source of new knowledge about society and culture. A field study may last for a few months, a year, or even two years or more, and it aims at developing as intimate an understanding as possible of the phenomena investigated. Many anthropologists return to their field throughout their career, to deepen their understanding further or to record change. Although there are differences in field methods between different anthropological schools, it is generally agreed that the anthropologist ought to stay in the field long enough for his or her presence to be considered more or less 'natural' by the permanent residents, the informants, although he or she will always to some extent remain a stranger.

Many anthropologists involuntarily take on the role of the clown in the field. They may speak strangely with a flawed grammar; they ask surprising and sometimes tactless questions, and tend to break many rules regarding how things ought to be done. Such a role can be an excellent starting-point for fieldwork, even if it is rarely chosen: through discovering how the locals react to one's own behaviour, one obtains an early hint about their way of thinking. We are all perceived more or less as clowns in unfamiliar surroundings; there are so many rules of conduct in any society that one will necessarily break some of them when one tries to take part in social life in an alien society. In Britain, for example, it is considered uncultured to wear white socks with a dark suit; still, it is perfectly conceivable that people who are not fully conversant with the local dress code do so. (In the field, anthropologists have been known to commit rather more serious mistakes than this.)

A different, and sometimes more problematic, role that can be assumed by the anthropologist in the field, is the role of the expert. Many fieldworkers are treated with great deference and respect by their hosts, are spoken to in exaggeratedly polite ways and so on, and can thus run the risk of never seeing aspects of society which the locals are ashamed of showing to high-ranking strangers.

No matter which role one takes on in the field – most ethnographers are probably partly expert, partly clown, at least in the early stages – fieldwork is extremely demanding, both in professional and in human terms. The tidy, systematic and well-rounded texts written by anthropologists are more often than not the end-product of long periods in the field characterised by boredom, illness, personal privations, disappointments and frustration: few anthropologists can state squarely that their fieldwork was a continuously exciting journey of exploration, full of pleasant experiences. In a foreign setting, one will usually master the language and the codes of behaviour poorly at the beginning, and one will feel helpless in many situations. Besides, one runs the risk of encountering suspicion and hostility, and it can be profoundly unpleasant for the body to have to cope with an unfamiliar climate, strange food and a different hygienic standard than one is accustomed to. Last but not least, it can be very trying for people with a middle-class 'Western' background (which would be the case for most anthropologists) to adapt to societies where being alone is considered a pitiful or pathological condition. Plainly, in many village settings one is never left alone. This problem is usually not a pressing one for the growing number of anthropologists who carry out their fieldwork in modern urban settings. In their case, the problem may be the opposite: in societies where people have TV sets and cars, and where time is considered a scarce resource, an ethnographer may quickly discover that his or her presence creates neither excitement nor curiosity among the natives, and that continuous immersion in local life is difficult. Urban fieldwork tends to be more discontinuous than village fieldwork, and often depends on more formal methods, such as the structured interview.

Even fieldwork in 'exotic' settings should not be romanticised. Among some Indian peoples in North America, a new profession has emerged in recent years: that of the professional ethnographic informant. Some cultural specialists may actually charge handsome fees for spending their time explaining the intricacies of myths and customs to visiting ethnographers.

IN THE FIELD

A principal requirement in fieldwork nonetheless consists of trying to take part in local life as much as possible. Anthropologists also use a variety of specified, formal and informal techniques for the collection of data (see, for example, Ellen 1984; Atkinson et al. 2007). Depending on the kind of fieldwork one is engaged in, structured interviews, statistical sampling and other techniques may be required to varying degrees. Most anthropologists depend on a combination of formal techniques and unstructured participant observation in their fieldwork.

Participant observation refers to the informal field methods which form the basis for most fieldwork, whether or not it is supplemented with other techniques. The aim of this method is to enter as deeply as possibly into the social and cultural field one researches; in practice one becomes, as Evans-

Pritchard remarks (1983 [1937], p. 243), a 'doubly marginal' person, in a sense suspended between one's own society and the society under investigation. During participant observation, one tries to immerse oneself into the life of the locals and tries not to be noticed, so that they can carry on with their own lives as usual. In this regard, the issue of hidden versus open observation has been discussed in the anthropological community. The ethical guidelines of the professional associations nonetheless state in no uncertain terms that it is unethical not to inform one's hosts what one is up to. The people explored must have the right to refuse to be subjected to anthropological analyses; in the case of hidden observation, they are deprived of this possibility.

There are many ways of doing fieldwork, and it is therefore difficult to provide a clear recipe for how to carry it out. For one thing, the anthropologist him- or herself is the most important 'scientific instrument' used, investing a great deal of his or her own personality in the process. The gender, age, 'race' and class of the anthropologist inadvertently influences the experience of fieldwork. A complementary source of variation is the greatly differing settings and topics investigated by anthropologists. We can concede that the methods must be tailored to fit the requirements of the subject, but it is difficult to be more specific. Evans-Pritchard once recalled his first attempts to learn about fieldwork in the early 1920s (1983 [1937], pp. 239–54). He had asked a number of renowned anthropologists how to go about doing it and had received various answers. First, he asked the famous Finnish ethnologist Westermarck, who said, 'Don't converse with an informant for more than twenty minutes because if you aren't bored by that time, he will be.' Evans-Pritchard comments: 'Very good advice, if somewhat inadequate.' Alfred Haddon said 'that it was really all quite simple; one should always behave as a gentleman'. Evans-Pritchard's teacher, Charles Seligman, 'told me to take ten grams of quinine every night and to keep off women'. Finally, Malinowski himself told the novice 'not to be a bloody fool'. Evans-Pritchard himself emphasises, later in the same account, that facts are themselves meaningless; in other words, 'one must know precisely what one wants to know' and then fashion a suitable methodology from the available techniques. However, it may equally well be argued that 'what one wants to know' often becomes apparent only after one has begun fieldwork, which shows why proper fieldwork takes a long time. There is – alas – no simple recipe for fieldwork.

Many anthropological accounts of the process of inquiry, and not least fieldwork, are probably strongly idealised. The expression 'participant observation', a vaguely defined research technique, may serve as a convenient blanket term to conceal both ethical, methodological and personal shortcomings in the actual research process. Many ethnographers probably develop a profoundly ambivalent, sometimes even antagonistic, attitude towards the people they study. When Malinowski's private diaries were published more than twenty years after his death (Malinowski 1967), they led to a long and heated debate. Malinowski, who was and is regarded as an outstanding ethnographer, turned out to have a less than flattering view of the Trobriand Islanders. His project consisted of understanding the islanders in their own terms, yet he personally (at least on a bad day) regarded them as unwashed savages. Frequently, he reports, he had to force himself to leave his hut in the morning for fieldwork. The question which has been raised in this context is whether it is possible to carry out good fieldwork among people one has this little respect for. The answer is obviously yes; and as long as one does not molest one's hosts in the field, there can be no rules against negative attitudes on the part of the anthropologist. At the end of the day, the value of participant observation lies in the quality of the empirical data one has collected, not in the number of close friends one has acquired in the field.

Common problems in fieldwork can be limited knowledge of the field language, gender bias (see Chapter 9) or the fact that one's main informants fail to be representative of the society as a whole. Concerning the latter point, it may be true that anthropologists in the past have tended to pay too much attention to the elite of the community (although elites in complex societies are understudied, partly because access to them is difficult; see Shore and Nugent 2002). Frequently chiefs, teachers and other untypical individuals are most efficient in offering their services to a visiting anthropologist, and the anthropologist may also unwittingly be attracted to these kinds of people because they resemble him- or herself. Gerald Berreman (1962) once wrote a confessional piece on his own field experiences in North India. He depended on an interpreter, and only after he had been at work for a while, rather unsuccessfully, did it become evident that the interpreter was a significant source of distortion in his fieldwork; not because he lied or was inadequate as an interpreter, but because of his position in the caste hierarchy. People did not talk as openly to him as they would to someone like Berreman himself, who was caste-neutral by virtue of being foreign, or to a local with a different caste membership.

Fieldwork does not have to be either capital-intensive or labour-intensive: as a research process it is cheap, since the only scientific instruments involved are the fieldworkers themselves and possibly an assistant. However, and this is perhaps the main point about fieldwork as a scientific method, it is time-intensive. Ideally, one should stay in the field long enough to be able to see the world 'from the native's point of view'. Even if this may be impossible, among other reasons because one cannot entirely bracket one's own cultural background, it can be a worthwhile aim to pursue. The strength of the anthropologist's knowledge can thus be said to lie in his or her mastery of both the local culture and a different culture (his or her own), and of tools of analysis, which makes it possible to give an analytical, comparative account of both.

The very strength of ethnographic field method can also be its weakness: it is demanding, and rewarding, partly because the ethnographer invests not only professional skills in it, but also interpersonal skills. The ethnographer draws on his or her entire personality to a greater extent than any other scientist. For this reason, many emerge from the field exhausted, but with a material of extraordinary richness and depth. At the same time, this degree of personal involvement has important ethical implications. Are friendships and other confidential relationships developed in the field 'real' or 'fake'? What are the moral obligations of the ethnographer towards the informants? The AAA (American Anthropological Association) and other professional bodies, as well as many university departments, have developed ethics codes for the protection of informants, who may disapprove of both the 'anthropologifica-tion' of their personal concerns and of their 'close friends from abroad' who suddenly vanish, never to return.

A different set of problems concerns professional bias caused by personal biography, which may lead ethnographers to see only those parts of social reality that make sense in terms of their earlier experiences. On the other hand, existential involvement in one's own research can also improve the quality of the work (Okely and Calloway 1992). In many cases, fieldwork is as profoundly personal as it is professional, and most anthropologists probably feel a lifelong attachment to their first field site. A topic rarely talked about, but probably not uncommon, concerns sexual relations between anthropologist and informant. An edited volume devoted to this topic (Kulick and Wilson 1995) is entitled, characteristically, *Taboo*.

THEORY AND DATA

The relationship between theory and empirical material, or data, is fundamental in all empirical science, including anthropology. No science can rely on theory alone (it then becomes pure mathematics or philosophy), just as it cannot rely on pure facts: in that case, it would be unable to tell us anything interesting. To put it differently, research has an inductive and a deductive dimension. Induction consists of going out there, 'watching and wondering', collecting information about what people say and do. Deduction consists of attempts to account for facts by means of a general hypothesis or theory. Suppose I were to explore the hypothesis that the rank of women in society is proportional to their contribution to the economy (see Chapter 9). Working deductively, I would develop an argument showing why this made sense. In the actual research process, however, I would have to shift to an inductive mode, exploring the relationship between the position of women and the economy in a number of existing societies. As soon as I came across one or several societies where there was no apparent relationship between the contribution to the economy and the relative rank of women, I would have to modify my initial hypothesis.

We may envision the search for this kind of general insight as a zigzag movement between the observation of fact and theoretical reasoning, where new facts modify the theory and (modified) theory accounts for the facts. Each time one shifts from theory to description of empirical process and back, one's insight has become a little bit more accurate.

If one were to reproduce everything one's informants said and to describe everything they did, one would be unable to falsify, or for that matter justify, specific hypotheses. One would virtually drown in details without being able to present patterns and regularities. The description of society would be as complex and ambiguous as society itself and therefore superfluous. The anthropological project consists, to a great extent, of imposing ordering patterns and regularities onto the observed material, and we depend on our own theoretical abstractions in order to do so. The challenge lies in saying something significant about culture and social life through these abstractions.

The choice of an accurate topic for investigation therefore is an important part of the preparation for fieldwork. At the very least, one should know if one

---

Challenging Dichotomies

A great part of anthropological theory rests on contrasting pairs, or dichotomies, used analytically to distinguish between ideal types (Weber's term) of societies and cultures. Some of the most widely invoked such dichotomies are: Small-scale/large-scale; oral/written; *bricoleur*/engineer; traditional/modern; status/contract; *Gemeinschaft* (community)/*Gesellschaft* (society).

An underlying assumption of this kind of dichotomy is the view that modern industrial society is unique and stands out in relation to all other societies, which, by comparison, are depicted as 'more or less the same'. Obviously, these dichotomies are inadequate as descriptive devices. First, traditional societies are, to say the least, not 'all the same' – the ancient kingdoms of India and pastoral societies of North Africa indeed have little in common. Second, this holds for modern societies as well. There are important differences between, say, Japan, the United States and France. Third, the very dichotomous distinction between 'types' of societies is untenable. In most if not all societies of the world, one would be able to identify 'modern' as well as 'traditional' aspects – not least in the age of globalisation.

The world as it is studied by anthropologists is not characterised by clear, 'digital' or binary boundaries, but rather by grey zones and differences in degree – analogic differences. It is not an archipelago of isolated cultures, but an unbounded system of multiple interrelationships. Why, then, should we bother with dichotomies at all? Strangely, perhaps, it seems difficult to do without them. Anthropologists have for a long time been aware of the inadequacies of rigid classificatory schemes, and they have often been discarded, but frequently only to re-emerge in new garb. Perhaps dichotomies are indeed necessary for the anthropological enterprise. If so, we should keep two critical points in mind: first, the models are not identical with the social world but a mere aid in organising facts from the social world; and, second, dichotomies may be envisaged as scales marked by differences in degree rather than as absolute contrasts.

is interested in, say, resource management or child-raising before embarking on fieldwork. Otherwise one will end up knowing too little about everything rather than knowing enough about something. Godfrey Lienhardt (1985), borrowing an analogy from Geertz, has compared the relationship between theory and ethnography to an elephant-and-rabbit stew. What is required, says Lienhardt, is one elephant of ethnography and one rabbit of theory. The art, as he sees it, consists in cooking the stew in such a way that the taste of rabbit is discernible in every spoonful.

ANTHROPOLOGY AT HOME

Anthropology has traditionally distinguished itself from sociology through (1) the emphasis placed on participant observation and fieldwork, and (2) studying chiefly non-industrialised societies. Sociology has concentrated on understanding, criticising and managing modern societies, whereas the historical task of anthropology has been to account for the variations and similarities in human existence and, to some extent, to rescue disappearing peoples from oblivion by recording their way of life in writing.

For a number of reasons, fieldwork in the anthropologist's own society or a similar one has become much more common since the founding period of the discipline. First, anthropology today faces a number of new challenges because of historical changes in the world, including the virtual disappearance of 'the tribal world' and the forces of globalisation – from the Internet to migration. It has become impossible to posit sharp distinctions between 'us' (moderns) and 'them' (primitives), not least because modernisation and 'development' have contributed to shrinking spatial distances and have blurred boundaries between cultures which formerly seemed relatively clear. What is 'home' and what is 'abroad' is no longer always clear. Second, analyses of tribal societies have inspired researchers to use similar analytical models when dealing with their own society, and have also provided a useful basis for comparison. It is easier to see what is unique to our own society when we have intimate knowledge of other societies, than it would otherwise be. There is an intellectual continuity, therefore, between 'tribal studies' and studies in contemporary cities. Third, there are many researchers competing for scarce research funds and far from everybody is able to raise funding for long-term fieldwork in a remote place. In addition, a number of governments in the Third World have grown sceptical of anthropologists. Anthropology is no longer a 'science of the tribal' or of the 'non-industrial world', but it remains a truly global science which may just as well study Internet use in Trinidad (Miller and Slater 2000) as Hindu nationalism (Frøystad 2005), adoption and kinship in Western societies (Howell 2007) or ethnic complexity in London (Baumann 1996).

One argument sometimes used against fieldwork in one's own kind of society is that the overall aim of the discipline is to account for cultural variation in the world. It therefore seems reasonable that one should study people who are, by common consent, seen as culturally remote. Another argument is that it is necessary to use our own society as an implicit basis for comparison, something which vanishes when we study our neighbours. On the other hand, thorough field studies of 'modern' societies have revealed that they are far more heterogeneous, in terms of culture and social organisation, than is generally assumed. Also, the distinction between 'the cultural self' and 'the cultural other' is no longer unproblematic. A German ethnographer may, in significant respects, have more in common with educated Kenyans than with Neo-Nazi skinheads from his or her own hometown.

A general argument in favour of anthropological research 'at home' is that the most fundamental questions we ask about culture, society and so on are equally relevant anywhere in the world. Sir Raymond Firth, then the undisputed doyen of British anthropology, expressed his own view in a lecture given on the future of anthropology in 1989: 'Since we can explore the anthropological problems anywhere, we might as well go to places where it is comfortable to spend some time' (Firth 1989). For his own part, Firth carried out much of his fieldwork in Tikopia, a tropical island in the Pacific (but, it must be conceded, he also did fieldwork in England). As a matter of fact, today's anthropology encompasses the whole world, including the areas which anthropologists call home. Fieldwork at home, like anywhere in the world, depends on the anthropologist's professional skills. In a familiar or semi-familiar setting, one has the advantage of mastering the language and cultural conventions better than in a culturally distant place, but one also tends to take too much for granted. This problem can be described as 'homeblindness', and it can be overcome, at least to a great extent, through proper training. The comparative, detailed study of cultural variation which forms the core of the education of an anthropologist enables us to study societies we believe to be familiar with roughly the same methods and analytical apparatus we would apply to distant societies.

INTERPRETATION AND ANALYSIS

When modern anthropology took shape in the early years of the twentieth century, there were still large chunks of the globe that had hardly been visited by Europeans, much less been subjected to systematic exploration. When Boas studied the Kwakiutl and neighbouring peoples on the north-west coast of North America, when Malinowski lived in the Trobriand Islands, when Bateson visited the Iatmul in New Guinea and when Evans-Pritchard went to live among the Azande, they could only prepare themselves to a limited extent through reading earlier studies from the region. They knew relatively little about the sites they were going to. The world has changed quite dramatically since then. There now always exist studies from the region one visits as ethnographer, although it may still be possible to come across smaller groups, notably in the Amazon basin or New Guinea, which have not been studied anthropologically and who have had limited or no contact with the outside world. More often than not, however, one can learn the language before leaving home, and there usually exists a large specialist literature devoted to the region, which must be consulted before embarking on fieldwork – and which one may hope to add to eventually, thereby contributing to the cumulative growth of knowledge which is the hallmark of any science, however it is defined.

The classic anthropological monograph from the 1920s to the 1950s typically dealt with a people's most important institutions, usually taking village fieldwork as its empirical point of departure. It frequently aimed at a comprehensive overview of 'the way of life' of a people, describing the interrelationship between religion, politics, the economy, kinship and so on. For a number of reasons, this model eventually went out of fashion. One obvious reason is that most anthropological studies now take place in complex large-scale settings and are not limited to villages. Another reason is the growing specialisation within the discipline, which has turned many professionals into highly specialised sub-disciplinary experts focusing, say, on medical systems, socialisation, public rituals or political rhetoric in particular societies. A third, related, reason is the fact that a wealth of general ethnography has already been carried out on most regions, so it is frequently unnecessary to begin from scratch. When Annette Weiner left for fieldwork in the Trobriand Islands in the 1970s, therefore, she did not endeavour to study every aspect of the Melanesian island society in detail: Malinowski and others had already done much of the groundwork, and she could relate her own work to lacunae or controversial points in earlier analyses of the Trobrianders (Weiner 1988). Her studies accordingly deal chiefly with the role of women and gender relations, and they engage in a critical dialogue with earlier work in the area (see Chapters 9 and 12).

Moreover, social theory is now being produced from within in many of the societies studied by anthropologists. Sociology, anthropology and other theoretically informed texts are now being written by the grandchildren of Radcliffe-Brown's and Kroeber's informants. This implies that today's anthropologists may, and are indeed forced to, engage in a dialogue with the society explored to a greater extent than their predecessors did. It also implies that anthropological studies may affect local communities directly. If someone today writes a monograph on, say, a South African neighbourhood, the book will necessarily influence South African society; it will be read by some of the 'natives', and thus becomes part of the social reality of the informants. This situation has created obvious ethical problems. It would not have occurred to Malinowski or Bateson that their books on Melanesia might have a direct influence on the societies in question (although Malinowski's work has for a long time been well known in the Trobriand Islands): they could write freely without taking such issues into account. This is no longer possible, at least if one's work is published in English or French.

THE ETHNOGRAPHIC PRESENT AND THE PAST

Anthropological texts are usually written in the present tense. Many of the most influential monographs were nevertheless written half a century ago or more, and in every single case the societies they deal with have changed radically since the original fieldwork took place. Frequently, moreover, fieldwork was carried out during an unusual, not a 'typical', historical period. Classic African anthropology was developed during the last phase of French and British colonialism, namely between the First World War and 1960. It has since been pointed out that this period was untypical because it was a time of a peculiar form political stability shaped by colonialism, which has been absent both before and afterwards in African societies.

Social anthropology has never tried to replace history. Anthropological analysis has traditionally been focused on social and cultural interrelationships at a particular point in time and, until recently, rarely emphasised the historical processes which have led up to the present. In the British, American and French traditions, the aim has usually been to account for the workings of a particular society or culture, not to try to explain how it emerged. Boas, Radcliffe-Brown and Malinowski were all critical of the rather speculative forms of cultural history which preceded modern anthropology. However, an appropriate response to the bad cultural history exemplified in much early anthropological writing would not be to discredit history as such, but rather to improve one's historical accuracy – as witnessed at an early stage in the work of the fourth 'founding father', namely Mauss, whose essay on gift exchange draws extensively on well-documented historical material from Norse, Indian and Roman society.

Although the historical dimension has come to prominence in much anthropological work since the 1980s, a majority of anthropological studies could probably still be described as synchronic 'snapshots'. We may use the term 'the ethnographic present' to characterise the literary tense involved. At the level of a purely analytical understanding, it is irrelevant *when* the Nuer, the Trobriand Islanders or the Swat Pathans enact a certain culture or form of social organisation as described in a monograph. The importance of the studies of these peoples does not lie primarily in their historical or genealogical explanatory power, but rather in their contribution to our understanding of differences and similarities of social life in general. They contribute to our comparative knowledge of forms of human life. As Kirsten Hastrup argues, the ethnographic present does not imply that timelessness is a feature of other societies, 'but we do stress that ethnographic knowledge transcends the empirical' (1992, p. 128) in that it deepens our understanding of the human condition in general.

There is also a clear methodological advantage involved in the synchronic study of social life. Anthropology may be described as the process whereby one wades into a river and explores it as it flows by, whereas historians are forced to study the dry riverbed. Lacking trustworthy time machines, we cannot engage in participant observation of the past.

On the other hand, many anthropologists have followed the lead of Kroeber and Evans-Pritchard in stressing the importance of knowing the history of a society and its contribution to the present. This can be especially rewarding – some would say absolutely necessary – in studies dealing with societies with a written history. Further, the connections between different societies, which are often crucial for the understanding of each society, can only be properly investigated historically (Wolf 1982). For example, it would be impossible to understand the industrial revolution in England properly without prior knowledge of the slave trade and the cotton plantations in the United States.

In sum, the ethnographic present and the historical dimension should not be seen as mutually exclusive. The critics of diffusionism, who correctly pointed out the importance of studying societies and cultures as more or less integrated systems and eschewed irresponsible speculation, tended to overemphasise the relative isolation and unchanging character of societies. To the extent that historical sources are available, they doubtless make important contributions to the contemporary understanding of single societies.

WRITING AND READING ETHNOGRAPHY

Although fieldwork remains the most important method of generating new knowledge in anthropology, the transmission of knowledge within the professional community generally takes place through the writing and reading of texts. Geertz (1988) argues, in a study of the writings of several prominent practitioners, that the most characteristic activity of anthropologists is writing, and he therefore calls attention to the way in which such texts are produced. Far from being neutral and objective descriptions and analyses of other people's customs and cultural systems, anthropological writings are shaped by each author's biography, literary style and rhetoric, as well as by the historical period in which they were written (such as colonialism) and, of course, by the character of the fieldwork. These aspects of the production of anthropological knowledge have often been understated or dismissed as irrelevant to the end-product: the monograph or academic article.

The approach to ethnography exemplified in Geertz's book may seem to undermine the authority of these works as sources of knowledge about society and culture, and to reduce them to mere literature. This was not Geertz's intention although it may have been an unintended side-effect: he argued for more professional reading, offering, through his examples, contexts of interpretation enabling the reader to appreciate the full significance of ethnographic texts. For example, he shows how Firth establishes his ethnographic authority by starting his famous 1927 monograph on the Tikopia with a lengthy descriptive literary passage 'marshaled with Dickensian exuberance and Conradian fatality' (Geertz 1988, p. 13) to communicate his familiarity with the society he then goes on to describe in strict sociological terms for the following several hundred pages. This observation does not mean that Firth's work is invalid, but that a different anthropologist would have written a different book – in other words, that the anthropologist as author is situated in the field and in his or her own text.

Several anthropologists (or meta-anthropologists) followed Geertz's lead (and went further than he did) in applying techniques from literary criticism to ethnographic writings (see Clifford and Marcus 1986; Manganaro 1990; James et al. 1997) and have suggested, for example, that Malinowski's style was indebted to Joseph Conrad, that Evans-Pritchard's representation of Africans was tainted by his colonial background and attitudes, that Ruth Benedict's wartime study of the Japanese, *The Chrysanthemum and the Sword* (1974 [1946]), had to be understood primarily in the context of the Second World War and not as a research monograph, and so on. A possible implication of this focus on narrative strategies and implicit agendas is that anthropological studies tend to be persuasive rather than convincing; that they evoke more than they describe; that they are shaped by the author's personal bias, not by the studied society; and that they create a 'suspension of disbelief' in the reader not so much because of the data presented but because of the author's style and rhetoric.

The recent interest in the writing of ethnographic texts does not necessarily lead to a conclusion this radical, and many have followed Jonathan Spencer's lead in criticising the 'textual turn' as a way of turning away from social reality (Spencer 1989). Geertz's aim was not to dismiss ethnography as fiction, but rather 'that we shall learn to read with a more percipient eye' (1988, p. 24). Some understanding of literary techniques and the importance of personal and historical contexts in the production of knowledge in the long run can only lead to more accurate comprehension than a naïve reading would. Such insights into the social conditions of the production of knowledge led, in the 1980s and 1990s, particularly in the United States, to a proliferation of 'experimental ethnographies' that tried to solve the problem of representing others in novel ways (see Clifford and Marcus 1986; Marcus and Fischer 1986), as well as 'postcolonial ethnographies' that are either written by members of the formerly colonised peoples or by foreign anthropologists arguing against previous understandings of the areas in question, which they see as informed by a colonial way of thinking, or at least by exoticism and stereotypes (see, for example, Guha and Spivak 1988; Gupta and Ferguson 1997).

THE PROBLEM OF TRANSLATION

In the earlier discussion of ethnocentrism, I remarked that we would not arrive at a satisfactory understanding of a society if we were to evaluate its achievements in relation to the standards and values of our own society. It therefore becomes a central challenge to connect analytical concepts to the alien social and cultural world dealt with. The related problems arising from this project are frequently spoken of as the *problem of translation*. How can we translate an alien way of experiencing the world into our own mode of thought; how can we be certain that we do not misinterpret or distort the society when we try to describe it in our own terms? And how can we be entirely certain that we understand the alien society and culture at all, imbued as we are with our own cultural background, concepts and values? These interrelated problems are fundamental to anthropology, and they are dealt with extensively in Chapter 15. For now, we will restrict ourselves to an outline of some dimensions of the problem.

Within the discipline of anthropology, it is necessary to use abstract terms such as kinship, social organisation, social control, religion and so on. These terms are necessary for the discipline to be comparative in its scope: how could it be possible to compare, say, the kinship system of the Trobrianders with that of the Yanomamö if one did not have a general concept of kinship? However, the abstract, technical terms used by anthropologists exist only rarely in the societies we study: they form part of our professional world, not theirs. How, then, can we justify accounting for an alien society in terms which are demonstrably not its own, if the aim of anthropology is to understand societies and cultures from within?

There are several possible solutions to this seeming paradox. A first step could be to distinguish between *description* and *analysis*. The descriptive aspect of an anthropological account is usually close to the native conceptualisation of the world (experience-near), and a major challenge lies in translating native concepts into the anthropologist's working language. When describing a social and cultural life-world, the anthropologist will often resort to direct quotations from informants, to give an account of the world as it appears from within. The analysis, on the other hand, will try to connect the society to other societies, at a theoretical level, by describing it in the comparative terms of anthropology. In other words, it will describe the society with concepts which do not exist in the society itself (experience-distant). What kind of 'kinship system' do the people have? How do they resolve 'conflicts'? What is the 'division of labour between men and women'? What is the role of 'religion and rituals'? How are 'power relations' structured?

The suggested distinction between description and analysis, although helpful, is not absolute. Even the description is necessarily shaped by the anthropologist's selection of facts and their own interpretations, and he or she can never become a native. In addition, it would plainly be impossible to include everything in a description, even if one's aim is to provide a comprehensive account of a society and one has a thousand pages at one's disposal.

EMIC AND ETIC

Let us look a little more closely at the relationship between the view from within and the view from the outside. Ethnographic description lies closer, in a sense, to the world as experienced by the informants than the analysis does, as the latter may ultimately aim at general statements about culture and society. This level – life as experienced and described by the members of a society themselves – is sometimes spoken of as the 'emic' level. Its counterpart, the analytical descriptions or explanations of the researcher, is the 'etic' level.

The emic–etic dichotomy was introduced into anthropology by Marvin Harris (1964, 1979), but it was first developed by the linguist Kenneth Pike (Headland et al. 1990), who derived the terms from the linguistic distinction between phonetics and phonemics, referring to the objective relationship between sounds and the meaning of sounds, respectively.

The 'native's point of view' is emic, whereas the analytical perspective of the anthropologist is etic. However, even if the anthropologist aims to reproduce reality the way it is perceived by the informants, there are three reasons why the result may never be an emic description. First, we must usually translate between two different languages, and the translation is different from the original. Second, we use a written medium to reproduce oral statements, and the meaning of utterances changes when they are transformed into writing. Third, the anthropologist can never become identical with the people he or she writes about. The only truly emic descriptions possible in anthropology are therefore accounts written by natives in their vernacular.

It is a common assumption that emic perspectives are wrong, whereas the etic perspectives are correct. This is an unfortunate way of framing the issue. The point is not whether the 'natives' or the 'scientists' are correct, but rather that social scientists have specialised interests and that the kinds of insight they aim at are frequently not identical with the interests of their informants in the field. There are a number of equally correct ways of describing a cultural and social system; one's choice must depend on one's interests. A further misunderstanding regarding the emic–etic distinction amounts to the idea that emic notions are 'concrete' whereas etic notions are 'abstract'. This may be the case, but it is not inherently true. As Geertz (1983) reminds us, many of the studied peoples use highly abstract, or experience-distant, concepts such as 'God', 'witchcraft', 'mortgage interest' or 'karma'.

However, a necessary condition for anthropological research to be meaningful at all is that the researcher knows something essential that the native does not know. He or she must have the ability to connect a local reality to a comparative conceptual apparatus, enabling a particular society to shed light on other societies and contributing to the growth of our total body of knowledge about social and cultural variation. There are 'strong' and 'weak' programmes in this regard: some anthropologists plainly see themselves as in a way like natural scientists in search of general theories and laws of culture and societies, while others are more strongly concerned with elucidating dimensions of a single society in great detail, doubting the validity of theories with a highly general scope. What all of them have in common, nevertheless, is an interest in the similarities and differences of forms of human existence, and confidence in the ability of anthropology to say something meaningful about it.

ANTHROPOLOGY AS POLITICS

Unlike university subjects like law and medicine, anthropology does not lead to a particular profession, and there are anthropologists practising in a growing number of professions. Only a minority teach and carry out research at universities. Many are involved in development cooperation, and probably an even larger number work in public administration, many of them being engaged with issues to do with ethnic diversity and multicultural society. There are also anthropologists working in publishing, in private enterprises, in hospitals, in the media and so on. An anthropological training, in other words, may be useful in a variety of professional practices. Here, we focus on the production of anthropological knowledge in the most powerful milieux of the profession, namely where the authoritative texts – monographs and articles – are written and evaluated, where appointments are decided and where reading lists are made; in short, the arenas where the discipline is being defined.

Anthropology, arising out of a particular kind of social environment, can itself be studied anthropologically. The knowledge offered to students is not developed in a social and cultural vacuum, and theoretical as well as empirical directions are decided through social cooperation, competition, the search for personal prestige and political decisions. Students, for their part, must be socialised (see Chapter 4) into a particular mode of reasoning and style of writing in order to succeed.

Anthropology may thus be regarded as a social and cultural field; and like any social phenomenon, it entails power disparities (see Bourdieu 1988 for a critique of academia along these lines; see also MacClancy 1996). This fact is frequently pointed out, and criticised, by students, who form the least powerful group in the academic world. In the 1970s it was thus commonplace for students all over the Western world to form informal 'countercultural' groups where they analysed and criticised what they saw as an inherent ideological bias in the subject. Notably, they argued that a feminist perspective was lacking, and that traditional anthropology was incapable of analytically coming to terms with coercion and exploitation. In this period, the dominant professional priorities were challenged. Above all, the critics stressed that anthropology, as a human science, is intimately related to society as such and that it is therefore influenced by power interests in society. Some Third World critics claimed that anthropology was simply an extension of the colonial ideology, trying to subjugate non-white peoples by incorporating their way of life into a Western body of knowledge. A related issue was the question of how knowledge advances. Are research environments fundamentally self-critical and ruthless in their impartial search for knowledge (Popper 1968 [1959]), or are they rather deeply conservative, since every new idea threatens to challenge their own claim to authority (Kuhn 1962)?

The radical students, and other critics of the anthropological practice, did contribute to a transformation of the discipline, even if it remains true –

perhaps necessarily – that it is being defined by a professional (or professorial) power elite. What is most remarkable about the kind of autocritique referred to is perhaps the willingness to apply insights from social science 'out there' to one's own situation 'in here'.

Finally, something must be said about the anthropological production of knowledge as a social process. Although fieldwork is emphasised as the main source of new insights, the production of anthropological understanding mainly takes place at universities and research institutes. The exchange of knowledge between anthropologists occurs at international conferences and through professional journals, doctoral dissertations and books. Since many anthropologists compete over prestige and power within their professional environment, a rather frenzied rate of publishing can be observed in parts of the international anthropological community. The American maxim 'Publish or perish!' is as valid among anthropologists as in other scientific disciplines. In other words, it may occasionally be the case that the 'love of knowledge' programmatically underlying scientific publishing is not necessarily the main motivation for publishing.

Of course, anthropology is about understanding social systems and cultural variation, not about the professional careers of individual anthropologists. It should nevertheless be kept in mind that this knowledge is not being produced in an ivory tower inhabited by pure vocational spirit; that fallible human beings of flesh and blood are responsible for the advancement of analysis; and that our modes of analysis, claiming universal applicability, should occasionally be applied to ourselves as well as to 'the Others'.

*   *   *

The population explosion that has taken place among anthropologists since the 1960s, perhaps especially evident in anthropological publishing, has made it difficult for any single individual to follow every development within the subject. The number of professional journals and monographs published annually is enormous, and we have also witnessed an increasing specialisation within the discipline. Through the development of a growing number of sub-disciplines, such as regional specialisations, medical anthropology, symbolic anthropology and development anthropology, the subject may seem threatened by fission. In the 1940s it was relatively easy to acquire an overview of the discipline; there were perhaps only 30 or 40 canonical books that it was necessary to relate to. Today the number of relevant studies is enormous and specialisation is inevitable. However, in this kind of situation it is more important than ever to retain a common core of shared concepts and some shared knowledge of culture and social systems if the discipline is to remain one. This book aims at presenting – and critically engaging with – the bulk of this common foundation, which makes it possible for anthropologists everywhere to have informed professional exchanges, even if their specialisations are very different. Had we lacked such a shared professional language, it would have been difficult to exchange ideas and experiences across the many specialisations and emerging sub-disciplines of anthropology, and ultimately, anthropology as a common project, or science, would cease to exist.

SUGGESTIONS FOR FURTHER READING

Gerald Berreman: *Behind Many Masks: Ethnography and Impression Management in a Himalayan Village*. Society for Applied Anthropology: Monograph no. 4, 1962.

John van Maanen: *Tales of the Field: On Writing Ethnography*. Chicago: University of Chicago Press 1988.

C.W. Watson, ed.: *Being There: Fieldwork in Anthropology*. London: Pluto 1999.

4   THE SOCIAL PERSON

The self is something which has a development; it is not initially there, at birth, but arises in the process of social experience and activity, that is, develops in the given individual as a result of his relations to that process as a whole and to other individuals within that process.

— *George Herbert Mead*

THE SOCIAL CHARACTER OF HUMANITY

The press occasionally reports stories about 'jungle children' who are discovered after allegedly having spent many years in a forest or similar wilderness, isolated from culture and human society. According to such stories – Kipling's novel about Mowgli, *The Jungle Book*, is the most famous one (and one which does not, incidentally, claim authenticity) – these children have been raised by animals, usually monkeys, and are therefore unable to communicate with humans. Normally, 'jungle children' are said to reveal a pattern of acting similar to animal behaviour; they growl, they are terrified of humans and they lack human language, table manners and other capabilities which render the rest of us culturally competent. Most of these stories are fictional (although a few have been well documented), but they can nevertheless be useful as illustrations of a crucial anthropological insight, namely the fact that human beings are social products. As Carrithers puts it, 'from infancy humans are directed to other human beings as the significant feature of their environment' (1992, p. 57).

What we think of as our human character is not inborn; it must be acquired through learning. The truly human in us, as anthropology sees it, is primarily created through our engagement with the social and cultural world; it is neither exclusively individual nor natural. All behaviour has a social origin; how we dress (for that matter, the mere fact that we dress), how we communicate through language, gestures and facial expressions, what we eat and how we eat – all of these capabilities which are so self-evident that we tend to think of them as natural, are acquired. Of course, humans are also biological creatures with certain unquestionably innate needs (such as those for nourishment and sleep), but there are always socially created ways of satisfying these needs. It is a biological fact that humans need food to grow and to survive; on the other hand, the food is always prepared and eaten in a culturally determined way, and food habits vary. Ways of cooking, seasoning and mixtures of ingredients which may seem natural to me may seem disgusting to you; and – a topic of great interest to anthropologists – food taboos are nearly ubiquitous but differ from society to society. High-caste Hindus are not supposed to eat meat at all; rule-abiding Jews and Muslims do not eat pork; many Europeans refuse to eat horse meat, and so on. It is also a biological fact that hair grows on our heads, but our ways to relate to this fact are socially and culturally shaped. Whether we let it grow, cut it, shave it, dye it, curl it, straighten it, wash it or comb it depends on the social conventions considered valid in our society.

In order for humans to survive in society, they depend on a number of shared social conventions or implicit rules for behaviour. For example, there is general agreement in Britain that one speaks English and not Japanese, that one buys a ticket upon entering a bus, that one does not wander naked around shopping centres, that one rings the bell before entering one's neighbour's house and so on. Most social conventions of this kind are taken for granted and therefore tend to be perceived as natural. In this way, we may learn something about ourselves by studying other societies, where entirely different conventions are taken for granted. These studies remind us that a wealth of facts about ourselves, considered more or less innate or natural, are actually socially created.

NATURE AND SOCIETY

Figure 4.1 depicts some central dimensions of human existence. The bottom left field presents humanity as a biological species. Typical characteristics of *homo sapiens sapiens* seen through this lens, through its shared biological features, could be its digestive system, its average length and body weight, its reproductive apparatus and its brain volume. Inborn aptitudes common to all humanity, such as the capability for language acquisition, also belong here. Anthropologists and others influenced by biology and, in particular, Darwin's theory of natural selection, argue that the list of inborn traits and potentials is much longer (Tooby and Cosmides 1992), and so do structuralists. In spite of recent advances in cognitive science, the general trend in contemporary social and cultural anthropology is nevertheless to emphasise 'nurture' over 'nature', and to emphasise the enormous variations generated, under differing circumstances, by our shared inborn apparatus.

The bottom right field depicts differences between humans which can be accounted for biologically. Until the 1930s or 1940s, it was commonly held that there are important genetic differences between human populations, that is 'racial differences', which account for some observable cultural variation. However, it has been shown that only a tiny proportion of the genetic variation in the world is related to what are conventionally thought of as racial variations (Cavalli-Sforza et al. 1994). To begin with, all humans have about 99.8 per cent of their genes in common. Of the remaining 0.2 per cent, 85 per cent can be found within any ethnic group, and 'racial' differences account for

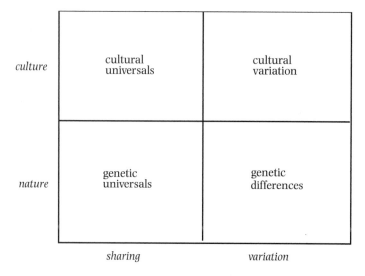

Figure 4.1   Four dimensions of human existence

only 9 per cent of 0.2 per cent, which amounts to 0.012 per cent difference in genetic material. Finally, quite a bit of this 'racial' variation is unrelated to physical appearance. For example, many human groups when adult lack the enzyme lactase, which is necessary for digesting milk. Following this criterion, North Europeans should be classified together with Arabs and some African peoples such as the Fulani, while South Europeans belong with other Africans and East Asians. The classification of humanity into races, based on physical appearance, is arbitrary and scientifically uninteresting. The study of race thus belongs to the anthropology of power and ideology, not to the area of cultural variation. It should be added that social scientists working within an evolutionary paradigm often called 'evolutionary psychology' (Buss 2004), tend to be more struck by the similarities than by the differences between human groups. Darwinist social science is, in other words, not tantamount to racist social science; it tends to look foremost at similarities, but also at variations *within* any group.

The top left field of Figure 4.1 refers to the shared cultivated, social dimensions of humanity, that is, the shared characteristics developed by humans through their lives in society; whereas the top right field represents cultural variation. Put together, these dimensions form the core of anthropological research. By demonstrating variations between the human qualities created in different societies, anthropology has often tried to show that there are large areas of human existence which biology cannot account for fully, since the inborn genetic variation between human groups is incapable of accounting for the enormous cultural variation in the world – on the other hand, it should not be ruled out that the latter variation might actually conceal uniformity at a deeper level (Brown 1991). There are evident biological limits concerning human potential: for instance, there is probably no society which has taught its members how to fly or to live eternally, or which has dispensed with the need for food and drink. In addition, there are ecological limitations to human potential. Anthropology generally does not see it as its task to account for these limitations, but rather focuses on the social and cultural dimensions, trying to elucidate variations as well as uniformities between discrete forms of human life. The relationship between anthropology and biological accounts of humanity is nevertheless the subject of debate. Some biologists-cum-anthropologists, the sociobiologists, hold that important aspects of human life ultimately have a genetic origin. Others, including most anthropologists, would rather argue that dimensions of existence which seem inborn, such as the differences between the genders, or even aggression and other emotions commonly seen as genetically determined, must be understood as social and cultural products. Evidence for this normally consists in a coherent account of a people where aggression is seemingly absent (as in Howell and Willis 1989) or, at a more general level, where the emotions displayed appear to be radically different from the emotions familiar from the anthropologist's own society (Rosaldo 1984; see Spiro 1986 for a universalist view inspired by Freudian psychology).

If we regard humanity in general, we may explore both similarities and differences between humans. Most biologists focus on the similarities. In the study of humans as cultural beings, the situation is more complicated. Certainly, anthropology necessarily deals with something all humans have in common, since we have already established that all humans are cultural creatures and relate to social conventions. On the other hand, many anthropologists have also been concerned with accounting for individual variations and with the uniqueness of particular societies.

Concerning the thorny concept of culture, this always refers to something shared, but there are two ways in which it is so. First, culture may refer to something universally shared – a shared quality of all humans is the fact of their culturedness (top left square of Figure 4.1). Second, culture is also used in the meaning of *a* culture (which is thus distinct from other cultures, a word which can be conjugated in the plural; top right square of Figure 4.1). Seen in this perspective, culture is a marker of difference between groups (who are differently cultured, so to speak), and not a marker of human universals. Both of these meanings of culture are commonly used – and sometimes confused.

LANGUAGE

'Language', the author William Burroughs famously said, 'is a virus from outer space.' Biologists have argued that although Burroughs is probably wrong, several components of the human speech faculty are related to other evolutionary features which humanity shares with other species. Chimpanzees who have been taught the meaning of a limited number of English words seem to form abstract concepts representing classes of phenomena such as 'car' and not merely terms for specific objects (Lieberman 1994).

Notwithstanding similarities with biologically related species, notably the great apes, verbal language is often seen as the main discriminating mark of humanity. No other species uses meaningful sounds in nearly as many ways as humans, and no other species is actually able to speak. In human societies, objects are named and classified, human acts are named, and abstract entities such as spirits and gods are named. The symbolic meaning and verbal form of each phenomenon are conventionalised and perpetuated throughout the speech community, and the interrelationship between concepts and symbols makes up a particular cultural universe within which people think and act. This makes language a cultural universal. In linguistics and evolutionary theory, an important controversy concerns the possible evolutionary basis of language. Darwinian linguist Steven Pinker has argued that language must have been adaptive in proto-human society (1993; see also Dunbar 1999), while the world's most famous linguistic scholar, Noam Chomsky, regards this view as pure speculation – he sees the issue as a 'mystery' rather than a 'puzzle'. Stephen Jay Gould, a leading Darwinan theorist, saw language as a side-effect of other evolutionary adaptations (Gould 2002). Whatever the case may be, language is universal, but at the same time people in different parts of the world obviously speak different languages, and in this sense language (in the meaning of *a* language), like culture, can be seen as a concept which describes differences rather than similarities between groups of humans.

However, just as much of the genetic variation in the world can be found within ethnic or national groups, there is much linguistic and cultural variation within groups as well. Earlier anthropologists, tending to stress the uniformity and integration of traditional societies, have frequently been criticised for overstating the cultural and linguistic uniformity within groups, suggesting that all members of a people share the same basic repertoire of knowledge and world-view and are equally linguistically competent. It has nevertheless been well documented that there are important differences in cultural repertoire, skills and indeed world-views within even small groups, even if they also share important cultural characteristics, such as a mother tongue.

CULTURE AND ECOLOGY

It is no longer common among professional anthropologists to regard some peoples are 'closer to nature' than others by virtue of their simple technology. It is a dogma in modern social and cultural anthropology that culture is the fundamental human diacritic, shared by all humans, and that it would be nonsense to claim that some peoples 'have more culture' than others. Humans in all societies are equally cultured, although in different ways.

On the other hand, a view which is far from uncommon in modern societies, and which may also occur among anthropologists, amounts to the idea that people with a simple technology tend to have an intuitive understanding of the processes of nature because they live 'closer to nature' than we do, whereas we moderns, for our part, have 'removed ourselves from nature' by placing a thick layer of alienating filters – computers, concrete buildings, highways and books – between ourselves and nature. Let us consider an example.

The BaMbuti pygmies of the Ituri forest in what is today north-eastern Congo (DRC) are traditionally hunters and gatherers with a simple technology and a social differentiation based on gender, age and personal qualities (Turnbull 1979 [1961], 1983; Mukenge 2002). Numbering about 30,000–40,000 people spread over a large area, they carry out hunting in two different ways: individually, with bow and arrow, and collectively, with nets. Women and children gather edible things, which are abundant. In their own view, any shortage of food is a result of laziness.

The BaMbuti live in small groups numbering about 20–30 persons and have a classificatory kinship system, which means that the same kinship terms are used to denote individuals who are differently (or not at all) biologically related. Rank is determined according to gender, age and personal authority, and the transition between life-stages is marked by elaborate rites of passage. Weddings are also important rituals, and divorce is discouraged. Although non-marital sex occurs, it is negatively sanctioned. Flirtation is subjected to strict rules.

Both men and women appropriate a wide variety of skills necessary for survival. The majority of these are culturally specific; they are not shared by the neighbouring Bantu-speaking peoples, most of whom are agriculturalists. Hunting techniques, the preparation of poison for arrows and techniques for honey gathering are among the most important male skills. Women have specialised knowledge about the plants in the forest and their uses: which are edible, which have healing qualities and which can be used in basket-weaving.

All men are initiated into a secret cult, the *molimo* cult, which gives them privileged access to higher powers. At important rites, the *molimo* trumpet is blown and ritual songs are performed.

In short, the lives of the BaMbuti are culturally ordered from beginning to end. In this sense, there is no reason to assume that they are 'closer to nature' than people in industrial societies are.

On the other hand, it is clear that the alterations they make to their natural environment are much less significant than those inflicted by people with a different mode of subsistence, be they agriculturalists or industrial peoples. Their population grows very slowly, and they do not alter the fundamental processes of the environment permanently.

From a different perspective, it is also tempting to conclude that the BaMbuti are closer to nature than, say, agricultural peoples or people living in Paris. Their religion is characterised by a deep reverence for the forest: after all, they subsist on what the forest 'gives' them, and they worship the spirits of the forest. Among agriculturalists, Claude Meillassoux has written (1967), there is instead a tendency to perceive nature as an enemy. Meillassoux, drawing on Turnbull's ethnography, argues that the BaMbuti perceive nature as a *subject* – they harvest its products and see it essentially as a friend – while the neighbouring farmers regard it as an *object* – as something they continuously modify and cultivate, and which they have to protect against natural hazards such as weeds and baboons.

On the other hand, it must be stressed that the BaMbuti, like Bantus or for that matter Frenchmen, take great pains to turn their offspring into something different from animals or members of another tribe: the children are to be transformed from their initial, unmoulded state to follow the proper way; they are to become real BaMbuti, neither more nor less.

TWO NATURES AND TWO APPROACHES

Anthropology has two main kinds of concepts about nature: external nature, or the ecosystem, and inner nature, or human nature. Both of these concepts represent the opposite of culture. What is cultural is always something other than nature, and culture always implies a transformation, and sometimes a denial, of that which is natural. Lévi-Strauss's axiom that all human societies distinguish between culture and nature is accepted by many anthropologists (but challenged by others, see the contributions to Descola and Pálsson 1996). Our non-humanised surroundings may sometimes appear as a major threat to human projects: they may threaten to destroy our crops, kill our livestock and so on. Every cultural project seems to imply a transformation of both external and human nature.

Senses and Anthropological Sensibilities

Karl Marx famously wrote that the five senses were the product not of nature, but of all of world history up to the present. Although Marx did not develop this thought further, he thus foreshadowed a set of problems which have often been overlooked by anthropologists: how does the use of the senses differ cross-culturally, how can smell, touch and sound be explored ethnographically, and what methodological problems arise from the variations?

A certain visual bias is evident in many – probably most – ethnographic writings. Descriptions of field settings usually concentrate on spatial organisation, buildings, plants and generally what meets the eye. Sounds, tastes and smells tend to be conspicuously absent, as noted by Mary Louise Pratt (1986). Constance Classen (1993) remarks that the Ongee of the Andaman Islands live in a world ordered by smell, and links the 'olfactory decline of the West' with the growth of scientific rationalism. Whereas a rose was associated with smell in antiquity and in medieval times, by the eighteenth century its main purpose had become 'to divert the eye and thereby divert the mind' (Classen 1993, p. 27). Paul Stoller has argued along similar lines (1989), indicating that the senses have been subject to a lot of scattered attention, but little systematic treatment, in anthropology. Stoller's work on the senses in society and culture range from embodied memories to the classification of smell, while David Howes (2003, 2004) is concerned equally with cross-cultural comparisons and the cultural specificity of the senses as social and cultural phenomena in particular societies.

In the pioneering monograph *Sound and Sentiment*, Steven Feld (1982) describes a people in New Guinea, the Kaluli, for whom sound and music are central cosmological categories. The Kaluli classify birds not only according to their appearance, but also according to their song. Indeed, Feld shows how sounds function as a symbolic system of meaning in Kaluli society. Song and music, thus, are considered highly important among the Kaluli. Speaking more generally, Walter Ong (1969; see also Stoller 1997) argues that oral societies, unlike literate ones, tend not to 'picture' the world and thus do not, in a strict sense, have a 'world-view', but rather 'cast up actuality in comprehensive auditory terms, such as voice and harmony'. Classen, comparing three oral societies, the Tzotzil of Mexico, the Ongee of the Andaman Islands and the Desana of Colombia, finds that they all have distinct ways of making sense of the world: 'the Tzotzil order the cosmos by heat, the Ongee by smell, and the Desana by colour' (Classen 1993, p. 122). In other words, the visual/aural dichotomy is too simple, but at least it points out the importance of studying the social use of the senses – and of reflecting critically on ethnography's over-reliance on sight and visual metaphors (Salmond 1982).

More recently, anthropologists have begun to explore a third sense, namely touch, systematically. In a wide-ranging, interdisciplinary reader titled simply *The Book of Touch* (Classen 2005), topics covered include the feeling of being tortured during the Inquisition, difficulties of handling children in an era obsessed by paedophilia, virtual touch in cyberspace and the disciplining of the soldier's body.

At the same time, culture is intrinsically connected with nature. Many peoples hold that nature furnishes the raw materials culture is based on, and that there is a strong relationship of mutual interdependence between the two. Nature also seems to be stronger and more permanent in character than cultural products, which by comparison appear as fragile, vulnerable and temporary. If one succeeds in presenting a particular social order as 'natural', one has indeed legitimated it.

Nature is often perceived as threatening and difficult to control, yet it is always necessary as the provider of raw materials for cultural products. At the same time it is ambiguous: it is simultaneously a source of legitimation and an opponent. In *After Nature* (1992), Marilyn Strathern describes a system of kinship and descent which is exceptional in that it gives individuals the option to replace 'natural' reproduction with (cultural) technologically controlled reproduction (test tubes, insemination, surrogate mothers, etc.). One palpable cultural result is a change in popular conceptions of what is cultural and what is natural. Strathern's book deals with kinship in the English middle class at the end of the twentieth century (see also Carsten 2004).

There are two principal ways of approaching the nature–culture relationship. On the one hand, one may study how nature and the nature–culture relationship is conceptualised in different societies; on the other, one may investigate how nature (the environment or inborn characteristics of humans) affects society and culture. Nature thus exists both as cultural representations of nature and as something outside of culture and society, yet influencing the ways in which humans live. As a biological species, we take part in ecosystems and modify them; as cultural beings, we develop concepts about our environment and place ourselves outside it.

INTERACTION AND ACTORS

Above all, social life consists of action, or interaction: if people ceased to interact, society would no longer exist. It may be useful for our purpose to distinguish the concept of *action* from the related concept of *behaviour*: behaviour refers to observable events involving humans or animals, whereas action (or agency), the way the concept is used here, implies that actors can reflect on what they do. It calls attention to the intentional (willed, reflexive) aspect of human existence. As far as we know, no other species apart from humanity is able to reflect upon its behaviour intentionally. Marx referred to this fact when, in *Capital* (1906 [1867–94]), he compares a human master-builder with a bee. The beehive may be more perfectly fashioned and more functional than the house constructed by the builder (at least if he happens to be so-so), but there is a qualitative difference: the human builder has an image of the house in his consciousness before starting on his work, and we have no reason to suppose that the bee starts from a similar image. It acts directly on pre-programmed 'instincts', and human actors do not.

The notion of agency thus implies that people know that they act, even if they do not necessarily know the consequences of their acts. In other words, it is always possible to do something different from what one is doing at the moment. This indeterminacy in agency makes it difficult to predict human agency; indeed, many social scientists hold that it is in principle impossible.

In anthropology and sociology, an acting person is frequently spoken of as an actor (or agent). This term can also include collective actors and is therefore semantically wider than words like 'person', 'individual' and so on. The state, for example, may be an actor. Further, *corporations* frequently appear as actors in anthropological studies. A corporation is a collective of humans which appears as an acting unit in one or several regards. In many societies, political parties, NGOs and trade unions are typical actors; in others, kin groups make up corporations (see Chapters 5, 7 and 11). The concept of the corporation must be distinguished from that of the *category*: a category of persons who have something in common at the level of classification without ever functioning as an acting unit.

The concept of agency, or action, can usually be replaced by the concept of interaction. Conceptualising whatever people are up to as interaction calls attention to the reciprocal character of agency, and most acts are not only directed towards other agents, but shaped by the relationship. The smallest entity studied by social anthropologists is not an individual, but a relationship between two (Leach 1967). In other words, the mutual relationship between two persons may be seen as the smallest building-block of society.

STATUSES AND ROLES

Common words in social science jargon, such as social convention, interaction, corporations and categories are highly abstract comparative concepts. They are useful in cross-cultural comparison, but they only very rarely form part of the native (or emic) vocabulary. This also holds true for an additional, useful group of concepts which have been developed to describe the various kinds of social relationships engaged in by humans. First, all members of society have certain rights and duties in relation to other members, and there are hardly two individuals who have exactly the same rights and duties. Second, each person has many different rights and duties in relation to different persons and different situations. In order to distinguish analytically between these aspects of social processes, it is customary to speak of social statuses.

A status is a socially defined aspect of a person which defines a social relationship and entails certain rights and duties in relation to others. Each person may have a great number of statuses, such as uncle, dentist, neighbour, customer, friend and so on. The social person is composed of, and defined by, the sum of these statuses. There are also social expectations connected with each status, which contribute to its maintenance through time. The relative importance of each status for the actor varies greatly. Membership of an ethnic or religious group, for example, may be so important to the actor that it affects his or her field of agency in nearly every respect. Other statuses, such as that of grandson in a society where kinship is relatively unimportant, have less significance for the individual – they define the person in a smaller number of situations and are marginal to his or her self-perception.

It can be useful to distinguish between *ascribed* and *achieved* statuses. Ascribed statuses cannot be opted out of; a 7-year-old boy cannot choose not to be, say, a second-grade pupil, a son and a child. Achieved statuses, on the contrary, are acquired by the actor. In modern societies, one's profession is usually considered an achieved status, but in many societies it is clearly ascribed (not chosen). A central notion in classic anthropology and sociology is the view that modern societies are qualitatively different from traditional societies in that many of the social statuses are achieved in the former, whereas most statuses are ascribed in the latter. Tönnies's (1963 [1889]) famous distinction between '*Gemeinschaft*' (community) and '*Gesellschaft*' (society), as well as Maine's distinction between contract and status societies, relates to this kind of duality. Later research has shown this kind of distinction to be simplistic, but it may still be useful as an analytical starting point.

A term which is closely related to the concept of status is the concept of role, and the two words are sometimes used as synonyms. In anthropology, however, the role is generally defined – following Linton (1937) – as the dynamic aspect of the status, that is, a person's actual behaviour within the limitations set by the status definition. A typical status in a modern society may be 'bus driver'; the role of the bus driver will then be defined by what one actually does as a bus driver.

Being the incumbent of a particular social status directs one's actions in specified ways. A princess, for instance, is expected not to drink beer late at night at seedy joints. A shaman among the Inuit is expected to establish contact with supernatural powers when necessary; a wife in the Trobriand Islands is expected to be sexually monogamous; a worker in a German factory is expected to register for work before 8:30 a.m. every weekday. When one breaks the rules and expectations connected with the role enactment of a status, other members of society may react by imposing sanctions or different forms of punishment.

SWITCHING BETWEEN ROLES

Thanks to status differentiation and the regular implementation of sanctions, social life has a certain degree of regularity and predictability. However, this predictability is far from total. If it were, social scientists would be outstanding prophets. The social status and its dynamic counterpart, the role, delineate some of the possible scope for the actor, by giving him or her certain rights and duties connected to expectations and possible sanctions. However, the social status of a person never defines his or her entire field of agency. This is partly due to the fact that a status never entails exact, detailed rules concerning how to behave in every situation, and also to the fact that the role is never identical with the status. One is, in other words, forced to improvise – for example, there are many, widely different ways of enacting the role of the father in every society, although the social definition of the status 'father' also entails certain expectations. Every status, however, is ambiguous in the sense that actors have to interpret it before enacting it.

In his major micro-sociological and existentialist work, *Being and Nothingness* (*L'Être et le néant*), the philosopher Jean-Paul Sartre (1957 [1943]) meticulously describes how actors reflect upon, define and enact statuses in frequently contrived and highly self-conscious ways. One of his most famous examples is the waiter at a Parisian cafe, who cautiously and professionally tries to exude 'waiterness'. By virtue of his gaze, his gestures and his elegant way of balancing a full tray of drinks while he swings, in a seemingly nonchalant way, through the kitchen doors, he gives a clear expression of embodying the status of the waiter, turning it into a role and thereby an art. However, if he were to maintain this role at home with his wife, she would presumably file for a divorce within a few weeks.

In his philosophical descriptions of role enactment, Sartre brings up a topic which has since been pursued by many sociologists and anthropologists. They have focused on the ability of actors to manipulate their statuses and thereby liberate themselves – not from the statuses as such, but from the apparent coercion certain statuses seem to imply. Actors may thus regard their status from a distance; they decide, within limits, which expression they give to it, in order to give their co-actors a certain impression of who they are. Through the study of role enactment, we may thus study aspects of the relationship between freedom and coercion in social life.

One of the most influential elaborations on role enactment and role distance in the literature is Erving Goffman's *The Presentation of Self in Everyday Life* (1978 [1959]). Drawing on a wide range of examples, the author shows how people determinedly use their more or less ascribed statuses and social relationships to pursue their own ends. In his descriptions of social processes, Goffman uses expressions from the theatre. He talks of actors, roles and performances, and distinguishes between the front-stage and the back-stage. His point in doing so is to show that there are situations we master well and feel relatively secure in, as when the (literal) actors, in their back-stage dressing-rooms, can 'truly be themselves', make jokes, display their true emotions and feel free from the strict requirements of their roles on stage. In the front-stage area, by contrast, impression management becomes important: the actor has to be self-consciously aware of the impression he or she makes on others, and tries to shape it in the desired ways. In this kind of situation, as in a formal interview or another kind of situation where one feels slightly uncomfortable for lack of complete mastery of the role, one will contrive to appear in a specific way through what Goffman calls impression management.

The notion of impression management was taken up by Barth in his ethnographic vignette on the social organisation of a trawler off western Norway (Barth 1966). The boat has a captain, a crew of five to eight fishermen, and a 'netboss' (*notbas*). All of them have a variety of statuses, but in the boat their professional statuses are, naturally, the most important. Each category of actors has specified tasks. The captain's job is to steer the boat and to supervise the others. The 'netboss' is expected to find schools of fish and to order the fishermen to drop the net when he 'feels' that there are large amounts of fish down below. The fishermen, for their part, carry out all the manual work.

With this simple status distribution as his point of departure, Barth describes the role play on the ship. He shows how certain aspects of the statuses are overcommunicated; that is, the actors place great emphasis on presenting these aspects in their impression management. The captain acts as a sturdy man with immense experience and a sound sense of judgement. The fishermen frequently gather on deck, watch the ocean and talk quietly together to display their eagerness to do a good job. The netboss, who plays the 'trickster' role, gives the impression of being endowed with great intuitive powers of partly mystical origins; he watches the weather for signs which are invisible to others, wanders restlessly about 'sniffing' for fish, and so on. In this situation, through deliberate overcommunication of certain role aspects, all the actors do their best to present themselves as fully competent carriers of their status.

Are we, then, identical with the roles we 'play'? Does social life largely consist of conscious impression management and, ultimately, manipulation? It may be tempting to criticise Goffman and his followers for giving the impression that social life consists of attempts to outsmart and see through the strategies of others, at the same time as one self-consciously projects a particular image of oneself, where no act seems authentic or sincere. This kind of criticism, even if it may have some relevance, is largely misplaced. Goffman's main point is the fact that there are social conventions defining everything we do as social creatures. Even to express the most powerful and sincere emotions, one has to follow specific, culturally defined rules prescribing how to express such emotions. Even the most spontaneous of acts must be channelled through a socially defined mode of expression if it is to be comprehensible.

Furthermore, even when one would like to violate the conventions of society there are a limited number of ways of doing so. Generally, criticism of social conventions is fairly common in modern societies. The conventions may then be described as 'straitjackets' or as a 'prison' preventing the true self from emerging. In the 1960s and 1970s, a large number of young people in many West European and North American societies rejected what they saw as 'empty routines' in order to live in a more 'natural, authentic' way. They let their hair grow, had extra-marital sex with several partners, rejected cultural practices which led to environmental deterioration and so on. Since then, it has been claimed by critics of these movements that two general social scientific lessons could be drawn from them. First, new social conventions were surprisingly rapidly developed by the long-haired rebels (Berger et al. 1973). For example, it was difficult to be accepted in the group unless one obeyed a certain dress code. Second, it has been argued that it turned out that people had little or nothing left in life when they had abandoned all 'empty routines'. In other words, everybody appears to depend on social rituals, conventions and routines to relate to.

POWER AND SOCIAL LIFE

A common criticism of role theory is its alleged lack of ability to deal with power relationships in society. For it is clear that social conventions, role expectations and the very distribution of roles and statuses in society contribute to systematic differences in power. Some actors are able to exert considerable power over others; some have very limited control of their own lives, let alone other people's. This dimension of social life is only dealt with indirectly in the work of Goffman and other role theorists.

Power is an elusive and difficult concept. The philosopher Bertrand Russell once said that power is to the social sciences what energy is to physics: it belongs to an exclusive handful of central concepts, but it is impossible to define it accurately. Russell is still right to the extent that no definition of power exists on which there is universal agreement. Yet, there are obvious and very significant differences between societies regarding power relationships, both in the public and the private spheres.

It can be useful to distinguish between two principal ways of conceptualising power. More generally, society as such may be conceptualised in two chief ways, which are discussed later as the actor perspective and the systemic perspective, respectively (see especially Chapter 6). Society may be envisaged either as the product of intentional, willed agency, or as the totality of institutional structures which condition all agency. If we see power from the actor perspective (Max Weber's principal view), it may be defined as an aspect of a social relationship, namely the ability to make someone do something they would otherwise not have done. If we look at power from a systemic perspective (as Marx did), it instead becomes crucial to show how power differences embedded in the fabric of society are, in fact, constitutive of those very social relationships. One cannot simply choose not to have a powerless status. On the other hand, one can certainly improve one's relative position, so it could be said that, although they must be kept apart for analytical purposes, both perspectives are useful, and most contemporary anthropologists switch between them in their analyses.

THE SELF

Another criticism that has been levelled against role theory is represented in the view that the self is an integrated whole and that it is artificial to 'chop it up' into separated roles. This may be the case – at least many modern individuals may feel that they are 'integrated persons' – but different social relationships nevertheless require of us that we develop specialised behaviour tailored to fit different situations. Few persons, presumably, behave identically when they are with their grandmother, their professor and their friends, respectively. Since the social person is constituted through his or her social relationships, and since these relations vary in their content, one must necessarily vary one's behaviour somewhat, through some degree of impression management, when confronted with different persons.

Usually this flexibility in social life does not lead to major problems for the individual actor, but quite often one meets conflicting expectations from different persons – which may present a problem when they arise simultaneously. Which status between two mutually exclusive statuses ought one to choose when one is forced to? Most adolescents in contemporary Western societies have presumably experienced this kind of awkward situation when they have unexpectedly met their friends while out with their parents.

Role theory, as exemplified above in Goffman's work, can be a powerful tool for describing social relationships, and its usefulness will be shown further later. We should nevertheless keep in mind that statuses and roles are theoretical abstractions from the ongoing process of social life, and are as such etic terms. Comparative research has indicated that all human groups have a concept of the self or the person (Geertz 1983; Mauss 1985 [1938]; Fitzgerald 1993), but this concept varies in important ways. In European societies, the self is usually conceived of as undivided (as in the word 'in-dividual'), integrated and sovereign – as an independent agent. In many non-Western societies, however, the self may be seen rather as the sum total of the social relationships of the individual. Indeed, as Strathern (1992) has argued in a comparison between the English and Melanesian kinship systems, the typical Melanesian view of the self is, sociologically speaking, the more correct one. In the highland New Guinea societies to which she refers, a human being is not perceived as a fully fledged person until he or she has acquired the basic categories of local culture. Personhood is, in other words, acquired gradually from birth onwards as the child becomes increasingly familiar with the shared customs and knowledge of society. In many central African societies, a similar notion may be discerned, since children who die do not turn into proper ancestral spirits: as their cultural competence is limited, and as they have yet to forge a sufficiently broad range of social relationships, their personhood is still only partial. Further – to return to Melanesia – a person is not considered dead until all debts are paid and the inheritance has been distributed. Only when all of the social relationships engaged in by the deceased have been formally ended can he or she be considered properly dead. Strathern concludes that Melanesians conceive of persons pretty much as social scientists do, as the sum of their social relationships – unlike the English, who tend to see persons as isolated entities.

The Latin term '*persona*', Mauss notes in his essay on selfhood (1985 [1938]), originally meant 'mask'. He attempts to show that the idea of the 'self' as something distinct from the 'masks' or roles that people took on appeared in Europe only after the spread of Christianity. Among the Zuñi (Pueblo) Indians, he writes, only a limited number of first names existed in each clan, and each incumbent of a particular name was expected to play a specified role in the 'cast-list' of the clan. In other words, they were not seen as autonomous individuals, but saw themselves as predestined to 'act out ... the prefigured totality of the clan' (Mauss 1985 [1938], p. 5).

PUBLIC AND PRIVATE SELF

It should be added at this point that the anthropological emphasis on everything public and social does not necessarily mean that nothing private and 'inner' exists. Many writers distinguish between the public and private self; the latter being the 'I' as it sees itself from the inside, which is not, of course, available for direct observation by an anthropologist. As Lienhardt (1987) has noted, several African peoples talk of identity in a way that is closely related to this distinction of ours. Using the metaphor of the tortoise, they distinguish between the public persona (the tortoise displaying its head and limbs) and the private persona (the tortoise withdrawn in its shell). Although the two levels of personhood are certainly related, it is difficult to reduce one to the other.

If the tools provided by role analysis are universally applicable – can be useful in the study of any society – they provide a mere starting-point if the aim is an understanding of differences as well as similarities between social and cultural systems. It has often been argued by anthropologists that some peoples lack a concept of the private persona (or, as we might put it, of personal identity). At the very least, it is certain that the relationship between private and public aspects of personhood varies greatly between societies. Even in the comparatively culturally homogeneous Western European and North American societies, there are important variations. Many Europeans are shocked at the ease with which North Americans may speak about their private lives to strangers. If we move further afield, the differences become more profound. In Indian society, Dumont (1980 [1969]) has argued, the individual is entirely subordinated to the collectivity and sees him- or herself not as an independent agent, but as a part of an organic whole.

Personal names may give a clue as to the concept of personhood prevailing in a society. Among the Cuna of Central America, Alford notes (1988), children do not acquire a proper first name until they are about 10 years of age. Geertz (1973) has described naming in Java as an extremely bewildering and complex affair to the outsider, where each person has seven different names pertinent in different situations. Compare this to the informality of North American society, where even complete strangers may address each other with a diminutive of their first, or 'Christian', name (Bill, Bob, Jim, Tommy, etc.). This kind of cultural difference, which may be significant, may not be evident from mere role analysis, but role analysis can help us in posing the relevant questions about cultural constructions of the self, since it helps in structuring observations of social life which may at first glance seem random and purely improvisational.

Brian Morris (1994) has suggested a threefold distinction between different aspects of personhood. First, a person can be identified as a human being, as 'embodied, conscious and as a social being with language and moral agency' (1994, p. 11). This kind of notion, he remarks, seems to be universal. Second, the person can be described as a cultural category. This kind of categorisation can be both more and less inclusive than the first. On the one hand, some societies will in many contexts exclude strangers, children and slaves from the rights associated with full personhood; on the other, non-human entities such as ancestral spirits and features of the physical environment may be included. Third, Morris discusses the human person as a self, the 'I as opposed to others', the construal of which exhibits vast cultural variations. Individuals proper, in Dumont's terminology (which I choose to follow here), see the origins of their agency as located within the ego, while many societies hold that the causes of human agency may be social, religious or suprahuman.

THE ANTHROPOLOGY OF THE BODY

The culturally specific has been emphasised in this review of personhood in a comparative perspective. Universalist alternatives, which focus on personality elements that are shared pan-culturally, include psychoanalytic views (like Obeyesekere 1981), evolutionary psychology (Barkow et al. 1992; Buss 2004) and some phenomenological approaches, particularly those inspired by the work of the philosopher Maurice Merleau-Ponty. His influential *Phenomenology of Perception* (1962 [1945]) points towards an alternative conceptualisation of personhood, as it focuses on the *embodied* self. 'The body', writes Thomas Csordas (1999, p. 172), 'has always been with us in cultural and social anthropology, but it has not always been a problem.' In this, he means that bodily practices have been described in ethnography since the beginning – circumcision, clothing, penis sheaths, toilet training, etc. – but that little attention was granted to the human body as a sociocultural entity until the 1970s, an important exception being the work of Mary Douglas on impurity, boundaries and classification relating to the body (1966, 1970). Much of the research on the body that has been carried out since then can be classified as medical anthropology (e.g. Martin 2001) or political anthropology (e.g. Bourdieu 1977), where cultural variations and power relations, respectively, are analysed in the context of the body partly as agent, partly as 'passive lump of clay ... upon which society imposes its codes' (Csordas 1999, pp. 178–9). Another fertile field of research concerns the relationship between the body, notions of personhood and technological change. Jeanette Edwards and others (Edwards et al. 1993; see also Wade 2007) have discussed how the Western idea of personhood will change as new reproductive technologies change the formerly given relationship between parents and child. Others have similarly investigated how information technology (such as the Internet) contributes to a redefinition of personhood in contemporary Western societies. From a different, but complementary point of view, Donna Haraway (1991) has argued that increasing technological control and scientific discourse about (especially female) bodies require counter-reactions stressing that bodies are not 'natural' but defined subjectively, from the inside. In this way, an ideological feature of modern Western societies, namely individualism, is re-formulated, this time in the context of a body politic. The recent growth of anthropological interest in the body can at least partly be seen as a reflection of a widespread concern with bodily issues in the anthropologists' own societies (from cosmetic surgery to surrogacy), and it therefore seems appropriate that a great deal of the contemporary research efforts linking the body with issues of personhood are ethnographically located to those societies, although important research is also being done on phenomena such as organ trafficking, which usually affects people in poor societies (Scheper-Hughes 2004).

*　*　*

This chapter has described social life in quite abstract and general terms, largely as models of interpersonal interaction. The study of the enactment of roles shows how people are, in principle, free to choose their actions within a socially and culturally defined framework which is by and large given. In the next chapter, we move on to some of the conditions under which people choose their actions; in other words, the main emphasis will be placed on the level of society rather than the level of the person.

SUGGESTIONS FOR FURTHER READING

Erving Goffman: *The Presentation of Self in Everyday Life*. Harmondsworth: Penguin 1978 [1959].
Richard Jenkins: *Social Identity*, 3rd edn. London: Routledge 2008.
Brian Morris: *Anthropology of the Self*. London: Pluto 1994.

5   LOCAL ORGANISATION

The people who live in any society may be unaware, or only dimly aware, that it has a structure. It is the task of the social anthropologist to reveal it.

— *E.E. Evans-Pritchard*

Much of the empirical material necessary for anthropological thinking and research is still obtained through studies of local communities. Most classic anthropological analyses are based on detailed descriptions of culture and social organisation in a delineated system, which could be a village or an urban environment. Anthropology has diversified in recent decades into a variety of new, specialised directions and, given the complexity (and often non-localised nature) of many contemporary fields, it has become clear that it may be necessary to consult sources which cannot be obtained through fieldwork (such as historical sources, statistics, media, formal interviews, etc.). Still, the holistic study of social life – the exploration of interrelationships between different aspects of social and symbolic systems through participant observation – remains a central concern, although the setting is today rarely an isolated village.

Two factors could be mentioned as partial explanations for the traditional anthropological stress on studies of small-scale localities. First, local communities are methodologically manageable units which can realistically be studied through participant observation. In a village or a relatively bounded local environment, most inhabitants know each other personally; they participate in, and reproduce, a social system characterised by face-to-face contact. In this kind of setting, it is possible for the anthropologist to become acquainted with most of the locality's inhabitants in the course of fieldwork. He or she can map out, without insuperable methodological difficulties, which actors find themselves in which relationships to which other actors, and can thereby develop a comprehensive picture of the patterns of interaction that make up the local community.

Second, local communities may be studied as though they were self-sustaining (although, in practice, this is almost never the case). Most of the activities of the inhabitants take place locally, many of their needs are satisfied locally, and the local community is being reproduced – maintained – through a period of time. It is thereby possible, using the methodological tools of anthropology, to study the interrelationships between different social institutions within the framework of local communities.

It must be stressed, however, that in fact virtually no local community is completely self-sustaining and unchanging through time. Doing fieldwork in a suburb of Oslo in 2009, I soon discovered that more than half of the adult population went elsewhere to work during the day, while many of the people who worked locally (largely in the civil service and other service professions) lived in other parts of the city. In the evenings, many of the youths went into the city centre for activities or entertainment. Indeed, to many of those who lived in the suburb, their transnational connections with relatives in Pakistan appeared to be more important than their ties to the local community. Furthermore, a large and growing number of anthropologists are concerned with the study of social systems of a staggering scale (nations, cities, regions ...), or systems with unclear boundaries and continuous social flux, such as airports, large sports events or Internet communities. However, the methods and logic of inquiry applied to large-scale and fluctuating systems are by and large the same as the methods used in small-scale systems, although they must frequently be supplemented by methods other than participant observation. This chapter draws most of its material from small-scale societies of the kind typical of classic anthropological studies, where basic tenets of the discipline were developed, which, I should argue, remain essential for the contemporary study of complex phenomena such as migration or city life.

The previous chapter concentrated on persons and interpersonal relationships. This chapter, on the contrary, presents different levels of social organisation between which it may be useful to distinguish in anthropological research – whether one's unit of study is a Bushman homestead, a nation-state or the transnational networks of Manchester United supporters. Whereas the previous chapter saw social life from the viewpoint of the individual, this chapter sees it from the viewpoint of society. In the next chapter, the relationship between individual and society is dealt with theoretically.

NORMS AND SOCIAL CONTROL

Every social system requires the existence of rules stating what is permitted and what is not. Such rules, whether they are stated openly or are simply followed by tacit consent, are called norms. They are activated in all fields of life; some are extremely important whereas others have a marginal importance. A key norm in many societies is the rule 'You shall not steal'. A somewhat less important norm, which is limited in scope to certain environments in modern societies, is 'You shall always wear a tie at work'. Some norms concern all members of society, others concern only small groups, while still others, such as the Universal Declaration of Human Rights, are intended to be valid for all humanity.

The existence of norms does not imply that there is total agreement on them or total obeisance towards them in any society. For instance, there may very well be a rule about virilocality (stating that a newly wed couple should move in with the groom's family; see Chapter 8) without it being followed by all members of society.

All norms have in common that they are connected with sanctions. In principle, both positive and negative sanctions exist. A positive sanction involves a reward for following the norms, while a negative one entails punishment for breaching the rules. However, the term 'sanction' is normally used about negative sanctions, that is forms of punishment ranging from mild to severe.

The ability to impose legitimate sanctions, whether punishments or rewards, represents a main source of power in all societies. It is therefore important to study the system of norms and sanctions in any social system. The norms reflect the basic values of society, while the kinds of sanctions applied to different norm-breaking activities give an indication of the relative importance of different values and reveal power discrepancies. For example, in some societies sexual unfaithfulness is considered more serious, and is punished more severely, than theft; in other societies, the situation may well be the opposite.

The system of sanctions applied when norms are violated can be called social control. Societal institutions such as the family, the village council, the police, the judicial system or the school system have social control as one of their appointed tasks: they aim to prevent the violation of social norms, and are endowed with power to apply appropriate punishment when such breaches happen.

One cannot expect all members of society to follow the norms. However, even when they are violated, norms are important, since they demarcate what is and what is not socially acceptable. Generally, people who violate norms will of course try to do so without being found out and subjected to sanctions. Further, norms change through time as society changes; some vanish, some are replaced by others, others are reinterpreted, and yet others remain but are accorded reduced importance. Blasphemy, for example, is still considered a violation of a norm in many Christian societies, but it is by no means as serious as it would have been only a hundred years ago. The social power of the church and the symbolic power of Christian dogma have been reduced.

One should keep in mind that although norms and sanctions give a clue as to the basic values and modes of thought and behaviour in a society, they cannot explain fully why people act the way they do. This is due to the fact that people do not always 'follow the rules', but also to the fact that norms, like role scripts, are not sufficiently detailed to specify exact instructions as to how to behave. In real life, people always have to improvise and take decisions for themselves, but in doing so, they refer to a culturally learnt system of 'oughts' and 'ought-nots'; that is, norms.

SOCIALISATION

Many anthropologists have studied child-raising, or socialisation, in a comparative perspective. Socialisation is the process whereby one becomes a fully competent member of society – where one acquires the knowledge and abilities required to function as a member of society. In many societies, the family has the main responsibility for socialisation. In societies with a complex division of labour, however, the responsibility is in practice divided between different institutions; for instance, the family, school, leisure clubs, sports associations, television and so on. All societies nevertheless accord the socialisation of children and adolescents great importance. Children not only have to learn the categories of language, they also have to learn when and how to use it. In addition, they have to acquire thousands of little bits and pieces of knowledge – manners and rules of conduct, whom to respect and whom to worship, and how eventually to manage on their own and lead a good life in accordance with the values of society. Socialisation is the chief way in which cultural categories are transferred from one generation to the next; in other words, it secures a certain cultural continuity.

Many anthropologists who have studied socialisation have argued that an examination of child-raising may reveal central features of society by showing how specific forms of behaviour and thought are gradually shaped in the members of society. It is, obviously, in the formative stages of life that cultural competence is acquired. Among social psychologists and anthropologists in the 1940s, it was a widespread view that the presumedly authoritarian, patriarchal German method of socialisation was an important contributing factor to the Second World War. However, studies of socialisation in traditional societies have been more widespread in anthropology than comparative studies of modern ones, and they have chiefly aimed at accounting for the interrelationship between patterns of socialisation and social organisation and culture in general. Some anthropologists have also investigated the possibility of cross-cultural invariants, or constants, in socialisation.

A famous study of socialisation, which draws parallels with the author's own society towards the end, is Margaret Mead's *Coming of Age in Samoa* (1978 [1928]). In this book, Mead describes how the personality of girls and young women is shaped in a cultural environment very different from our own, in a Polynesian island. Among other things, Mead shows how the girls are socialised into a more relaxed and flexible view of sexuality than those with whom she compares them, namely middle-class girls in the USA. Further, she claims that the absence of strong individual competition makes it easier for Samoans than for Americans to reconcile themselves with their lives and be at peace with the world. The problems of everyday life are easy to understand and grasp, and they usually have a simple solution, she says. She also claims that adolescence in Samoa is not characterised by personal crises and confusion:

[Adolescence] represented no period of crisis or stress, but was instead an orderly developing of a set of slowly maturing interests and activities. The girls' minds were perplexed by no conflicts, troubled by no philosophical queries, beset by no remote ambitions. To live as a girl with many lovers as long as possible and then to marry in one's own village, near one's relatives, and to have many children, these were uniform and satisfying ambitions. (Mead 1978 [1928], p. 129)

In her comparison with the early twentieth-century North American society in which she lived, Mead argued that socialisation in Samoa created more harmonious and balanced personalities than the American system was capable of. Her general theoretical (and political) point was that important aspects of the personalities of humans, far from being inborn, are created through the dynamic interplay between individual and society, and feed into the 'ethos' of the culture. Since cultures are different, they create persons differently.

Mead's research has been criticised severely from several quarters. Although the general theoretical framework, the 'culture and personality' school developed mainly by Mead's teacher and friend Ruth Benedict, has largely been abandoned, the main thrust of the criticism has focused on the quality of her ethnography. Derek Freeman, an Australian anthropologist who carried out research in Samoa for many years, was her sharpest critic (Freeman 1983). His image of Samoa differs sharply from the idyllic society presented by Mead, where children are taught love and friendliness and where social harmony prevails. Freeman depicts a society where the pressure to conform is extremely strong, and where deviants and 'dropouts' of different kinds develop profound personal problems. He shows that the suicide rate is unusually high, and that certain mental disorders are quite widespread among persons who fail to conform. He even intimates that several of Mead's informants were deliberately lying to her, laughing behind the back of the gullible anthropologist when she left the beach to write up her notes.

According to Freeman, *anomie* is a major problem in Samoa. Anomie, a concept developed in Durkheim's classic study of suicide, refers to that feeling of alienation which is caused by inability to believe in, or to live up to, the values of society. This condition creates a sense of emptiness and meaninglessness. Durkheim believed that anomie would be most common in urban societies, but later anthropological research has shown that it can well exist in apparently tightly integrated 'traditional' village societies – which are integrated only for those members of society who fully master and are faithful to its basic values, not for the misfits, the powerless and the marginalised. Freeman's position was underpinned by a view of nature based on evolutionary biology, a perspective that Mead had devoted a large part of her professional life, and perhaps particularly her study of Samoa, to questioning. The debate following Freeman's book, published after Mead's death in 1978, was unusually acrimonious and framed within the classic nature/nurture controversy (see Hellman 1998). Most of the contributors to the debate had never been to Samoa; however, Samoan specialist Lowell D. Holmes concluded, in defence of Mead, that 'the validity of her Samoan research was remarkably high' – considering her young age and sketchy training in ethnography (Holmes 1987, p. 103).

Whether ultimately founded in society or nature, the ultimate goal of socialisation is to ensure that the actor internalises the values, norms and forms of behaviour upon which society is founded. When a norm is internalised, it is literally turned into something 'inner'; it becomes a personality trait. The norm 'Thou shalt not kill' is internalised among most of us: it is a matter of course that we normally do not kill other humans. Our language is also internalised: we speak English, French, Arabic or whatever is our vernacular, without reflecting that this is actually what we do. This also goes for elementary table manners and a number of other cultural customs. As mentioned earlier, it is perhaps chiefly through comparison with other societies that we can hope to discover such traits in our own: like the members of any society, we have a general tendency to take them for granted. This means that we have internalised central aspects of the culture where we grew up, and that perhaps we need the view from afar provided by anthropology in order to discover them. This 'view from afar' can then be brought back home, as in Allison James' studies of English children (James 1993; James and James 2004), which among other things shows that the peer group pressure to conform among children is extraordinarily strong, something which facilitates the internalisation of norms, but also leads to the painful exclusion of those who fail to conform.

LIFE-STAGES AND RITES OF PASSAGE

It is common to assume that we are 'the same person' throughout our existence. Perceived this way, personal identity appears as something unchangeable; as a constant core in an otherwise changing world. This issue is ultimately a philosophical one, but central aspects of it can be explored anthropologically. As noted by Jenkins (2008, p. 50), moreover, there is 'not always harmony between how we see ourselves and how others see us (or how we imagine they do)'. In later chapters, it will be shown how class, gender, age and ethnicity contribute to shaping the social identities of actors in a multitude of ways in different situations; for now, we simply deal briefly with one way in which a person's identity changes through time.

All societies distinguish between life-stages in the lives of their inhabitants (see also Chapter 9). Everywhere adults have rights and duties that differ from those of children, whose rights and duties are not the same as those of old people. Many societies distinguish between a greater number of stages than these; in modern North Atlantic societies, for example, the period known as 'youth' or 'adolescence' has eventually been recognised as a 'natural' stage in one's life, while among the Maasai of Kenya and Tanzania, a young boy passes through several stages before being accepted as a fully developed *moran* or warrior.

All societies must find a way of solving the problem of transition from one stage to the next. How can one tell with certainty when a girl has become a woman or when an adult has become an elder? The solution is usually to be found in rites of passage. These rites tend to be strongly dramatised public events whereby an individual or an entire age cohort moves from one status to another. The most important are usually those that mark the transition from child or adolescent to adult man or woman.

In traditional societies, these rites of passage, or initiation rites, are frequently characterised by the temporary suffering, trials and deprivation of the participants. In many of the societies anthropologists have studied, circumcision of the genitals or body tattoos function as visible signs indicating that one is henceforth to be regarded as an adult person. The rite of passage can thus be seen as an endurance test, forcing the candidates to show that they deserve full responsibilities and rights as adults. They also frequently acquire important ('secret') knowledge relevant for adult life during the phase of transition, which transforms them into a new kind of social person. Common forms of rites of passage in modern societies are confirmation, bar mitzvah or first communion, marriage and funerals, all of which mark stages in a person's development as a social being. Such rites are dealt with in greater detail later (Chapters 9 and 14). However, an important rite of passage in middle-class life, usually not thought of as such, is clearly also marked by the day of retirement from work, since people living in wagework societies derive much of their self-esteem, their social networks and their standing in society from work. Indeed, at many workplaces, the retirement of a colleague is celebrated with a solemn, bittersweet reception, where drinks are served, speeches given and gifts exchanged, displaying many of the characteristics of ritual more narrowly conceived.

Persons who are in a phase of transition are frequently surrounded by taboos, prohibitions and strict rules of conduct. In some societies, they are kept in isolation for weeks. One reason for this strictness may be that the rites of passage themselves, although they are necessary for society, can be seen as a threat to the social order and to the dominant power relations in society. When one is a child, one represents no threat: one has a secure and unquestionable social status as a child; as an adult, one normally has an equally well-defined place in society. When one is wedged halfway between the two stages, however, it may seem as if 'anything might happen' (Turner 1967). During a rite of initiation, which may last for weeks, one is in a certain sense located *outside* of society; one is neither child nor adult. Anomie is a real danger, since the candidates are for the first time able to see themselves – and society – from the outside, and perhaps reflect critically on society and their role in it. Perhaps, indeed, the extended adolescence typical of contemporary modern societies may fruitfully be seen as a very long rite of passage.

So far, the development of the social person has been described as an interplay between individual and society. We now move a step further and turn towards the social organisation of communities, looking at who does what with whom, and how societies are maintained (and change) through time. A central concept in this regard is the social institution. This could be defined as a custom, a system of social relationships, including power relations, or a set of rules for conduct which endures through a long period and which, in a certain sense, exists independently of the persons enacting it. When, say, a nuclear family is dissolved because of death, divorce or the children's departure, the institution of the nuclear family is not affected. When a king dies and his son replaces him, this usually has little effect on the institution of monarchy.

Society exists through its institutions; when they cease to function, society changes, sometimes in fundamental ways. After the French Revolution, the monarchy was replaced by a new institutional arrangement in the domain of politics, namely the republic. And when aboriginal Australian societies have been subjected to genocide, displacement or the enforced introduction of wagework and a monetary economy, so that formerly important institutions have ceased to function, these societies have either been dramatically transformed or have vanished from the face of the earth. Note that societies may disappear without their inhabitants necessarily disappearing: they may simply be incorporated into another group or, in the case of many minorities, 'greater society'. In other words, social institutions may be a highly relevant focus for the study of change as well as continuity.

THE HOUSEHOLD

The smallest building-block in social anthropology is not the isolated actor but a relationship between two. The smallest social system is thus the dyadic relationship. There are few systems of this modest compass in the world; and there are relatively few social activities which take place within the framework of a system this narrow. When the fieldworker arrives in a locality, therefore, he or she will usually soon find out that the smallest and most easily accessible social system where intensive and important interaction takes place is the household. In many cases, the anthropologist will actually be a guest in a household during fieldwork. Therefore, and because households (although they differ in their composition) exist in every society, it seems reasonable to begin an empirical study by exploring this social system.

A household usually, but not always, consists of people who are relatives; it also frequently, but not always, consists of people who live under the same roof. The most common definition of a household is as follows: a household includes those persons who regularly eat their main meals together. The reason that a shared domicile does not form the chief criterion is simply the fact that many peoples have living arrangements whereby men, women and youths live in different huts.

The following examples, one from West Africa and one from the Caribbean, reveal important differences between household structures and may hint at the significance of such variation for other differences and similarities between societies.

The Fulani (French: *peul*) are cattle nomads who number altogether around 27 million and who live – scattered, often nomadically – in most of the Sahel region in West Africa from Senegal to the Sudan (Stenning 1962; Riesman 1998). The Fulani household traditionally tends to consist of a nuclear family (husband, wife and children) or a compound family (husband, wives and children). The cattle herds are owned by the man. The household is an economic unit and has collective responsibility for animal husbandry. It is also responsible for the socialisation and economic support of the children until they marry and form new households. When all the children have married, the household eventually dissolves.

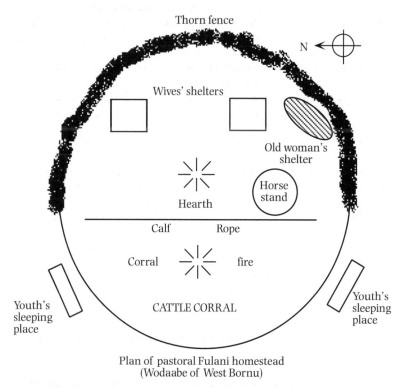

Plan of pastoral Fulani homestead
(Wodaabe of West Bornu)

Figure 5.1   A typical Fulani household (Stenning 1962)

There are two things to be noticed here. First, the household changes, or evolves, according to an established pattern; it goes through a developmental cycle. Second, the Fulani household is flexible and can change its composition if this is required for economic or other reasons.

Let us first look at the developmental cycle of the household. The life of the nuclear family begins, by definition, when the first child is born. If it is a son, he receives his first calf on the same day as he is named, seven days after his birth. When he is between 7 and 10 years old, he is circumcised. At this stage he is old enough to work as a shepherd; he is also given several animals from his father, as the foundation of his own herd. A few years later the boy is introduced to his bride-to-be, who has been selected by the two pairs of parents. She moves in with him and stays there until she becomes pregnant. She then moves back to her own family, where she says for about two years, giving birth and nursing the baby with the assistance of her kin. When she finally returns with the child, the couple form their own household.

The Fulani are Muslims, and the men are allowed to have up to four wives. A household may, in other words, be comparatively large at the zenith of its cycle. Then it 'peels off' as the children begin to move out with their animals, eventually shrinking to comprise just the original, old couple. The kind of physical continuity witnessed in the households of many settled agricultural peoples, where the same dwelling house and the same fields may have belonged to many consecutive generations, does not exist among nomads. Yet it is obvious that the household, seen as a social system, has a constant structure and that the changes are cyclical, not irreversible. We may therefore talk of it as a social institution which reproduces itself through the generations.

The Fulani household and the cattle herd are intimately related to each other. Ideally, the herd ought to grow at the same rate as the family; each time a son is old enough to herd, the herd itself ought to grow accordingly. However, this does not always work in practice and there are several factors which may disturb the viability of the household. Some are climatic and environmental; others are related to the organisational features of the household.

A minimum of cattle is required for survival. Stenning estimates this as 21 cows and one bull for a couple with no children, but it is extremely demanding for a couple to herd them alone, in addition to carrying out all the other tasks. At the early stage of the developmental cycle of the nuclear family, the household is thus only barely viable. Frequently such a household will temporarily merge with that of the man's father, until his oldest son is able to work as a shepherd. Such an alliance with the husband's father's household can be especially important during the dry season. During this period, the Fulani are scattered over a large area; during the rainy season, they live in larger kin groups and can more easily share the work.

The situation for the new household improves as the sons grow up and can contribute their labour. In other words, the household's viability depends on the relationship between two factors: labour power and other economic resources, notably cattle and available pastures. From this it follows that the size of the herd is decisive in a man's ability to have several wives (and, to some extent, vice versa). Further, a man is permitted to divorce a wife who has few or no children, since he needs labour power for his growing herd. The position of the woman in the Fulani household is thus much more uncertain than that of the man. He alone owns everything they have of value, namely the cattle herd.

The herd should not grow too large either. There are limits as to how many animals a limited number of persons can herd; moreover the land is impoverished if there are too many animals in an area.

Marriage among the Fulani is more of an economic institution than it is in industrialised societies. The spouses have mutual obligations in that the man is obliged to ensure that the herd grows and is in good health, while the woman is obliged to give birth and socialise children. If either of them neglects their duties, the other party is entitled to divorce.

The Fulani household is a self-sufficient economic unit which passes through specified, standardised stages of varying degrees of viability. The difficult art of sustaining this kind of household consists of keeping the labour–cattle relationship above the lower limit, even at difficult times of drought or disease. If food is scarce, the woman may divorce; if labour (that is, healthy children) is scarce, the man may divorce.

Since the time of Stenning's fieldwork around 1960, significant changes have taken place in the Sahel region, but Fulani peoples (who pass by different names in different regions) remain highly mobile and geographically dispersed, and are still associated with cattle and animal husbandry generally (Oppong 2002).

In modern societies as well, household viability can be a useful concept. When a European household is dissolved because the breadwinner(s) are unable to pay the mortgage, we are witnessing a household which falls below the lower limit of viability. Among the urban poor in the USA, moreover, household viability is a central concern, creating a kinship pattern sometimes described as 'matrifocal', where the unemployed men have a relatively peripheral place in the household.

A CONTRADICTION-RIDDEN HOUSEHOLD

Household structures tend to be constant through a period of time, although different household forms may coexist in the same society and important structural changes may also entail changes in the household composition. When the household structure changes dramatically, this is usually an indication of other changes in the social organisation. In European societies, the shift from extended families to nuclear families in the nineteenth and twentieth centuries was generally accompanied by a shift from agrarian to industrial production. In some societies, for example among the Bushmen (San) hunters and gatherers of southern Africa, the household structure changes periodically in response to climatic and economic changes. During dry periods they are small and flexible; during wet periods they join together in larger bands. The kind of household to be considered now is flexible in a different way. Put bluntly, it is extremely difficult to keep it together.

The Lesser Antilles of the West Indies are tropical islands largely populated by the descendants of slaves brought there from Africa to work on plantations. They are Christian (mostly Catholic), and the typical household structure is the nuclear family (see R.T. Smith 1956; P.J. Wilson 1978 for classic studies). In many of the villages of this area, the inhabitants get their livelihood from a combination of agriculture and fishing – both for subsistence and for marketing – as well as miscellaneous forms of wagework and petty trade. The rates of migration from the West Indies to the US, Canada and Western

Europe have been very high since the Second World War, and more than half of the families in many of the islands have relatives living abroad temporarily or permanently (Castles and Miller 2003; Olwig 2007).

Although the nuclear family is considered the ideal in the Caribbean, few in Providencia, the island studied by Peter J. Wilson (1978), live in stable nuclear families. The strongest social bond is that between mother and son, and many sons are reluctant to leave their mother. Moreover, many couples live together without marrying, many married men have mistresses and women frequently have children with several men. It is far from uncommon for a woman to remain in her natal household after having children.

The problems associated with household stability can be summed up as follows. A woman has strong moral commitments towards the household she lives in, to her own children and to the men with whom she is in regular contact. Usually women till the land. A man, for his part, has strong commitments towards his mother, his wife, his children, his male friends, the mother(s) of his children and possibly his mistress(es). With so many obligations in different directions, it is practically impossible for a man to fulfil all of them satisfactorily. The most common domestic conflict arising in this kind of society is directly caused by the strong normative pressure on the man to spend his money outside of the household in which he lives: on his male friends, his mother and his mistress.

Women are also entitled to become dissatisfied with their adult sons, since they depend strongly on their economic contributions to the household, given that their own menfolk are unreliable. It is quite common for close relationships between men and women, and between men and their children, to be severed. This is not due to some 'irresponsible mentality' among male West Indians, but is rather related to structural contradictions. Both men and women are faced with irreconcilable expectations.

The relationship between the household and the kin group is frequently conflict-ridden. In the West Indian example, this contradiction is expressed as a conflict between the husband–wife and the mother–son bond, but it is nearly always the case that actors have obligations towards relatives outside the household. Many live in households dominated by persons who are not their relatives (frequently they are relatives by marriage, in-married or affines). If a woman lives with her husband's relatives, she is often entitled to move 'home' to her parents if she feels mistreated. For his part, a man can use great resources to take care of his mother at the expense of his wife and children. We will return to this problem in Chapters 7 and 8.

THE VILLAGE

Virtually no household is entirely self-sufficient. There are always a number of problems which must be solved outside of the household, concerning politics, religion, economy, children's marriage and other central aspects of existence. Even the relatively autonomous Fulani household depends on other Fulani in matters of politics, religion and marriage, and it depends on non-Fulani for trade. In complex modern societies, characterised by strong institutional differentiation, comparatively few needs are taken care of in the household. From Facebook communities to the job market and the cafe on the corner, members of such societies are participants in many social networks of varying scale; some small and tight, some vast and dispersed. The household is nevertheless always related to other households and to social institutions existing at a higher systemic level, such as a local community or a state. At this stage, we shall focus on the village as a social system at a higher level of scale than the household.

The Dogon, who number slightly less than a million individuals, live on the dry savannahs of south-eastern Mali, near the border with Burkina Faso (Beaudoin 1984), in an area where nomadic Fulani also live. They are sedentary farmers and cultivate millet, fruit and vegetables. They live in villages which traditionally make up independent political entities. These villages are in many ways self-sufficient, with their own farmers, political leaders, craftsmen, fields and public rituals. The autonomy of the villages is evident through the fact that political conflicts in the area are frequently conflicts between villages, caused by disagreements over land rights or disputes at the marketplace, where inhabitants from different villages meet.

The settlements in the Dogon villages are divided according to lineage membership. Each lineage has rights to cultivate specific fields and lives in a delineated part of the village. Political power is distributed among the lineages so that a member of each belongs to the council of elders, which is the highest political authority. Its leader is called the *hogon*. He is judge and chairman, and also exerts religious authority. The council of elders meets almost daily to discuss village problems ranging from land disputes, inheritance cases, crimes or conflicts with neighbouring villages, as well as planning upcoming religious festivities.

The village council and the *hogon* traditionally have exerted political authority over problems above the level of the individual household. (Today state institutions are gradually taking over many of their traditional tasks.) They are entitled to receive presents from the inhabitants, but are also committed to paying compensation to inhabitants who have suffered various damages. The *hogon* has many of the same kinds of power as the state in modern societies. He metes out punishment when the law is broken, he is 'prime minister' and 'archbishop', and he is responsible for redistribution. The presents he receives from the members of the community can be seen as taxes, and he is obliged to redistribute them for the common good. Such mechanisms for redistribution, which exist in most societies (see Chapter 12), ensure that households which are not in themselves viable may still survive.

The Dogon villages are also integrated along other lines than the purely political and judicial ones. The religious cults, in which all adult men participate, are significant. It is considered important to establish and nurture a sense of continuity with the past, and all lineages of a village can refer to a distant ancestor who allegedly founded their current settlement. The soil is spoken of as ancestral land and it cannot be sold. In this way, the Dogon villages become very stable. In- and out-migration have traditionally been uncommon. This pattern has been widespread among many African agricultural peoples, but during the twentieth century, and particularly since the Second World War, it has changed, largely due to colonialism and the growth of a state educational system and a capitalist labour market. In the case of the Dogon, in recent years cultural tourism has become a main source of income and contact with the Western world, contributing to increased mobility and cultural change.

FLEXIBILITY AND FISSION

The Yanomamö, or Yanomami, who live in the forested hill areas straddling the border between Brazil and Venezuela, represent a different pattern regarding village organisation (Chagnon 1983; Lizot 1984). They are horticulturalists, which means they practise a simple form of agriculture with neither draught animals nor plough, and their most important working tool is the digging stick. Their form of production is also called swidden agriculture, meaning that people burn off the vegetation in an area before planting it in order to eradicate weeds and enhance the soil. A swidden plot of land may be used for a few years before the soil is temporarily so impoverished that people have to move on to a new area. Swidden agriculture is particularly widespread in the Amazonas region, in south-east Asia and in Melanesia.

Also because of the danger of war with other villages, the Yanomamö villages are moved relatively often, frequently quite long distances. In addition, they move short distances in order to be near the gardens currently under cultivation. Among the Yanomamö, a garden has a lifespan of four to five years. In other words, their villages are much less permanent as physical structures than those of the Dogon.

The Yanomamö villages are, materially speaking, composed of a *shabono*, a single, large communal hut which may shelter between 50 and 400 persons. Most of the inhabitants are relatives. They practise a system of marriage that we would call bilateral cross-cousin marriage (see Chapter 8), which means that a young woman must marry a man who is recognised as her mother's brother's son and her father's sister's son. Their kin terminology is classificatory; in other words, they use the same kin terms to describe large categories of persons (see Chapters 7 and 11).

The Yanomamö have a less complex division of labour than the Dogon; it generally follows gender and age. The youngest and the oldest are entitled not to work, while the women are mainly responsible for agricultural activities and only the men go hunting.

The village headman and the shaman are the highest authorities in the villages. Neither of these offices is hereditary; they are achieved through

The Yanomamö Controversy

For many years one of the most popular teaching texts in anthropology undergraduate studies worldwide has been Napoleon Chagnon's *Yanomamö*, originally subtitled *The Fierce People* (1983, first published in 1968). A portrayal of an Amazonian people, their kinship system and economic practices, but also giving ample attention to violent feuds, raids for women and use of hallucinogens, I remember the book as a mesmerising read during my first year in anthropology, and it keeps appearing in several places in this very book, notwithstanding the following story.

In autumn 2000, controversy broke out regarding Chagnon's work among the Yanomamö. An investigative journalist named Patrick Tierney had written a book called *Darkness in El Dorado* (2000), and several leading anthropologists, among them Terence Turner, who also worked among Brazilian Indians (the Kayapó), reacted strongly upon reading the unpublished manuscript. Tierney accused the American research group, of which Chagnon formed part, of various forms of unethical behaviour towards the Yanomamö, ranging from manipulating his evidence of widespread violence among the Yanomamö to upsetting social cohesion by instigating conflict. It was eventually proven that the most serious accusation, namely that the research team had deliberately spread measles in a eugenic experiment worthy of a Josef Mengele, was false. Chagnon and his defenders, among them many prominent sociobiologists, argued that the criticism was a part of a plot against the 'scientific approaches' in anthropology that Chagnon advocated. A believer in objective science and Darwinian explanations of cultural behaviour, Chagnon felt victimised by what he saw as the postmodernist, relativist mainstream of cultural anthropology. At the same time, the doyen of American cultural anthropology, Marshall Sahlins, published a very critical essay focusing on Chagnon's research methods. Although Sahlins agreed that Tierney's accusations were partly wrong, he castigated Chagnon for treating the Yanomamö disrespectfully and unethically, and ultimately misrepresenting them as far 'fiercer' than they in fact were (Sahlins 2000).

Dust settled, but the Tierney–Chagnon controversy revealed a discipline severely divided and deeply troubled in its self-identity as a science. As Robin (2004, p. 164) observes, no middle ground could be found between believers in quantitative methods and falsification of hypotheses, and humanist interpreters (see Borofsky 2005 for the full story).

outstanding personal qualities and through successfully competing for power with others.

Since the division of labour is rather simple, it might be thought an advantage for each household to run its own business independently. However, there are sound reasons for the Yanomamö to stick together in larger groups. First, there are necessary tasks which have to be done collectively, such as hunting and rituals. Second, the Yanomamö are periodically involved in feuds with their neighbours, and naturally there is both strength and security in numbers when they are regularly faced with this kind of situation. Exactly how widespread war is among the Yanomamö, is a matter of intense dispute among anthropologists (Lizot 1994; Borofsky 2005); the present description is chiefly based on Napoleon Chagnon's controversial, but influential research.

One of the main reasons for feuding is the quest for women. Villages which are successful in military terms thus tend to grow. When the Yanomamö village has reached a certain size, however, it is split as one or several lineages move out and build their own *shabono* elsewhere. There is always a conflict prior to this kind of village fission, but Chagnon (1983) argues that conflicts do not lead to fission before the village has reached at least 200 inhabitants. There must therefore be another reason for the fission apart from the conflict itself. In this context, Chagnon argues that only a limited number of people can be organised politically on kinship principles when the division of labour is as limited as in this case. His argument is strengthened by the fact that villages where the inhabitants are close (biological) kin prove to be more stable than those where people are less closely related. In the stable villages people tend to be related to each other in several ways simultane-ously, because the same lineages have exchanged women for generations and therefore have stronger moral obligations vis-à-vis each other than is the case in less stable villages. Whether the strong solidarity witnessed in certain villages is a result of multiplex social relationships creating bonds of trust, or of 'kin selection' (solidarity with biological relatives), is a controversial issue to which we shall return later.

SOCIAL INTEGRATION IN VILLAGES

In all of the societies discussed so far, kinship has a privileged place in the social organisation. Among the Fulani, the father–son relationship forms the very spine of the social organisation, since the fathers are responsible for the sons acquiring their own herds. In Providencia, the mother–son relationship is such a strong bond that it affects life in the nuclear family adversely. The Dogon are physically organised along kinship lines; both place of settlement and land rights follow the lineage, each lineage has a political representative, and the distribution of political power follows kinship lines. Finally, among the Yanomamö, kinship is the main principle of loyalty and belonging, and the powerholders in this society are dependent on being able to draw on support from their kin to maintain their position. Kinship is thus a fundamental organising principle in these (and other) societies.

The role of the village council and *hogon* of the Dogon, or the headman of the Yanomamö, often consists of mediating between kin groups with opposing interests. However, they are also responsible for 'foreign policy'. There is no legitimate authority outside of the village, and each village is thus an independent political unit. To the villagers, the village is the centre of the universe. Family, livelihood, childhood memories, physical protection and future all lie there. (Here we should keep in mind that the tense is the ethnographic present. Neither the Dogon nor the Yanomamö are today unaffected by the state and capitalism. Yanomamö society has experienced serious disruptions due to increased, unwanted contact with gold-diggers and others from the outside world, but at the same time, one of their leaders, Davi Kopenawa Yanomami, who speaks fluent Portuguese, is a leading figure in the transnational indigenous rights movement.)

One may ask why the Fulani do not live in villages. The general answer is that the pattern of settlement in any society depends on a number of factors. The Fulani live in an area where, traditionally, there has been little competition over land rights. The savannah between the Sahara and the lusher coastal areas of Western Africa has always been thinly populated. The Fulani have had no competitors, there has been no imminent threat of war and they have depended on large grazing areas per household. They have also been flexible enough to unite in larger entities when required; the wet season has been a period for intensive ritual activities. In addition, like other pastoralists, they have always lived in a complementary trade relationship with sedentary farmers. In fact, it can be ecologically disastrous to enforce village organisation among cattle nomads, as some colonial and postcolonial regimes have tried in African countries. In Chapter 11, we shall nevertheless see how dispersed nomadic peoples may merge into larger entities when threatened by an external enemy.

SUGGESTIONS FOR FURTHER READING

Margaret Mead: *Coming of Age in Samoa*. Harmondsworth: Penguin 1978 [1928].
Karen Fog Olwig: *Caribbean Journeys: An Ethnography of Migration and Home in Three Family Networks*. Durham, NC: Duke University Press 2007.
Colin Turnbull: *The Human Cycle*. New York: Simon & Schuster 1983.

6   PERSON AND SOCIETY

To say that societies function is trivial, but to say that everything in a society is functional, is absurd.

— *Claude Lévi-Strauss*

The person is a social product, but society is created by acting persons. In the previous chapters, this apparent paradox has been illustrated in several ways. It has also been made clear that there will always be some aspects of society which change and some aspects which remain the same, if we regard the entire system through an extended period. In this chapter, we draw some theoretical lessons from these themes, and also propose a model of the relationship between person and society on the one hand, and the relationship between structure and process on the other. These two dichotomies are fundamental elements in the analytical framework developed in subsequent chapters.

SOCIAL STRUCTURE AND SOCIAL ORGANISATION

The totality of social institutions and status relationships makes up the social structure of society. It has been common to assume that this structure, in a certain sense, exists independently of the individuals who at any point in time happen to fill particular positions. Radcliffe-Brown expressed it like this in a much-quoted statement:

The actual relations of Tom, Dick and Harry or the behaviour of Jack and Jill may go down in our field note-books and may provide illustrations for a general description. But what we need for scientific purposes is an account of the form of the structure. (1952, p. 192)

Social structure may thus be perceived as the matrix of society, emptied of humans; the totality of duties, rights, division of labour, norms, social control, etc., abstracted from ongoing social life. The point of this kind of conceptualisation is to develop an abstract model of a society which brings out its essential characteristics without unnecessary details, which may be used comparatively and which shows that social institutions exist independently of the individuals inhabiting them at any given point in time. A principal concern of Radcliffe-Brown and his students was to point out the functions of social institutions, to show how they supported and contributed to the maintenance of society as a whole. The general function of religion, for example, was held to lie in its ability to create solidarity and a sense of community, and to legitimate power differences. The chief function of the ancestral cult of the Dogon may thus be said to be that it creates societal continuity and family solidarity, that it ties actors to the land through strong normative bonds and that it indirectly prevents revolt or revolution against the social order. The function of household organisation may be said to be, in nearly every society, to create stability, reproduction through procreation, and to secure the continuity of values, norms and conventions through socialisation. When external influences, such as the introduction of capitalism, change the conditions of existence for households, one might say – within this analytical framework – that the original household organisation has become dysfunctional: it is no longer practical and so eventually disappears. Within a structural-functionalist mode of thought, all social institutions thus appear as functional; if they are not functional, they vanish.

In classic structural-functionalism, deriving from Durkheim and Radcliffe-Brown, society was often thought of as a kind of organism, as an integrated whole of functional social institutions. Kroeber (1952 [1917]) described culture in a similar vein, by comparing it to a coral reef where new coral animals literally build upon their dead relatives. Seen as a whole, the coral reef (culture) is qualitatively different from the sum of its parts, and its form develops and changes gradually without the knowledge of the individual polyps (actors).

The existence of certain social institutions was thus explained by reference to their function. Certain peoples believed in witchcraft, it was said, at least partly because the belief indirectly strengthened social integration and the stability of society – without the actors' knowledge of this function of witchcraft (see Chapter 15). In his theory of primitive religion, Durkheim therefore argued that when people believe that they worship supernatural powers, they really worship society.

Several problems have been pointed out in relation to this kind of argument. One obviously problematic aspect of structural-functionalism is the belief that a description of social structure might be tantamount to a good description of social life. If this were the case, we would have to expect people to act diligently and predictably according to a pre-established system of norms and sanctions. Of course this is not the case, as anyone who has done fieldwork knows. People break the rules, make exceptions, interpret norms in different and sometimes conflicting ways, and so on. An example could be the pattern of settlement among the transhumant reindeer-herding Sami of northern Scandinavia (Pehrson 1964; Paine 1994). According to the Sami, a woman ought to join her husband's household at marriage (the technical term for this is virilocality). However, in practice only about half of them actually do so, and there are often good, pragmatic reasons for making an exception. Pehrson thus draws the conclusion that the transhumant Sami actually do not have a rule about post-marriage residence. Ladislav Holy and Milan Stuchlik (1983,

p. 13) do not agree in this. They argue, rather, that the rule of virilocality definitely exists, since the Sami themselves say that the woman ought to join the man's group, even if the rule is often violated. This is obviously a valid point. In many societies, sexual infidelity is quite widespread, even if most of the persons in question would agree that there is a rule to the effect that such a practice is morally objectionable.

Raymond Firth (1951) tried to resolve this problem through proposing a distinction between social structure and social organisation. The structure, according to this perspective, is the established pattern of rules, customs, statuses and social institutions. Social organisation, on the other hand, is defined as the dynamic aspect of structure; in other words, what people actually do: their decisions and patterns of action within the framework of the structure. This distinction is analogous to the distinction between status and role, and allows for a messier, less neatly ordered social world than an exclusive reliance on a structural understanding would allow.

Firth's innovation represented an attempt to conceptualise social process; that is, society and social life seen as something which happens rather than something which is. This distinction does not imply that actors continuously break the rules and norms valid in their society, but rather that systems of rules do not specify exactly how people are to act. Even perfect knowledge of the Bible is certainly not adequate if we wish to understand how Christians act; and those who began studying the Qu'ran following the 2001 Al-Qaeda terrorist attacks in the USA probably missed the point. The move from structure to process expressed through Firth's model made a more truthful realism possible in ethnographic descriptions than in classic structural-functionalism, and it would exert a strong influence on later anthropological theorising.

SOCIAL SYSTEMS

The term 'social system' has been used a great deal here with no further definition. It can be defined briefly as a set of social relations which are regularly actualised and thus reproduced as a system through interaction. A social system is further characterised by a (more or less) shared normative system and a functioning set of sanctions; that is, a certain degree of agreement or enforced conformity concerning the oughts and ought-nots of interaction within the limits of the system.

Until now, we have dealt empirically with social systems at three levels: the dyadic relationship, the household and the village or local community. Do these levels thereby represent different cultures? If an actor engages in a relationship with her husband, in another relationship with her family and in a third relationship with her village, does that make her a member of three cultures? Of course not. But different social statuses are activated in the three cases, and the kinds of relationship engaged in may vary greatly. There are aspects of life which can only be shared with one's spouse, and there are other events (such as public rituals) which would not be meaningful unless they are public. Culture may thus be understood as that which makes it possible for two or several actors to understand each other. It is not a 'thing' which one either has or does not have, and it can be relevant to talk of degrees of shared culture. Similarly, every actor is integrated, or participates, at several systemic levels in society. An adult may be a member of a nuclear family, a profession, a political grouping and a nation. One may also conceptualise one's 'levels of belonging' in more geographic, or spatial, terms: one is a member of the nuclear family, a neighbourhood, a town, a province and a nation. There are also many other possible ways of delineating systemic levels in society. These systems exist only to the extent that they are maintained through regular interaction.

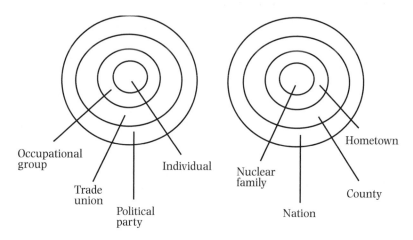

Figure 6.1   Two ways of conceptualising group membership in modern
              societies

The ethnographic examples of the previous chapter reveal several systemic levels. Among the Fulani, the household, the kin group and the larger group assembling in the rainy season are relevant and important systemic levels which exist (or are activated) under particular circumstances. In the Caribbean village, the natal household remains an important systemic level for the male actor throughout his life. Among the Dogon and Yanomamö, on the contrary, the household, the lineage and the village seem to be the most important systemic levels. As regards many communities deeply integrated into large-scale social systems, it may be argued that the market and the State are the crucial systemic levels, although kinship and small groups remain important in such complex societies as well.

Distinctions between relevant systemic levels depend on which persons are related in which ways to which others. Put simply, it concerns which groups persons belong to, and what is the purpose of these groups. In anthropological studies, the analytical interests of the anthropologist are also important.

Should one concentrate one's research efforts on the household, the kin group, the village, a network centred around a pub or an Internet chat group, a trade union, a factory or the nation-state? An obvious answer is that one might begin by finding out how the inhabitants of a society themselves relate to their different webs of relationship; what appears as most important to them, and with whom do they carry out important tasks?

It is important to be able to distinguish between social system and social structure. A social system is just as abstract as the social structure, but it refers to a different kind of phenomenon. Social systems are delineable sets of social relationships between actors, whereas social structure (usually) refers to the totality of standardised relationships in a society. Both of those concepts may, however, be conceptualised as socially created channels and frameworks for human action, which provide both opportunities and constraints.

THE BOUNDARIES OF SOCIAL SYSTEMS

If we define a social system as a set of social relationships which are created and re-created through regular interaction, it makes sense to say that the boundaries of the system lie at the points where interaction decreases dramatically. In a relatively isolated village community, as among the Dogon in precolonial times or the Yanomamö before the 1960s, it would be appropriate to say that the relevant social system stops at the village boundary. The interaction engaged in by the inhabitants with outsiders is (traditionally) sporadic and relatively unimportant. Religion, family life, politics and production have all taken place within the limits of the village. However, concerning some activities, such as trade, the village appears as a sub-system; as a part of a larger system. Systemic boundaries are in this way not absolute, but relative to a particular kind of social context or a set of activities. Unless this is kept in mind, it would be difficult to delineate the boundaries of most social sub-systems in the contemporary world; in their different ways, they may link up with vast entities such as world Islam, the Internet or the global commodity market.

Society, if we think of it as an integrated whole, may also be divided analytically into various sub-systems. In the Dogon village, one such sub-system is the religious and ritual one, in which certain but not all members of society take part. Another sub-system, involving a different set of actors for different ends, would be the lineage organisation; a third would be the household, and so on. The relationship between such sub-systems is of great importance in anthropological research, since we aim at an understanding of the intrinsic connections between different social institutions and activities.

NETWORKS

The term 'social network' has in recent years entered the everyday vocabulary of many societies. In day-to-day speech, it refers to an ego-centred set of relationships, as when people talk of 'my social network'. It may also be used to refer to a set of relationships activated for a particular end, without necessarily being organised around a single person. The analytical meaning of the term 'social network' is thus related to the meaning of social systems; generally, we may say that a network is a person-dependent kind of social system which depends on continuous activity to be reproduced. The social networks activated through the Internet, from chatgroups to Internet communities on Twitter, Facebook and so on, illustrate this point well. Unless one makes an effort to keep the communication going, one ceases to be part of the community.

The first anthropologist to use the expression 'social network' was John Barnes, originally an Africanist, who carried out fieldwork in Bremnes, western Norway, in the early 1950s (Barnes 1990 [1954]). Since the hamlet lacked unilineal corporate groups of the kind he was accustomed to from his African research, he needed other analytical tools to grasp the mechanisms of integration. To begin with, he noted that each person in the parish belonged to several groups; the household, the hamlet, the churchgoers, the professional group and so on. For analytical purposes, Barnes identified three kinds of social fields in Bremnes. First is the territorially delineated field, which is hier-archically organised through public administration. Second is the economic field, which consists of many mutually dependent but formally independent entities, such as fishing boats, fish oil factories, groceries and so on. These two fields have a certain stability through time, to some extent independently of the actors. The third social field Barnes delineated, however, 'had no units or boundaries; it had no co-ordinating organization. It was made up of the ties of friendship and acquaintance which everyone growing up in Bremnes society partly inherited and largely built up for himself' (1990 [1954], p. 72). These ties existed between social equals, and were continuously modified as actors changed their circle of acquaintances.

A main point in Barnes's study is that this kind of society lacks the stable corporations typical of African village societies. An important contributing reason for the lack of corporations in Bremnes, he argued, was the bilateral kinship system: kin reckoning which includes both the mother's and the father's side.

I have my cousins and sometimes we act together; but they have their own cousins who are not mine and so on indefinitely.... Each person is, as it were, in touch with a number of other people, some of whom are directly in touch with each other and some whom are not. (Barnes 1990 [1954], p. 72)

It is this kind of system of relations that Barnes proposed calling social networks. Here it should be noted that networks often have no boundaries and no clear internal organisation, since any person may consider him- or herself the centre of the network.

Barnes further holds that one of the most important differences between small communities and large-scale societies is the fact that the networks are denser in the former than in the latter. When two people meet for the first time in a large-scale urban society, it is quite rare for them to discover that they have many common acquaintances; in small-scale societies, on the contrary, 'everybody' knows each other in many different ways – through kinship, common friends and neighbours, shared school experiences, professional life and/or intermarriage.

The network has a fleeting and impermanent character. The term is therefore most appropriate in descriptions of social fields, or sub-systems, which primarily exist by virtue of ties between concrete persons, and which therefore are transformed, or disappear, when those persons for some reason cease to maintain the ties. The network may be a more useful descriptive term than more rigid concepts such as 'social structure', when the locus of study is a large-scale social system. Indeed, theorists of globalisation such as Manuel Castells (2009) have gone so far as to suggest that the contemporary era, 'the information age', is generally characterised by flux, instability and shifting boundaries, and that it may therefore be described as 'a network society' (see also Hannerz 1992).

SCALE

It is often said that anthropologists have traditionally studied 'small-scale societies' as opposed to 'large-scale societies'. But what is scale as such? It could be seen as a measure of social complexity in a society (see, for example, Barth 1978; Eriksen 2007a). The scale of a society can be defined as the total number of statuses necessary for the society to reproduce itself. If we compare the Yanomamö village with the Caribbean one, it becomes evident that the latter exists on a larger scale than the former. The Yanomamö community is small in size and relatively simple in terms of its division of labour. In the Caribbean village the division of labour is more complex: there are ties of mutual dependency between a large number of persons because of professional specialisation, and the village is intrinsically linked to systems of much larger scale (the state, remote localities through migration, etc.). If we move on to industrial societies, the level of scale is enormous: the mutual dependency may encompass millions of persons. If some of their statuses cease to contribute to the upholding of the system, it will change: if, say, all the bus drivers in the Netherlands go on strike, this will, directly or indirectly, affect the lives of most of the Dutch.

Scale may also be regarded as a measure of relative anonymity: the larger the scale, the fewer the actors of the system one knows personally. We now turn to an example indicating the possible uses of the concept of scale.

Case Noyale is a village on the south-western coast of Mauritius, an island-state in the Indian Ocean (Eriksen 1998). About 700 individuals live in the village, which has approximately 170 households. The main source of livelihood is fishing, but many villagers have other work. Some work at a sugar plantation nearby, some are independent farmers, some work at a hotel

5 kilometres away, and so on. The village has a grocery, a few small shops, a post office and a dispensary.

In a certain sense, one may say that Case Noyale is a social system of relatively small scale. The division of labour and the specialisation in the village itself are limited, and there are few local organisations with specialised aims. Virtually all of the villagers know each other.

On the other hand, it is ultimately not very helpful to regard Case Noyale as an isolated small-scale system. About 20 per cent of the adults work outside the village, and several of those who work within it (including the Catholic priest and the schoolteacher) live elsewhere. The fishermen sell their catch to an intermediary, a *banian*, who drives to and from town daily. Several of the teenagers of the village attend secondary school at Rose-Hill or Quatre-Bornes, towns which are about an hour away by bus. The inhabitants receive much of their knowledge about the outside world through radio and television; the school has state funding; the products sold in the grocery are largely imported from abroad, and so on.

From this sketch, it can be extrapolated that scale can be highly relevant in the study of agency. Scale sets limits to the scope of options for action, but simultaneously it is the product of action. In Case Noyale, the first teenager who went to secondary school became a participant in a system of larger scale than his friends were involved in. Every time someone files a court case at the District Court of Rivière Noire, he or she activates a level of scale higher than is common. To most villagers at most times, however, the village of Case Noyale is the relevant social system. This is where they go to primary school, work, sleep, eat and buy food. However, Case Noyale may also be regarded as an integrated part of the nation-state of Mauritius (school, public transportation and other facilities are organised at a national level, and the fish is eventually sold at the national fish market) and even, in some respects, as a part of the global economic system, since the backbone of the Mauritian economy is the sugar industry.

In order to say anything meaningful about the scale of a society, it is necessary to investigate social relations carefully. Above all, we must identify which tasks the members of society are faced with and which options they have in carrying them out. If these tasks – subsistence, socialisation, politics, religion and so on – depend on many actors with specialised statuses, the scale is by definition larger than would be the case in a society where nearly everybody knows nearly everything. Scale is also, as we have seen, situational in the sense that all actors move from situations of small scale to those of larger scale, and back again, on a daily basis.

NON-LOCALISED NETWORKS: THE INTERNET

In *The Internet: An Ethnographic Approach* (2000), Daniel Miller and Don Slater remark that the Internet transcends dualisms such as local/global and small scale/large scale. In this, they mean that online communities of, say,

Trinidadians (their ethnographic focus) can be based on close interpersonal relationships even if the participants are scattered around the world (due to the extensive migration of Trinidadians). To some extent, ethnographic studies of Internet users raises problems reminiscent of those encountered by Barnes when he came to Bremnes from Southern Africa. Where were the corporate groups? he asked. Where was the gravitational point of the community? Regarding the Internet, a similar question may be: 'In which sense do online communities exist?' They come into existence only when people log on, quite unlike local communities, which exist in more materially imperative ways. An interesting issue thus concerns the degree to which Internet participation creates binding commitments similar to those created in offline settings. The Internet is a decentred, unlocalised 'network of networks' (Hannerz 1996) which may seem to operate according to a different logic from other social networks.

Many studies of Internet users so far have confined themselves to online research. While this research strategy may in many ways be rewarding, anthropologists usually ask research questions which require them to collect other kinds of data as well. Notably, the relationship between online activities and other social activities needs to be studied if we are going to understand the place of the Internet in people's lives. In their study, Miller and Slater have participated online with Trinidadians, made household surveys of computer use, carried out structured interviews with businesspeople, politicians and other elite persons, been hanging out in cybercafes and so on – in brief, they employed a wide variety of methods in order to assess the impact of the Internet on Trinidadian society. Some of their findings are surprising. For example, Trinidadians do not customarily distinguish between online and offline life, between the 'virtual' and the 'real'; to them, all their activities form a seamless whole. Also, they are far from being 'de-territorialised' online, but on the contrary tend to overcommunicate their identity as Trinidadians. The Internet actually enhances their national and, in many cases, religious identity. It also turns out to be a good medium for intimate conversations.

Subsequent developments of the Internet lend support to Miller and Slater's views (see also Miller and Slater 2003). Contrary to what many expected in the 1990s, the Internet did not evolve into a kind of marketplace or a source of information only; the services which have grown the fastest, are driven by the desire to communicate with others, ranging from global services such as Facebook to more specialised forums like the Open Anthropology Cooperative. In other words, the Internet has evolved into a medium for social interaction rather than just consumption.

The newness of information technologies such as the Internet should not lead us to believe that everything about it is new. Ethnographic studies of Internet users tend to ask similar research questions to those asked in studies of local communities or localised urban networks, and the methods employed also tend to be similar. But it is equally important to keep in mind that information/communication technologies such as the Internet, mobile phones and satellite television create new frameworks for communication and interaction. In a sense, as Miller and Slater say, the far/near, small-scale/large-scale and local/global dichotomies are dissolved; but instead, other issues arise – concerning place, commitment, trust and, not least, the boundaries of the network. If it is difficult to delineate the boundaries of, say, Bremnes or Case Noyale, the problem of delineation is even greater here. This is a kind of question which needs to be addressed by anthropologists today, as they bring their skills in network studies and participant observation to new areas.

GROUP AND GRID

Distinctions between small-scale and large-scale societies are still used in social anthropology, even if this kind of distinction is problematic as most actors are involved in social fields of large as well as small scale. Mauritian village life does not preclude having 500 Facebook friends or regular interaction with Australian tourists, or consuming Burmese rice, or corresponding with foreign anthropologists via e-mail; just as the nuclear family and the personal friendship remain very real possibilities for the inhabitants of Germany.

Another way of classifying societies, which concentrates on the principles of social control rather than size and complexity, has been proposed by Mary Douglas (1970, 1978). In many of her theoretical studies in anthropology, sociology and social philosophy, she draws on a classificatory scheme that runs along two axes (Figure 6.2), which she labels 'group' and 'grid'. Along the 'group' dimension, persons and societies may be classified according to their degree of social cohesion, while the 'grid' dimension describes the degree of shared classifications or knowledge. Purely personal notions, which are not shared with others, belong below zero. Strong group indicates that other persons exert strong pressure on the individual; strong grid indicates that people are rigidly classified at the societal level, which leaves little space for individual idiosyncrasies.

One 'strong grid, strong group' society is, in Douglas's view, the Tallensi of Ghana as described by Fortes under colonialism. 'Here the public system of rights and duties equips each man with a full identity, prescribing for him what and when he eats, how he grooms his hair, how he is buried or born' (Douglas 1970, p. 87). Such societies, Douglas argues, are strictly conformist, strongly integrated and create rigid boundaries vis-à-vis outsiders.

Another kind of society is the 'weak grid, strong group' one, which Douglas exemplifies by describing the situation in some Central African societies during late colonialism (that is the 1950s; see also Chapter 16). In these societies, contradictory demands are placed on people; they must be obedient, but also strive for individual excellence. They are expected to till the land of their ancestors, but also to earn money, which can only be achieved through migration. Internal differentiation is unclear and ambiguous, unlike the strong 'ritualisation' of social relationships in the previous type.

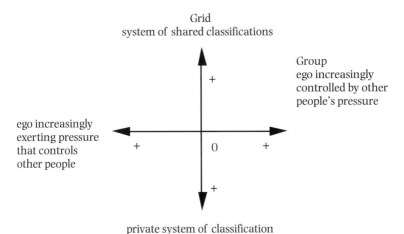

Figure 6.2   Grid and group (Douglas 1970, p. 84)

The third societal type exemplified in Douglas (1970) is the kind she calls 'strong grid', where group cohesion is weak. This is a sort of society, she argues, which might be better described in terms of temporary networks than in terms of corporate groups; where there are no chiefs and no rigid boundaries. Nevertheless, she notes, the meanings and classifications of society are shared.

The 'strong grid' type also has another variant, which can be described as the 'big-man system' (see Chapter 11), oscillating from the left to the right on the upper half of the diagram. The big man, a self-made leader in a small-scale society, tries to exert as much pressure as possible on his subjects, but as his power grows, so does their discontent, and they pull him towards the right.

Where do industrial (and postindustrial) societies belong in Douglas's scheme? It is not easy to say and, admittedly, my brief summary is a simplification of her account. In reality, societies are spread out on the diagram, so that some groups or some social contexts belong, say, in the top left slot while others might be placed in the top right corner. In the view of some, industrial societies are generally 'weak group, weak grid': they are individualistic and anonymous, and thus others exert little social control over ego; and they are internally differentiated in such a way that boundaries between categories of persons, and between society and the outside world, are unclear. However, another perspective might rather maintain that industrial societies are 'strong group' because of the power of the state in exerting pressure on its citizens. Douglas suggests, for her part, that there are remarkable similarities between 'some Londoners' and Mbuti pygmies. Both modern individualists and egalitarian hunter-gatherers may tentatively be placed close to zero on the vertical axis ('complete freedom' in Douglas's terms). A small, homogeneous and strongly integrated nation-state, such as Iceland, can perhaps be placed squarely in the top half of the diagram, while loosely integrated urban societies (Los Angeles perhaps), would cluster around the vertical axis and – if social disintegration is strong – mostly in the bottom half. Rich eccentrics, homeless people and other 'outsiders', such as artists, belong largely below zero. On the other hand, religious cults and other strongly integrated groups in modern societies, like Jehovah's Witnesses, could be firmly placed with the Tallensi in the top right area of the diagram.

Douglas's scheme can be very instructive as a tool for thinking about humans in society. It is simple, non-evolutionary and can be fruitful for investigating the relationship between cohesion and other dimensions of social life, such as cosmologies. Its central premises are Durkheimian, and Douglas states explicitly that too little sharing and too weak social control (in other words, a condition approaching zero) is tantamount to anomie and disintegration. While role analysis and models of scale and networks take the social actor as their point of departure, Douglas's work reveals a distinctly systemic approach. A possible implication of the model could be that people who are not fully integrated are pathological and that social and symbolic integration is the 'aim' towards which every society strives. Douglas emphasises that 'societies' do the classifying, and though people relate to it individually and may even create a private classificatory system, what matters sociologically is the shared system of knowledge and norms.

SOCIETY AND ACTOR

The founder of Social Darwinism, Herbert Spencer (1820–1903; he also coined the term 'social structure'), proposed that social relationships ought in general to be founded on voluntary contracts between individuals. Spencer was an early proponent of a school of thought which may be called individualist, as opposed to collectivist. Individualist thought (or methodological individualism) is often associated with Max Weber, whereas collectivist thought (or methodological collectivism) is associated with Marx and Durkheim. The difference between these approaches to social life has been stated succinctly by Holy and Stuchlik (1983, p. 1), who say that anthropologists try to find out either what it is that makes people do what they do, or how societies work. Most anthropologists probably claim that they do both, but there is an important difference between the perspectives. I shall later distinguish between actor-centred and system-centred accounts, and it will become clear that the two approaches may indeed lead to different, if complementary, kinds of insight.

Actor-centred accounts, which stress choice, goal-directed action and individual idiosyncrasies, emerged in European social anthropology in the 1950s as critiques, often inspired by Malinowski and Weber, of the then dominant structural-functionalist models. The structural-functionalists regarded society as an integrated whole where the social institutions 'worked together', more or less in the same way as body parts are complementary to each other. The individual was not granted a great deal of interest, and individual agency was seen more or less as a side-effect of society's reproduction of itself.

'Can "society" have "needs" and "aims"?' asked the critics rhetorically, and replied in the negative. Society is no living organism, they said; it is only the arbitrary result of that myriad of single acts which take place. Further, they pointed out that it is misleading to use biological metaphors in the description of society. The sharpest critics of structural-functionalism instead emphasised that society existed largely by virtue of interaction. Norms, therefore, were to be seen as a result rather than as a cause of interaction (Barth 1966).

The structural-functionalist concept of function was also subjected to severe criticism. Already in 1936, Gregory Bateson had written that the term 'function' is an expression from mathematics which has no place in social science (Bateson 1958 [1936]). Functionalist explanation, it was later remarked (Jarvie 1968), is circular in that the premises contain the conclusion. Since the observed facts by default have to be 'functional', all the social scientist has to do is to look for their functions.

It is a truism that social institutions are functional in the sense that they contribute to the survival of society, since they are themselves part of the society that survives. This does not, however, explain *why* a given society develops, say, either monotheism or a witchcraft institution, or why some societies are patrilineal whereas others are matrilineal. In other words, structural-functionalism promises to *explain* cultural variation, but succeeds only in *describing* the interrelationships between institutions.

From a different perspective, Edmund Leach (1954) pointed out that societies are by no means as stable as one would expect from a structural-functionalist viewpoint. His analysis of politics among the Kachin of upper Burma reveals a cyclical system, where the political institution in its very structure carries the germ of its own destruction. In this regard, it is far from stable or 'functional'. In contemporary anthropological research, which stresses change and process just as much as stability, structural-functionalism is not an option as a research strategy, but its influence continues to be felt, particularly in its emphasis on the interconnections between different institutions in society. It should also be noted that, in spite of its theoretical shortcomings, structural functionalism, with its holistic emphasis on the interconnection between different institutions, provided a good scaffolding for writing ethnography.

THE DUALITY OF STRUCTURE

Obviously, actors make decisions, and it is equally obvious that societies change. However, actors do not act entirely on their own whim: there are bound to be structural preconditions for their acts. There are phenomena which cannot be imagined as purely individual products, which are inherently collective phenomena. Religion is often mentioned in this context, as well as language and ritual. None of them can be thought of as aspects of individuals: on the contrary, religion, language and morality are social preconditions for the production of individuals. Anthropologists who stress the role of individuals in the making of society would answer that morality, language and religion certainly exist, but that they cannot help us in predicting action and that they cannot be taken for granted as given facts either. They change: we must look into what people actually do, and why they do it, in order to understand what these phenomena mean and why they are maintained or transformed through time.

It may sometimes seem as though the contrast between individualist and collectivist accounts is a chicken-and-egg kind of problem. The individual is in many regards a social product, but only individuals can create societies. What we must do therefore is to distinguish clearly between the two perspectives and try to see them as complementary. Neither individual nor society can be conceptualised without the other aspect.

The theoretical sociologist Anthony Giddens (1979, 1984) has tried to reconcile these two main dimensions of social life, agency and structure, through his general theory of structuration. The problem Giddens sets out to resolve is the same one that has been posed in various ways in earlier sections of this chapter: on the one hand, humans choose their actions deliberately and try their best to realise their goal, which is a good life (although, an anthropologist would add, there are significant cultural variations as to what is considered a good life). On the other hand, humans definitely act under pressure, which varies between people, contexts and societies, and which limits their freedom of choice and to some extent determines the course of their agency.

Giddens's very general solution to the paradox can be summarised in his concept of the *duality of structure*. Social structure, he writes, must simultaneously be understood as the necessary conditions for action *and* as the cumulative result of the totality of actions. Society exists only as interaction, but at the same time society is necessary for interaction to be meaningful. This model combines the individual and the societal aspects of social life, at least at a conceptual level. The craft of social research, in Giddens's view, largely consists of relating the two levels to each other. His model, and related models (of which there are many), try to reconcile the idea of the free, voluntary act and the idea of systemic coercion.

In an influential book on the social construction of everyday life, Peter Berger and Thomas Luckmann (1967) deal with many of the same problems as Giddens. Inspired by the social phenomenology of Alfred Schütz and Karl Mannheim's sociology of knowledge, their point of departure is the fact that humans are, at birth, thrown into a pre-existing social world, and they re-create this world through their actions. In addition, Berger and Luckmann emphasise the ways in which each new act modifies the conditions for action (what Giddens calls the recursive character of action). The Greek philosopher Heraclitus said that a man cannot enter the same river twice, because both man and river would have changed in the meanwhile; Berger and Luckmann would hold that a man cannot undertake the same act twice, since the first act would change the system slightly.

The social system, or structure, would consist of the process of ongoing interaction, but it also consists of frozen action. Both social institutions and material structures such as buildings and technology are products of human action. However, they take on an objective existence and appear as things, as taken-for-granteds upon which humans act: they determine conditions for agency. In this way, Berger and Luckmann argue, the institutionalisation of society takes place and society, although the product of subjective action, becomes an objective reality exerting power over the individual consciousness. Thereby they answer their own main question, namely that of how living human activity (a process) can produce a world consisting of 'things' (social structure and material objects).

Just as Kroeber's metaphoric 'coral reef' (1917) reproduces itself while slightly modifying itself through every new cultural event, human action relates to earlier human action in the reproduction of and change to society. New acts are not mechanical repetitions of earlier acts, but at the same time they are dependent on earlier acts. The first act determines where the next begins, but not where it ends.

Berger and Luckmann's influential perspective is consistent with Marx's notion of labour and the 'freezing' of social life; he once wrote that the dead (labour) seizes the living (labour) through its material traces and products. The creative aspect of human activity is sedimented as dead material, be it a building, a tool or a convention. Social life, and the eternal becoming of society, can thereby be seen as an immanent tension between ongoing human action and the social institutions' limiting effect on the options for choice; between the solid (structure, institutions) and the fleeting (process, movement).

SOCIAL MEMORY AND THE DISTRIBUTION OF KNOWLEDGE

Societies can be delineated through enduring systems of interaction and through the presence of shared social and political institutions with a certain continuity through time, although neither boundaries nor continuity are ever absolute. A related feature of integration, which emphasises the cultural rather than the social, concerns knowledge and acquired skills. Whereas it was for years common to assume that the members of a society (at least a small-scale society) shared the same basic outlook and values, detailed ethnographic evidence, as well as critical voices from various camps (which, for the sake of brevity, could be labelled Marxist, feminist, postcolonial and postmodernist), have revealed that knowledge is unevenly distributed and that members of a society do not necessarily have shared representations.

The issue concerning to what extent culture is shared within society is a complex one, which has led to a lot of heated debate, some of it based on mutual misunderstandings; let us therefore initially make it clear that sharing at one level does not necessarily imply sharing at another. Societies may appear both as patterned and as chaotic, depending on the analytical perspective employed and on the empirical focus. Language, for example, is by definition shared by the members of a linguistic community, but this certainly does not mean that everybody masters it equally well. Indeed, oratorical skills are an important source of political power in many societies. The unequal distribution of linguistic skills, and its consequences for power in society, is shown in a very simple and instructive way through the influential work of Basil Bernstein (1972) and William Labov (1972), two sociolinguists. Briefly, Bernstein wanted to explore why working-class children in Britain generally had poorer school results than middle-class children. He found that the language acquired in working-class homes was less compatible with the standard version used in schools than the language spoken in middle-class homes was. The dominant code of society – that considered 'proper English' – was thus identical with the sociolect of the middle class. Meanwhile Labov, in a study of black children in the US, showed that the linguistic difference between blacks and whites did not represent a lower 'cognitive complexity' among black children, but rather that their way of expressing complex statements differed from the dominant idiom in such a way as to impair them in school. The linguistic code favoured in schools, in Labov's analysis, was not 'more sophisticated' than the black sociolect, but rather a hidden mechanism for ensuring white middle-class dominance.

Key Debates in Anthropology

In the mid 1980s, Tim Ingold (1996) reports, he felt a lack of vitality regarding debate about 'the theoretical and intellectual foundations' of social anthropology. In his view, the discipline suffered from three problems: first, it had become fragmented into narrow specialisations with few overarching debates between the sub-fields; second, there were few new academic appointments at the time, leading in turn to a paucity of fresh ideas; third, Ingold claims, anthropologists no longer seemed to engage with major issues of wide public relevance. In order to address this problem, Ingold initiated a series of annual debates hosted by the University of Manchester, where colleagues and students from the whole country were invited. The debates, organised by the Group for Debates in Anthropological Theory (GDAT), were structured in an unusual way: two anthropologists were asked to support a particular 'motion' and two were asked to oppose it. At the end, the audience were asked to vote for and against the 'motion'. Although this form has an ironic edge – truth is not decided through democratic voting – these polemical debates doubtless contributed to a revitalisation of the general theoretical debate in social anthropology. The first six debates

▶

(from 1988 to 1993) have been published in book form (Ingold 1996). The topics and results are as follows.

- *Social anthropology is a generalising science or it is nothing.* For: 26. Against: 37. Abstentions: 8. *Comment:* The problem was probably the term 'science' and not the term 'generalizing'; many felt uncomfortable with the implied association with natural science.
- *The concept of society is theoretically obsolete.* For: 45. Against: 40. Abstentions: 10. *Comment:* Surprisingly many felt that we can no longer use the word 'society'. On the other hand it may be theoretically obsolete and yet useful in practice, although it is a far from accurate technical term.
- *Human worlds are culturally constructed.* For: 41. Against: 26. Abstentions: 7. *Comment:* This is a take on the classic 'nature/ nurture' issue: what is inborn and universal; what is cultural and variable? Most British anthropologists still seem to favour nature, but a generation ago, they would have won even more comfortably.
- *Language is the essence of culture.* For: 24. Against: 47. Abstentions: 7. *Comment:* Although a clear majority held that non-linguistic aspects of culture are essential, the result might have been very different 20 years earlier in Britain (when structuralism was influential) or today in the United States, where cognitive and linguistic anthropology remain important.
- *The past is a foreign country.* For: 26. Against: 14. Abstentions: 7. *Comment:* The proposed motion is ambiguous (it quotes the title of David Lowenthal's book, which again quotes from a novel), and the debate largely concerned whether the interpretation of past events is reminiscent of the interpretation of other cultures.
- *Aesthetics is a cross-cultural category.* For: 22. Against: 42. Abstentions: 4. *Comment:* Does beauty exist (as philosophers from Plato to Kant believe), or can it be dissolved into merely cultural notions of beauty? Convincing win for the relativists here.

Social inequality is reproduced at the symbolic level through the transmission of different kinds of knowledge through socialisation. It has been customary to believe that all members of a 'primitive' small-scale society by and large obtained the same body of knowledge and skills, but anthropological research has revealed that social differentiation and political power in such societies is just as closely related to differences in knowledge and mastery of symbolic universes as in modern complex ones. 'Secret knowledge' is only for the cream of the initiates. Moreover, such self-reproducing patterns of difference are difficult to eradicate even if one actively tries, as has been done in social democratic societies, to ensure that every member of society has access to roughly the same body of knowledge and skills. They are intrinsic to social organisation and the division of labour, and the differences in the transmission of knowledge are connected with other social differences to which we shall return in later chapters.

There are many ways of accounting for differences in skills and knowledge within societies. Feminists have tended to follow one or both of two lines of argument: (1) women experience the world differently from men because they are women; (2) it is in the interest of patriarchy (male rule) to keep socially valuable skills away from women. Analyses inspired by Marxism tend to link the study of knowledge and skills to that of power and ideology (see Chapters 9, 11 and 14), while social anthropologists inspired by Durkheim may relate such differences to the complementary division of labour, which thereby contributes to the integration of society. It should be noted that the designation of 'valuable knowledge' and, more generally, the very definition of the world, is a form of power (see Bourdieu 1982; see also Chapter 15). Nonetheless, values and rules of conduct are taken for granted as much by the powerful as by the powerless, and their taken-for-grantedness can contribute to explaining the maintenance of a social order which might otherwise appear as unjust – they make the social order appear natural and therefore inevitable – as well as accounting for some degree of cultural continuity.

Paul Connerton, in a study of social memory (1989), argues for a distinction between three kinds of memory: personal memory (which is to do with biography and personal experiences), cognitive memory (which relates to general knowledge about the world) and, importantly, habit-memory, which is embodied, or incorporated, rather than cognitive. Connerton argues that habit-memory is, in highly significant ways, created and reproduced through bodily practices embedded in rules of etiquette, gestures, meaningful postures (such as sitting with one's legs crossed), handwriting and other acquired abilities, which the actors do not normally perceive as cultural skills but rather as mere technical abilities or even 'social instincts'. He particularly emphasises rituals as enactments of embodied knowledge. Like Foucault (1979) and Halbwachs (1999 [1925]) before him, Connerton stresses the social and political implications of bodily discipline in reproducing values, 'inscribed' knowledge and social hierarchies. Arguably, this kind of knowledge has been understated by scholars working in diverse fields, including anthropology, where knowledge that can be verbalised tends to be privileged.

In an attempt to explain the transmission, spread and transformations of social representations, Dan Sperber (1996) has proposed what he calls an epidemiology of representations. Using an analogy from medical science, but also obviously drawing on Lévi-Strauss, Sperber stresses that representations spread in a different way from viruses, which are simply duplicated. 'For example', he writes (1989, p. 127), 'it would have been very surprising if what you understand by my text were an exact reproduction of the ideas

I try to express through this means.' Knowledge and skills therefore, in Sperber's analysis, change (are transformed) slightly each time they are transmitted through communication, although the actors may be unaware of this happening.

Although the mode of communication depends on a number of factors, including communication technology, the basic 'epidemic' character of knowledge transmission is, in Sperber's view, universal. Interestingly, he offers a method for the study of representations which does not presuppose direct access to the minds of the actors, by focusing on that which is public and communicated, yet enables the researcher to identify both variation and change, and – perhaps – properties of the mental make-up of the informants. The epidemiological model, further, seems to overcome shortcomings of some other approaches to knowledge in its ability to account for both sharing and variation, both continuity and change.

AGENCY BEYOND LANGUAGE AND SELF-CONSCIOUSNESS

Notions of choice and freedom are common in actor-centred accounts of social life. We should therefore keep in mind that far from all action is chosen in a conscious sense. Much of what we do is based on habit and convention, and in most situations it does not occur to us that we could have acted differently. In an influential, but also convoluted work on the organisation of society, Pierre Bourdieu (1977; see also Ortner 1984) discusses the relationship between reflexivity or self-consciousness, action and society. Like the other theorists discussed in this section, he wishes to move beyond entrenched positions in social science and provides a critical review of positions he deems inadequate. In a discussion of interpretive anthropology (particularly the American school of ethnomethodology), Bourdieu stresses that one should not 'put forward one's contribution to the science of pre-scientific representation of the social world as if it were a science of the social world' (1977, p. 23). And he continues:

Only by constructing the objective curves (price curves, chances of access to higher education, laws of the matrimonial market etc.) is one able to pose the question of the mechanisms through which the relationship is established between the structures and the practices or the representations which accompany them. (1977, p. 23)

In other words, for a full understanding of society, it is not enough to understand the emic categories and representations of society. Indeed, at least in this regard Bourdieu comes close to Evans-Pritchard's research programme, which consisted of studying the relationship between emic meanings and social structure.

Bourdieu's concept of culturally conditioned agency has been extremely influential. He uses the term 'habitus' (originally used by Mauss in a similar way) to describe enduring, learnt, embodied dispositions for action. The habitus is inscribed into the bodies and minds of humans as an internalised, implicit programme for action. At one point, Bourdieu defines it as 'the durably installed generative principle of regulated improvisation' (1977, p. 78). The habitus can also be described as embodied culture, and being prior to self-conscious reflection it sets limits to thought and chosen action. Through habitus, the socially created world appears as natural and is taken for granted. It therefore has strong ideological implications as well as cultural ones and, we should note, it refers to a layer of social reality which lies beyond the intentional. Informants cannot describe their habitus in the course of an interview, even if they want to. Drawing on his own fieldwork as well as recent research in neuroscience, Robert Borofsky (1994) builds on Bourdieu's perspective in distinguishing between *implicit* and *explicit* knowledge. Implicit memory, which is unintentional and not conscious, cannot be reproduced verbally, but is nevertheless a form of cultural competence which informs action.

In several of his books on epistemology, Bourdieu criticises social scientists for overestimating the importance of representations and reflexivity in their comparative studies of society and culture. This cognitive, and especially linguistic, bias, Bourdieu argues, is characteristic of our occupational specialisation and tends to lead us to ignore the fact that the social world is largely made up of institutionalised practices and not by informants' statements. Other anthropologists have also pointed out that the social world is underdetermined by language; in other words, that there are large areas of social life and of cognition which are not only non-linguistic, but which cannot easily be 'translated' into language. The transmission of knowledge and skills, Maurice Bloch (1991, 2005) argues, consistently with Connerton, frequently takes place without recourse to language. Many cultural skills can only be explained by showing them in practice. In other words, if an over-reliance on interviews is a methodological pitfall, an overestimation of the linguistic character of the social world is an epistemological error.

* * *

We have now introduced some of the most fundamental theoretical issues of social science, including anthropology. It should be noted that after the critique of structural-functionalism in the 1960s, anthropology has made a distinctive move in two directions: first, there has been a shift from emphasis on structure to emphasis on process – change is now seen as an inherent quality of social systems, not as an anomaly; second, there has been a no less significant shift from the study of function to the interpretation of meaning. As an implication, anthropology has in the eyes of many moved away from the social sciences in the direction of the humanities. Be this as it may, it is beyond doubt that contemporary anthropologists often are cautious about positing explanatory accounts of social processes, and concentrate instead on understanding and translation.

SUGGESTIONS FOR FURTHER READING

Peter L. Berger and Thomas Luckmann: *The Social Construction of Reality*. Harmondsworth: Penguin 1967.

Mary Douglas: *How Institutions Think*. London: Routledge 1987.

Erving Goffman: *The Presentation of Self in Everyday Life*. Harmondsworth: Penguin 1978 [1959].

7   KINSHIP AS DESCENT

No society (I believe) is bloody-minded enough to ban sex from marriage, and there is an obvious convenience in combining the two; but sex without marriage one can have and one does.

— Robin Fox

Generations of anthropologists have been flabbergasted at the intricate kinship systems existing in many 'primitive' societies. Several famous examples of such complicated systems are to be found in the Australian aboriginal population, whose kinship systems were studied systematically already in the 1870s by the self-taught ethnographers Lorimer Fison and William Howitt (1991 [1880]). These peoples, traditionally hunters and gatherers, have the simplest technology in the world. They lack metals, domesticated animals and writing, and in most cases they do not even have the rudiments of agriculture. Nonetheless, many of these nomadic groups have kinship systems so complex that it may take an outsider years to comprehend them fully. They can name a large number of different kinds of relatives, they have accurate rules determining who can marry whom, and the groups are subdivided in intricate ways into moieties, clans and sub-clans.

The study of kinship has always been a core topic in anthropology. Towards the end of the 1940s kinship was so central, especially in British social anthropology, that despairing outsiders, American cultural anthropologists and, not least, students, spoke ironically of the subject as 'kinshipology'. Many non-anthropologists continue to react with incomprehension regarding the great interest in kinship still prevalent in twenty-first-century anthropological research.

What is it about kinship that makes it so important? The simple answer is that in very many (some would say all) societies kinship is the single most important social institution. The kin group, in many cases, takes care of one's livelihood, one's career, one's marriage, one's protection and one's social identity. Chapter 5 offered a first glimpse of the importance of kinship, and indicated that there is a close interrelationship between the kinship system and other aspects of social organisation. In some cases, what anthropologists describe as the kinship system may indeed be coexistent with social organisation, since the members of society, and most of their activities, may first and foremost be organised along kinship principles. In other societies, kinship has given way to other principles of organising politics, religion, the economy and so on, but it continues to be a crucial part of people's identity and their webs of commitments to others. At the same time, Godelier (2009) is doubtless right in stating that no society is based merely on kinship: other mechanisms for cohesion, such as exchange and symbolic rituals, are necessary as well.

There are many social ways of organising, and thinking about, kinship. Although it is a widespread notion in North Atlantic societies (and quite a few others) that kinship is related to biology and blood ties (Schneider 1984; Strathern 1992; Holy 1996), anthropological research generally analyses it as cultural classifications of interrelatedness and as aspects of group formation. This chapter introduces some central features of kinship seen as social organisation, and discusses different ways of reckoning kin. In the next chapter, the focus is on marriage systems and symbolic aspects of kinship.

INCEST AND EXOGAMY

All known human societies prohibit sexual relations between persons who are classified as close blood kin, which includes at least the father–child, mother–child and sibling relationships. This does not of course mean that such relations do not occur, but rather that there is a norm prohibiting it. This universal rule is often spoken of as the incest taboo. There are significant cultural variations concerning who is included in this taboo; in many societies, persons others might regard as very distant cousins are included in the prohibition; similarly, people classified in the West as first cousins may, in unilineal kinship systems, not be seen as closely related at all. Sanctions against violations of the incest prohibition are not universally strong; however, marriage between close kin is always strictly prohibited.

Why is the incest prohibition universal? Since the time of Tylor and Freud, several explanations have been put forward. Several anthropologists have pointed out the social advantages of the rule, including the expansion of the group through the inclusion of new members and the forging of alliances across kin boundaries (see Chapter 8).

A functionalist explanation of the incest taboo, common among non-specialists, is that widespread incest would lead to biological degeneration through the transmission of inheritable disease, and that functional mechanisms preventing incestuous practices are therefore called for. This kind of explanation is not satisfactory. Notably, it does not explain what it is that makes people reject incest, since they are in many cases ignorant of its possible negative effects on the genetic material.

Some anthropologists, following the lead of Edward Westermarck (1862–1939), have argued that people who have grown up together will scarcely feel mutual erotic attraction, while others have invoked the blanket term 'instinct' to explain why close kin do not feel sexually attracted to each other. Lévi-Strauss has argued that men, at least in classificatory kinship systems, divide the women surrounding them into two mutually exclusive categories, 'wives' and 'sisters', and that only the former are seen as potential sexual partners. He holds that the exchange of women between kin groups is, when all is said and done, an effect of reciprocity, which is a fundamental structure of the human mind, be it conscious or unconscious.

Some anthropologists have even argued against the use of the term 'incest' at all (Needham 1971a, 1971b), since its meaning varies cross-culturally. Most would nevertheless agree that it is a useful concept, referring to sexual intercourse between persons who are locally (emically) defined as close relatives. In a magisterial overview of the state of kinship studies, Godelier (2004) argues that the incest prohibition is indeed universal and a means to distinguish human societies from the non-human – in other words an important element in human self-identity as something distinctive from the rest of nature.

There are societies which prescribe their members to marry their relatives, though never the very closest ones. This kind of practice is called endogamy; one marries inside the group. The opposite practice, whereby one marries outside of the group, is called exogamy. The two concepts are relative: the Yanomamö are endogamous at the level of the ethnic group (they do not marry non-Yanomamö) but exogamous at the level of the clan. They are divided into a number of exogamous clans (named groups with a common ancestor), and are required to marry persons who do not trace their genealogy to the same ancestor as they do. Since they reckon kinship along the male line (patrilineality), father's sister's children and mother's brother's sister do not belong to one's own clan (they are cross-cousins) and are thus classified as marriageable. Among many Arabic-speakers in the Middle East, and in parts of the Indian subcontinent, on the contrary, marriage with one's father's brother's child (one's parallel cousin) is considered desirable and widely practised. In a sense, most human groups are both endogamous and exogamous to varying degrees: one is expected to marry 'one's own kind', but not someone classified as a close relative. Who is a close relative and who is not is naturally culturally specified, although the people classified as parents, children and siblings in Europe are virtually everywhere seen as close kin.

CORPORATE GROUPS

Kinship concerns much more than the reproduction of society and the transmission of cultural values and knowledge between the generations, although these aspects are certainly important. Kinship can also be important in politics and in the management of everyday affairs. In many societies, a man needs support from both consanguineal kin (blood kin) and from affines (in-laws) in order to follow a successful political career. In other societies, family members join forces in economic investments. Among the Hindus of Mauritius, for example, it is common for groups of brothers and cousins to set up a joint business. Although there may be no formal rule to the effect that one has to be related to run a business together, kinship can give a practical advantage. One can usually trust one's relatives, since they are tied to oneself through webs of strong normative obligations.

In many societies, especially stateless ones, the kin group usually forms, along with locality, the basis for political stability and for the promotion of political interests (see Chapter 11). The group is tied through mutual bonds of loyalty and can often function as a corporation in situations of war, as well as in peaceful negotiations over, say, marriage payments or trade. In this kind of society, marriage does not take place between single individuals on the basis of personal preference, but between groups.

Inside the kin group, norms specify roughly how one is to behave towards different categories of kin. These norms prevent the dissolution of the group and ensure that people carry out their duties. The entire division of labour may thus be organised on a kinship principle. Corporate kin groups tend to be unilineal, which means that new members are recruited on a genealogical principle, either becoming a member of the father's kin group (patrilineal system – common) or the mother's kin group (matrilineal system – less common).

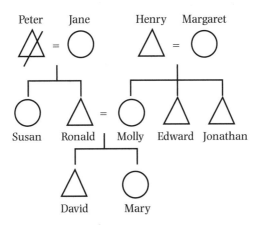

Figure 7.1   Kinship symbols

A triangle denotes a man, a circle a woman, and the sign of equation denotes that they are married (sometimes depicted by a horizontal line connecting the two from below). A horizontal line connecting two persons from above indicates that they are siblings. A diagonal line through a symbol indicates that the person in question is dead. In other words, Ronald is married to Molly, and their children are David and Mary. Ronald's sister is Susan, and Molly's brothers are Jonathan and Edward. Ronald's mother is Jane, and his father Peter is dead. Molly's parents are Henry and Margaret.

INHERITANCE AND SUCCESSION

Group membership, politics, reproduction and social stability have been mentioned as important aspects of kinship. A further important dimension of the kinship institution is the judicial one: it is no coincidence that a large part of the anthropological kinship vocabulary derives from Roman law.

Blood is thicker than water, it has been said in many parts of the world (though not everywhere), and the famous return of the biblical lost son was celebrated with a great feast. Fratricide and patricide are considered the most serious crimes imaginable in many of the world's societies, Cain's slaughter of Abel being the paradigmatic tale of betrayal in the Judeo-Christian world, and parents have always meddled in the marriages of their children – both before and after their consummation. These nearly perennial issues are tied to the fact that kinship is connected with inheritance and succession. Both institutions are to do with the transmission of resources from one generation to the next. Inheritance concerns the transmission of property, while succession refers to 'the transmission of office' (Rivers 1924), transmission of specified rights and duties as ascribed statuses.

All societies have rules regulating who is to inherit what when someone dies, although these rules are often contested or interpreted in varying ways. There is no universal link between the kinship system and the rules of inheritance in societies. There are patrilineal systems of descent where men and women are equals in terms of inheritance, and there are systems which give priority to one of the genders, usually the male. In some societies the eldest son receives a larger part of the inheritance than his siblings (primogeniture); others follow the opposite principle and give priority to the youngest son (ultimogeniture). Whereas the corporate principle functions in an integrating way, inheritance is a source of potential disruption, since it reveals conflicts of interest among the relatives.

Rules of succession are often closely linked with the principle of descent. In patrilineal systems, a son (or a younger brother) will frequently take over the commitments of the deceased; in matrilineal systems, a man commonly succeeds his mother's brother. However, it should be remembered that many forms of succession do not follow genealogical principles at all, for example in societies where chiefs and shamans are appointed or elected on the basis of personal merit. This is the case among the Yanomamö and in many other small-scale societies.

WAYS OF RECKONING KIN

Formally, there are six possible principles for the transmission of kin group membership and other resources from parents to children (Barnard and Good 1984, p. 70). As already noted, the same principle does not have to hold true for succession, inheritance and descent, although the three are frequently lumped together, particularly in patrilineal societies.

1. *Patrilineal.* Transmission of membership and/or resources takes place unilineally through the father's lineage.
2. *Matrilineal.* Transmission of membership and/or resources takes place unilineally through the mother's lineage.

3. *Double*. Some resources are transmitted through the father's lineage, others through the mother's lineage. The two lineages are kept separate.
4. *Cognatic*. Resources can be transmitted through kin on both mother's and father's side (bilaterally).
5. *Parallel*. Rare variety whereby men transmit to their sons and women to their daughters.
6. *Crossing* or *alternating*. Rare variety which represents the opposite of the previous one: men transmit to their daughters, women to their sons.

This simplistic typology should not lead anyone to believe that, for instance, persons in patrilineal societies 'are not related to' their mother's relatives. Practically all kinship systems organise kin relations on both the mother's and the father's side, although rights, clan or family names and group membership frequently give priority to one side. In a patrilineal society, one's commitment to the father's lineage is, in most situations, stronger than one's commitment to the mother's. In many societies, moreover, classificatory kinship terminologies complicate any view of there being a simple relationship between biological and social relatedness. These terminologies lump together persons with varying degrees of biological relatedness under the same kinship term, so that, for example, all boys of the same generation and the same clan are called 'brothers'.

COGNATIC OR BILATERAL DESCENT

In most of Europe and North America, kin on both sides are in principle regarded as equally important. Both mother's and father's relatives of both genders are our relatives, and we often do not distinguish systematically between the two lineages terminologically. In English, for example, we do not have separate kinship terms for father's mother and mother's mother (but such distinctions exist in the Scandinavian languages, for example).

Most of these societies have traditionally given the father's side a priority, since the father's surname has been passed on to the children. However, in recent years, many women have begun to retain their maiden name after marriage, and often the children's family name therefore becomes that of the mother. In some countries, such as Norway, children now automatically get their mother's family name unless the parents sign a joint application to the contrary.

As shown in the example of Bremnes in the previous chapter, it is difficult to organise stable corporate groups within the framework of a bilateral kinship system. The kin group cannot be clearly delineated, since ego's relatives will always have relatives to whom ego is unrelated. Most societies which are constructed about incorporated kin groups therefore base them on a unilineal principle. However, in some parts of the world, particularly in the Pacific, cognatic corporate groups do exist. They are constructed on an eclectic basis, drawing pragmatically on both matrilateral and patrilateral kinship.

A cognatic or bilateral way of kin reckoning creates problems in the construction of genealogies as well. For each generation one moves back in time, the number of kin is doubled. We have two parents, four grandparents, eight great-grandparents, sixteen great-great-grandparents and so on. Genealogies thus tend to be shallow in this kind of society – most persons are unable to name ancestors more than three or four generations back and, as mentioned, corporations based on kinship are relatively rare. Instead, it could be said that class endogamy, particularly among the upper classes, often forms the basis of group solidarity and a pooling of resources reminiscent of the logic of kinship corporations.

For a long time, bilateral kinship received little attention in social anthropology, despite the fact that a third of the world's kinship systems are bilateral. This could be a result of the tendency, particularly strong in British anthropology in the post-war years, to see unilineal descent as the main mechanism of social integration in traditional societies.

PATRILINEAL DESCENT

The lineage in a patrilineal system includes, at least, ego's siblings and father, father's siblings and the children of the men in the group. Father's sister's children, however, do not belong to ego's group, but rather to her husband's group.

The lineage is usually larger than this, and its size depends on the structural or genealogical memory of the group. If one includes, say, every descendant of a shared ancestor seven generations back, the group will naturally be much larger than if one starts reckoning at an ancestor only three generations back. This kind of difference is not caused by mere variation in memory or forgetfulness, but is rather related to organisational features of society. In a society with a long genealogical memory it is necessary, or at least possible, to organise fairly large kinship-based networks and corporate groups – much larger ones than societies which stop their kin reckoning two or three generations back. An example of the latter kind of society would be the Bushmen of the Kalahari, where the social group is small and genealogies are shallow (Barnard 2007). Let us consider an example illustrating what patrilineally based kin groups may do.

When the Dogon settled in south-eastern Mali where they live now, each village was, according to the myth, founded by several brothers, who were the ancestors of one or several present-day clans (Beaudoin 1984). All of the descendants of an ancestor live in the same hamlet, called a *ginna*. The word '*ginna*' is used about the clan's land, about the family house where the clan chief (*ginna bana*) lives and about the smaller houses where the households are based. Most of the land is managed and distributed among the heads of household, by the *ginna bana*. The concept of *ginna* thus groups what anthropologists see as property, place of residence, social rights and duties, and politics, in a single kinship term.

Only men and their children are members of the lineage. The wives/mothers belong to other lineages which are based elsewhere. Marriage is usually organised by the two fathers, who strengthen informal ties of friendship in this way. The Dogon are exogamous at the lineage level. Divorce does occur; as the patrilineal principle is all-encompassing, the father and his lineage are entitled to keep the children when this happens.

Since kinship is formally only recognised through the father, every Dogon has kinship obligations towards a limited number of relatives, notably close male agnates (patrilateral kin); that is, one's father, brothers and father's brothers.

In addition to the patrilineal principle of descent, the pattern of residence is virilocal. This means that the newly married settle in the man's household or at least in his *ginna*. In this way, all of the most important resources controlled by the Dogon men – land rights, politics, children and relatives – are concentrated in the same geographical place.

The system seems to be most beneficial to the men, who control the most important resources. Women in patrilineal and virilocal societies are outsiders and are often associated with danger; in some African societies, they are still today vulnerable to witchcraft accusations. Their own agnates may be far away in a different village, and in a certain sense they live among strangers throughout their married lives. Married women thus represent a threat to the cohesion of the lineage, since they are strangers within the community. This reminds us of the potential conflict, mentioned in Chapter 4, between the household and the lineage. The man's loyalty becomes divided, and sometimes difficult situations may arise, where he may have to choose between loyalty to his lineage and to his nuclear family.

Patrilineal systems are capable of concentrating all valuable resources in a single principle, namely the principle of descent through the agnatic line: succession, inheritance, property rights, place of residence, marriage partner, children and political rights. Many societies, particularly in the Middle East and North Africa, further practise parallel cousin marriage, meaning that a male ego if possible should marry his father's brother's daughter. This system, if and when it functions according to the rules, certainly creates powerful and compelling forms of integration, since each individual will be related to other members of the in-group in several different ways. In the words of Emmanuel Todd: 'the endogamous community family is probably the anthropological environment which more than any other in the history of humanity integrates the individual' (1989, p. 140). We now turn to looking at matrilineal systems, which present a less neat picture.

MATRILINEAL SYSTEMS

Although most peoples in the world are classified by anthropologists as either patrilineal or cognatic, many groups, particularly in Melanesia, Africa and North America, are classified as matrilineal.

It is a common misunderstanding that matrilineal kinship systems are simply inversions of patrilineal ones, where women have taken the place of men. Some may even believe that matrilineality is the same as matriarchy. This is wrong. In matrilineal societies, just as in patrilineal ones, men tend to hold formal political offices and control important economic resources. This implies that matrilineal systems have to be more complicated than patrilineal ones. In Figure 7.2, the difference between a simplified patrilineal and a simplified matrilineal system is illustrated. Biologically, the kin relations are identical on both sides of the diagram; in practice, however, we see that person A belongs to a kin group composed in a very different way from person B's group.

The Trobriand Islanders, who were first studied by Malinowski during the First World War, are one of the most thoroughly studied matrilineal peoples in the world. The inhabitants of Kiriwina (the largest of the Trobriand Islands) are all members of matrilineages, which form four matriclans altogether. The most important task of the clan, which includes several lineages, is to arrange marriages. The lineage, which collectively owns land, magical incantations and other resources, is the most important corporate group in Trobriand society (Weiner 1988).

Both female and male relatives of mother, mother's mother and mother's mother's mother (etc.) belong to one's matrilineage. One's father, however, belongs to a different lineage, namely his own matrilineage. So far, the matrilineal system appears as a mirror-image of the patrilineal one.

However, the political power remains with men, although descent is traced through women. Each matrilineage has a male chief. Moreover, important resources are transmitted through inheritance from men to other men, usually from mother's brother to ego. The mother's brother also acts as an authority to his sister's children, while the father is expected to be kind and gentle (Malinowski 1984 [1922]) – quite the opposite of the general situation in patrilineal societies. Further, the Trobrianders are virilocal: the newly wed couple settle with the man's family, not with the woman's.

The Trobrianders are horticulturalists, and the staple food is the yam (a tuber rich in carbohydrates). However, each household does not primarily cultivate yams for its own consumption – a source of early puzzlement for Malinowski. Rather, they grow yams for their matrilineal relatives. A man and his household thus grow yams for the man's sister. (Women also grow some yams for daily consumption in gardens allocated to this purpose.) The islanders also give yams to other relatives, and a man may redistribute yams given to his wife by her brothers. The purpose of this traffic in yams may be seen to be purely symbolic – as a tangible reminder of kin obligations – but it has a political aspect as well. The woman's husband controls the yams and he is obliged to repay her brother for them – either by giving him presents or through political support. A man with several wives thus has good opportunities for acquiring political power, since he receives a lot of yams not required for food, which may thus be invested.

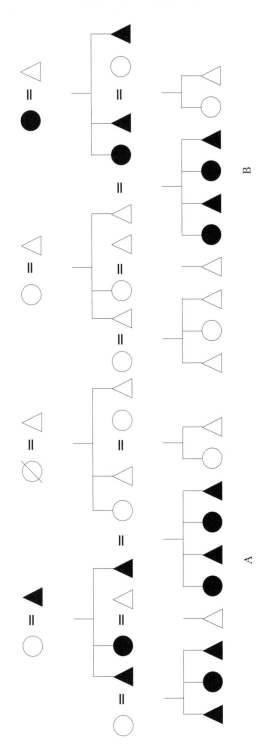

Figure 7.2 Patrilineal system (A) and matrilineal system (B)
Shaded symbols stand for members who belong to the same lineage.

109

At this point we leave the Trobrianders, whose exchange system will be dealt within some detail in Chapter 12. At this point we should note that matrilineal systems in general create a sharper conflict between household and lineage than patrilineal ones. The most important male authority in the socialisation of children, the mother's brother, lives outside the household; and the head of household has profound obligations towards his sister, who also lives outside the household. The fact that the Trobrianders are virilocal (which is not common among matrilineal peoples) complicates matters further.

Matrifocality

A well-known example of a 'very consistent matrilineal system' (Radcliffe-Brown's expression) is the Nayar people of the Malabar coast, southern India. Among the Nayars, stable nuclear families do not exist, and the man has no rights in his children – only in his sisters' children (Gough 1959). According to custom, the marriage is broken off after only a few days, and the woman is later allowed to take lovers. Her children belong to her matrilineage, and the men concentrate their efforts on socialising their sisters' children.

In addition to being matrilineal, this kind of arrangement can be described as matrifocal. This is not a kinship term, but rather a description of a household type. It entails, simply and literally, that 'the mother is the focal point'. The term is used about households where the father for some reason is peripheral; where the marriage bond is unstable, as in many Caribbean societies or – as an extreme case – among the Nayars. Matrifocality is rarely relevant for inheritance and succession, group formation and kin terminology. The phenomenon may occur in patrilineal as well as matrilineal and cognatic societies. It has been pointed out that, in modern societies such as the USA, matrifocality is particularly widespread among the poorest.

DIFFERENCES BETWEEN THE SYSTEMS

Let us now sum up the central differences between matrilineal and patrilineal systems of descent.

Both kinds of systems are usually dominated politically by men. Inheritance, particularly land rights, often follows men. In patrilineal societies, such rights are transmitted from father to child (frequently from father to son); in matrilineal societies, they are transmitted from mother's brother to daughter's son.

Ascription of group membership varies along the same lines. In a matrilineal society, ego will be a member of the same kin group as his or her mother, mother's mother, mother's brother, mother's brother's children, etc.;

in a patrilineal society, one belongs to the same group as one's father, father's father, father's brother, father's brother's children, etc.

In patrilineal systems, the wives of the men ensure the continuity of the group; in matrilineal systems, the men's sisters do so.

In certain societies, ego can take over certain rights through his or her father and others through the mother, but wherever kin-based corporations exist, one of the principles is nearly always followed in this respect. In certain rare cases, furthermore, one is a member of two lineages, one patrilineal and one matrilineal. This kind of system (dual descent) should not be confused with cognatic or bilateral kin reckoning. Among the Herero of Namibia, for example (Radcliffe-Brown 1952), everybody is a member of two separate lineages – a matrilineal one through the mother and a patrilineal one through the father. Some rights are vested in the patrilineage and others in the matrilineage. Thus the men ensure the continuity of the patrilineages (their sons and daughters become members of their patrilineage), while the women, similarly, ensure the continuity of the matrilineage.

CLANS AND LINEAGES

So far, I have used the terms clan and lineage without defining them. In much of the professional literature, they are used nearly as synonyms, although clans tend to be regarded as larger, less tightly incorporated groups than lineages. As a general rule, however, a lineage consists of persons who can indicate, by stating all the intermediate links, common descent from a shared ancestor or ancestress. A clan encompasses people who assume shared descent from an ancestor/ancestress without being able to enumerate all of these links. Among the Pathans of Swat valley, northern Pakistan, thousands of persons regard themselves as members of the patrilineal Yusufzai clan, assuming by general consent that they are agnatic descendants of the mythical Yusuf without being able to 'prove' it (Barth 1959).

Thus lineages are generally historically more shallow, and as a consequence smaller, groups than clans. In many societies, including the Trobriand Islands and Swat valley, several lineages considered to be related occasionally form alliances and thus appear as clans – as kin groupings at a higher systemic level.

Anthropologists have developed concepts about several kinds of clan organisation, but we should keep in mind that these notions are our own and not those of the informants. One widespread form is the conical clan, which is hierarchically ordered with a centralised leadership (Sahlins 1968). There is one recognised leader, usually the oldest man of the lineage, at each level, and the clan as a whole has a chief at a higher level. Conical clans are typical of relatively stable chiefdoms, which nevertheless – unlike states – are based on kin loyalty, not on loyalty to the law or to the flag.

Another model of clan organisation, which has been very influential in studies of African peoples, is the segmentary clan, which has largely been studied as a political form of organisation. The Nuer of southern Sudan, who were studied by Evans-Pritchard in the 1930s (Evans-Pritchard 1940, see Chapter 11), are probably the most famous example of a segmentary clan organisation.

Unlike the conical clan system, the segmentary clan is non-hierarchical; it is acephalous (literally 'headless'), meaning that it has no recognised leader but is composed of structurally equal lineages and sub-clans. All members of the clan regard each other as relatives, but they have clear notions about relative genealogical distance: some are close relatives, while others are more distant. In peaceful periods, and when grazing land is abundant, the household may function as an autonomous unit, more or less like the Fulani household. If a feud with another group develops, or if there is a drought, the lineages and sub-clans may unite at a higher level, temporarily, as corporate groups.

These two types of political clan organisation are the most elegant ones at the level of models, but they are not the only ones extant. In the New Guinea highlands it is quite common for the local group to be organised as an independent, patrilineal, exogamous clan with customary rights to a territory. Such a group, which may include a few hundred or a thousand persons, does not usually consider itself as related through kinship to another group. Further, such patriclans are often scattered over a large area, provided potential rules of virilocality are not strictly enforced. Besides, ethnographic research indicates that the principle of shared descent is less important to many Melanesian and South Asian peoples than it is in segmentary African societies (Carsten 1997).

BIOLOGY AND KINSHIP

At this point, a few words need to be said about a trend inside and (especially) outside of anthropology which places a great emphasis on kinship and, unlike most social and cultural anthropologists, sees it as being primarily biological. This perspective on kinship has already been mentioned in passing several times, and it is time to give it a slightly fuller treatment. Within this tradition of evolutionary thought, it is assumed that the single most important driving force in human action is the drive for reproduction. Men do their utmost to spread their genetic material, and women seek men who can protect them and their offspring while the children are small and defenseless. Culture and society, including kinship systems, develop more or less as side-effects of these inborn needs. (One of the most extreme statements of this position belongs to Richard Dawkins, who has claimed, famously, that we organisms are mere survival machines for our genes; Dawkins 1976.) Solidarity between family members can thus ostensibly be explained by the fact that they have shared genes. It would therefore be rational, from a genetic point of view, for a man to die for two of his brothers or for four of his first cousins.

The most influential theorist of sociobiology in its early incarnation, Edward O. Wilson (1975, 1978), originally regarded the social sciences as

Kinship and Genetics

With the advances in research and knowledge about human DNA, notions about kinship, race and ethnicity are being destabilised (Carsten 2004; Wade 2007). The typical social and cultural anthropological approach to genomics and genetics, as opposed to approaches in physical anthropology, does not consist in asking what research on DNA, and individual DNA testing, can tell us about who we 'really' are. Rather, anthropologists are studying the implications of varying public understandings of genetics, taking their cue from scholars like Emily Martin (2001) and Marilyn Strathern (1992), who have studied cultural appropriations of science as ideological constructions with implications for the ways people think about what is natural.

Looking into the public understandings of genetics in a number of European countries, the contributors to *Race, Ethnicity and Nation* (Wade 2007) take anthropological kinship studies as their point of departure. This makes sense since kinship is a foundational principle in every society, and arguably is a basic underlying principle for notions about race, ethnicity and nationality, along with territorial identity.

This book shows that ideas of kinship and relatedness vary significantly. Writing from the Basque country (Euskadi), Porqueres (2007) points out that although Basque nationalism has shifted from an ethnic and racial to a territorial and linguistic focus, kin relatedness is conceptualised as emerging not only from genetic kinship, but also from 'living on the same land'. Howell and Melhuus (2007), in a chapter from Norway, compare transnational adoption (whereby persons born abroad are being 'kinned') to the restrictive Norwegian legislation concerning assisted fertilisation, which reveals that, to Norwegians, 'knowledge of biological origin has enormous emotional significance for individual persons' (Howell and Melhuus 2007, p. 67). Other chapters look at media storylines about hybridity and individuals discovering 'who they really are' through DNA testing, Spanish adoptive families and their views of cultural origins, Lithuanian notions of kinship and ethnicity, and the intricacies of race and identity in the UK. In sum, this research shows the continued importance of anthropological perspectives on kinship in an age where the boundary between nature and culture seems to have shifted in this respect.

the most recent branches of biology, which have not yet been fully integrated into their 'mother science'. For obvious reasons, this kind of argument had to be met with strong reactions among cultural and social anthropologists (see Ingold 1986, pp. 68–73, for a scathing dismissal; see also Rose and Rose 2001; Eriksen 2006), who usually emphasise the non-biological aspects of human existence and who saw Wilson's 'new synthesis' as an unwelcome and irrelevant intrusion into their domain. In *The Use and Abuse of Biology*, Sahlins (1977) argues against sociobiology on the basis of a cultural relativist position. He shows, among other things, that the actual kinship systems studied by anthropologists in no way support the idea that solidarity between humans is strongest where there is shared genetic material. Indeed, many kinship systems create enduring and strong commitments between people who are not what we would call 'blood relatives' (see also Carsten 2004; Howell 2007). Homosexuality, which exists in most societies, also seems difficult to explain within this framework. In later work, Wilson (1998) modified his views, and called for cooperation across disciplinary boundaries rather than subsuming one (anthropology) under the other (biology).

Generally, anthropology inspired by Darwinism has become less determinist and more nuanced since the1980s (see Whitehouse 2001 for an excellent collection; see also Durham 1991). Culture is no longer regarded as an epiphenomenon, and nobody would seriously claim today that cultural phenomena are necessarily 'biologically functional' or adaptive. It nevertheless remains a fact that adherents of Darwinist views of humanity, often described as 'evolutionary psychology' (Buss 2004), tend to emphasise uniformities presumably founded in genetic dispositions (sex, violence and kinship are typical topics), which challenge the sociological and cultural relativist underpinnings of mainstream anthropology, often in provocative ways.

In spite of attempted *rapprochements* between sociocultural and biological anthropologists (e.g. Dunbar et al. 1999), there remain deep tensions between their respective accounts of kinship. One of the most controversial studies in this regard is arguably Martin Daly and Margo Wilson's work on family violence (Daly and Wilson 1988, 1998). A main argument in their work, supported by statistical material from several Western societies, is that step-parents are more likely to harm children than biological parents, because they do not share a genetic lineage with them. Sociocultural anthropologists have tried to interpret their findings in other ways, arguing that the social relations in a family with a step-parent are likely to be systematically different from families where both are biological parents. In support of this view, Signe Howell's (2007) research on transnational adoption of children introduces the term *kinning* to denote the social construction of kinship, where there was initially none, between the adopted child, the adoptive parents, their families and their wider social surroundings. Although the Darwinians do have a point, they often appear to underestimate the flexibility of human social life.

The most common view among social and cultural anthropologists is expressed clearly by Holy (1996), in an introductory text on kinship. He notes that many peoples in the New Guinea highlands become relatives by virtue of sharing food, and that their relationship to their mother seems to be based on her role as someone who offers food rather than as the person who brought one into the world. After some further examples of variations in cultural ideas about kinship, he concludes:

All societies have their own theories about how women become pregnant. As these theories may ascribe widely different roles to men and women in procreation, the notions concerning the relationship between the child and its father and the child and its mother may differ considerably from society to society. (Holy 1996, p. 16)

* * *

This chapter has chiefly described kinship through descent, inheritance and succession, and has indicated how corporations can be formed on the basis of notions of shared descent. In the next chapter, we move a step further and consider the importance of marriage for descent and kinship in general.

SUGGESTIONS FOR FURTHER READING

Janet Carsten: *After Kinship*. Cambridge: Cambridge University Press 2004.
Ladislav Holy: *Anthropological Perspectives on Kinship*. London: Pluto 1996.
David M. Schneider: *A Critique of the Study of Kinship*. Ann Arbor: University of Michigan Press 1984.

8 MARRIAGE AND RELATEDNESS

They are our enemies, we marry them.
— *Nuer proverb*

There are no societies based on kinship, nor has there ever been.
— *Maurice Godelier*

Seen from a male point of view, women are a scarce resource. No matter how male-dominated a society is, men need women to ensure its survival. In matrilineal systems, the men's sisters carry out this work; in patrilineal societies, their wives do it; and in cognatic or bilateral societies, sisters and wives each do part of the job, seen from a male perspective. A man can have a nearly unlimited number of children – in theory, he can beget several children every day – while a woman's capacity is limited to one child per year under optimal conditions and, moreover, in many societies, child mortality limits the number further. From the perspective of human reproduction, one may thus state baldly that sperm is cheap while eggs are expensive. This simple fact may be a partial explanation of the widespread tendency to the effect that men try to control the sexuality of women, as well as the tendency for men to regard the women of the kin group as a resource they do not want to give away without receiving other women in return.

There may be several reasons why men often want many children. Frequently, they need the labour power of the children for their fields or herds; and children can also form the basis of political support or be seen as an old age insurance policy. There are also biological explanations for the male 'drive to reproduce', which, for all their possible merits, fail to account for variation and historical change.

In many societies, polygyny (a system where a man can have several wives) has been widespread. Polyandry (where a woman can have several husbands) is much rarer. In fact, in the 'Ethnographic Atlas Codebook', compiled from survey data on 1231 societies, polyandry occurs only four times; 186 were classified as being monogamous; polygyny occurred occasionally in 437 cases; while polygyny was common in 588 societies (Gray 1998). Now, regarding the marriage institution as such, its rationale is evidently, at least partly, its efficacy in producing and socialising children. Comparatively and historically speaking, romantic love is rarely seen as an important precondition for a good marriage. Rather, marriage in most traditional societies tends to be arranged by kin groups, not by the individuals concerned; if the parties happen to like each other, this may be seen as a kind of bonus. Whether or not persons choose their spouses, marriage is very commonly perceived as a relationship between groups, not primarily between individuals.

The ideology prevalent in North Atlantic societies to the effect that marriage should be built on pure love, which may even transcend class boundaries, is peculiar if seen in a comparative perspective. Among the Maasai, for example, the famous cattle nomads of East Africa, it is seen as a distinctive disadvantage if the romantic love between the spouses is too powerful. In this society, marriage is chiefly seen as a business relationship, the purpose being to raise children and make the herd grow. If the spouses fall in love, the result may be jealousy and passionate outbursts with adverse effects on business. Many Maasai women regard marriage as a necessary evil (Talle 1988). On the other hand, it is not true, as some believe, that high divorce rates exist only in modern societies. Divorce occurs in most societies in the world, and some 'traditional' peoples have higher divorce rates than the inhabitants of any European city.

DOWRY AND BRIDEWEALTH

In European and some Asian societies, the dowry has traditionally been an important institution (it is sometimes described as an 'Indo-European institution'). It means that the bride brings gifts from her family into the marriage, often household utensils, linen and other things for the home. The institution can be seen as a compensation to the man's family for undertaking to support the woman economically. A dowry can also be an advance on inheritance. In some societies, the payment of dowry entails a considerable economic burden. The costs associated with having daughters marry are a main cause of the high rates of female infanticide in India.

Bridewealth (sometimes called 'bride-price') is more common than dowry in many societies, particularly in Africa. Here, the groom's kin is obliged to transfer resources to the bride's kin in return for his rights to her labour and reproductive powers. The payment of bridewealth establishes the rights of the man in the woman and her children. If the bridewealth is not paid, the marriage may be void, and disagreement over bridewealth payments is traditionally a common cause of feuds among many peoples.

In societies where bridewealth is common and the agnatic kin group is strong, the levirate may occur. This means that a widow marries a brother of the deceased (the *levir*), and in this way the patrilineage retains control of the woman and her children after the husband's death. The sororate, where a widower marries a sister of the deceased, is not a simple inversion of the levirate: in most cases it means that the woman's kin group has committed itself to replacing the dead woman with a living one.

Payment of bridewealth creates several kinds of moral bonds between people. First, it creates a contractual tie between lineages, being a sign of mutual trust. When the bridewealth is paid over a long period, for example through bride-service whereby the groom works for a certain period for his parents-in-law, the bonds are strengthened further. Second, the system of bridewealth strengthens solidarity within the paying group. Frequently, several relatives must contribute to the payment of the price, and often the groom must borrow from his relatives. Such loans may create long-term debt and moral obligations on the part of the groom towards his kinsmen.

MOIETIES AND MARRIAGE

Exogamous groups must by definition obtain women from outside. It is a fact that property, inheritance and political office tend to be transferred between in most traditional societies, and that men often take the formal decisions regarding who is to marry whom. So even if the pattern of residence should be uxorilocal (that is, the groom moves in with the bride's family), the woman's brothers and other male relatives tend to determine her matrimonial destiny, even if they live with their wives in a different village.

The simplest form of woman exchange would consist in the exchange of sisters: I give my sister to you, and you give me yours in return. In lineage societies, it is corporations rather than persons who exchange women. If a society consists of two kin groups who regularly exchange women between them, the society is divided into moieties. Frequently, moieties have a division of labour in addition to exchanging women.

The moiety system of exchange is widespread among Australian peoples. In studies of these marriage systems, it has been pointed out that the outcome of a moiety system is eventually a kind of classificatory cross-cousin marriage. It happens like this: in a fairly small group, like the Kariera of Central Australia, all members of society define themselves as relatives. They reckon patrilineal descent and are organised in two exogamous 'marriage classes'. They can marry anyone of the right gender who is not classified as a sibling. The Kariera, like the Yanomamö and many others, have a classificatory kinship terminology, which means that they use a single term to describe many different persons, in this case everyone belonging to the same gender, generation and clan, independently of biological kinship. The Kariera thus use the same term to describe a father, his brothers and other males of the same generation and same clan. One cannot marry persons considered as siblings, a category which includes those analytically labelled classificatory parallel cousins (father's brother's and mother's sister's children).On the other hand, father's sister's children and mother's brother's children, and everyone included in the same category, that is everybody who we would call classificatory cross-cousins of the opposite gender, are marriageable.

Seen through a certain period, this kind of system takes on the form of a moiety system based on two patriclans which exchange women between them. A man marries where his father married, which is into his mother's patriclan.

Both father's sister's children and mother's brother's children belong to this clan, since father's sister also married into that clan.

A similar example, which may further illustrate the logic of exchange within a moiety system, is provided by the Yanomamö. A Yanomamö man marries a person classified as father's sister's daughter and/or mother's brother's daughter. A woman, similarly, marries a person classified as father's sister's son and/or mother's brother's son. The patrilateral parallel cousins belong to one's own group, as do the matrilateral parallel cousins, since mother's sister by definition is married to father's brother. Remember that we are talking about a classificatory kinship system and not a system which distinguishes terminologically between people of varying degrees of biological relatedness.

The Yanomamö use the term *suaböya* about all marriageable women, who are classificatory mother's brother's daughters and/or father's sister's daughters. However, although there are only two kinds of same-generation women in Yanomamö terminology – wives and sisters – they distinguish in practice between 'close' and 'distant' cross-cousins. Many parents therefore try to marry their children into lineages with whom they want to forge alliances.

Through a statistical analysis of several Yanomamö villages, Chagnon (1983) has argued that political stability is highest where the biological kinship bonds are strongest. Obviously, the members of groups which have exchanged women for several generations are related in more ways – both in terms of kinship and other obligations – than persons who have a purely classificatory kin relationship. Further, it is obviously in the interest of women to marry 'close' cross-cousins as they live in the same village as themselves. Thus the women can be close to their brothers, whom they may need for protection.

The ideal model of cross-cousin marriage among the Yanomamö, as depicted in Figure 8.1, would create a very stable system where the inhabitants of the *shabono* were very close relatives. However, in practice the Yanomamö are often forced to develop links beyond the confines of the village, both to reduce the danger of war (see Chapter 11) and to look for wives. As a consequence, the inhabitants of the *shabono* are less close relatives than they would ideally be, according to Chagnon's biologically oriented model of analysis.

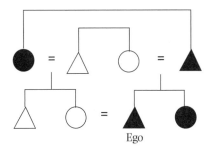

Figure 8.1   Bilateral cross-cousin marriage among the Yanomamö
The shaded persons belong to ego's patrilineage. The model is strongly simplified; in reality, a much larger number of persons would be involved.

EXCHANGE AND RANK DIFFERENCES

Many peoples traditionally practise the cyclical exchange of women between more than two groups, so that, say, clan A gives women to clan B, which gives women to clan C, which gives women to clan D, which in turn gives women to clan A. Within this kind of system, a woman can only be 'paid for' with another woman.

A system where three or more groups are mutually linked through some kind of cyclical exchange of wives may be on a larger scale than moiety systems, since it depends on a greater number of relationships to function. Such a system, where one distinguishes categorically between wife-givers and wife-takers, is called an asymmetrical alliance system, whereas moieties constitute a symmetrical alliance system. While the latter implies equality between the groups, an asymmetrical alliance often, but not necessarily, implies rank differences between the groups. This system of exchange thus contributes both to the cohesion of society, through the establishment of enduring ties between clans, and to the reproduction of hierarchical relations.

The Kachin of upper Burma traditionally practise exogamy at the level of the patrilineage (Leach 1954). Their rules for wife exchange reveal a more complex and more hierarchical social organisation than that of the Yanomamö. Among the Kachin, wife-givers ('*mayu*') have higher rank than wife-takers ('*dama*').

The Kachin, who are rice cultivators, are divided into three main categories of lineages: chiefly, aristocratic and commoner. Women move downwards within this system as every lineage is *mayu* to those with lower rank than themselves. The *dama* is obliged to pay bridewealth to its *mayu*, but is usually unable to pay immediately. Frequently, therefore, the groom has to work for years – sometimes for the rest of his life – for his higher-ranking parents-in-law. In this way, since wives are 'expensive', the rank differences between *mayu* and *dama* are reproduced and strengthened through time.

All of the examples so far have dealt with exogamous marriage systems. Group endogamy also exists, particularly in highly stratified societies where considerable resources are transmitted through marriage. European royal families and Indian castes are thus known to be endogamous. However, we should remember that endogamy and exogamy are relative terms. All peoples are exogamous at least at the level of the nuclear family; conversely, few peoples would encourage their children to marry anybody without any discrimination. Even in societies such as the United States, where individual freedom of choice is stressed as a virtue, 'race endogamy' is common. So is, incidentally, endogamy regarding social class.

DESCENT AND ALLIANCE THEORY

A principal point in the study of marriage rules and practices concerns politics, alliances and stability. Since all groups are exogamous at some level, marriage necessarily creates alliances outside the nuclear family, the lineage or the clan. These kinds of alliances have been emphasised by many anthropologists, who have implicitly or explicitly argued against those who regard descent- and lineage-based solidarity as the most fundamental facts of kinship.

New Guinea and the Anthropologists

New Guinea is the second largest island in the world (after Greenland), with a total area of 810,000 square km (the size of Great Britain, by comparison, is 244,046 square km). The population numbers about 7 million (2010), and since 1975, the island has been divided between the western half, Irian Jaya, which belongs to Indonesia, and the eastern half, the independent state Papua New Guinea.

New Guinea has a great number of endemic species of plants and animals, that is, species which do not exist elsewhere. The landscape is dramatic and varied, containing barren swamps as well as jagged mountains and deep valleys which make large parts of the island relatively inaccessible. However, human settlement in both lowland and highland New Guinea dates back several thousand years. Most of the many hundreds of ethnic groups of New Guinea are traditionally horticulturalists, who have settled in scattered pockets from the coast to valleys located up to 4000 metres above sea level. Many of the peoples, especially in the highlands, keep large herds of pigs.

The linguistic variation in New Guinea is exceptional. Over 700 languages are spoken, and 500 of them – the highland languages – do not seem to be related to any other language groups and are also, in most cases, mutually unintelligible. As noted by Knauft (1999, p. 1), although 'Melanesia has a population of under eight million people, it includes an amazing one-quarter of the entire world's languages and associated cultures'.

The coastal areas, where Melanesian languages are spoken, have been known to outsiders for centuries, both to Malayan and Indonesian sailors and, later, to Europeans. The highlands were virtually unknown until the twentieth century. Actually, they were generally assumed to be uninhabited until the first aeroplanes crossed the highlands, revealing a multitude of small settlements in secluded valleys and on high plateaus. As late as 1938, a group of natural scientists led by Richard Archbold accidentally discovered the orderly settlements of a very large ethnic group, the Dani. Crossing a hilltop just before dusk, the expedition was amazed to discover a fertile valley full of little fires and neatly cultivated gardens. Although missionary activity, the state, anthropological research and the spread of the monetary economy have later, especially since the 1960s, come to influence life in the highlands, many aspects of traditional culture and social organisation remain strong.

▶

Since the discovery of the New Guinean highland peoples by Europeans, New Guinea has been the object of intense attention by anthropologists, who immediately saw the island as an enormous resource for the young comparative science of culture and society – containing, as it did, many relatively isolated 'Stone Age' peoples displaying a great cultural variation. The inflow of anthropologists has eventually led to a certain irritation among many New Guineans, who feel that the anthropologists see them as ethnographic curiosities or even as relics from a bygone age. These issues are addressed by Knauft (1999), who asks how contemporary anthropological research in Melanesia can move from a situation where one 'looks at the primitives to a postcolonial project where research is carried out with as much as about the people in question'. As an example of the latter approach, which is becoming increasingly common, Hviding (1996, 2006), working in the nearby Solomon Islands, has for years collaborated with islanders in compiling stories as well as ethnobotanical material, and devising schemes for ecological sustainability.

Some innovative, classic studies of kinship, notably Evans-Pritchard's (1940) and Fortes' (1945) studies of the Nuer and the Tallensi, respectively, focused strongly on descent-based corporations. They showed how groups with shared unilinear descent – be it factual or fictitious – were cohesive and could be mobilised politically (see Chapters 7 and 11). This corporate group, united through shared ancestry, was seen as the fundamental fact of kinship in stateless societies.

Several anthropologists reacted against the elegant logical models of segmentary clans presented by this group of Africanists (Kuper 2005). In particular, this was the case with those who had done fieldwork in New Guinea, where it had initially been expected that the patrilineally based communities would be organised in segmentary lineages, as was the case in much of Africa. However, it soon transpired that New Guinean societies included persons who did not belong to the patrilineage, and that they lacked the mechanisms of fusion and fission that had been described for the Nuer and the Tallensi (Barnes 1962). The Chimbu of highland New Guinea, for example, could just as well be described either as a cognatic system with a patrilineal basis, or as a patrilineal system with many exceptions. Thus the general validity of the models proposed by Evans-Pritchard, Fortes and others was questioned on empirical grounds – and it was concluded that they had probably exaggerated the importance of the unilineal descent groups at the cost of underestimating the importance of cognatic and affinal (in-law) ties. An interesting detail in this regard may be the fact that the anthropologists who focused on the structured, systemic aspect of kinship were associates of Radcliffe-Brown, while the critics who stressed the primacy of practice over abstract structure, notably the Africanist Audrey Richards (1956), but also Firth, tended to be students of Malinowski (Kuper 1996).

ELEMENTARY AND COMPLEX STRUCTURES

In one of the most influential books ever published about kinship, *The Elementary Structures of Kinship* (1969 [1949]), Lévi-Strauss challenges descent theory in a more theoretically principled way than Malinowski's students did. Unlike the structural-functionalists of the British school, Lévi-Strauss did not regard shared descent, but rather the development of alliances between groups through the exchange of women, as the fundamental fact of kinship. Taking his cue from structural linguistics (which saw the relationship between sounds as fundamental to language) and the sociology of Marcel Mauss, where reciprocity was seen as a fundamental fact of human life (see Chapter 12), Lévi-Strauss develops a highly original view of the institution of kinship. Indeed, he argues that the very formation of society occurs when a man gives his sister away to another man, thereby creating ties of affinity.

A central element in Lévi-Strauss's perspective is the idea that all kinship systems are elaborations on four fundamental kin relationships: brother–sister, husband–wife, father–son and mother's brother–sister's son. Lévi-Strauss regarded this 'elementary structure', or 'kinship atom', inspired by similar structures from structural linguistics (see Figure 8.2), as being fundamental to kinship and thus to human society as such. Some societies are constructed directly on the 'elementary structure', including societies based on classificatory cross-cousin marriage as well as societies based on asymmetrical alliances. 'Complex' systems, in Lévi-Strauss's terminology, add further relationships to the four fundamental ones as determining factors in marriage. He argues that elementary systems have positive rules; they not only specify who one cannot marry, but also who one can marry (as among the Yanomamö). Complex systems, prevalent in modern societies and based on individual choice, have only negative rules and are therefore unable to create long-term alliances between kin groups.

The mother's brother is a key figure in Lévi-Strauss's kinship atom. Granted the universality of the incest prohibition, and granted that men control women, the production of children ultimately depends on his willingness

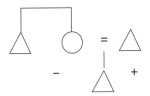

Figure 8.2   The kinship atom

to give away his sister. Inspired by an earlier argument by Radcliffe-Brown (1952), Lévi-Strauss argues, further, that the relationship between a man and his maternal uncle is crucial. If the spouses are intimate, the wife will have a distanced relationship with her brother and vice versa. If one has a close, tender relationship with one's maternal uncle, the father will be a strict and severe person and vice versa. The 'severe uncle' usually appears in matrilineal societies.

Lévi-Strauss's argument is complex and covers much ground, both theoretically and empirically. An important point, pertinent to the earlier discussion about descent and alliances, is nevertheless that his line of thought implies that alliances between groups are more fundamental for the reproduction of society than shared descent. Affinality is thus a universal key to the understanding of the integration of society. The nuclear family, which was earlier considered to be the smallest building-block of kinship, becomes a secondary structure within this schema, since it presupposes the brother–sister relationship and affinality.

PRESCRIPTIVE AND PREFERENTIAL RULES?

As remarked, Lévi-Strauss regarded the principle of cross-cousin marriage as a fundamental expression of reciprocity between kin groups with an elementary kinship system. These groups would also, according to him, have positive as well as negative marriage rules. Such elementary systems, moreover, would have unilineal descent systems and would exchange women at the level of the group.

The Oxford anthropologist Rodney Needham, an early translator and critic of Lévi-Strauss, held that the latter's model was only valid in societies with prescriptive marriage rules, even if a distinction between prescriptive and preferential systems (proposed by Needham) was not elaborated in *The Elementary Structures of Kinship* (Needham 1962). Lévi-Strauss repudiated Needham's interpretation, and stated in no uncertain terms that he regarded the kinship atom as a universal elementary structure, that his theory about the exchange of women was valid for all unilineal societies, and that the distinction between prescriptive and preferential systems was irrelevant. In practice, he argued, so-called prescriptive systems are preferential, and in theory so-called preferential systems are prescriptive. Prescriptions thus only exist at the normative level, and in practice such rules are never followed 100 per cent.

It thus seems necessary to distinguish between categorisations of persons one can and cannot marry (such as rules of exogamy) and cultural preferences concerning whom it is particularly beneficial to marry. To individuals, marriage practices may be perceived as prescriptive rules if their parents arrange the marriage, but at a societal level it would be misleading to use this model as a description of the overall practices. What Lévi-Strauss speaks of as prescriptive rules simply amount to the categories through which the members of society think; Needham's distinction makes it possible to distinguish between these categories and the strategies actors follow to achieve specific, culturally defined aims.

Even perfect knowledge of categories and rules does not enable us to predict how people actually will act, and at this point we might recall Firth's distinction (Chapter 6) between social structure and social organisation. Rules and norms are not identical with the social application of rules and norms.

Most kinship phenomena can probably be interpreted from an alliance perspective as well as a descent perspective. Both alliances and descent are aspects of every kinship system, although, as Kuper (2005) has remarked, descent theorists largely concentrated on societies where agnatic lineages were especially important in the organisation of society, whereas alliance theorists were more concerned with the study of societies where the forging of alliances between kin groups was crucial. It is nevertheless quite possible to identify important cross-cutting alliances in societies usually thought of in terms of descent groups.

KINSHIP, NATURE AND CULTURE

In many societies, it is customary to think of kinship in terms of biology. Europeans generally see themselves as more closely related to their siblings than to their cousins, and more closely related to first cousins than to second cousins. Classificatory kinship seems to be more or less absent in this kind of society. However, even this kind of society has kin terms which derive from social organisation rather than from biological kinship. Among the Yanomamö, all of the women of one's patrilineage are regarded as 'father's sisters', and all of the men in mother's patrilineage are regarded as 'mother's brothers'. In the parental generation of ego, only two kinds of men and two kinds of women exist: fathers, mother's brothers, mothers and father's sisters. Among the Kariera and several other Australian peoples, all members of a moiety of the same generation and gender can be spoken of with the same kin term. All 'brothers' are brothers for nearly all practical purposes, even if they do not have shared biological descent.

In most European kinship terminologies, some affines are labelled 'uncles' and 'aunts', namely those who have married our parents' siblings. In many Indo-European languages, moreover, there is no terminological difference between biological and affinal uncles and aunts. The European kinship terms brother-in-law and sister-in-law may also refer to two different kinds of relatives. A brother-in-law may be the brother of ego's spouse; he may also be ego's sister's husband. Kin, in other words, do not come naturally; they must be created socially, and this is at least partly fashioned so as to facilitate tasks to be solved and to create order in an otherwise chaotic social world.

Arguing against those who have emphasised the biological foundations of kinship, Needham (1962) and Schneider (1984) have argued that kinship is an invention with no necessary connection with biological facts, and they both stress that in a certain sense, kinship is the invention of anthropologists. At least, the examples in this chapter have shown that the kinship system in a society does not follow automatically from biological kin relations. When descent is important in order to justify claims to land, it may be common to manipulate genealogies. Laura Bohannan (1952) has dealt with this in a study of the Tiv of Nigeria, an agricultural people organised in landholding segmentary patriclans. In this society, the structure and origins of the lineage are frequently consciously manipulated for the benefit of the interests of the living. Anne Knudsen (1987, 1992), writing about kinship, vendettas and mafia in Corsica, shows that of the total number of cousins (male collateral kin) a person has, only a small proportion is socially activated. Only the kinsmen one has shared interests with are in practice reckoned as kinsmen. Frequently, those cousins who are genealogically the most distant ones, become the closest ones in practice. Geertz (1988, p. 8) puts this openness of 'facts' to manipulation and interpretation in a more general way when he refers in passing to the North African mule, 'who talks always of his mother's brother, the horse, but never of his father, the donkey'.

Despite the importance of the objections against a biologically based view of kinship, it remains a fact that important forms of kinship are universally (or nearly universally) framed in terms of biological descent, although other forms of kinship – classificatory, affinal, symbolic – may be more important in a variety of circumstances.

SOME COMMON DENOMINATORS

As we have seen, there are many different ways of resolving the problems associated with kinship, but all societies have some common denominators: all have rules regulating incest and exogamy. In all societies, alliances are forged between persons or descent groups, whether their importance is marginal or significant. All societies also seem to have developed a social organisation where mother and child live together during the first years of the child's life (a possible exception being societies with a high density of kindergartens). All societies have also developed functioning reproductive institutions, and all have rules of inheritance.

Further, many societies have also developed forms of local organisation, with political, economic and other dimensions, which are based on kinship. Both religion and daily rules for conduct in such communities may be based on respect for the ancestors and ancestral spirits (see Chapter 14). Differences in power are also often related to kinship. Kinship, indeed, is often the master idiom for talking about society and human existence. What, then, is the role of kinship in societies which lack corporate kin groups, prescriptive marriage rules and ancestral cults?

KINSHIP AND BUREAUCRACY

It is doubtless correct that kin-based forms of organisation continue to be important in many societies after having gone through processes of modernisation, that is, after the inhabitants have become citizens and taxpayers, wageworkers and TV audiences. In most modern states, family dynasties exist in the realm of finance (and sometimes in politics), and genealogies remain important to individual self-identity. The nuclear family is an important institution in modern societies, and in many such communities kinship is decisive for one's career opportunities, political belonging, place of residence and more.

The capitalist labour market, however, is ostensibly based on voluntary labour contracts and individual achievement – not on kinship commitments and ascribed identity. It is therefore customary to regard the kin-based organisation as a contrast, and possible threat, to the bureaucratic organisation characteristic of both the labour market and the system of political administration in modern state societies. Kin-based organisation is based on loyalty to specific persons, while bureaucratic organisation ideally is based on loyalty to abstract principles, notably the law and contractual obligations. Kinsmen may be obliged to help each other out, whereas bureaucrats have committed themselves to following identical procedures and principles no matter who they are dealing with. According to a kinship ideology, it is appropriate to treat different people differently; according to a bureaucratic way of thinking, everybody is to be treated according to identical formal rules and regulations. When a person of high rank employs one of his kinsmen, others may call this practice nepotism (literally, particularism favouring nephews), that is, 'unfair' differential treatment on the basis of kinship. According to a kinship logic, such a differential treatment is not unjust, however, but is rather an indication of loyalty and solidarity. The two logics, which coexist in virtually every society today, are thus difficult to reconcile in theory – they represent opposing moralities.

Max Weber (1978 [1919]) was the first social theorist to write systematically about the differences between kinship-based and bureaucratic organisation. His point of departure was the industrialisation of Europe, and he demonstrated a clear interrelationship between the Industrial Revolution, the growth of anonymous bureaucratic organisation based on formal rules and the weakening of kinship bonds. Although he was critical of some aspects of bureaucracy (he feared the inflexibility of the 'iron cage' of bureaucracy), Weber regarded this form of organisation, based on anonymous principles of equal treatment and a clear distinction between a person's professional and private statuses, as a distinctive advance over the particularistic principles that had dominated earlier. Talcott Parsons, Weber's main intellectual heir in the mid-twentieth-century Anglophone world (Parsons 1977), regarded modern societies as achievement-oriented and universalistic, as opposed to 'traditional' societies, which he saw as ascription-oriented and particularistic. This distinction means that a person's rank and career opportunities in a modern society depend on his or her achievements and achieved statuses, and that equal treatment for all (notably equal civil rights and equality before the law) is an important principle. In a traditional society, on the contrary, Parsons held that ascribed statuses, frequently connected with kinship, were more decisive; in other words, that it was less important what a person did than what he or she was. The theory of bureaucracy, in this form, thus can be seen as an elaboration on themes introduced in nineteenth-century social science, through dichotomies like *Gemeinschaft–Gesellschaft*, status–contract and so on.

Dichotomies of this kind are always simplistic. First, it is definitely not true that particularistic principles are absent in modern societies, notwithstanding their bureaucratic organisation. Second, anthropological research has shown that there exist many 'traditional' societies which are highly achievement-oriented, where individual achievements are more important than lineage membership. This is the case, for example, among many hunters and gatherers, as well as in highland New Guinea. Further, the very term 'traditional societies' is inadequate since it lumps together a mass of highly diverse societies – from a Quechua village in the Andes to the Chinese empire.

On the other hand, dichotomies of this kind can be useful as conceptual tools and, provided we do not confound them with descriptions of an empirical reality, they can be helpful in the process of organising facts. We should never forget, though, that they are ideal types (Weber's term); stylised, abstract models of aspects of the world, which are never encountered in their pure form 'out there'.

The relationship between kin-based and bureaucratic organisation must always be explored in an empirical context. Then we will discover that the two principles very often function simultaneously; that they are not mutually exclusive in practice. A person may support both ideals of formal justice *and* kinship solidarity in different situations (see e.g. Herzfeld 1992).

METAPHORIC KINSHIP

A lesson from the study of bureaucratic organisations is that the introduction of universalistic principles (formal rules, contracts, etc.) does not simply do away with particularistic principles: the two sets of rules coexist, just as individualism has not made the family superfluous, although many of its former functions have been taken over by other institutions. Let us now consider whether a kinship way of thinking may have survived in other, less obvious ways in modern state societies.

Owing to industrialisation and the integration of large, heterogeneous populations in nation-states, it has in many contexts become impractical to maintain clan- or lineage-based social organisation. In this kind of society, everybody is dependent on a large number of persons one is not related to, and each person is responsible for his or her life, largely without support from the kin group. The labour contract has replaced the clan land and the family trade, and social mobility is high. A marriage ideology based on individual choice has replaced the former lineage-based marriages. The monetary economy and the ideology of universal wagework has turned questions of subsistence and place of residence into individual and not collective issues.

This has led many, among them many social scientists, to believe that kinship has ceased to be important in modern societies. This is clearly not true even at the level of interpersonal relations; class structures are being reproduced quite efficiently through the medium of kinship. Moreover, kinship has important symbolic dimensions in addition to its potential as a vehicle of social organisation. Kinship is, in most known human societies, a main focus for subjective belongingness, sense of security and personal identity. In these areas, it seems clear that kinship has at least partly been replaced by metaphoric kinship ideologies such as nationalism or other 'imagined communities' such as religion. Nationalism presents the nation as a metaphoric kin group. Like lineage ideologies, it is based on a contrast between 'us' and 'them', and, although it may be internally egalitarian and universalistic, it favours particularism in relation to other nations (see Chapter 18). The nation may also function as a *de facto* lineage in certain judicial contexts. If a citizen dies with no personal heirs, the state inherits the estate. The state may also assume the parental responsibility for children in certain cases.

A decisive difference between nationalism and actual kinship ideology is the fact that the nation encompasses a large number of people who will never meet personally; it promotes an anonymous, abstract community between people who do not know each other. If we wish to develop an ideal-typical distinction between societies of large and small scale, it may be useful to place the boundary at this point: if important aspects of one's existence depend on people one does not know, one belongs, in important respects, to a social system of large scale.

KINSHIP IN ANTHROPOLOGY TODAY

Whether metaphorical or not (and whether or not this difference makes a difference), kinship remains a core concern in anthropology. In his overview of the anthropology of kinship, Holy (1996) reminds his readers that not all anthropologists agree about the ubiquity and universal character of kinship. However, since the days of Morgan and Maine, many practitioners of the discipline have seen kinship as a human universal although most accept that it varies somewhat between societies. This view, Holy argues, rests on three assumptions:

(1) That 'kinship constitutes one of the institutional domains which are conceived to be universal components or building blocks of every society'

(Holy 1996, p. 151). The others, he adds, are an economic system, a political system and a system of belief.

(2)   The second assumption is the notion that 'kinship has to do with the reproduction of human beings and the relations between human beings that are the concomitants of reproduction' (1996, p. 152).

(3)   Finally, there is the view that 'every society utilises for various social purposes the genealogical relations which it assumes to exist among people' (1996, p. 153).

Holy then goes on to show that all three assumptions are questionable: the degree and form of institutional differentiation varies from society to society; reproduction and biological relatedness carry varying meanings and social implications; and the ways and extents to which genealogical connections are traced, also vary considerably. Important variations between concepts of personhood and of relatedness may be glossed over by an over-insistence on the primacy of kinship, whether it is seen as chiefly biological or not. In the years following the publication of Holy's book, research on kinship has revealed an even greater variation than he suggested, leading Janet Carsten (2004), among others, to suggest replacing the term at least partly with the wider concept 'relatedness'.

Be this as it may, the empirical salience of kinship in most societies – notwithstanding important variations – ensures its place as a main focus of anthropological research today, not least in studies of complex, modern societies, where its significance has probably been underestimated in social theory. The field of kinship studies is also, naturally, a main fighting ground between biological determinists and culturalists. Whatever complementarities may exist between biological or evolutionary perspectives on humanity and perspectives that posit the primacy of social constructions (and I believe these complementarities to be of considerable potential), kinship has proved resilient to attempts at integrating these views. Few themes in anthropology provoke more heated debates than questions relating to the biological versus the socially constructed in kinship.

KINSHIP AND GENDER

To round off these two chapters about kinship and marriage, it seems appropriate to linger briefly on the relationship between kinship and gender. During the heyday of 'kinshipology', up to the 1960s, anthropologists, with a few notable exceptions, were not particularly interested in gender as a differentiating principle. When reading the classic studies of Boas, Kroeber, Malinowski, Radcliffe-Brown, Evans-Pritchard and Fortes today, the absence of analyses of gender and the social and cultural production of gender differences is striking. In studies of kinship, a male perspective is often taken for granted. Certainly, women have a place in these studies; they sometimes appear as wives, mothers and sisters, but rarely as independently acting persons. They appear as resources which society (that is, male society) controls; they are exchanged between groups, are married, accused of witchcraft and so on. Additionally, classic anthropological studies of kinship have rarely explored how particular kinship systems create particular kinds of gender relations – what sort of ideology justifies men's power over women – or even reflected on the fairly obvious fact that a kin relationship is often a gender relationship as well.

Today there exists a growing literature which tries to see social life from a gender-neutral perspective or even with an explicit female bias. Since the 1970s, many important studies on the fundamental importance of gender as an organising principle in society and culture have been published, and some of these studies are discussed in the next chapter. However, relatively little of this literature links up with the study of kinship (but see Collier and Yanagisako 1987; Howell and Melhuus 1993; Carsten 1997; Stone 2009). For if Lévi-Strauss is right in that the sister–brother relationship is fundamental in the social production of kinship, it is surely not without interest that this kin relationship is also a gender relationship. The following two chapters deal with various criteria, starting with gender, that are used to classify people into mutually exclusive categories, which more often than not entail differences in power.

SUGGESTIONS FOR FURTHER READING

Linda Stone: *Kinship and Gender: An Introduction*, 4th edn. Boulder, CO: Westview Press 2009.
David Pace: *Lévi-Strauss: The Bearer of Ashes*. London: Routledge 1983.
Emmanuel Todd: *The Explanation of Ideology: Family Structures and Social Systems*. Oxford: Blackwell 1989.

9   GENDER AND AGE

All animals are equal, but some are more equal than others.
                                        — *George Orwell*

In all societies, there are differences in power between persons. There is not a single society where all adults have exactly the same influence over every decision, where everyone has exactly the same rights and duties. Social differentiation and inequality are, in other words, universal phenomena. The ideas of the eighteenth and nineteenth centuries about the 'original primitive society', where all humans supposedly had the same rank and were political equals, was completely devastated when the first professional ethnographers returned from the field. Even among very small groups, and even among peoples with very simple technology, differences in rank existed. Unlike what many armchair anthropologists and philosophers had believed small-scale societies do not lack internal differentiation. Marx and Engels were thus right in assuming, in the mid-nineteenth century, that there are universal criteria for social differentiation, which are the distinctions between older and younger people, between men and women and between insiders and outsiders, 'us' and 'them' (the latter is dealt with systematically in Chapters 17–18).

Not all social differentiation entails unequal access to rank and power, and it may therefore be useful to distinguish between vertical and horizontal differentiation. The vertical dimension refers to inequalities in power or rank, while the horizontal dimension refers to those aspects of social differentiation which do not express unequal rank – differences which may, for example, be expressed through the division of labour. Most forms of social differentiation nevertheless have a vertical or hierarchical aspect, which is frequently contested by people encompassed by these forms.

Of course, the differences in forms of differentiation are huge. In small-scale societies with a limited division of labour, such as hunter-and-gatherer societies, social differentiation is simple and may be defined in a few cases mostly by age and gender. In many horticultural and agricultural societies, religious leaders and chiefs have recognised statuses setting them apart from the rest of the people, although those statuses are not necessarily hereditary. In more complex agricultural communities, there tend to be hereditary political offices, often supported by a professional bureaucracy and professional soldiers, and there may be huge differences between the rich and the poor. In some societies, ascribed statuses (such as caste in India) are decisive in formal social differentiation; in others, achieved statuses may be more important in determining a person's social rank and place in society.

There are many possible analytical approaches to such criteria for social differentiation as gender, age, class and caste. Some of the most vigorous debates in anthropology have indeed dealt with issues related to differentiation, power and rank. This and the following chapter, which discuss some of the most widespread criteria for differentiation and approaches to them, are therefore far from exhaustive.

SEX AND GENDER

There are two fundamentally different ways of regarding gender differences. On the one hand, there are certain biological differences between men and women; the genitals look different and function differently, women give birth to children, men usually have larger bodies, and so on. At this level, it is customary to use the term 'sex' instead of gender.

On the other hand, in practice, gender differences are codified and institutionalised socially and culturally, and it is largely this kind of difference anthropologists focus on, which is distinguished from (biological) sex by using the term 'gender'. All human societies conceptualise differences between men and women, and all consider such differences to be important in certain regards. However, there are important variations in the ways the relationships between men and women are perceived and practised, and therefore it is difficult to generalise about gender. Gender can best be studied as a relationship – men are defined in relation to women and vice versa – and this relationship is conceived of differently in different societies.

For many years, gender was relatively neglected in anthropological research, which is perhaps surprising, since gender identity may well be the most fundamental basis for personal identity. Malinowski, who has often been praised for his detailed ethnography, actually neglected important women's institutions completely and exaggerated the contribution of men to the reproduction of Trobriand society (Weiner 1988). In many other classic studies too, social agents are more or less seen as equivalent to social men. This kind of perspective may be called androcentric (*andros* is Greek for man). Since the emergence of a distinctively feminist anthropology in the early 1970s (Rosaldo and Lamphere 1974), however, gender has become a central dimension of much anthropological research. For this to happen, several myths first had to be debunked, foremost of them the idea of an original matriarchy. Evolutionist thinkers had claimed that human societies went from matriarchy to patriarchy (probably confusing matriarchy with matrilineal kinship), an idea which had not been properly dismissed. Early feminist anthropologists argued, on the basis of ethnography, that such notions, which are widespread among many peoples, are probably myths created by men to justify their own power over women (Bamberger 1974).

The relative powerlessness and allegedly universal subjugation of women have also been subjected to a great deal of comparative research, forming the basis of debate both in favour of and against Western notions of 'discrimination' and 'power'. It has been argued that although women in many societies are deprived of formal political power, they may exert considerable power domestically and indirectly. It has also been suggested that the concepts of anthropologists dealing with discrimination may be ethnocentrically biased. Even if women in traditional Middle Eastern societies appear to be discriminated against and powerless from a European (ethnocentric) perspective, they may perceive their situation otherwise.

Some of the current anthropological research on women does not primarily deal with the 'position of women', but instead concentrates on different aspects of the male–female relationship in different societies. Several anthropologists have even discovered that not only women but men, too, are gendered (e.g. Herdt 1987; Gilmore 1989; Archetti 1999; Robinson 2008).

Gender is omnipresent and easily visible; perhaps this is one reason why it has suffered neglect from anthropologists who have regarded it as 'natural'. However, like kinship and ethnicity, although it can be said to have a biological basis, gender is not natural and immutable, but socially created. The great cultural variation regarding conceptions and conventions about gender reveals this. Probably all societies hold notions about the 'naturalness' of certain gender differences, but such ideas are themselves cultural constructs and not a part of nature, and are frequently contested from within. A contemporary anthropological perspective on gender would thus not try to answer the question 'what is gender really?', but would rather look into 'the social and cultural construction of gender ... [and] the relationship between constructions of maleness and femaleness' (Strathern 1988, p. 69).

GENDER IN THE DIVISION OF LABOUR

Even in societies with a simple division of labour and little occupational specialisation, women's work is distinguished from men's work. We have already seen examples of this from the Yanomamö and the Fulani. The most typical cases of communities where a division of labour based on gender is the most important are nevertheless hunter-gatherer, or foraging societies, and here it may be worth noting that humanity has consisted exclusively of hunters and gatherers for the greater part of its existence.

Some readers may have noted the use of the cumbersome term 'hunters and gatherers' instead of simply 'hunters'. The reason for this terminology is actually an increased understanding of the importance of gender. Among such peoples, men usually hunt and women usually forage. For a long time, anthropologists and other outsiders believed that hunting was the main source of livelihood among these groups. The men of these societies spoke incessantly about hunting, and visitors were given the impression that this was the single most important activity. Detailed research on nutrition among some hunter-gatherers, notably in Southern Africa, nonetheless revealed that the most important source of nutrition are tubers, insects, edible plants and small creatures gathered by the women, while the men's hunting activities are irregular, uncertain and form no reliable basis for subsistence. Among a Bushman group studied by Richard Lee (1968), it was documented that the inhabitants received two-thirds of their nourishment from what was brought in by gathering. Nonetheless, the men saw their society as a hunting society, and the women's routine work was not given the same symbolic importance accorded to hunting.

It seems reasonable to assume, as a hypothesis, that the influence of women is most significant where their economic contribution is important. In a classic work, Ester Boserup (1970) compared the division of labour in a number of agricultural societies with regard to gender. Her main conclusion, which was surprising to many at the time, was that women in many societies, especially in Africa and in communities which do not use draught animals, carry out the bulk of the agricultural work. An African farmer is typically a woman. It also seems that their influence is generally greater in these societies than in places where they are chiefly responsible for the domestic sphere. Boserup's controversial conclusion is that the political position of women in farming societies is generally weakened when new mechanical technology is introduced, since this technology tends to be controlled by men. In addition, land is usually controlled by men. Boserup argues that the position of women is weakened when their economic contribution is reduced; this is nevertheless a thorny issue. For what is an economic contribution? As indicated, foraging may be less spectacular than hunting, and less ritualised and talked about (just like housework in industrial societies), but it is an economic contribution nonetheless. The following ethnographic example may illustrate the relationship between gender relations, the economy and the realm of ideology and power.

The Mundurucú are a group of about 10,000 who live in the south-eastern Amazon basin (Murphy and Murphy 1985). Their traditional way of life is comparable to that of several other Amazon forest peoples. They are politically incorporated at the level of the village; each village, with between 50 and 100 inhabitants, is politically autonomous. They are horticulturalists and grow tubers, fruit and vegetables, apart from fishing and hunting. That is, the men go hunting.

The division of labour is based on gender. The men are responsible for clearing the ground, but planting, weeding and harvesting are women's work. The women also gather wild fruits and nuts, while men and women cooperate in fishing. The Murphys write:

The men think of themselves essentially as hunters, not as gardeners or fishermen, the religion is oriented towards hunting, and the spirit world is closely associated with the species of game. It is the skillful hunter who is honored, not the industrious tiller of the soil. (Murphy and Murphy 1985, p. 88)

In fact the horticultural activities are more important, from a nutritional point of view, than both hunting and fishing, and these activities are also more labour-intensive. The issue, however, is not purely to do with nutrition: power and prestige are also at stake. If, therefore, it is considered a more valuable thing to shoot a single mammal than to grow a tonne of taro, it does not necessarily make a difference that the taro is more important to the group's survival than the animal is.

Mundurucú society is politically dominated by men. Like men in many male-dominated societies, they tell stories of an original matriarchal social order when 'everything went wrong', before 'things were set right' by a mythical, male cultural hero. This myth of matriarchy must be considered an important aspect of their ideology: together with the disproportionate emphasis put on hunting as a means of livelihood, it contributes to legitimating male supremacy. Nevertheless, it may be noted that if the Mundurucú had regarded female subordination as natural, there would be no need for such ideological myths: the stories are told as warnings that the women may rise again unless the men are vigilant.

Why, one may still ask, do men have political and economic supremacy in most known societies, when it is not true that men necessarily contribute more than women to the physical survival of the group? Let us consider some attempts to account for this more or less universal power discrepancy.

THE PRIVATE AND THE PUBLIC

Although women may carry out as much or more work than men, they are nearly universally responsible for domestic work (notwithstanding the middle classes of industrial societies) – child-raising, cooking and cleaning. Men, on the contrary, tend to be responsible for the household's dealings with the outside world. In hunting and gathering societies, they have to protect the woman and her infants from dangers; in more specialised societies, they tend to hold political and ritual offices. Some anthropologists have seen a principal cause of the subordination of women in the fact, ultimately rooted in biology, of women's lack of physical mobility during pregnancy and suckling. These impediments to free movement serve to link the woman to the home while the man is free to roam the public space. It has thus been suggested (Rosaldo 1974; see also Davidoff 1998) that power discrepancies between the genders are related to the distinction between the public and private spheres in society: men control the former and women are confined to the latter. The Murphys' monograph on the Mundurucú suggests that such a distinction may have something to recommend it. In the Mundurucú village, only women and children live in huts; all men live in a men's house. This house has no walls; it is constructed as a large leaning roof supported by long poles. Its open side faces the village, so that the men can at any time follow events there. The woman's place is at home and in the fields, while the men's place is in the public space, where decisions of importance for the whole village are taken.

Ortner and Whitehead (1981) have added to this perspective that there is a general tendency to the effect that women are, rightly or wrongly, culturally associated with private and particularistic projects, while men are associated with the public and common good. They argue:

[This] relates to a widespread sociological distinction suggested by Rosaldo (1974): Nearly universally, men control the 'public domain', where 'universalistic' interests are expressed and managed, and, nearly universally, women are located in or confined to the 'domestic domain', charged with the welfare of their own families. (1981, p. 7)

The public/private distinction has been criticised as ethnocentric (Collier and Yanagisako 1987; Moore 1993) – it is said to be meaningful in modern societies but not necessarily in others – but it is nevertheless well established and implicitly assumed in much comparative research on gender.

DOMINANCE AND SUBMISSION

Is the subordination of women universal – do women everywhere have a lower rank and less power than men? The most common answer is yes, but the question is far from unproblematic. First, there are very significant variations between gender relations in different societies, ranging from nearly complete equality (as among the Chewong of Malaysia; see Howell 1989), to societies where the women's influence over their own lives seems very limited. Second, concepts such as 'rank', 'subordination' and 'discrimination against women' are themselves problematic. Perhaps, it has been suggested, the anthropologist's own cultural background creates an unhealthy analytical bias here, in that he or she assumes, as a matter of fact, that equality is desirable, while many of the people studied by anthropologists insist that the genders ought not to be equal but should rather be complementary. This predicament is evident, perhaps more strongly than anywhere else, in research on immigrant minorities in Europe, where the complementary gender roles of migrants from the Middle East and South Asia exist in the same social space as the egalitarian gender roles of the majority. Finally, it is not entirely certain that men and women understand the same thing by power and power discrepancies. Perhaps women in many cases care little about what the men see as prestige objects?

One group frequently mentioned as marked by a high degree of gender equality is traditional Hopi society in what is now the south-western United States. 'When traditional Hopi women are asked "Who are more important, women or men?", a common reply is "We are, because we are the mothers", with the qualification that men are important, too, as the messengers to the gods' (Schlegel 1977, p. 186).

The Hopi, a North American Indian people famous for having preserved important aspects of their traditional culture, have a matrilineal kinship system. Unlike in most matrilineal societies, a woman's brothers and mother's brother are not strong authorities impeding her freedom of movement and agency. The spouses are considered equally valuable and complementary, and the lineage as well as the household has a female head.

On the other hand, men have formal political and religious power at the level of the village, although, as Schlegel remarks, 'women do not hesitate to speak their minds' and, as 'Hopi men readily admit, women usually get their way' (1977, p. 195). At an intermediate level between the household and the village is the clan, which is led by a brother–sister pair.

The traditional division of labour among the Hopi is unexceptional, comparatively speaking. Only the men go hunting, and only the women grind flour; however, they share the agricultural work. Schlegel thus suggests that there may be a cultural, and not an economic, cause for the high level of gender equality among the Hopi: 'Where the ideological focus of a culture is life, and both sexes are believed to be equally necessary to the promotion of life, devaluation of either sex is unlikely' (1977, p. 205). Could this be adequate as an explanation? It is true that some male-dominated societies regard the woman's role in reproduction as marginal; the male seed is seen to play the crucial part. In many patriarchal or otherwise male-dominated societies (as in the New Guinea highlands), it is generally believed that women produce the soft, perishable parts of the body, while the men produce the hard parts, the skull and bones. But could this kind of gender ideology be the *cause* of inequality between the genders, or is it rather the *effect* of such an institutional order? No general answer to this question is proposed here; suffice it to note that in actual social process, ideology and practice function together and can only be separated analytically. In other words, it is not easy to point out what it is that determines what.

What does it mean that women tend to be 'subordinated'? Even in otherwise egalitarian societies, women rarely, if ever, hold high religious office. Among the Mundurucú, only men are allowed to play and even see the sacred trumpets used in ritual – in many societies elsewhere too, for example in West Africa, women are not allowed to play musical instruments; and even among the Hopi, only men can be high priests. On the other hand, it is not obviously true that priesthood is the ultimate expression of power in society. In fact, women who are deprived of public office – be it political or religious – have been known to exert considerable informal power. During my own fieldwork in societies which are ostensibly strongly male-dominated, I have often met men who sincerely complain that their wives, who control the domestic domain, decide everything about their lives.

In an intriguing study of a Portuguese local community in the Saloio area outside Lisbon, carried out about a decade before the 'carnation revolution' of 1974, Joyce Riegelhaupt (1967) analyses the relationship between male and female power in a society where male power is officially all-pervasive. At the time of her fieldwork in the 1960s, the subordination of Portuguese women was established by law, in the domestic as well as in the public sphere. Nearly all political offices were held by men. However, Riegelhaupt discovered that women in this community were, in practice, sometimes more powerful than men.

The explanation for the strong position of women in this community seems to lie in the division of labour, which paradoxically allows women a more public role than their husbands. The men are responsible for agricultural work, while female members of household divide their time between housework, child-raising, some agricultural work, marketing and shopping. Since the men work in the fields, only the women stay in the village during the day. They then meet in the shops, where they may exchange information and develop networks. They also travel to Lisbon to sell food and other goods, and in this way are able to develop networks outside the village as well. The men, for their part, have much less contact with each other, since they work in isolation on their separate plots.

As the women market the family's produce, they are central to the domestic finances. They are also important in politics, despite their formally marginal position. Most political issues in the locality concern the maintenance of and improvements to public infrastructure; mending roads, installing water pipelines and so on. It is necessary to have personal contacts with the authorities in order to achieve this. Thanks to their wide-ranging networks, the women frequently succeed in persuading the wives of local political leaders to talk their husbands into taking the right decisions.

There is, in other words, a great discrepancy between *rules* and *practices* in this case. The law and official ideology state that men ought to be in charge of politics and the domestic economy. In practice, the women may sometimes seem to exert more power than their spouses in both respects. The Saloio example indicates that the subordination of women cannot be assumed *a priori*, and it also serves as a reminder that even perfect knowledge of the explicit norms of a society does not enable us to predict how people will act, and that informal power may take on a different form than formal power structures imply.

MEN:WOMEN::CULTURE:NATURE?

This subheading is shaped like a structuralist formula. It reads like this: 'Does the relationship between men and women correspond to the relationship between culture and nature?' A simple colon refers to a relationship, while a double colon refers to a relationship between sets of relationships (see Chapter 15).

In many societies, women are seen as being closer to nature than men, who are considered more cultivated than women. Like nature, Ortner notes in a classic article inspired by Lévi-Strauss's structuralism (Ortner 1974), women are regarded as undomesticated, wild and difficult to control. Therefore they represent danger (to men) and must be domesticated. Ortner mentions three related, universal aspects of female existence which may lend support to this widespread cultural view. (1) The body of the woman and its biological functions (birth, menstruation, suckling) make it necessary for her to spend more time on 'species behaviour' than the man, who is freer to concentrate on 'purely cultural projects'. (2) The body of the woman and its functions place her in social roles which are regarded as 'lower' than those of men (cooking, cleaning, etc.). (3) These two aspects of female existence give her a mental structure which is different from that of men and which is seen as being closer to nature. This point, we should note, is reminiscent of the public/private distinction. It also suggests that women are seen as passive while men are seen as active, which is a very widespread notion in ideologies of gender, whether concerning the sexual act, the transmission of culture or the respective roles of the genders in the upholding of society. In modern nationalist ideologies, too, women are often depicted as the passive guardians of tradition and the family, while the men go out to fight for and build the nation (Anthias and Yuval-Davis 1989).

Following this line of thought, biological differences between men and women form the starting-point for gender inequality; for example, her association with small children (who are also considered imperfectly cultured) draws her towards nature. In patrilineal and virilocal societies, it may be added, women also come from the outside; they belong to a different kin group from the one in which they live. All of this indicates that – and may contribute to explaining why – women are often regarded as more natural, less cultural, than men.

On the other hand, women everywhere obviously have cultural roles; in many societies it is actually the role of women to maintain and transmit tradition, and it is often considered natural that women should be more strongly religious than men. In parts of the Mediterranean, further, men tend to be considered sexual 'forces of nature' and, for this reason, women are themselves seen as to blame if they are raped – they ought to be cultured enough to protect themselves from the male, who is allegedly unable to contain his sexual drive. Nevertheless, there is a wealth of ethnographic support for Ortner's general assumptions, namely the fact that women give birth, nurse babies and menstruate gives them an ambiguous and sometimes 'dangerous' cultural position between nature and culture.

The notion that 'man is to woman what culture is to nature' is controversial, and most scholars agree that the model is simplistic. It has also been pointed out that the cultural distinction between nature and culture may not be as universal as Ortner, drawing on Lévi-Strauss, assumes. It may still be good to think through, however, as an aid to interpreting complex ethnographic material. The general notion that one's enemies or subordinates are somehow closer to nature than oneself is far from uncommon, and it is certainly not restricted to the male–female relationship. According to the racist ideology which served to justify slavery in North America, blacks were closer to nature than whites and were therefore better suited for hard physical work (Wade 2002); but simultaneously they were 'like children', unable to handle responsibility and freedom. In this way, the framing of social inequality in a culture–nature dichotomy can be an important ideological instrument legitimating power differences.

'WOMEN'S WORLDS' AND 'MEN'S WORLDS'?

If we accept that there are systematic differences between women and men – whether we attribute the differences to biology, socialisation or ideology – we must also admit that men and women may experience the world in different ways (related to what Ortner calls different 'mental structures'). This was the point of departure for Edwin Ardener when he wrote that the 'problem of women has not been solved by social anthropologists' (1977, p. 1). The problem of women is not identical with the problem of the 'position of women', he continues, but rather concerns the methodological and theoretical problems raised by women in relation to anthropological research. Notably, Ardener claims that women in many societies appear to behave in a shy and quiet way, and are difficult to engage in conversation on topics interesting to the anthropologist. He speaks of them as 'muted' – not literally, but in the sense that women tend to communicate in ways not immediately intelligible to anthropologists (be they male or female), while men more easily talk about their society in ways familiar to anthropological reasoning: the male cultural universe, Ardener intimates, is closer to the anthropological one than the female cultural universe. In his view, it is anthropology *as such* which has a male bias, not individual anthropologists. This argument, which has been influential in later research on gender, is reminiscent of Ortner's and Whitehead's distinction between the particularistic woman and the universalistic man. If Ardener is correct, women's worlds are generally more difficult to explore than men's worlds. Whatever the case may be, it is clear that women and men may experience the world differently in many societies. In research in the Caribbean, it has indeed been argued that women and men represent opposing moralities: women try to enhance their *respectability* while men strive to improve their *reputation* (P. Wilson 1978), and the two value systems entail two quite different ways of perceiving the world. However, although the two moralities are associated with gender, they are not irretrievably linked with gender. There are 'bacchanal women' – '*femmes fatales*' – who look for ways to improve their reputation, and there are also stable and predictable men who rarely touch alcohol and take their children to church every Sunday (Eriksen 1990).

This kind of society, marked by strong tensions between the genders, seems paradoxical, since it appears to be based on two, partly irreconcilable value systems. The truth is probably that similar paradoxes are common, if less visible, in other societies as well, and that it may be fruitful to explore such moral dualities by focusing on gender. Such an approach brings us far from the original preoccupations of what is 'really' male and female (the search for essence), and shows that the study of gender as a social construction is an important dimension in the study of society as such.

SEXUALITIES

The examples above suggest that if sex is fixed, gender is fluid; and this is indeed the orthodox view in social and cultural anthropology. Since sex is only culturally available as gender (that is, cultural constructions of sex and their accompanying social practices), this seems to indicate that maleness and femaleness may vary indefinitely. In a lively discussion of late-twentieth-century developments in the anthropology of gender, Henrietta Moore remarks that a problem remains in spite of attempts at relativising gender, namely 'the inconvenient fact that people have bodies that are present in a differentiated binary form' (1999, p. 154; see also Moore 1994). She then goes on to discuss body mutilation (tattooing etc.) in contemporary Western societies, transsexualism and homosexuality as practices that seem to pose a serious challenge to this 'binary form' or male/female contrast. It has time and again been shown that gay men are, in many societies, classified as an 'intermediate' gender – neither wholly male nor wholly female, and in many societies there is a widespread notion that lesbians are somehow biologically different from heterosexual women. In the emergent field of inquiry known as 'queer theory', this kind of reasoning is developed to great sophistication, in that the relationship between genitals, gender identity, sexual identity and sexual practices is problematised (Kulick 1998; Boellstorff 2007). This is a field where careful attention to the facts is crucial, even though direct observation sometimes be difficult. During a campaign against AIDS in Norway, the anthropologist Bjørge Andersen coined the term 'Men who have sex with men' in order to reach men who did not define themselves as gay. (The term later became the name of an ultimately ill-fated Oslo rock group.)

As Moore drily comments, the 'available anthropological data actually suggests that most people do not find their gender identities particularly fluid or open to choice' (1999, p. 158), but she also demonstrates the instability of the sex/gender boundary, paying particular attention to recent developments in the Euro-American part of the world. The uncertainty and reflexivity characteristic of gender relations and gender identities in this kind of society could further be said to form part of a more encompassing phenomenon, namely that of reflexive identity in general, where the self is seen as a project, not as something given once and for all (Giddens 1991). Just as it has become difficult to state squarely what it means to be a good man or a good woman, other identities – be they national, ethnic, religious or professional – are also subject to scrutiny and negotiation. Plastic surgery, which in the space of a few years has become very widespread in the affluent Western societies, can frequently be seen as an attempt to change an identity which is usually perceived as no less imperative and absolute than gender, namely age.

AGE

Like gender, age is a universal principle for social differentiation and classification. Ageing is an inevitable and irreversible biological process but, like gender, age is to some extent socially constructed. In many societies a person's rank rises as he or she becomes older, regardless of gender. Indeed, Holy remarks, with 'the exception of a few hunting and nomadic societies in which survival depends on the physical ability to move around ... the nonindustrial societies emerge as distinctly old-age oriented' (1990, p. 167). In industrial and postindustrial societies, by contrast, old people do not have a particularly high authority by virtue of age: they are no longer achievers and are therefore less valuable in societies like these, which place a high value on individual achievement. In addition, the rapid pace of cultural change in modern societies renders much of the wisdom and cultural competence of old people obsolete.

Advanced age is often associated with deep experience, wisdom and a sound sense of judgement. In many societies, old men are the political rulers and old women are perceived as less 'threatening' than younger ones, since they have grown more 'cultivated' and are further removed from nature than younger women are. They no longer menstruate, they no longer have children; they are 'drier' and do not represent a 'threatening' sexual force. Old women in some societies may exert more direct political power than young men. Societies where the old in the main control the political domain are called gerontocracies.

Similarly, children and adolescents are often considered imperfect in the sense that much of their immanent humanness has yet to be realised – while they may also, for the same reason, be considered 'innocent', a condition which is a form of perfection. They have yet to be socialised, and therefore know neither sin nor virtue.

In most societies, criteria other than gender and age contribute to distinguishing between categories of people, but there are also societies which only use those criteria, in addition to personal merit. It therefore seems clear that gender and age are more fundamental criteria for social differentiation than, for example, caste, class or ethnicity.

AGE GRADES AND AGE GROUPS

In some societies where age is an important principle of differentiation, there are several degrees, or institutionalised stages, between youth and old age. The Baktaman of New Guinea thus distinguish between seven age grades among men, and the ritual passing from one grade to the next entails a promotion in relative rank (Barth 1975). Men of the seventh grade possess virtually the entire body of knowledge extant among the Baktaman, including various forms of secret knowledge (which is transferred through consecutive rites of passage), and it therefore seems 'natural' that they should have control over the political domain.

In this way, age may function as a vertical principle of differentiation. It may also function horizontally, by dividing the population (usually males only)

Life-Stages as an Analytical Category?

All societies distinguish between different life-stages. Van Gennep's, Turner's and others' studies of rites of passage indicate how the process of socialisation inevitably creates ruptures in life, whereby persons pass from one stage to another, entailing new statuses, rights and duties. But are such life-stages universal? This view has been argued by Colin Turnbull (1985), who presents five life-stages he considers as universal. If he is correct, life-stages may be used as comparative concepts; that is to say, we may expect to find the same stages in all societies.

Turnbull's life-stages are as follows.

Childhood is marked by dependence on others and fast acquisition of cultural categories.

Adolescence is described as that period between childhood and maturity when one develops sexual maturity and is gradually preparing for full social responsibility.

Youth is seen as the stage between adolescence and adulthood, which is largely described as a period of higher education. Indeed, Turnbull himself admits that this is not a universal life-stage.

Adulthood, the fourth phase (or, in many societies, the third one), seems 'more boring', Turnbull claims, than the previous ones; it is full of responsibility, work and routine.

The final life-stage is old age, a period in which, Turnbull writes, a physical and mental defects may set in, but when the 'heart and soul' are more vital than ever before, since old persons have such a great deal of experience.

Does aging and the passage between life-stages, then, entail more or less the same thing in different societies, as Turnbull intimates? Many anthropologists would deny this. On the other hand, it remains true that a great deal of research exists on initiation from childhood to adulthood, whereas relatively little attention is paid to transitions to old age (Sokolovsky 2004).

into peer groups who belong to the same age category. In societies lacking criteria for internal differentiation other than age, gender and kinship, such as the pastoral Nuer and Maasai societies of East Africa, men (and sometimes women) are organised into age sets of people who are not defined as kin, but who were circumcised at the same time. A special kind of solidarity, reminiscent of kinship, exists within these groups, and often age sets have special collective obligations. The formation of such sets contributes to strengthening social cohesion and integration in society, since they cross kin boundaries (see also Chapter 11). In some modern state societies, schoolmates may develop comparable ties of solidarity, not least in the upper echelons of the English class system, where, for example, old Etonians of the same cohort are expected to support each other.

AGEING INTO A GENDERED PERSON

Gender and age have both biological and cultural aspects. Age is not necessarily directly correlated with gender. Among the Bakweri of Cameroon, for example, it is nearly impossible for a man to get married before he reaches the age of 40, since he must have property and political influence to find a wife. Women, on the other hand, are married shortly after sexual maturity.

Children are often considered relatively sexless, and their socialisation frequently aims at achieving a double end: to turn them into members of society, and to turn them into men and women. For this reason, rites of passage for girls and boys usually differ markedly.

Among the people who live near Mount Hagen in highland New Guinea (Strathern 1988), it is a common view that infants are born with both male and female properties. For them to become women and men, they have to go through a long process of learning, which culminates in a series of puberty rites. Among the boys, in particular, this ritual is highly demanding. According to the Hagen people themselves, this is due to the fact that the boys have to be worked more than the girls to become properly gendered persons, that is, functioning social agents. The girls need to be transformed less through cultivating rites, since they are considered to carry the necessary growth potential in their bodies already. As mentioned, men are often seen as active, women as passive.

After such rites of initiation, children are clearly differentiated by gender in most societies. Such rites may take place at the onset of puberty or earlier. In some Middle Eastern societies, both boys and girls may go to the public bath with their mothers; after initiation, however, the boys are not even allowed to see naked women. Rites of initiation may entail circumcision of the genitals, tattooing or other visible, physical alterations, making it possible at a glance to distinguish insiders from outsiders and 'complete' humans from 'incomplete' ones. In many societies, the candidates are also subjected to great trials during the period of initiation, frequently physical pain, to give them the opportunity to prove that they are worthy of the responsibility and the rights given them as grown members of society. Among the Nuer, the initiation of boys includes the cutting of six parallel stripes across the brow from ear to ear. The cuts go 'to the bone' (Evans-Pritchard 1940), and the boys are expected not to show evidence of pain during the ordeal.

RITES OF PASSAGE

The term rite of passage (*rite de passage*) is associated with the name of Arnold van Gennep, who published the book *Les Rites de passage* already in 1909 (van Gennep 1909, 1960). Through such rites, van Gennep wrote, society reproduces itself. People are given new statuses without the social structure changing, and the public character of the ceremonies gives the members of society an annual reminder of the fellowship, rights and obligations provided by society. Later, Victor Turner (1967, 1969, 1974) developed van Gennep's perspective further by looking closely into the phases and levels of meaning provided by these rites among the Ndembu of what is now Zambia. A general point in Turner's analysis is that the rites of passage simultaneously function as permitting integration into society *and* give the participants a mystical experience of oneness with the spiritual world and with the 'societal organism'.

Turner follows van Gennep in dividing the rites into three phases: separation, liminality and reintegration. Separation is characterised by the individual's or group's movement away from a fixed point in social structure towards something unknown. When the breach is completed, the participant enters a liminal phase, an ambiguous stage where he or she is in a certain sense placed outside society, 'betwixt and between' (Turner 1969) two stable conditions. This puts the actor in a dangerous position. Society runs the risk that the actor refuses to be reintegrated and rejects its values and power hierarchies, while the individual for his or her part risks anomie and social homelessness. Turner writes that in nearly every society, a person in a liminal phase is 'structurally if not physically invisible in terms of his culture's standard definitions and classifications' (1974, p. 232). This difficult and dangerous liminality is nevertheless necessary in order to 'clean off' the earlier statuses of the individual, to make him or her ready to be reborn as a new category of social person.

The Kaguru are a matrilineal people numbering about 200,000, living in central Tanzania. Their main ethnographer, T.O. Beidelman (1971), writes that if a boy dies immediately after circumcision he cannot be buried in the ordinary way, since he will have died neither as a child nor as an adult, but as a liminal, indeterminate kind of person, or even non-person.

The final phase in rites of passage is reintegration. During this phase, the candidates return as virtually new persons with new statuses, rights and duties.

Beidelman provides detailed descriptions of initiation rites among the Kaguru, and it is easy to identify the three phases analysed by Turner in these. The rites entail both moral education and physical alterations for both genders, but their content differs. The boys, who are 10–12 years old, are led away from the village into the bush (separation), undressed and shaved. Their foreskins are then removed surgically, and the adult men who have accompanied them then begin to teach them riddles, songs and myths which encapsulate the essence of the Kaguru world-view. After circumcision, the boys have to remain in the temporary camp in the bush for a certain period (liminality), and during this period the adult men arrange various trials for them: they move about in the bushes at night making lion growls, tell them that they might die after circumcision, and so on. This prolonged phase is, of course, the liminal one. Finally, the boys are taken back to the village where they are given new names (reintegration).

Unlike the boys, Kaguru girls are not regarded as being fundamentally transformed after initiation. Whereas the boys are taken out into the bush together, girls are initiated separately and in isolation in huts in the village, but they too are circumcised and given moral education, although to some extent they learn other things than the boys do.

The liminal phase gives the boys in Kaguru society (and in many other societies) powerful common experiences; they have gone through trials together and have become adults together. Frequently, such shared experiences create life-long ties of solidarity; as previously mentioned, such ties are sometimes institutionalised and serve as a mitigating political factor in societies which are otherwise based on lineage organisation.

MARRIAGE AND DEATH

Most anthropological studies of rites of passage deal with initiation rites. Rites relating to marriage and death are nevertheless also important. They move persons from one status to another and serve as collective reminders – just like initiation rites – of the cohesion of society, its moral values and the legitimacy of authority. In kinship-based societies, marriage gives important opportunities for forging alliances between kin groups and symbolises the continuity of society.

The mortuary rite marks the last important rite of passage in the life of any human being. Among the Kaguru, mortuary rites are associated with two problems. First of all, one must ensure that the deceased is safely transferred from the land of the living to the spiritual world. Recently deceased persons, like adolescents in the bush, are 'betwixt and between' and must therefore be approached with great caution. They cannot be controlled as one controls living people, yet at the same time they are sufficiently close to the living to influence them. In other words, they must be established as properly dead people as quickly as possible lest they may remain 'undead' and dangerous.

A Kaguru who has died is shaved all over (like a novice during initiation); men are laid on their right side, women on their left. Both genders are buried with their heads facing left, towards the spiritual world. Dead bodies are buried in great haste since they are considered polluting and dangerous, but the mourning period lasts for at least four days. At the end of this period the second problem associated with death turns up, namely the question of inheritance. In this situation, the issue does not merely concern how to make a good deal for oneself, but also which social ties are to be strengthened and which are to be weakened. There are social obligations, property and social statuses to be redistributed at a death.

The challenges faced at a death are perhaps universal. First, death must be given a symbolic, perhaps religious, content to make it possible for the survivors to reconcile themselves with it; and, second, one must ensure that life goes on, that is, that society continues to exist more or less unaltered after a death.

RITES OF PASSAGE IN MODERN SOCIETIES?

Some North Atlantic readers may have the impression that rites of passage exist 'out there' and not 'among ourselves'. This is not the case, but it is doubtless true that such rites have a diminished importance in modern societies.

In West European societies, four major rites of passage have traditionally been important, although three of them seem to have lost some of their significance since the late twentieth century. While the funeral is still a social event of great importance, baptism, confirmation (or first communion) and marriage have become both less widespread and, in most of Europe, less important. In part, this is due to the fact that these rituals are associated with a religion whose role in the daily life of Europeans has diminished; another partial explanation is that these rituals are no longer socially important for individuals in marking the transition from one status to another. In the Protestant societies of Scandinavia, candidates for confirmation were traditionally obliged to learn by rote a considerable amount of biblical knowledge, and failing was a real and deeply shameful possibility. At the confirmation party afterwards, young people received 'adult' presents such as a suit and a watch – in parts of Scandinavia, cigarette cases and sets of false teeth (often made of whale ivory) were also common gifts as late as the 1930s – which signified that they were now to be considered grown-ups with full responsibilities. As confirmation takes place when children are around 14, it is easy to understand why its importance has decreased: while, in the past, they were expected to earn their own living after confirmation, there is no longer a dramatic change in their lives following the rite. Perhaps a similar explanation holds for the reduced importance of the marriage rite in societies where serial monogamy is becoming the norm rather than the exception?

Concerning age as a criterion of differentiation, it is interesting to note that, in many contemporary North Atlantic societies, youth is valued much more highly than advanced age. From presenters on television to politicians, the average age of high-prestige individuals has steadily decreased since the last decades of the twentieth century. The cultivation of youth as a desired condition can be seen as a consequence of a social form oriented more towards the future than towards the past, where change can be seen as a good thing, and where culture changes fast enough to render traditional knowledge obsolete. Interestingly, the tendency to place a high value on youth occurs in societies where the average age of the population is increasing due to declining birth numbers and improved health.

*   *   *

An important difference between gender and age as principles for social differentiation is the fact that one more or less automatically changes membership between age groups, while very few change their gender. In gerontocratic but otherwise egalitarian societies, boys may simply await their coming of age to achieve full political rights; they may be eligible to sit on the elders' council and may eventually become powerful ancestral spirits. This is not an option available to women in many societies.

As this chapter has shown, the division of labour in society is fundamental to social differentiation, and the relative complexity of the division of labour may indicate the complexity of social differentiation. It has also been shown that social differentiation cannot be studied independently of politics and ideology. Both gender and age tend to be associated with politics and the division of labour, but they usually function together with other factors. In the next chapter, we consider some such criteria which contribute to the kind of complexity mentioned, namely caste and class.

SUGGESTIONS FOR FURTHER READING

David Gilmore: *Manhood in the Making*. New Haven, CT: Yale University Press 1989.
Sherry Ortner: *Making Gender: Politics and Erotics of Culture*. Boston: Beacon Press 1997.
Victor W. Turner: *The Ritual Process*. Chicago: Aldine 1969.

10   CASTE AND CLASS

For unto every one that hath shall be given, and he shall have abundance; but from him that hath not shall be taken away even that which he hath.
— *Holy Bible (King James version), St Matthew 25: 29*

Like gender and age, caste in the Indian subcontinent refers to ostensibly inborn, ascribed characteristics. In theory, changing one's caste membership is as difficult as changing one's gender.

The concept of social classes is different, and not only because classes exist in many different kinds of societies, while caste is usually associated with Hinduism and India. Although many social scientists have demonstrated that most people in class societies take over their parents' class membership (if one is a working-class child, it is likely that one remains in the working class), there is a great deal of mobility between the social classes, both in theory and in practice. In many societies, class membership is emically considered an achieved and not an ascribed status.

The relationship between caste and class is complex, and both concepts are difficult to define accurately. Let us begin with the concept of caste.

THE CASTE SYSTEM

The caste system encompasses aspects of both 'culture' and 'society'; that is, it is both a symbolic system associated with Hinduism, and a set of rules and practices regulating social organisation, interaction and power in societies in the Indian subcontinent.

The caste system can be defined as a system dividing all of Hindu society into endogamous groups with hereditary membership, which are simultaneously separated and connected with each other through three characteristics: separation regarding marriage and contact; division of labour in that each group, at least in theory, represents a particular profession; and finally hierarchy, which ranks the groups on a scale dividing them into high and low castes.

The caste system thus entails a ranking of people according to ascribed statuses, it provides rules regulating the interrelationships between members of different castes, and it creates mutual dependence of the castes through the division of labour, which implies that certain tasks can only be carried out by members of specified castes.

Regarding ideology and religion, the caste system is based on notions of ritual purity and impurity, which serve to justify the segregation and division of labour between the castes. The variations in ritual purity imply, among other things, that a member of a high caste will be polluted if he or she eats food prepared by a member of a low caste, and that only members of the Brahmin caste are entitled to conduct religious rituals. Each caste has its own rules for good conduct; for example, high castes tend to be vegetarians and to abstain from alcohol.

VARNA AND *JĀTI*

It is common to think of the caste system as a hierarchy dividing the entire Hindu population into four main groups, the *varnas* (a Sanskrit word meaning 'colour'). The Brahmins (priests) have the highest rank, followed by the Kshatriyas (warriors and kings), the Vaishyas (merchants) and the Shudras (artisans and workers). Outside the *varna* system proper, at the very bottom of the ladder, are the Dalits, sometimes still spoken of as Untouchables, labelled thus by the British because a high-caste person had to go through an elaborate purification ritual after having touched such a polluting person. Members of the three highest *varnas* are called 'twice-born' because they have gone through a ceremony entailing spiritual rebirth.

Such a description of the caste system, although it is not incorrect, is simplistic and ultimately misleading. First, it should be noted that there are also non-Hindus who belong to castes; India's approximately 140 million Muslims have their own castes (usually low ones), and the many ethnic groups sometimes called 'tribals' tend to be classified as, and treated as, Dalits. Some of them, partly for this very reason, have converted to Christianity or Buddhism. Caste, moreover, also exists in non-Hindu societies in the Indian subcontinent, from Buddhist Sri Lanka to Muslim Pakistan.

Furthermore, and more significantly, this fivefold partition of the Indian population is highly abstract and has a relatively modest significance in daily life. The Indian social anthropologist M.N. Srinivas wrote already in the early 1950s: 'The real unit of the caste system is not one of the four *varnas* but *jāti*, which is a very small endogamous group practising a traditional occupation and enjoying a certain amount of cultural, ritual and judicial autonomy' (1952, p. 24). There are thousands of *jātis* in India; they all represent an hereditary profession or craft (even if it is no longer practised) and have long-standing commitments to the other *jātis* in the area as well as a special place in the ritual hierarchy. Most *jātis* are relatively small, but some are large and internally differentiated groups with asymmetrical alliance patterns between the lineage segments.

At an intermediate level between the *jātis* and *varnas*, we find the all-Indian occupational castes, for example the Lohar caste of blacksmiths, which includes local *jātis* all over India.

The practical function of the *varna* system is mainly to make it possible for members of local *jātis* to locate themselves hierarchically in relation to *jātis* in other parts of the country; additionally, it represents a fixed, abstract hierarchy and value system founded in the main interpretations of Hinduism. Like Indian Christians and Muslims, Dalits do not have a place in the *varna* system proper, but they all tend to belong to *jātis*. Members of the lower *jātis*, comments Srinivas (1952, p. 30), have always tried to improve their rank 'by adopting vegetarianism and teetotalism, and by Sanskritizing [their] ritual and pantheon'; this process of caste-climbing, he adds, has led to the spread of a remarkably uniform value system in the subcontinent. In other words there seems to be widespread agreement concerning values and criteria for distinguishing a low caste from a high one.

THE *JAJMANI* SYSTEM

The traditional *jāti*-based division of labour in Indian villages is called the *jajmani* system. It consists of a set of traditional rules about the exchange of products and services between the members of different castes. In other words, each caste has specific commitments towards the others. Seen from a systemic perspective, one may say that the village is maintained as a social system thanks to the interdependence between the castes; seen from an actor-perspective, one may say that it creates significant structural constraints on individual opportunities. The *jajmani* system is ideologically connected with and justified through religion, and thus contributes to maintaining notions about purity and impurity and about relative rank within the caste system. The fact that members of the sweeper caste actually do sweep and clean toilets is interpreted as evidence that they are in fact polluting; at the same time, they have to sweep and clean toilets because they are perceived as polluting. In this way, the social and symbolic aspects of caste are interconnected, and contribute to reinforcing each other by creating a correspondence between ideology and practices.

Traditionally, little money circulated through the *jajmani* system, which largely consisted of complementary exchanges of goods and services. Frequently, no exact account was kept of these prestations, since each caste had specified duties toward the others. In modern India, it is usually impossible to make the *jajmani* system function according to traditional practice. First, the monetary economy has made it possible to buy all kinds of services and commodities from people with whom there is no *jajmani* relationship. Second, changes in Indian society have created a large number of new occupations which are not legitimated or even described in the *jāti* system. Third, the incorporation of Indian villages into a larger capitalist market and state bureaucracy has weakened the ties between the *jātis*. Urbanisation and social change have made the *jajmani* system impractical. It did integrate the social system at the scale of the village with a stable economic system and division of labour, but it does not work properly in large cities like Mumbai or Bangalore, with a high economic rate of change, huge inmigration and a very complex division of labour. This does not imply that every connection between *jāti* and profession has vanished in these cities, only that this connection is more tenuous, ambiguous and open to manipulation than in the traditional village, and increasingly irrelevant in people's everyday affairs.

CASTE AND SOCIAL MOBILITY

The relationship between caste and other criteria for social rank may be complex in other, more 'traditional' settings as well. F.G. Bailey's classic studies of 'caste-climbing' and political conflict in the village of Bisipara (Orissa, eastern India; see Bailey 1968) reveal some of this complexity. His perspective is largely an actor-centred one, while most research on India has tended to focus on systemic properties.

In Bisipara, the *jajmani* system was still more or less intact when Bailey carried out his fieldwork in the 1950s, but some disruptive elements had entered from outside. Notably, the village had been integrated into the modern Indian state in the sense that important political career opportunities were now available to members of the low castes (a kind of policy which has expanded considerably in later decades). Bailey describes different kinds of political conflict and competition within the village, and we shall look more closely at two: caste-climbing and caste conflict.

A person has three possible ways of improving his or her situation. They may try to change caste membership (which is exceedingly difficult in a small village), try to improve their own caste's relative rank, or dismiss the entire caste system and try to build a career outside it.

The distiller caste in Bisipara had improved its economic condition steadily for decades, but this did not automatically lead to an improvement of its ritual purity. One may be economically well-off and ritually polluting and vice versa, although there is often a correlation between wealth and ritual purity. The leaders of the caste thus tried to convert their economic capital into ritual purity. First they had to purify their own practices through what is generally known as Sanskritisation. They ceased to perform typical low-caste rituals (such as animal sacrifice) and adopted Brahmanic rules in other respects as well, becoming vegetarians and so on.

For the distillers to be recognised as a high caste, however, they also had to improve their position within the *jajmani* system, and this was the most difficult part. Each caste which entered into a *jajmani* relationship with the polluting distillers risked being surpassed by them in the local hierarchy; on the other hand, the distillers were able to pay well for services. Eventually they succeeded – after having passed through several rungs on the ladder – in having Brahmins perform ritual services for them and were thereby considered a clean caste, but at the cost of a considerable amount of money. They converted a high economic position into a high ritual position.

This kind of social mobility, we should note, does not challenge the caste hierarchy as such; rather, it openly endorses it. The type of political conflict described in Bailey's work as caste conflict is of a different kind.

The Pan caste was a lowly, ritually polluting and poor caste whose leaders were inspired by Gandhi's ideals of caste equality. On several occasions they had tried to enter a temple reserved for the high castes, but had been evicted. They then built their own temple and declared themselves a clean caste. This strategy was not accepted by the other castes in Bisipara, who saw it at a blatant breach of rules, and it did not help in improving the socially defined rank of the Pan caste.

To the Pan caste, the strategy followed by the distillers was not feasible for economic reasons. Thus some of them began to follow a third course of action, trying to improve their rank through a rival value hierarchy, namely the civil service. By exploiting the quotas for the ritually impure in local government, they succeeded in climbing socially within a hierarchical scale where criteria other than caste membership and ritual purity were relevant.

From this sketch of social mobility in an Indian village, we see that there are three scales of rank, functioning partly independently of each other: the economic system, the caste system and public administration. Different resources are at stake within the respective systems, but all of them entail power differentiation, are legitimated through different principles and are partly incommensurable. The Brahmins of Bisipara did not recognise the Pan rise to prestige through public administration; however, through climbing in local government, members of the Pan caste became able to exert some power over Brahmins.

It should also be noted that while it proved possible to convert economic power into ritual purity, it is not possible to convert political power (in the public sector) into similar prestige. This seems to be caused by the workings of the *jajmani* system, which combines economic and ritual factors but does not include the state sector.

CASTE: A KIND OF SOCIAL STRATIFICATION?

Research on caste has always focused on the Indian subcontinent. However, it has been argued that the concept of caste can fruitfully be transformed into a comparative concept with a wider scope. Let us consider two examples of this view.

In connection with his study of politics in Swat valley, north-western Pakistan, Barth (1959, 1981) describes the system of stratification in the valley. Although the Pathans are Muslims, in this area they are so strongly influenced by their Hindu neighbours that they are divided into hereditary status categories associated with varying degrees of purity, which may well be described as castes. The division of labour in Swat valley resembles a *jajmani* system: there are relations of interdependence and mutual obligations including 'saints', landowners, priests, craftsmen, herdsmen, peasants and 'despised groups' (which correspond to the Dalits in Hindu society).

However, the caste system of Swat is not related to, or justified through, a religious superstructure. On the contrary, there is a direct contradiction between the caste system and Islam, which teaches that all are equal before God. Since the Pathans are not Hindus, Barth argues that their castes are chiefly an aspect of social stratification and of the division of labour.

This view of caste as an aspect of social structure, which Max Weber also endorsed, has been challenged by Louis Dumont (1980, pp. 208–12). According to Dumont, in order to understand caste it is necessary to view it as an integrated part of a social and cultural totality; one cannot therefore talk of castes in isolation from the particular cultural context in which they have emerged. The presence of 'castelike systems' in non-Hindu societies is accounted for by the spread of some aspects of the caste institution. To Dumont, these 'imitations' of the caste system in Swat, among Christians in Kerala (south-west India) and among Buddhists in Sri Lanka and elsewhere, are encompassed by, and influenced by, Hindu culture without fully taking part in it. In sum, Dumont argues that caste is an aspect of Indian culture and has to be understood within a Hindu sociocultural totality. The very concept of 'stratification', Dumont has elsewhere argued (1986), is moreover an individualistic European concept which does not make sense in the hierarchical societies of the Indian subcontinent.

Gerald Berreman (1979) has taken a more radical stance than Barth in trying to make the caste concept a comparative one. He argues, among other things, that there are castes in the United States, describing the American blacks as an 'impure caste'. Notwithstanding the official ideology of meritocracy, which holds that everyone controls their own destiny, he claims that blacks belong to a hereditary low-rank category, with low-ranking professions and polluting power if they touch members of the pure castes (whites). Before Berreman, Kroeber also argued the usefulness of a similarly wide concept of caste, which would clearly be unacceptable to Dumont, who sees it as intrinsically related to the totality of Indian society and culture.

Dumont's perspective on caste is a systemic one, while Barth and Berreman place greater emphasis on the actor's available options. In the latter approach, it becomes possible to find important similarities between blacks in the USA, Swat Pathans and Hindu villagers, although their respective cultures differ greatly. Berreman has also criticised Dumont's view of caste as a 'Brahmanic view' (Berreman 1979; see also Burghart 1990; Quigley 1993) more or less uncritically reproducing the views of those in power. In other words, the former does not see Indian society as a totality whose members necessarily are encompassed by a relatively uniform world-view. Others, including Pauline Kolenda (1985), have shown how members of low castes consciously develop liberating ideologies in direct opposition to the caste system, many even converting to Buddhism, Islam or Christianity.

CASTE IN CONTEMPORARY INDIA

The caste system has a religious, or spiritual, and a practical, social aspect. It has significance for the religious position of people and their ritual practices, for their marriages and alliances and for their possibilities in professional life. It is nevertheless impossible to maintain the caste system unaltered in contemporary India, and there are four main reasons for this. First, the introduction of new professions complicates the classification of people according to *jāti*. Second, in many contexts wageworkers are hired on the basis of qualifications (achieved statuses) rather than caste. Third, Indian authorities actively try to level out the differences between castes through quotas for 'Scheduled castes' and 'Scheduled tribes' in the public sector. Fourth, urbanisation makes it difficult to classify the people one meets, and makes it possible for many Indians to escape from a stigmatised identity by moving to a city where nobody knows them.

Within Hinduism itself, attempts have also been undertaken to eradicate the caste system. An important reformist movement, Aryanism, has worked towards this end since the nineteenth century, and Mahatma Gandhi tried to modify the caste hierarchy by, among other things, renaming the Untouchables 'Harijans', which means children of God. Today, Dalit organisations (rejecting what they see as Gandhi's patronising term for them) militate for the actual abolition of caste.

Despite these and other attempts to abolish the caste system, or at least mitigate its effects, it remains very much alive. The marriage ads in the *Sunday Times of India*, for example, are classified according to caste membership. Although the *jajmani* system may be on the wane in many parts of India, the caste system retains a number of functions in the ritual and social spheres. In a study of caste and religion in the city of Kanpur, north India, Frøystad argues that her upper-caste informants 'constantly classify people as either above, on a par with, or inferior to themselves' (2005, p. 269), showing through detailed ethnography that caste relations are more fundamental to Indian society than the Hindu–Muslim divide, which nevertheless plays an important role in politics.

CLASSES AND STRATA

Gender and age function everywhere as principles for the social differentiation and classification of people. Systems based on caste and/or class in addition are more complex in their structure and tend to have a more complex division of labour.

The term 'social class' is usually applied to capitalist societies, although classes, strictly speaking, exist in other societies as well. The most influential theory of social classes was developed by Karl Marx in the mid-nineteenth century. In his very wide-ranging studies of historical societies, especially

Caste Outside of India

From 1940 to 1917, following the abolition of slavery in the European colonies, several million Indians were transported to remote colonies where they settled permanently. The cause for this mass migration was the need for fresh manpower in the plantations after the freeing of the slaves. Many have argued that these Indians, tempted by promising labour contracts, were virtually shanghaied, and that their actual situation in the plantation colonies were scarcely better than that of the slaves had been. Hugh Tinker (1974) has described the system of indentureship as *A New Form of Slavery* (see also Mintz 1974). Most of the Indians came from Bihar and Uttar Pradesh – some of the most impoverished parts of India – but a fair number were also Dravidian speakers from Tamil Nadu and Andhra Pradesh. The descendants of these Indians still live in the former plantation colonies, and they are particularly numerous in Mauritius (65 per cent of the total population), Guyana (c. 55 per cent), Fiji (c. 40 per cent), Trinidad and Tobago (c. 40 per cent) and Suriname (c. 35 per cent).

There exists a large anthropological literature on this Indian diaspora, and many scholars have raised questions pertaining to cultural continuity and change. Regarding the caste system, for example, it was modified from the day of departure, since dietary restrictions were impossible to maintain on board ship, and since the division of labour in the colonies soon made the *jajmani* system obsolete. In some of these societies, notably in Mauritius, some castes are nevertheless still endogamous and play a political role, but in others, such as Trinidad, the various subgroups have for most practical purposes merged into a single category of 'Indo-Trinidadians'. Even in Trinidad, however, only Brahmins can become orthodox (Sanatanist) priests. In Mauritius, further, there was a revival of caste consciousness in political contexts towards the end of the twentieth century, and the low castes formed their own interest groups.

The experience from the Indian diasporas, where neither *jajmani* systems nor *panchayats* (caste councils) have survived, but where notions of caste continue to exist, seems to indicate that the caste system can be both flexible and adaptive, and that it is by no means certain that social and cultural change will eradicate it. On the other hand, it is certain that caste has a very varying significance as a criterion for rank and differentiation – both in India and among Indians overseas. To some persons, caste membership may define their place in society in great detail; to others, it may be relevant only at religious festivals and, perhaps, during election campaigns.

capitalist ones, the term class had a privileged place, since the dynamics of class relationships, according to Marx, were decisive in historical change.

Marx defined the classes in relation to property. The ruling class in any society is the one whose members control the means of production (land, tools, machinery, factories and the like) and who buy other people's labour power (that is, employ people). Below this class, one would usually find classes of farmers and independent craftsmen, as well as wageworkers who have to sell their labour power to survive. In modern industrial societies, we usually speak of three important social classes: the bourgeoisie, or capitalists, who own the means of production; the petty bourgeoisie, whose members own their means of production but do not employ others; and the working class, whose members sell their labour power. In addition, there are lumpenproletariats of unemployed, criminals, homeless people, etc., as well as an aristocracy whose members live off the interest from property (usually land).

There are considerable, systematic rank differences between people even in societies where equality is emphasised at the level of ideology. In practice, class differences tend to be reproduced over the generations, so that children take on their parents' class membership, although there is always a certain social mobility. Whether or not such differences are necessarily connected with ownership of means of production, they are very important from a systemic as well as an actor-centred perspective. It should nevertheless be noted that the majority of social scientists support a way of thinking about inequality which, contrary to Marxism, does not give priority to economic property as an explanatory variable. This is sometimes labelled the theory of social stratification, and is associated with Max Weber. Weber, writing half a century after Marx, argued that there were several, partly independent criteria which together gave a person a specific rank and that property was not necessarily the most important one. Political power and intellectual prestige could, for instance, be just as important in a given society.

Human Security as a Topic for Anthropologists

'Human security', writes Oscar Salemink (2010), 'is a relatively new concept that usually defines security along economic dimensions ("Freedom from want"), physical and political dimensions ("Freedom from fear") and ecological dimensions ("Freedom for future generations to inherit a sound natural environment").' As a 'people-centred security concern' it constitutes a shift away from the focus on the state as the locus and subject of (military, political) security, towards the individual as the locus and subject of (the right to) 'human security'. Originally a concept developed by the UNDP (United Nations Development Programme) in a bid to expand the scope of human rights policies and interventions, several anthropologists have seen it fruitful to incorporate the concept in their own research.

▶

Being a problem-oriented discipline, anthropologists who look at security naturally spend most of their time researching forms of insecurity (see Eriksen, Bal and Salemink 2010). Anthropologists describing the lives of small, tightly knit groups in Africa, Melanesia and South America have showed, sometimes inadvertently, that they live in a state of almost continuous anxiety. Anything from warring neighbouring tribes to poisonous snakes or crop failure could put their lives in jeopardy any day of the year.

If we move to more hierarchical, complex societies, they also seem to offer little more by way of security for their members. It is sometimes said of Egyptians that they tend to die of anxiety in middle age, usually connected with money problems, more specifically an almost chronic inability to look after their relatives properly economically. Ethnographies from India show that many Indian women live in constant fear of male violence, men worry about dowry payments for their daughters and a thousand lesser expenses, and that everybody fears downward mobility, whether individual or collective.

Security naturally refers to much more than this – and this could be said to be the strength and the weakness of the concept. Most individuals are, presumably, secure in some respects and insecure in others. Every society, group and individual on earth has its way of dealing with questions of human security. Nobody is immune. Non-believers often assume that religious people have a greater existential security than they do themselves, but such a generalisation is unwarranted. If one belongs to a religion with a notion of hell, or divine intervention, or both, then one had better mind one's step.

Moreover, it is often assumed that insecurity is more pronounced in the global era than it was formerly, given the fundamental vulnerability, the proliferation of risks, the environmental crisis, AIDS, the alienating individualism of neoliberalism, fears of terrorist attacks or outbreaks of war, or the loss of faith in canonical tradition, including religious salvation and protection from supernatural entities, that are assumed to accompany this era. A cursory look at the historical and ethnographic records do not support this view. The risk of being the victim of a terrorist attack for a citizen of Amsterdam in the early twenty-first century can safely be assumed to be much less than the risk of being bitten by a poisonous snake for an Azande in the 1920s. The threats of starvation, disease and war in the poorer countries, horrible as they are, were unlikely to be much less in pre-modern times than is the case today. An anthropology focusing on human security might, perhaps in a manner akin to an anthropology of happiness (Thin 2008), contribute not only to the catalogue of problems facing humanity, but also to their resolution, while at the same time addressing fundamental aspects of what it means to be human.

An important difference between perspectives on classes or strata concerns the significance placed on conflict. Class theory is nearly always a kind of conflict theory, seeing the conflicts between different classes as fundamental. Marx saw class struggle as the most central factor in social change, since successful class struggles eventually led to changes in the relations of production (property relations) and qualitative changes in the social order.

Both Marxist thought about social class and other theories of social strata or classes have been criticised for being ethnocentric. Dumont's criticism of the wide-ranging analytical uses of the term 'caste' is representative of this kind of argument. Whereas some would hold that all societies are stratified and that concepts of classes or strata are therefore universally useful, others would stress that the concepts themselves are linked with capitalism and relate intrinsically to modern state societies.

We return to some of the economic and political aspects of social strata and classes in later chapters. At this stage, we concentrate on class as a principle for social differentiation and classification. The following example, which shows the introduction of capitalism in a formerly feudal society, indicates that there may indeed be important interrelationships between economic change and cultural change.

During the first half of the nineteenth century, an important shift took place in San José, Puerto Rico (Wolf 1969 [1956]). Instead of chiefly growing food for their own consumption, the farmers increasingly began to grow one main product for the world market. The most important product was coffee, for which there was a growing demand. Several problems had to be solved, however, for the production to become profitable. The landowners had to increase their areas under cultivation, and thus they also had to expand the labour force. They also had to find a source of credit (a bank or similar institution) to fund the expansion.

As long as land was abundant, it was difficult to find wageworkers, since people preferred to cultivate their own plots. Gradually, however, the coffee-growers established control over most of the available land and eventually it ceased to be a commons: all land now had to be purchased; it was commoditised. This new situation led to the proletarianisation of a large number of formerly independent smallholders: they became dependent on selling their labour power.

Wolf describes the confrontation between the two systems – the capitalist one, based on purchase, sale and interest, and the traditional one, based on subsistence production – as a cultural conflict, a clash of opposing value systems. The locals described the Spaniards (most of the coffee-growers and money-lenders were Spanish) as mean and individualistic: 'They rob other people's money, but then they just sit on it. They don't spend it', and they 'don't give people subsistence plots on which to grow things to eat' (Wolf 1969 [1956], p. 178). The Spaniards, for their part, described the Puerto Ricans as lazy, drunken and unable to plan their life properly.

When this new, specialised economy was fully developed, it became possible to distinguish between four social classes in San José:

1. *Peasants*. They own a little land, cultivated on a family basis, and sell the surplus on the market, but are unable to generate enough surplus to expand their production.
2. *Middle-sized farmers*. They own more land, buy labour to grow it and make a larger profit than needed to sustain their lives.
3. *Rural proletarians*. They own no land and earn their living through selling their labour.
4. *Landowners*. They are specialised coffee-growers, buy labour on a large scale and make large profits.

Here the social classes are definitely defined in relation to the means of production. The hacienda owners rank highest; the propertyless lowest. In many traditional societies, we should note, it is impossible to rank people according to ownership of means of production, since land frequently cannot be sold or bought. Among the Dogon, we should recall, the village headman (the *hogon*) decides who is to cultivate which plot and land rights are tied up with kinship. In hunter-and-gatherer societies, there is no systematic difference in access to means of production; for example, all men have a bow and arrow. In Chapters 12 and 13 we look more closely into these major differences in the economic organisation of societies, and their connections with political power and social organisation in general; at this point, it is sufficient to note how economic differences, and the social organisation of production (division of labour), have ramifications in the cultural sphere and engender important differences in the classification of individuals.

'CULTURAL CLASSES'

In many contemporary societies, it may be difficult to argue that access to means of production is the main criterion for the class divisions, and in this respect, Weber seems to be right *contra* Marx. Notably, large population segments in industrial societies are public servants or 'white-collar workers' – they are neither capitalists nor workers. Many highly salaried directors of companies, for instance, own only a negligible number of shares in the firm they manage. This may necessitate a less rigid concept of class than the one developed by Marx, who wrote at a time when the main twofold division of Western societies into capitalists and working class was clearer than it is today.

In Wolf's analysis of Puerto Rico, it is apparent that actors rank each other according to their symbols of wealth: what makes a difference in the ways people classify each other could thus be whether someone owns a bedspread, whether the women of the household ride a horse or a mule, whether they eat their bananas plain or with milk. In Puerto Rico at this time, such markers were interpreted as being linked with differential access to property. However, this need not be the case. As the economist Thorstein Veblen showed more than a century ago (Veblen 1953 [1899]), Americans may strive to acquire status symbols, as a form of impression management, to give the impression that they are better off than they actually are. Veblen famously spoke of this kind of behaviour as 'conspicuous consumption'.

Later, Pierre Bourdieu developed a systematic and very influential theory of 'cultural classes' reminiscent of Veblen's perspective, taking France as his chief empirical example (Bourdieu 1984 [1979]; see also Jenkins 1993). A principal idea in Bourdieu's work is that power is connected with symbols, and that the ruling class in any society is, by default, the class which decides the ranking of symbols and the form of dominant discourse; in other words, the class that controls the criteria for good taste. Someone who knows the codes for decent behaviour, 'proper' speech, good taste in art and music and so on has a surplus of symbolic capital. Bourdieu admits that such differences are often connected with economic inequality, but he has analysed them as power systems in their own right, seeing symbolic capital as relatively independent of economic and political capital. In many societies there are people, such as politicians and intellectuals, who possess a great deal of symbolic capital and wield considerable power without owning means of production.

In his meticulously researched study of 'taste' in French society, Bourdieu stresses its social origin. Contrary to popular notions to the effect that taste is somehow inborn, his observations show

that the cultural needs are created by education: our study demonstrates that all cultural practices (museum visits, attendance at concerts, exhibitions, talks, etc.) and preferences within literature, painting or music are closely connected with the level of education (which is measured as academic title or number of years at educational institutions) and social origins. (Bourdieu 1979, p. 1)

Differences in taste thereby express 'objective class differences'. For example, Bourdieu shows that knowledge of classical music is strongly correlated with education and class background, and argues that the very definition of good taste is a manifestation of power which confirms and strengthens rank differences, as well as giving a certain prestige in itself. Just as an unclean caste in India may change its way of life in a bid to improve its rank in the caste system, 'upstarts' in modern class societies may try to appropriate as many symbols as possible that indicate good taste. Bourdieu calls this kind of strategy 'conversion of capital'; it may be possible, in other words, to convert economic capital into symbolic capital (cultural prestige). In France, for instance, aristocratic titles may sometimes be purchased. The parallel with the rise of the distillers in Bisipara should be obvious.

Although there is usually a clear connection between economic and symbolic capital, the two are not congruent: some have much of the former but little of the latter, and vice versa. This is why conversion may be an interesting strategy for actors who wish to increase their prestige. Whether the chief form of conversion follows one direction or the other depends, of course, on the dominant value system in society.

COMPLEXITY IN SOCIAL DIFFERENTIATION

A general principle in studies of stratification, class and social differentiation, is the rule of cumulation. This 'rule' holds that if someone is economically wealthy, he or she probably also has a good education, good health and secure employment. This line of thought has been well documented, particularly in sociological research on modern industrial societies. As anthropologists, we nevertheless need to be aware of the variation between societies regarding both criteria for rank and perceptions of rank. Although wealth nearly always provides high rank, it is not necessarily more important than, for example, ritual purity. Advanced age may give high or low rank; female gender may be completely disqualifying or nearly irrelevant, and so on.

Further – as indicated earlier in this chapter – there are often contradictions between different criteria for rank, which can be interpreted as conflicts between value systems or between principles for the legitimation of power. A typical example is the conflict, prevalent in many African societies, between age and education. Old men in the village try to retain their power, which is legitimated through tradition, while young men returning from college may insist that their educational, achieved qualifications are superior and entitle them to higher power than their elders.

Different criteria for rank, or principles for differentiation, thus do not overlap completely. The social hierarchy in Bisipara, for instance, may well be conceived of as a system based on no less than five pyramids which can be distinguished analytically and which influence each other and interact to varying degrees: caste, wealth, local government, gender and age.

These principles for differentiation function simultaneously, but their relative significance can rarely be predicted. Sometimes their significance is situational. This means that in some kinds of situations, such as during a religious festival, caste membership is more important than any of the other criteria. In other situations, economic power may be the most important criterion, and so on. Does a rich woman from a relatively impure caste, for example, rank higher or lower than a poor Brahmin? It is impossible to give this question an unambiguous answer, but it hints at the complexity of social classification and differentiation, and shows the necessity of detailed ethnography.

POWER AND THE POWERLESS

The last two chapters have to a great extent dealt with power and influence. Social differentiation, whether it is based on gender, age, class or caste, creates and reproduces differences in power. Often such power differences may lead to revolt and protests among the powerless, and sometimes these revolts may lead to permanent changes in the power relations of society. The French Revolution is often cited as an example of such a change: after this momentous event in European history, the privileges of the nobility and royal family were eventually replaced by formal principles of equality and democracy.

As this chapter has suggested, albeit mostly indirectly, there may be quite varying notions within a society about justice, good and bad and, ultimately, what the world looks like. Societies, in other words, are internally differentiated, not only in economic and political terms but also in cultural terms. Yet certain fundamental values are usually widely agreed upon, whether they are tacit or explicit. Even people who seem profoundly oppressed frequently support the dominating ideology, even if it may be said to contribute to their oppression. Any ideology attempts to make a certain perspective on society appear 'natural'; if it succeeds, people will perceive their own place, and the dominant hierarchy, as natural. This was the basic mechanism Marx had in mind when he wrote that the ruling ideas of society are the ideas of the ruling class.

The distinction between actor perspectives and systemic perspectives is indispensable when we look at inequality and differentiation, and both caste and class systems can be studied profitably through a conscious switching between the two perspectives. One is born into a caste and/or a class; the caste or class structure is a systemic property, but each actor relates to his or her position of relative power or powerlessness in an independent, unpredictable way. It is therefore necessary to grasp the duality of social process – it is simultaneously the product of agency and the objective condition for agency – in the study of power. This is shown in the next chapter.

SUGGESTIONS FOR FURTHER READING

Louis Dumont: *Homo Hierarchicus*, 2nd edn. Chicago: University of Chicago Press 1980.
Kathinka Frøystad: *Blended Boundaries: Caste, Class, and Shifting Faces of 'Hinduness' in a North Indian City*. New Delhi: Oxford University Press 2005.
Karl Marx and Friedrich Engels: *The Communist Manifesto*. New York: The Modern Reader 1968 [1848].

11   POLITICS AND POWER

Politics is parasitical on other social relationships.
                                           — *M.J. Swartz*

Politics is linked with power; both the power that people exert over each other, and the ways in which society wields power over people by imposing institutionalised constraints on their agency – constraints ranging from property taxes and traffic rules to torture and genocide. However, politics also has to do with the prevention of lawlessness and insecurity; that is, it concerns law and order, the implementation of the rights of persons, conflict resolution and social integration.

Politics can be identified analytically in all societies, but by no means all societies that anthropologists have studied have political institutions distinct from other societal realms, or even emic concepts that might easily translate as 'politics'. In modern state societies, it may seem relatively easy to delineate what is politics and what is not. Political science, developed to study politics in such societies, deals with the formal political institutions; with a legislative assembly, local administration, voting patterns and other aspects of society recognised as political. In non-industrial societies, it may be far more difficult to single out politics as something distinct from the ongoing flow of social life. In industrial or postindustrial society, we think of politics as something they *have*; a specialised set of institutions. In societies with no centralised state, the political system may rather be seen as something intimately woven into other aspects of existence. Very often in stateless societies, kinship and religion are in practice indistinguishable from politics. That institutional differentiation which is characteristic of modern societies is absent in many others (Godelier 1975). This implies that it would often be fruitless to look for identifiable political institutions which could be compared with, say, parliaments or city councils. Instead, political anthropologists have to look for the political decision-making mechanisms – they must find out where and how the important decisions are being made, who is affected by the decisions, what rules and norms govern political action, how hegemony is challenged, and what possible sanctions the rulers of society dispose of.

A central problem in classic political anthropology, which was largely developed by 'the British school' from the 1930s to the 1960s, was simply the naïve but pertinent question of how stateless societies were at all integrated: why they did not just fall apart due to lack of a central authority, how they managed to resolve conflicts and how peace was maintained. Today, following decolonisation and the emergence of the postcolonial state in the South, many studies in political anthropology instead focus on the relationship between the state and local communities, often showing how inhabitants of such communities resist dominance from the state (e.g. Kapferer 1988; Scott 1999) or how the state seeks to dominate populations through drawing on cultural notions widespread in the population (Wolf 1999; Krohn-Hansen and Nustad 2005).

Although complex modern societies are also dealt with here, this chapter takes politics in stateless societies as its point of departure and discusses how chiefs and 'big men' acquire their positions of authority, how the inhabitants of uncentralised, 'acephalous' societies resolve conflicts with no courts or judicial apparatus, and how power can be seen as the prize in political games. Seen from the vantage-point of a modern state, it may seem as though the political integration of tribal peoples like the Nuer, the Pathans and the Yanomamö is extremely tenuous and fragile; the fact is that many of these groups have revealed a remarkable structural stability, which has lasted longer than most European polities have existed, although they are now to varying degrees integrated into the state and capitalist economy.

Some political anthropologists emphasise how different societies are integrated (systemic perspective). Others instead stress how individuals make strategies to promote their interests (actor perspective). In this chapter, it will become clear why both kinds of perspectives can be useful. The empirical material discussed illuminates the tension between agency and social structure, as well as the differences between kinship-based politics and politics based on formal institutions.

POWER AND CHOICE

Since the study of power is essential to political anthropology, the concept of power must be discussed briefly. One of the oldest and still most influential definitions of power is that of Max Weber, who wrote that it 'is the ability to enforce one's own will on others' behaviour' (1978 [1919]); that is, the ability to make someone do something they would otherwise not have done. According to Weber, people have power over each other. Other concepts of power, including those inspired by Marxist scholarship, would also include structural power; that is power relations embedded in the division of labour, the legislative system and other structural features of society. It immediately seems to make sense to talk of 'systemic' or 'structural' power in many contexts: the obeying of norms and implicit rules may easily be seen as a form of structural power – it is not easy to tell *who* it is that forces me to hold the fork in my left hand and the knife in my right. However, if we include any action dictated by cultural convention in our definition, power risks becoming diluted and synonymous with conventions, norms and, ultimately, culture. It may therefore be fruitful, in the realm of political anthropology at least, to follow Weber in distinguishing between power, authority (*Herrschaft*) and influence, the latter being a 'milder' form of power presupposing tacit acquiesence. Authority, in Weber's view, is taken for granted and needs no justification, while power proper can potentially be challenged and therefore must be defended.

The differences between ways of conceptualising power correspond to the differences between actor-oriented and systemic perspectives. The great challenge of all social science, one might say, consists in trying to do justice to both.

Do people, when all is said and done, act under some form of coercion, or are they free to choose their course of action? In a sense, both statements are correct. We choose our actions, but not under circumstances of our own choice. If you live in a capitalist society and are penniless, you cannot choose to invest in the Taiwanese electronic industry. One cannot easily choose to dethrone and replace the chief in a society where political offices are hereditary, and a Tiv woman cannot buy herself a plot of land as long as Tiv customary law states that only men have land rights (see Chapter 12).

On the other hand, actors make choices whenever they can. It may be beyond my ability to buy a factory, but I can choose between depositing my salary in my bank account or spending it on expensive Norwegian beer. And although it was impossible for the Saloio women (Chapter 9) to achieve formal political positions, they were able to exert considerable influence or power through informal channels.

This implies that virtually all humans have some potential power or influence, however narrow their field of autonomous action. However, this resource, like all others, is unequally distributed. We should further be aware that power is a problematic phenomenon to explore comparatively, since the peoples we study may lack concepts corresponding to our concepts of power.

POWERLESSNESS AND RESISTANCE

The reverse of the coin, powerlessness, is also an important aspect of social life. It is not the same as a modest amount of power, but should rather be conceptualised as the absence of the ability to exert power. 'Muted' groups (Chapter 9) are powerless in this sense. Because of lack of communication channels, lack of organisation or similar poverty in resources, they are prevented from promoting their interests in efficient ways. In Michel Foucault's terms, powerless groups are subjugated by the dominant discourses of society; the ways in which everyday language structures the world and confirms a set of values (see also Chapters 14 and 15).

The sociologist Steven Lukes (2004) has suggested that power be studied at three levels. First, it can be identified in decision-making processes, that is, where decisions are actually being taken. This is the simplest perspective on power, which focuses on factual, observable events. Second, power can also be studied by looking at non-decisions; that is, all of those political issues which are dealt with within the political system but which are not addressed explicitly.

The third level on which power can be studied, which Lukes argues is often ignored by social scientists, is that including 'muted' or powerless groups, whose interests never even reach the level of negotiations. Such interests lack a voice in public life; they are marginalised and made invisible. This kind of perspective on power has been common in feminist scholarship and also in research on indigenous populations. Research on muted groups has nevertheless also shown that such groups, apparently powerless and marginalised, often develop their own strategies to increase control over their own existence. James Scott (1985) has thus shown how poor peasants may maintain a fairly high level of autonomy by systematically sabotaging impositions from the authorities. The notion of resistance in Scott's work on peasants in South-East Asia subsequently became fashionable in anthropological studies of a wide range of phenomena. Scott defines the 'weapons of the weak' like this:

> Here I have in mind the ordinary weapons of relatively powerless groups: foot dragging, dissimulation, desertion, false compliance, pilfering, feigned ignorance, slander, arson, sabotage, and so on.... They require little or no coordination or planning; they make use of implicit understandings and informal networks ... (Scott 1985: xvi)

Historical studies of slavery in the Americas (see, for example, Lewis 1983), moreover, reveal that similar strategies were widespread there as ways of retaining some autonomy under conditions of extreme oppression.

IDEOLOGY AND LEGITIMATION

Unless they rule through sheer terror and violence or threats of such, as many political regimes do, the powerholders in any society must in one way or other justify or legitimate their power. Among the Mundurucú, the men justify their power vis-à-vis the women by referring to myths describing how they gained control over the sacred trumpets. In Hindu society, the Brahmins may justify their power by referring to ascribed statuses and sacred texts, while in parliamentary democracies the legislating assemblies may refer to the 'will of the people' as embedded in election results when they initiate unpopular policies.

It is common to assume that power discrepancies in non-industrial societies follow tradition and ascribed statuses, whereas achievement is more important in industrial societies. This point of view has been criticised from several perspectives. First, it is not true that achievement counts for everything in industrial societies: social background and family networks may be extremely important in maintaining a particular power structure there, just as in non-industrial societies. Second, there are also great differences within the vast and inaccurate category of non-industrial, or 'traditional', societies in this regard.

The ascribed/achieved distinction may nevertheless be an important one in the comparative study of politics, provided we do not link it categorically to specific societal types. This dichotomy is rather an aspect of every political system. How important are personal qualities and individual agency in various political systems, we may then ask, and how important are those aspects which are hereditary and follow ascription?

The idea that all individuals in modern democracies have the same opportunities to achieve power is often regarded as an ideological (mis)-conception. Similarly, notions regarding what is 'for the common good' are often seen as expressions of ideology. In a more general vein, we may state that political authority rests on ideological legitimation: it must be justified. If the justification is accepted by the population, we may, following Weber, talk of legitimate authority.

Like power, culture and other core concepts, ideology is a difficult word to define. For now, we will adopt the suggestion that ideology is that aspect of culture which concerns how society ought to be organised; in other words, it concerns politics, rules and the distinction between right and wrong. Ideology is a normative kind of knowledge; it may be implicit or explicit, and it may be challenged.

Although there seem to be groups in every society which are relatively powerless, there tends to be widespread acquiescence in the values a society is based on – even among the people who seem to be losing out because of them. Many Marxist theorists, including Marx himself, have described this phenomenon, whereby people seem not to be aware of their own good, as 'false consciousness'. Because of considerable power disparities in society, the powerful are able to promote their own world-view much more efficiently than other groups and to give it an air of 'naturalness', thereby making deeply ideological notions part and parcel of the taken-for-granteds of society.

The notion of false consciousness has an immediate appeal. It seems likely that oppressed groups do not know their own good; otherwise they would have revolted, would they not? On the other hand, it is far from easy for an anthropologist, an outsider to society, to argue convincingly that a group is the victim of delusions of which its members are not themselves aware. On which grounds can researchers claim that they know the 'objective interests' of a group better than they themselves do?

It is rarely necessary for an anthropologist to take a stance regarding the issue of false consciousness. In comparative studies of political systems, it is in principle irrelevant whether the anthropologist thinks the group is 'right' or 'wrong' in its world-view and ideology. Above all, the anthropological study of politics is concerned with showing how political systems function and how people act or are prevented from acting within them, as well as indicating the relationship between ideology and social practice. It should nevertheless be kept in mind that actors rarely see the full context and consequences of their acts, and that an analytical task of anthropologists consists in working this out.

INTEGRATION AND CONFLICT IN KINSHIP-BASED SOCIETIES

Because of Evans-Pritchard's classic study of political organisation among the Nuer of the southern Sudan (1940), this nomadic people was for decades virtually a paradigm case in the study of politics in stateless societies. We shall therefore look at the political dynamics of the Nuer, writing in the ethnographic present, in some detail.

The Nuer are cattle nomads with an economic livelihood as well as an ecological environment reminiscent of the Fulani. Not only do cattle form an important part of their economy, they are also central in Nuer myth and symbolism.

Although the Nuer live in small local communities, every individual has ties of solidarity tying him or her to other people scattered over an enormous territory. Each has obligations and commitments towards his or her patrilineal kin; but is also tied to other groups.

First, a Nuer is a member of an agnatic lineage. Several lineages together form a sub-clan, and several sub-clans form a clan. This principle – the division of clans into equivalent sub-clans and lineages at several levels – is called 'segmentation'. From a male Nuer's perspective, loyalties and commitments generally decrease with growing genealogical distance (see Figure 11.1).

A different principle for dividing up Nuer groups is the territorial one, which usually corresponds roughly to kinship; at least Nuer men tend to live near their close male relatives. Although not everyone who lives in a Nuer village belongs to the same clan, each village is associated with a clan in roughly the same way as European nation-states are associated with ethnic groups.

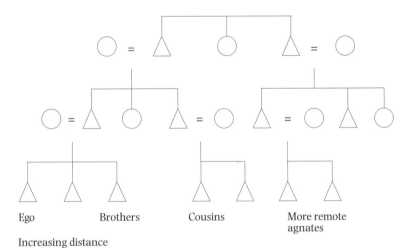

Figure 11.1   Degrees of genealogical distance in a patrilineal system (Sisters and female cousins are not included in ego's generation.)

In addition to these overlapping principles for belongingness – agnatic kinship and place of residence – each Nuer man has obligations towards his age-mates; the men with whom he was initiated , as well as his affines (members of clans into which his siblings and himself have married) and possible trade partners. These cross-cutting ties, which create complex systems of loyalties that cannot be reduced to mere concentric circles, reduce the danger of feuds between lineages. The local community is recruited through agnatic kinship, matrilateral kinship and affinality (Gluckman 1982 [1956]). If a man becomes entangled in a blood feud based on agnatic kinship loyalties, he thus runs the risk of having to direct his revenge towards his nearest neighbour and collaborator. Many Nuer therefore try to avoid open conflict with other lineages as far as possible.

Despite the mitigating effects of this mechanism, feuds occasionally do burst out among the Nuer. The cause may be disagreement over bridewealth, suspicion of cattle theft or murder. A feud may last for years, occasionally flaring up in violence, and one reason for its prolonged character is the existence of ties of mutual obligations between the feuding groups.

SEGMENTARY OPPOSITIONS

Because of the political commitments entailed by kinship among the Nuer, conflicts rarely involve only two people. Usually, they would at least be helped by their closest agnatic kin. In larger conflicts, such as murder or disagreements over grazing rights, the kin group is united at a higher level. The general principle is 'myself against my brother; my brother and I against our cousins; our cousins, my brother and myself against our more distant agnates' and so on, until one reaches the level of the whole Nuer tribe, which is united against the Dinka, the traditional arch-enemy (with whom the Nuer nonetheless appear to have fairly recent common origins; see Newcomer 1972; Southall 1976). Interestingly, during the wars in Sudan, pitting 'Arabs' from the North against 'Africans' in the south, the Nuer and Dinka have periodically united at a yet higher level of segmentation against the Muslim government of the Sudan.

This form of organisation is called a system of segmentary oppositions. Evans-Pritchard describes it like this:

A tribal segment is a political group in opposition to other segments of the same kind and they jointly form a tribe only in relation to other Nuer tribes and adjacent foreign tribes which form part of the same political system, and without these relations very little meaning can be attached to the concepts of tribal segment and tribe. (1940, p. 147)

The largest units – the tribes – thus only exist when they are in conflict with other tribes. It is thus through conflicts that the Nuer are integrated politically at various levels.

In a segmentary political system, the reach of the political community is flexible and depends on the scope of the conflict. If the Nuer had aristocratic lineages or even a king, the situation would naturally have been different. A necessary condition for segmentation is the equality, or equivalence, of the segments at each level: lineage A corresponds to lineage B, clan X to clan Y, and so on. It is therefore impossible to state unambiguously which group a Nuer belongs to: group membership is conditional on the situation.

One answer to the question of why the Nuer are not perpetually in conflict with one another – since the potential for conflict is ample and no central government or legislative system exists – is the presence of cross-cutting ties. However, they also have an institution reminiscent of a court of justice in the 'leopard-skin chiefs' (also known as men of the earth), who are not chiefs in the ordinary sense but who are generally respected as neutral intermediaries in situations of conflict. The leopard-skin chief listens to both parties and makes what he deems an appropriate settlement. However, there is no formal system of sanctions forcing people to follow his advice.

The leopard-skin chief usually comes from a small lineage and is thus considered a 'neutral' go-between in situations of conflict. However, he may often have acquired considerable wealth in cattle as payment for his services, and therefore has to be seen as a political actor, and an important one at that, although he is officially placed outside the political conflicts. This kind of ambiguous position, being outside and inside politics at the same time, is not unusual for religious leaders.

Like the Yanomamö (Chapters 5 and 7), the Nuer are primarily integrated through kinship, and they reproduce political stability both through shared descent and through alliances with other kin groups, thus reflecting the duality of kinship described in earlier chapters. Unlike the Yanomamö, as we have seen, they are organised in a segmentary way, which means that they have potential for corporate political action on a larger scale than the former. It should nevertheless be pointed out that we have dealt with both peoples in the ethnographic present, and in fact that the Nuer have for many years been fighting the Sudanese government, while the Yanomamö have, largely successfully, negotiated with Brazilian and Venezuelan state authorities over land rights. While thousands of Nuer live as refugees in the United States and elsewhere (Shandy 2007), Yanomamö leaders have appeared on international television and have participated in global conferences for indigenous peoples. It is thus no longer entirely accurate to state that the limits of the Yanomamö polity can be drawn at the point where it is no longer possible to organise a larger number of people along kinship lines.

The notion that one's loyalty is connected to many concentric circles which are activated in different situations is not only relevant to the study of stateless societies, but can also be applied to contexts in modern complex societies. The French nationalist leader Jean-Marie Le Pen once presented his own loyalties as a set of segmentary oppositions, stating that he preferred his daughters to his nieces, his nieces to his neighbours, his neighbours to people from other parts of France and so on. In general, politics in complex societies may often be illuminated through models of segmentary oppositions. Every citizen belongs not only to the nation or the ethnic group – in different political situations both larger and smaller groups may be capable of demanding one's loyalty. In Europe of the European Union, one might add, citizens can similarly be Barcelonians, Catalans, Spaniards and Europeans in different situations. Here, too, the principle of conflicting loyalties applies, since European citizens are also, for example, environmentalists, jazz lovers or lesbians.

ASCRIPTION VERSUS ACHIEVEMENT

Melanesia includes New Guinea and many other smaller islands to the east, including the Trobriands. The border between Melanesia and Polynesia is conventionally located at Fiji; Polynesia consists of a great number of islands in the southern Pacific, covering a vast area from New Zealand to Hawaii. Melanesia is an enormously diverse area regarding language and culture, while Polynesia, which was peopled much more recently, is more homogeneous. Although the Melanesia/Polynesia boundary is frequently contested in the academic literature, it will serve us well here as a general division.

Traditional Melanesian societies are generally autonomous village units integrated on the basis of kinship (Sahlins 1963; Knauft 1999). There are tendencies of segmentation, but it is rare for the groups to form alliances at a higher level than that of the village. In other words, they are by and large politically integrated at the village level. The political leaders of Melanesian societies are characteristically 'big men', individuals who have acquired power because of their personal qualities.

Polynesian societies are different. Many of them have traditionally developed states with hereditary, royal leadership. In Hawaii, New Zealand (Aotearoa in Maori) and elsewhere, there were professional armies, tax collectors and bureaucrats. This kind of division of labour was rare in Melanesia.

Leadership in Melanesia depends on personal achievement. Within every village, there is competition between men who wish to become 'big men'; who aspire to make decisions on behalf of the village and wish to be respected and powerful. Such a status is acquired through the exchange of gifts with a large number of people, thereby creating ties of mutual obligation with as many persons as possible. A 'big man' should therefore have many relatives and several wives as a starting-point for his networking. When an established 'big man' dies, a new group of younger men will start competing to build similar positions.

Traditional Polynesian societies were ruled by feudal landlords rather than by 'upstarts'. The leaders belonged to royal or aristocratic lineages (in most Melanesian societies all lineages are equal), and the authority of the king was seen as the will of the gods. The surplus produced by the farmers was sufficiently large for the aristocrats not to engage in manual work. When a chief died, his position was immediately filled by a younger kinsman. Contrary to the Melanesian system, power in this system is thus institutional and not individual.

In a classic article, Marshall Sahlins (1963) compared the two systems. It appears that they reach their respective critical points in very different – some would say opposite – ways. The egalitarian, achievement-oriented Melanesian system makes it possible for enterprising individuals to obtain power by forging interpersonal ties of reciprocity with other people. When a man wants to expand his area of influence, he has to start giving presents to strangers, sometimes in villages other than his own. During the first phase, he will get nothing in return: it takes time to build up confidence. Moreover, this kind of enterprise is risky for the 'big man'. In many cases his own kin and co-villagers will eventually begin to grumble about giving him gifts without receiving enough in return, since he invests the surplus 'abroad' in a bid to expand his sphere of influence. In some cases this kind of situation may lead to the downfall of the 'big man': he might be deposed, killed or chased from the village.

The problem immanent in the Polynesian order is of a different kind, but this system also carries germs of instability. Gradually the professional state bureaucracy grows larger; thus the taxes must be increased and there is a risk of reaching a point where the burden on the taxpayers becomes so heavy that they revolt against the aristocracy.

These two contrasting examples reveal an important difference regarding the level of political integration. The Melanesian system is kinship-based, egalitarian and characterised by equality and achievement, although it may be less individualistic than Sahlins assumed (Knauft 1999: 144). The Polynesian system, by contrast, is hierarchical and ascription-based, founded on differences between the aristocratic and commoner lineages. The Melanesian system collapses when the principle of equality is not taken care of sufficiently, while the Polynesian order folds when the institutionalised hierarchy is no longer capable of legitimating itself.

An important difference concerns the ability of the respective societal types to accumulate economic surplus. The swidden agriculture practised in Melanesian societies did not make it easy to produce much more than the requirements for subsistence, while the irrigation technology developed in some of the larger, volcanic Polynesian islands made it possible to support a class of full-time soldiers and bureaucrats. If such a large surplus had been generated in a Melanesian society and had been channelled in the direction of a 'big man' and his family, one might well conclude that the outcome could have been a political system of the Polynesian type. Indeed, Sahlins remarks (1963; see also Keesing 1981), there were tendencies in some Melanesian societies, such as the Trobriand Islands, towards the development of hereditary, ascription-based political power and thereby a firm distinction between aristocratic and commoners' lineages. The necessary condition for such a development is the production of a surplus sufficient to make a division of labour possible where a segment of the population does not need to engage in agricultural work at all. These 'transitory' cases may point to some of the preconditions for the development of a state.

This comparison reveals differences in legitimation as well as limits to the number of people who can be integrated into different kinds of polities: it appears from Sahlins' analysis that the centralised Polynesian system was able to integrate many more people than the egalitarian Melanesian one. It possessed powerful means of coercion in the form of soldiers supported materially by agricultural surplus; and it had a class of professional administrators similarly fed. The Polynesian system described by Sahlins (and, admittedly, criticised by later scholars for being simplistic; see Sand 2002) could be seen as a case of what Claessen and Skálnik (1978) have spoken of as 'the early state', which, as Skálnik (1992) has later remarked, serves to nuance the simplistic dichotomy often invoked between 'state societies' (that is, 'ourselves') and 'stateless societies' (that is, 'the others').

POLITICS AS STRATEGIC ACTION

So far in this chapter, politics has been analysed from a largely systemic point of view. Although the focus has to some extent been on remarkable individuals, such as 'big men', the underlying question has been: how are societies integrated? Let us now raise a different question, namely: how do actors go about maximising political power?

It may be convenient to distinguish between two complementary definitions of politics. First, politics can be defined as agency; as the establishment of authoritative decisions involving the exertion of power. Second, politics may be seen as a system, in which case the word refers to the circulation of power and authority in a society. If the first definition is used, politics appears as competition between individuals or groups. In Bailey's view, thus, the rules that create a political system concern 'prizes, personnel, leadership (teams), competition and control' (1969: 20). If the second definition is used instead, the ultimate purpose of politics lies in its integrative power.

In the discussion of the Melanesian 'big man', it became clear that individual motives of fame and personal gain among 'big men' indirectly create political cohesion in Melanesian communities. If we were to apply such a perspective consistently, we would give the impression that 'societies' do not exist as anything other than the unintended consequences of a mass of strategic actions. Simultaneously, of course, actors have to lay their strategies within a system (or society) which places constraints on their course of action. This duality of social life has been discussed earlier; we will now examine its relevance in the study of political processes.

The Pathans of Swat valley in north-western Pakistan are cereal farmers (Barth 1959). A tiny minority of the population, the Pakthuns, own virtually all of the land, while the majority of the rest of the population are their tenants. The Pathans are patrilineal, and all formal political power is vested with men. Only sons can inherit from their fathers, but all sons have rights of inheritance, unlike in societies where the eldest son (primogeniture) or the youngest son (ultimogeniture) inherits the family property. There is a desperate shortage of land, and, at the time of Barth's research, the most important political issues in Swat valley concerned competition over land rights. In such disputes, lineage segments may appear as political corporations. Unlike the Nuer, however, the Pathans do not usually align themselves with close agnates, but rather with distant ones. The reason is that, because of the rules of inheritance, the Pathans' plots of land border those of their close agnates and so they compete to expand into each other's land. The Pathans thus align themselves with distant agnates, whose plots are far away and therefore uninteresting, against close agnates. In this way, 'politics makes strange bedfellows' in Swat valley. (Brothers, however, do not compete for land: the norm of fraternal solidarity is stronger than the drive for expansion.)

In order to expand his fields, a Pakthun needs a large political following: he needs many clients. They can cultivate his fields and can be mobilised as soldiers if need be. Clients and land are thus the main resources competed for. Since there is no arable land not already under cultivation, the competition for clients and land can truly be seen as a zero-sum game: what one actor gains, another loses. Moreover, Barth emphasises, the game is played between individuals, not among lineage segments. Alliances and blocs are formed situationally by individual actors on a pragmatic basis.

More than fifty years after Barth's fieldwork, these tensions and conflicts over land rights are still relevant in Swat valley, but because of the political instability in the region, which borders on Afghanistan, current concerns in the area are chiefly related to the armed conflict between the Pakistani state and the Taliban, which enjoys some support in the region, and with the unrest along and across the border to Afghanistan.

MAXIMISATION OR CLASS STRUGGLE?

Barth's classic study of politics among the Swat Pathans focuses on individual strategies for maximisation: how individuals invest their resources, how they try to outwit each other to maximise value (locally defined as land and clients). In a reinterpretation of Barth's analysis, Talal Asad (1972) argues that the power disparities of the Swat were such a fundamental characteristic of the political system that an analysis which did not take them into account had to be misleading. First and foremost, he refers to the unequal access to land, which keeps a majority of the population in poverty and powerlessness. He also points out that the patron–client system prevents the clients from developing class-consciousness which might lead them to revolt. Since they are themselves divided by loyalty to different patrons, they are unable to organise their interests as a class. Rather than fighting the oppressors, they fight each other.

Asad proposes to replace Barth's individualist theory-of-games perspective with a Marxist analysis focusing on property and power disparities. It is evident that the two approaches raise fundamentally different questions, both of which are relevant to the study of politics but which lead to very different conceptualisations of the political field. Asad presents a systemic perspective where individual acts become relatively uninteresting since they follow from the systemic parameters; Barth's analysis zooms in on the individual actor's strategies, whereby the systemic form becomes chiefly a result of action. Both interpretations are valid, but the controversy reveals that different analytical approaches imply diverging descriptions of any given society.

THE POSTCOLONIAL STATE

The politics and political culture of complex state societies are dealt with in greater detail later, notably in the context of contemporary cultural complexity in Chapters 16–19. Nevertheless, a few aspects of state politics are considered here, partly to avoid the impression that most societies in the world of the early twenty-first century are stateless. They certainly are not, although the role of the state varies greatly between local communities – from being nearly irrelevant in everyday life to being an imposing presence in most public situations. Some, like Pierre Clastres (1977; see also Graeber 2004), would regard the emergence of the state, and the enforced incorporation of non-state peoples into the state, as the most important watershed in cultural history. The main lesson to be learnt from the examples discussed here, apart from their ethnographic and historical value, lies in the comparative models and approaches to politics they exemplify. Today, the modern state is present and is articulated to varying degrees in local communities nearly everywhere in the world. The general tendency, most textbooks on politics in Third World societies would argue, is for localities to be subjugated to state legislation and surveillance. In Max Weber's famous words (1978 [1919]; cf. Giddens 1985), where it exists the state has a double monopoly on taxation and on the legitimate use of force, although globalisation has reduced the direct power of the state in many realms (Eriksen 2007). It ensures new power constellations and places new demands on its subjects or citizens, and it very often uses force or the threat of force in order to ensure loyalty and obedience among groups that question its legitimacy.

The following example may be interesting as it displays a kind of process rarely studied by social scientists concerned with the state, namely one of progressive liberation of the state from the people.

The Central African state of Congo (Brazzaville), studied by Kajsa Ekholm Friedman (1991, 1994), became independent from France in 1962. It was thinly populated and rich in natural resources. Nevertheless, the country has experienced a nearly continuous economic decline throughout its period of independence; in the early 1990s the state was disintegrating in highly visible ways: schools, hospitals and roads were not being maintained, corruption and nepotism were serious obstacles to bureaucratic efficiency, and the state apparently did nothing to alleviate the misery of poverty-stricken areas. In many ways, the state was absent from public affairs in the country. Yet the public service was a very large employer, and since the means of production were state-owned, the state had ample funds.

Ekholm Friedman's analysis focuses on two levels: the state organisation, government and its employees; and actors situated in local communities. The state itself, she argues, has liberated itself from the people by ensuring an independent source of income through foreign trade and aid from donor agencies. Unlike the traditional African chiefs, with whom she explicitly compares Congo's contemporary rulers, the latter do not need to ensure the support of the country's inhabitants: they can do without the citizens' taxes and do not require their services as soldiers. Borrowing a metaphor from development sociologist Goran Hyden, Ekholm Friedman compares the Congolese state with a balloon floating above the country.

The state administration is based on patronage rather than meritocracy, with kinship as the most important principle. Thus a few very large extended kin groups control the entire state bureaucracy and are morally required to employ their relatives. As a result, Ekholm Friedman notes, many highly educated Congolese prefer to stay abroad after completing their studies, since they will never get a job with the state.

TACIT ACQUIESCENCE

Why do the people not revolt against such injustice? The answer, in Ekholm Friedman's analysis, lies in their cosmology and local organisation. Because of economic changes and migration, the local clan is no longer able to organise people in corporate groups. Further, Congolese tend to consult witchdoctors, clairvoyants or religious leaders rather than forming trade unions when they have a problem. Indeed, Ekholm Friedman places a great emphasis on the 'magical world view' prevalent in Congo in accounting for the citizens' tacit acquiescence in the excesses of the ruling families, showing how Congolese political movements have rapidly been transformed into religious cults.

David Kertzer writes:

Whether looking at historical accounts or at the world today, one is most struck not by the rebellions of the oppressed who rise up to destroy the political system that exploits them. Rather it is the overwhelming conformity of the people living in such societies that is most impressive. (1988, p. 39)

Kertzer accounts for this situation by emphasising the role of rituals and ideology in making the social order appear natural and inevitable; his term for this is 'mystification' (see also Chapter 14). It is doubtless true that dominant discourses and habit-memory (see Chapter 6), instituted through bodily practices and commemorative ceremonies in Connerton's phrase (1989), are often important legitimising instances. However, the curious feature of the Congolese situation is that the state, unlike the Polynesian chiefdom, does not seem to exploit and oppress its citizens: it simply ignores them.

It should also be noted that tacit acquiescence is not a universal phenomenon. Not least in South and Central American countries, social movements and peasant revolts aiming at the establishment of a more just political and economic order have been widespread, and have sometimes been successful in changing the social order and dominant power relations (Gledhill 2000). In Asian societies too, including China, India, the Philippines and Vietnam, powerful social movements organising peasants have been, or are, politically important. Perhaps the comparative lack of success of such movements in many African countries can be accounted for through Ekholm Friedman's study? Her work reveals a state which is both strong and weak; it fails to mobilise people, but is tightly organised and controls a great deal of wealth. Indeed, Ekholm Friedman concludes that the changes in Congo, both at the state level and in local communities, represent some of the least well-functioning combinations of modernity and African tradition conceivable. The inhabitants fail to organise their interests politically; the clan has ceased to function as a network channelling jobs, political organisation and social security; but the newly emancipated individuals have no abstract labour market to turn to. The state administration, for its part, legitimates and reproduces its power through kinship organisation, but it has severed the traditional ties of mutual obligations that the aristocratic lineages used to have with their subjects.

Yet another strategy is revealed in David Graeber's work on the Tsimihety of north-western Madagascar. Graeber describes them as 'masters of evasion' (2004: 55) and argues that this ethnic group, numbering around a million, largely successfully negotiates its relationship with the modern Malagasy state on its own terms, refusing subordination. Describing the Tsimihety as anarchists, Graeber describes their politics as a 'conscious rejection of certain forms of overarching political power which also causes people to rethink and reorganize the way they deal with one another' (2004: 56).

POLITICAL VIOLENCE

Many contemporary societies are less peaceful than the disintegrating Congo Brazzaville studied by Ekholm Friedman (where, incidentally, ethnic violence has since broken out) or the Tsimihety. One society associated with violent politics for several decades was Northern Ireland.

Allen Feldman (1991), writing about paramilitaries and militants in Northern Ireland during 'the Troubles' (which lasted from the late 1960s until the peace treaty of 1998), is concerned with the ways in which people are conditioned to committing violence; to using their bodies as tools for a cause, risking death in the act. Feldman scarcely discusses the large-scale political aspects of the conflict, but focuses narrowly on the experiences and narratives of those most immediately involved: the paramilitaries. His monograph 'is about the instrumental staging and commodification of the body by political violence' (Feldman 1991, p. 8), and shows how the political subject is created 'within a continuum of spaces consisting of the body, the confessional community, the state, and the imagined community of utopian completion: United Ireland or a British Ulster' (1991, p. 9).

Long quotations from paramilitaries of the militant Provisional Irish Republican Army (IRA) and Irish National Liberation Army (INLA) support the author's argument about the ways in which the body is being turned into an object or an instrument; the vocabulary developed to talk about bodies, living or dead, is particularly striking. Euphemisms for killing, including 'to do [someone]', 'to knock his cunt in' and 'to fill him in', are frequently used in their narratives. Important, concerted forms of resistance developed in prison further indicate the importance of the body as political instrument, and Feldman thus analyses 'the Dirty Protest' (refusal to wash), 'the Blanket Protest' (refusal to wear the prison uniform) and the recurrent hunger strikes. These ways of circumventing the prison's control over the inmates' bodies, which is evident in frequent beatings and in intimidating forms of physical surveillance, through objectifying one's own body in illegitimate ways, are seen, following Foucault, as ritualised acts of collective resistance whereby each individual inmate – especially in the case of hunger strikes – gives his individuality to the community and relinquishes control over his own body. The dramatised contrast between Loyalist and Republican, between Protestant and Catholic, is thus brought to a climax not only through the violent acts, but also through the hardships and humiliations experienced in prison.

Feldman, it should be noted, does not purport to explain the conflict in Northern Ireland; but he gives an understanding of why some of the inhabitants have committed themselves to violent action. He analyses political violence as a result of particular bodily experiences codified through an antagonistic political ideology. In this way, violence, which has in recent years become a central focus for anthropological theorising (Scheper-Hughes and Bourgois 2003), becomes understandable. In relation to the earlier discussions about agency and structure in politics, it should also be noted that Feldman's model encompasses both dimensions in its focus on the socially conditioned body – which simultaneously expresses aspects of the person and of the social system. Political violence takes many forms. The marginalisation and muting of large groups through terror, torture and massacres has been dealt with by Michael Taussig (1984), who writes about the many silent, powerless victims of colonialism and postcolonial state violence in South America. Political violence as civil war has been analysed in a study of Sri Lanka by Bruce Kapferer (1988), who shows how the image of the demonic Tamil is created and nurtured by Sinhalese nationalists who draw strategically on particular interpretations of ancient Sinhala myths and sacred texts to support the view of Tamils as devils. In a study of Hutu refugees from Burundi in Tanzania, Liisa Malkki (1995) shows, on the basis of detailed informants' narratives, how particular images of the past amalgamate into a 'mythico-history' emphasising enmities and deprivations in relation to the other main ethnic group in the region, the Tutsis. In a similar vein, but using a different kind of material, Peter van der Veer (1994) describes how militant Hindus in India developed a certain interpretation of the past in order to justify strong anti-Muslim sentiments, culminating in the Ayodhya riots in 1992–93. (Later, particularly in Chapter 17, the appropriation of the past for political purposes is discussed further.)

In anthropology, the concept of war, a characteristic form of political violence, has – not surprisingly – proved difficult to define comparatively (Descola and Izard 1992) since wars differ greatly in character. A war in the New Guinea highlands, for example, does not necessarily result in many casualties (Knauft 1990), quite unlike the wars engaged in by European states in the twentieth century. Bruce Knauft, further, enumerates as many as six distinct kinds of violence routinely classified as 'Melanesian warfare', ranging from violence between Europeans and Melanesians during colonialism to 'the ongoing local violence of gangs or *raskols*' (Knauft 1996, p. 137).

Human Rights in Anthropological Perspective

In debates over human rights, universalistic and relativistic perspectives may clash. On the one hand, one may argue that human rights are a universal good which should be promoted worldwide, and which should not, therefore, be regarded as the product of a particular kind of society. On the other hand, one may point out that human rights undoubtedly were developed in Europe in modern times, and that the Universal Declaration of Human Rights of 1948 is therefore anything but universal, but rather a child of modern European social philosophy. If one follows the latter argument, it may be seen as an ethnocentric error to claim that our human rights should be introduced and defended with the same vigour in African and Amazonian societies as in West European ones. According to this kind of logic, every society must be understood in its own terms, since every culture contains its own concepts of justice and rights. According to the first, universalistic line of thought, it would nevertheless be inhuman and arrogant to deny tribal peoples and other non-Europeans human rights only because they happen to have a different history from ourselves. In fact, the American Anthropological Association (AAA) issued a statement in 1948 about the incipient Declaration of Human Rights, arguing that it appeared to be ethnocentric.

Decades later, an anthropology of human rights has been developing in the interstices between legal and political anthropology, social philosophy and transnational law studies (Wilson 1997; Cowan et al. 2001; Mitchell and Wilson 2003; Goodale and Merry 2007; Goodale 2009). No longer concentrating on the relationship between universalistic and particularistic norms, the bulk of this research investigates

▶

the dynamics of human rights discourses and practices in particular local contexts. Unlike earlier ventures into the field (e.g. Renteln 1990), current research takes as its point of departure not 'the tribal world' but the contemporary world of states and legislative systems. Drawing on his own work in Guatemala and South Africa, Richard A. Wilson (1997) calls for a comparative anthropology of human rights that explores the different ways in which rights discourses and practices are appropriated locally, and which also indicates which kinds of conflicts arise as results of attempts at implementing human rights, often interpreted in divergent ways, in different societies. While much of the contemporary anthropological research on human rights deals with gender issues, violence and 'human security', the substantial literature on minority problems in contemporary Europe is also immediately relevant for anthropological approaches to human rights: the right to cultural identity may clash with individual rights, since minority leaders may overrule claims to autonomy from their members. Group rights may therefore be at odds with individual rights. The 'right to a cultural identity' would then, perhaps, have to be supplemented with 'the right not to have a cultural identity'.

In 1999, incidentally, the AAA issued a new statement on human rights, stating in no uncertain terms that it 'reflects a commitment to human rights consistent with international principles', adding 'but not limited by them' (quoted from Goodale 2009, p. 102). By this caveat, it is probably meant that cultural identities should still be allowed to flourish in so far as they are compatible with 'international principles'.

What about political violence as such? Do violent events as different from each other as those in Ayodhya, in Burundi and in Belfast have enough in common to merit comparison? Perhaps Feldman's analysis, focusing on the fusion of bodily experience and a powerful demonising ideology, can be useful as a starting-point for comparison (see also Krohn-Hansen 1994, 2009). For it is a sad fact that anthropologists will probably have to try to understand political violence for many years to come, probably forever.

A note on research ethics may be appropriate here. When doing research on contentious matters, open conflict or even situations of war, anthropologists are not just responsible for their own security, but also that of their informants. Time and again, anthropological research has been appropriated by authorities who do not necessarily have benign intentions towards the ethnographer's people. Since anthropologists are no better equipped than others to predict future developments than others, it can be difficult in this kind of situation to live up to the professional ethical guideline stating that one should 'do no harm'. As Oscar Salemink has showed in a detailed analysis of the interrelationship between ethnography and politics in Vietnam since the mid nineteenth century, ethnographic findings were often used by colonial (French) or neocolonial (American) powers to control and subdue minorities. Notably, Salemink (1991, 2002) describes how the detailed ethnographic work of the French anthropologist Georges Condominas was used to track down and capture minority leaders. Of course, Condominas could hardly be blamed, but this and similar stories should be read as a call for caution.

* * *

Anthropology is a holistic discipline in the sense that it aims at an understanding of the interrelationships between different aspects of culture and society. Later chapters draw on these preliminary insights into political processes and develop them further. Questions to do with ideology, power and legitimation are returned to, and politics in complex state societies is also explored further. The next chapter, which deals with exchange and consumption, thus integrates perspectives on politics with perspectives on the economy.

SUGGESTIONS FOR FURTHER READING

Fredrik Barth: *Political Leadership among Swat Pathans*. London: Athlone 1959.
Pierre Clastres: *Society against the State*. Oxford: Mole 1977.
John Gledhill: *Power and its Disguises. Perspectives on Political Anthropology*, 2nd edn. London: Pluto 2000.
David Graeber: *Fragments of an Anarchist Anthropology*. Chicago: Prickly Paradigm Press 2004.

12 EXCHANGE AND CONSUMPTION

Money is to the West what kinship is to the Rest.
　　　　　— *Marshall D. Sahlins*

Just as the anthropological study of politics is markedly different from the discipline of political science, economic anthropology distinguishes itself in important ways from the economic sciences. Anthropologists have always – at least since Malinowski – wished to call attention to the ways in which the economy is an integrated part of a social and cultural totality, and to reveal that economic systems and actions can only be fully understood if we look into their interrelationships with other aspects of culture and society. Just as politics ought to be seen as part of a wider system which includes non-political aspects as well, the economy cannot be properly studied as an isolated 'sector'. It has to be demonstrated in which way it is a cultural and social product, and this task can be undertaken in modern societies as well as traditional ones, although the economic system of modern societies is widely seen as 'rational', detached from other aspects of social life, and based on impartial market principles. An early contribution to the anthropology of consumption, entitled *The World of Goods* (Douglas and Isherwood 1978), tries to give an anthropological answer to the question of why people in modern societies want commodities. The drive for consumption witnessed in these societies is far from natural, even if it is taken for granted within economic science and the media. Why is it, for example, that people want to eat food A instead of food B, if it can be shown that both are equally nutritious and even that food B is less expensive? The full answer must be sought in an analysis of the cultural categories of the society in question, not in an analysis of 'rational choice' and maximisation of value. For although it may be true that people everywhere try to maximise value, what is considered valuable varies both cross-culturally and within societies.

Apart from providing valuable insights into other peoples' economic life, anthropological studies of consumption and exchange can show that the capitalist way of arranging the economy is far from the only possible way. The capitalist economy, by now hegemonic and almost universal, is a newcomer to the world. Seen from the perspective of cultural history, humans have been hunters and gatherers for about 90 per cent of their existence, and horticulturalists or agriculturalists for most of the remaining time. If we envision the history of humanity as a full day and night, modern industry appeared just a minute before midnight, and the Internet was invented a moment ago. This is one main reason that this chapter takes non-capitalist economies as its initial point of departure (see Carrier 2005 for a more comprehensive overview).

In anthropology, the economy may be defined in at least two markedly different ways. One is systemic, and sees the economy as the production, distribution and consumption of material and non-material valuables in society. The other is actor-centred, and focuses on the ways in which actors use the available means to maximise value. These two perspectives, sometimes labelled substantivist and formalist views, respectively, correspond to the two perspectives on politics demonstrated in the last chapter and, indeed, to a general tension in social science between actor-oriented and system-oriented accounts. Just as Dumont argued against what he sees as an ethnocentric conceptualisation of caste (Chapter 10) and Asad argued against an actor-oriented account of politics in Swat (Chapter 11), Sahlins (1972) has argued against the model of the 'rational agent' (*homo economicus*), a premise on which much economic science rests, as a comparative concept. Individuals who maximise value and base their economic behaviour on cost–benefit calculations, he contends, are characteristic of capitalist societies, but the very concept of the maximising individual is meaningless in societies where the unit of production is not the individual, but rather the household. Drawing on the agricultural economist Chayanov's findings among Russian peasants, Sahlins argues that peasants do not maximise profits, but instead work just enough to survive and to generate an adequate surplus; they are 'optimisers, not maximisers'. Against this, a 'formalist' would nonetheless reply that this proves only that peasants have different economic priorities from, say, stockbrokers; that the values they maximise are different from those of people in capitalist societies, not that their economy functions on qualitatively different principles. Leisure time, it could thus be argued, may be a 'value' which can be 'maximised'.

This controversy concerns differences and similarities between people in societies ('Are the others basically like "ourselves" or are they qualitatively

---

Consumption in a Capitalist World

Any comparative approach to consumption would indicate clearly that the economy does not simply consist in methods for material survival. Let us consider food. Why is it that the steaks of the middle classes are rarer than those of the working classes? Why did no *haute cuisine* develop in Africa when it did in Asia as well as Europe (Goody 1982)? Why did the inhabitants of Båtsfjord (northern Norway) start eating shrimps in the 1970s – an insectlike creature which had formerly been used exclusively as bait and was considered 'inedible' (Lien 1988)? And why do many North Americans refuse to eat horse meat (Sahlins 1976)?

▶

When we ask this kind of question, it becomes evident that consumption concerns much more than the mere satisfaction of inborn needs. This is, perhaps, more easily observable in modern than in traditional societies, since the consumer has more choice there (it is not entirely without reason that this kind of society is often called 'consumer society'). However, traditional societies have their own 'consumer cultures' and are, besides, increasingly integrated into a capitalist system of exchange. People in the whole world watch television, buy food, sweets and clothes in the shop: they consume. Through satisfying needs for food, clothes, etc. in culturally circumscribed ways, they communicate to others who they are – sometimes through conspicuous consumption. A theory which restricts itself to arguing that consumption amounts to the rational satisfaction of needs, not questioning how these needs are perceived locally, cannot explain why some prefer blue trousers to red ones, or why pictures of weeping Gypsy children are regarded as vulgar by the educated middle classes in Europe (Bourdieu 1984 [1979]). In order to find answers to this kind of question, an anthropological approach to the economy is necessary – it becomes necessary to study consumption as a cultural system.

With the emergence of an increasingly globalised world (Chapters 16–19), patterns of consumption seem to merge in certain respects; people nearly everywhere desire similar goods, from cellphones to ready-made garments. A precondition for this to happen is the more or less successful implementation of certain institutional dimensions of modernity, notably that of a monetary economy – if not necessarily evenly distributed wagework and literacy. The ever-increasing transnational flow of commodities, be they material or immaterial, creates a set of common cultural denominators which appear to eradicate local distinctions. The hot-dog (halal or not, as the case may be), the pizza and the hamburger (or, in India, the lamb-burger) are truly parts of world cuisine; identical pop songs are played in identical discotheques in Costa Rica and Thailand; the same Coca-Cola commercials are shown with minimal local variations at cinemas all over the world, Dan Brown volumes are ubiquitous wherever books are sold, and so on. Investment capital, military power and world literature are being disembedded from the constraints of space; they no longer belong to a particular locality. With the development of the jet plane, the satellite dish and more recently, the Internet, distance no longer seems a limiting factor for the flow of influence, investments and cultural meaning. At the same time it is necessary to be aware that, notwithstanding these flows, millions of people are wholly or partly left out of the world of transnational consumption: they have little or no purchasing power.

different?'), as well as addressing the perennial issue of fashioning context-free concepts that are useful for purposes of comparison. We shall keep the problem in mind while considering a few examples as well as some central issues in the anthropology of exchange.

THE ECONOMY AS PART OF A SOCIAL TOTALITY

The Trobriand Islanders are matrilineal, but virilocal horticulturalists. The first and most famous of Malinowski's monographs about this people, *Argonauts of the Western Pacific* (1984 [1922]) is chiefly a study of one of the most famous and striking social institutions in the region, namely the *kula* trade, which is a large-scale trade network in shell bracelets and necklaces. Not only the *kula* trade, but also other aspects of the Trobrianders' economy were the subject of great interest and wonder when Malinowski returned with his material from the islands after the First World War. He showed, contrary to widespread expectations, that 'savages' were by no means driven by lowly material needs in everything they did, that they had a sophisticated religion, and that a complex kinship system and a multitude of regulated practices upheld society and contributed to the fulfilment of far more needs than the purely biological ones. In *Argonauts*, Malinowski also argues against those who supposed that 'savages' were extremely 'rational' individualists who acted on pure, unmitigated self-interest. The Trobriander, he writes:

... works prompted by motives of a highly complex, social and traditional nature, and towards aims which are certainly not directed towards the satisfaction of present wants, or to the direct achievement of utilitarian purpose.... [A]ll, or almost all of the fruits of his work, and certainly any surplus which he can achieve by extra effort, goes not to the man himself, but to his relatives-in-law. (Malinowski 1984 [1922], p. 61)

Someone walking about in a Trobriand village just after harvesting will notice large heaps of yams displayed in front of many of the huts. This, as noted earlier, will not be the household's own produce, but rather obligatory gifts received from kin and (possibly) political clients. The size of these heaps of yams thereby gives an indication of who is particularly powerful in the community. Malinowski tells of an especially important chief in the village of Omarakana, who had 40 wives and received 30–50 per cent of the total production of yams in Kiriwina. The exchange of yams, in other words, does not just contribute to reproducing social bonds and ties of kinship, it also has an easily discernible, indeed physically visible political aspect.

In a capitalist economy, money is the common denominator for what is commonly thought of as economic activity, and it serves to single out an economic institution in those societies as something apparently separate from the rest of society. This kind of boundary may nevertheless be contested from an anthropological viewpoint, since it fails to include, for example, unpaid domestic work in the economy. The association of money with value (as in the term 'value creation') was, moreover, criticised already by Marx who, in the first chapter of *Capital* distinguished between exchange-value and use-value. The latter had no monetary equivalent; it was the value experienced through using (or consuming) an object or a service. As Graeber (2005) points out, anthropologists – like others – use the term value in three different ways, usually without distinguishing between them: (1) values in the philosophical or sociological sense (as in 'family values'), (2) value in the classic economic sense, and (3) value in a specific linguistic sense, where 'value' refers to 'a meaningful difference' (as in 'values of variables' in quantitative research). In other words, even in institutionally differentiated societies like ours, the economy has no objective boundaries.

In many societies, including the Trobriand Islands, there is no general term denoting the 'economy' as an institution separated from social life in general. When a man performs garden magic to make his yams grow, when he works hard for months just to give away his crop and when he exchanges shells with distant partners through the *kula* trade, he does not speak of this as an 'economic' activity: all of it is seen as a general part of his existence. With the Trobrianders, as with many other peoples, rights in women and children have an aspect which Westerners might call economic, since wives provide both labour and yams from one's affines. But nobody would claim that women and children, seen from the viewpoint of the Trobriand man, are solely an 'object of investment' to be regarded purely as an economic asset. When we single out the 'economic' aspect of the social life of the Trobrianders, therefore, this is in a sense an artificial abstraction, since it does not exist in Trobriand society itself. We nevertheless depend on this kind of abstraction for comparison to be possible in anthropology, even if it does not form part of native cultural categories.

In principle, a capitalist economy recognises only one form of commodity exchange, namely market exchange based on the laws of supply and demand. Among the Trobrianders, a multitude of forms of exchange (about 80, according to John Davis [1992]) are included in what we would translate as 'trade', and some of the most famous varieties are the following.

Gimwali is market exchange, reminiscent of capitalistic commodity exchange. Pigs, vegetables and other foodstuffs are traded and bargaining is accepted. *Laga* is payment for magical incantations bought from non-relatives. *Pokala* is usually a kind of tithe; yams or similar paid to one's social superiors. It can also refer to payment for magical incantations bought from relatives. *Sagal* is food which is distributed free of charge at public events such as funerals. *Urigubu* are yams given to one's sister's or mother's husband. *Wasi* is the exchange of fish for vegetables which takes place between coastal and inland villages.

Kula, finally, refers to the cyclical exchange of two kinds of valuables: shell necklaces and shell bracelets. The trade takes place over a large area of the south-western Pacific. The necklaces circulate clockwise, the bracelets anti-clockwise. The *kula* trade takes place both locally, within each island, and between the islands. The most valuable objects travel furthest. The people who travel with the shells are agents or partners of powerful men, usually aristocrats, in the various islands. *Kula* valuables are always named after their former owners.

It is difficult to argue that the *kula* trade is 'profitable' in a narrow economic sense. The rule is actually that one exchanges two objects of exactly the same value. When a deal is completed, one may keep the bracelet or necklace for a while – perhaps several years – before putting it into circulation again. What is the purpose of this trade?

Malinowski writes somewhere that the Trobrianders seem to exchange *kula* valuables 'for the sake of it', but elsewhere he argues that they have to be understood as token prestations, as a kind of symbolic valuable. He is not clear, however, as to what they symbolise. Pursuing the analysis of the *kula* trade further, Weiner (1988) argues that its main source of motivation is the quest for fame. The names of earlier owners are connected to *kula* shells, and the most valuable shells remain in circulation for a long time. In accordance with this reasoning, Jerry Leach (1982) has pointed out that the Trobrianders are generally proud of the existence of a book like *Argonauts of the Western Pacific*: like their own *kula* trade, this book contributes to increasing their fame. The *kula* trade, as with other forms of trade among the Trobrianders, may be classified as an economic activity, but its significance has ramifications far beyond what is usually thought of as the economy.

GIFTS AS TOTAL SOCIAL PHENOMENA

When a Trobriand Islander gives yams to his affines, he does not demand an immediate counter-prestation. The yams could thus be classified as a gift. The same could be said of the pocket money given by a European father to his daughter. She is not expected to pay it back. However, in both cases, the givers do anticipate some kind of counter-prestation. The Trobriander expects his affines to help him when necessary, and the European father may expect some kind of gratitude or even that the daughter will feel responsibility towards him when he grows old and frail.

Many of the world's economies, not least in Melanesia, have traditionally been described as 'gift economies' (Strathern 1988); that is to say that the distribution of goods takes place with no fixed price. Within the household and the lineage, goods are distributed according to individual needs and rights, and gifts are also an important means of making contact with outsiders: a means of creating peace, friendship or, as in the case of the Melanesian 'big man', political loyalty. If it is true that friends make gifts, Sahlins writes (1972, p. 186), gifts make friends as well. In societies where the exchange of gifts is very widespread, this contributes significantly to systemic integration. In a shrewd analysis of some of the categories of Norwegian culture, Eduardo Archetti (1991 [1984]) notes that whenever one buys a cup of coffee for someone in a university canteen, the recipient will hold out a few coins in payment the moment one returns with the drink. Archetti interprets this as an unwillingness to enter into a morally committing relationship with others. To accept the coffee as a gift would imply a vague debt of gratitude which Norwegians are reluctant to incur with new acquaintances.

Some criteria are necessary if a transaction is to be defined as gift-giving. Apart from the absence of a fixed price, the return gift or prestation should not be given at once. Only when these conditions are met is gift exchange socially integrating by its creation of webs of vague obligations on the part of large numbers of people. In some societies, such as the Polynesian ones Mauss describes in his famous essay on the gift (1954 [1924]), virtually everyone in a local community has vague long-term obligations towards each other, connected with gift exchange. Reciprocity can thus be seen as the 'glue' of society.

Gifts exchanged on an everyday basis between friends and relations are of a different kind to gifts exchanged publicly, which take on a political significance. For the latter, the term 'ceremonial gift exchange' may be appropriate, defined as a practice whereby which 'items of value are publicly displayed and given to partners on a reciprocal basis over time' (Strathern and Stewart 2005: 230).

The gift is a characteristic expression of reciprocity. The obligation to give implies the obligation to receive; the recipient again commits him- or herself to making a counter-prestation to the giver. The analytical interest of a gift thus lies chiefly in its social and cultural aspects, not in the purely economic aspect. Mauss describes a particularly important category of such gifts as *prestations totales* or total social phenomena: they involve the entire person and embody, by symbolic association, the totality of social relations and cultural values in society. Through such *prestations totales*, 'all kinds of institutions are simultaneously expressed: the religious, judicial, moral and economic' (Mauss 1954 [1924], p. 1). In modern societies, the exchange of wedding rings is, perhaps, the ultimate *prestation totale*.

POTLATCH, RECIPROCITY AND POWER

A famous social institution which was once widespread on the north-western coast of North America is known in the literature as 'potlatch' (Boas 1897; Mauss 1954 [1924]; Benedict 1970 [1934]). The potlatch was practised by Kwakiutl groups and their neighbours. These peoples were prosperous hunters and fishers, and lived in more hierarchical societies than is common among groups with this kind of livelihood. The aristocrats within the system continuously had to defend, and to try to improve, their relative rank by giving spectacular gifts to each other. This phenomenon, which could be described as competitive gift exchange, contains a mechanism for acceleration. When chief B received a gift from chief A, he would have to surpass the latter through his return gift. This competition could, in some cases, culminate in the destruction of considerable material wealth. Each winter the chiefs invited each other to large parties, where abundant food and drink were served and lavish presents were given to the guests. In addition, they destroyed valuables, throwing salt fish away and setting fire to tents and carpets; in the old days, Boas wrote around the year 1900, they even threw slaves into the sea to show off their wealth.

At the return party, the hosting chief would have to surpass the previous host in destructive capabilities. The chief who could afford to destroy the most achieved the highest rank in the regional hierarchy.

Institutions similar to the potlatch exist among many other peoples. The purpose of the waste is to establish a political hierarchy with oneself on top. Mauss (1954 [1924]) has identified a milder form of potlatch in the French custom of trying to surpass others by giving lavish wedding presents. Mauss describes the potlatch institution as a 'perverted' form of the more widespread phenomenon of reciprocity, an important social institution in all societies.

Mauss's essay on the gift has been extremely influential in later anthropological theorising on reciprocity and exchange. In Lévi-Strauss's theory of kinship (1969 [1949]; see also Chapter 8), a principal axiom is the universality of exchange, a notion indebted to Mauss, as a fundamental human mode of existence. Marriage systems, politics and everyday social interaction alike have been analysed in terms of exchange, both in Mauss's wide sociological sense and in a more restricted 'economic' sense, and this shows clearly the empirical shortcomings of a division of the social world into political, economic, religious and other 'sectors'.

In his studies of symbolic power, Pierre Bourdieu has also drawn on Mauss and the social logic of reciprocity. In his Kabyle ethnography (the Kabyles are Berbers in Algeria and Morocco), he describes a situation where 'the generalization of monetary exchange' enters into a relationship formerly defined through reciprocity:

[A] well-known mason, who had learnt his trade in France, caused a scandal, around 1955, by going home when his work was finished without eating the meal traditionally given in the mason's honour when a house is built, and then demanding, in addition to the price of his day's work (one thousand old francs), an allowance of two hundred francs in lieu of the meal. (Bourdieu 1977 [1972], p. 173)

Here, the mason was trying to convert a personal ritual gift to a decontextualised and quantifiable economic sum. Bourdieu explains that the mason thereby exposed 'the device most commonly employed to keep up appearances by means of a collectively concerted make-believe', the pretence that the economic transaction really amounted to a generous exchange of gifts. In pursuing this line of analysis, Bourdieu in a sense turns Mauss on his head, by focusing on the ways in which gifts and 'total social phenomena' conceal power relations and exploitative practices. Like Archetti's Norwegian in the university cafeteria, the mason insisted on market exchange rather than gift exchange.

The kind of social integration and mutual obligations created through reciprocity are not necessarily beneficial to everyone involved. Indeed, feudal lords in medieval Europe frequently sustained their power by offering gifts to their subjects. It could also be argued that development aid from North to South is a subtle technique of domination, intended to ensure the continued submission of Southern governments to global policies pursued by the rich countries. The former dictator of Uganda Idi Amin clearly understood this aspect of reciprocity when, some time in the 1970s, he was reported to have sent a shipload of bananas as emergency aid to crisis-stricken Britain.

In some interpretations of Mauss's work on gift-giving and reciprocity in general, the institution of the gift is seen as constitutive of society as such. While the principle of gift-giving is certainly important – Lévi-Strauss, it should be recalled, based his theory of kinship on it – Mauss did not see it as the only principle of integration. He also wrote on sacrifice (Hubert and Mauss 1964 [1898]; see also Chapter 14). The meaning of sacrifice, in Mauss's view, was to establish a particular kind of relationship to divine powers, but it also served to integrate society.

A more radical view was introduced in Annette Weiner's influential *Inalienable Possessions* (1992; see also Godelier 2009), which argues against the view usually associated with Mauss and Lévi-Strauss, according to which reciprocity is a fundamental social act. In Weiner's view, reciprocity and exchange can often be seen as surface phenomena that serve as a foil for the ultimate concern of the people concerned, which amounts to the protection and preservation of assets that are felt to represent their very personal identity – that is, their inalienable possessions.

FORMS OF DISTRIBUTION

Gifts are socially integrating at the same time as they define and reconfirm specified relationships between individuals. Commodity exchange in a capitalist system works in a different way. When buying food at the supermarket, it is exceedingly likely that one will not remember the face of the cashier later; or if you do, she is unlikely to remember you, having received payment from hundreds of customers during the week.

In an important study aiming at explaining the historical transition to capitalism, Karl Polanyi (1957 [1944]) distinguishes between three different principles in the circulation of material goods, or forms of distribution: reciprocity, redistribution and market exchange. Reciprocity is the dominant principle of distribution in gift economies such as those found in the egalitarian societies of Melanesia. Such communities are to a great extent integrated through the principle of reciprocity; through those mutual obligations created by gift-giving.

Redistribution means that a central actor (such as a chief or a state adminis-tration) receives goods from the members of society, which he commits himself to redistribute to them. This kind of system confirms and strengthens the legitimacy of the ruler, as well as creating a social safety net for the needy. Redistribution is thus centralised and can be described as a hierarchical principle of distribution, whereas reciprocity is a decentralised, egalitarian principle of distribution.

The third form of distribution is the market principle, which is based on a contractual relationship between the exchangers. The market is anonymous and involves abstract rules about contractual liberty (that is, one can choose one's trading partners). It normally creates an impersonal form of interaction.

Although the market principle dominates in modern capitalist societies, redistribution in feudal societies and reciprocity in egalitarian small-scale societies, in Polanyi's scheme one form of distribution does not exclude the others. In most societies, all three principles are at work in different situations and different social fields, as witnessed in the Trobriand example, although their relative significance varies. Polanyi's point is that the principles of distribution are adapted to fit very different kinds of society.

In Polanyi's and Sahlins's view (Sahlins 1972), the redistribution principle supports a centralised and hierarchical political structure, while the market principle is capable of integrating an enormous number of people in a single web of exchange as it is anonymous and based on abstract rules, and reciprocity proper creates solidarity on the basis of horizontal interpersonal obligations. As Bourdieu's Algerian example shows, however, this kind of typology makes sense only at an idealised model level since all societies embody a variety of exchange forms. Looking at contemporary urban society, it is also easy to see that all three principles are at work. Reciprocity is alive and well among friends and relatives; redistribution takes place through the agency of the state; and the market principle regulates exchange in most other realms. Add to this the fact that every society has an informal sector (Hart 1973, 1999) which is only partly monetarised, where services and goods are exchanged between acquaintances outside of the formal economy – this could be anything from helping one's brother-in-law build a garage to buying drugs on the street – and the picture becomes more complex still.

MONEY

Reciprocity, or gift exchange, is more important as an economic institution in kinship-based societies than in modern state societies, and can be a key to an understanding of fundamental differences. However, what we may think of as market exchange is certainly not uniform either, and it functions in different ways in different societies.

In most places, there are rules regulating what can be sold and purchased and what cannot. Even in modern capitalist societies, there is general agreement that there are values which cannot be bought – love, friendship and loyalty, for example. Still, it is easy to see that the scope of a capitalist market economy is much greater than that of a village market; not only with respect to its scale and the selection of goods, but also in the sense that all commodities are comparable: they are measured on a shared scale, namely that of money. A collection of short stories becomes 'equivalent' to two pints of bitter because they have the same price (or exchange value, in the Marxist terminology). Money renders different goods and services comparable by measuring their value on a shared scale.

As the example of the Trobriand Islands shows, the exchange of goods and services may be much more complicated than this and may thus involve a wider repertoire of social relationships. How can three hours of work be compared with a suckling pig or a bag of rice if one cannot measure them on a common scale? In many traditional societies, barter has been a common form of exchange. 'Primitive money', or special-purpose money, has also been widespread, the functions of which are reminiscent of money in modern societies. In large parts of pre-colonial West Africa, cowrie shells functioned as a kind of money, insofar as one could buy food and other subsistence items for them. The sale and purchase of labour and land, however, are frequently unthinkable in traditional societies, where land is tied to the kin group and labour cannot be measured (not least because time cannot be measured on a shared, objectified scale; see Chapter 15). Special-purpose money has functioned as a means of payment in a restricted way: some, but not all material goods and services could be mediated by them. Thus special-purpose money, unlike the general-purpose money characteristic of the contemporary world, has not functioned as a value standard: it has not been capable of measuring and comparing all kinds of material goods and services on a common scale.

In traditional societies, there are often different categories of goods that are incommensurable in value, that circulate in different, relatively closed spheres. We now turn to considering an example of such an economy and its transformation, which also gives an indication of general changes taking place in traditional subsistence economies being integrated into the capitalist system of production and exchange.

ECONOMIC SPHERES AMONG THE TIV

The Tiv are traditionally farmers who live in the savannah belt of central-eastern Nigeria (Bohannan and Bohannan 1953; P. Bohannan 1959). They are patrilineal and also transfer land rights along the patrilineage. As in many other kinship-based societies, it was not possible for Tiv to buy and sell land before colonialism, since the land ultimately belonged to the ancestors. Personal identity was, as one might expect, intimately tied to the lineage land.

The Tiv grew cereals, fruit and vegetables and kept livestock. They produced food for subsistence in addition to a surplus which was either redistributed or sold in the market. Their system of distribution was multicentric, which is to say that economic resources were distributed according to different principles and did not form a uniform 'single market'. (The opposite of a multicentric economy is a unicentric system, where one institution, usually the market, dominates completely.)

Until about the Second World War, the Tiv had three economic spheres, or centres, in their economy. They were ranked morally. The lowest was the subsistence sphere, where cereals and other foodstuffs, kitchen utensils, spices and tools circulated. These commodities were exchanged in the market and were thus commensurable: they were the same kind of products.

The second sphere was the prestige sphere. Here cattle, brass rods, magical paraphernalia, slaves and a highly valued, imported textiles circulated. In this sphere, brass rods functioned as a means of payment.

The third and highest sphere was where women and children were exchanged. Generally, a person could only be paid for with another person. If my lineage received a woman from yours, you could only be repaid with another woman from my lineage. Payment, obviously, did not have to take place immediately.

Within each sphere, exchange was considered morally neutral, which was to say that someone did not become subject to condemnation for exchanging fowls for pots, or brass rods for magical aids. Problems arose only with exchange *between* the spheres, when values were converted. Since there was no common denominator encompassing all three spheres, there were no rules as to the amount of subsistence goods required to pay for prestige goods. It was considered foolish and irresponsible to convert downwards, selling off brass rods for grain, for example – this was possible, but not a well-advised thing to do. Prestige objects were an indication of symbolic capital and were comparable to, say, aristocratic titles in Britain or France, or ritual purity in Hindu society. To rid oneself of brass rods therefore entailed a qualitatively different loss than selling off one's agricultural surplus. Similarly, only a desperate lineage would sell off its women for brass rods, since the ultimate aim of Tiv men was to have as many wives and children as possible.

With the effective colonisation of the interior of Nigeria from the early twentieth century onwards, great changes took place in Tiv society. The colonial government created a peaceful situation (*pax Britannica*) enabling villagers to extend trade networks over much larger areas than had been possible earlier. The Tiv now had access to hitherto unknown imported goods, and trade became on the whole much more important than it had been formerly. Many Tiv left the subsistence economy entirely and became small capitalist farmers producing specialised crops, notably sesame seeds, for the international market. Those crops were sold for money (general-purpose money, that is pounds and shillings), which was now spent on food and other necessities.

The introduction of general-purpose money had important consequences for Tiv society, and the monetary economy proved to be irreconcilable with the former, rigid distinction between spheres of circulation. Money entered the system at all levels, and in a matter of a few years, all sorts of commodities alike could be measured on a common scale. By the 1950s, Paul Bohannan reports (1959), the Tiv used money as a value standard even when engaged in direct barter: even when they exchanged 10 lbs of tomatoes directly for a chicken, they agreed that the price for both was 5 shillings and that they were therefore equivalent. Money, in other words, became a common denominator for all goods. Eventually bridewealth began to be paid in cash. Many felt this was a devaluation of women, since the new practice indicated that they were a commodity of the same kind as pots and chickens.

In accordance with the distinction between actor perspectives and systemic perspectives employed elsewhere, it should be noted that Bohannan's analysis of change in Tiv society represents a typical systemic perspective. Change, in his analysis, is caused by exogenous factors (outside factors) modifying the system as a whole. In an actor-oriented analysis of the breakdown of economic spheres in another African society, the Fur in western Sudan, Barth (1967) instead emphasises endogenous factors of change. He shows how an enterprising individual (an entrepreneur) discovers new, profitable ways of exchanging goods through conversion between spheres, and the result is roughly the same as in Tiv society; a breakdown of the moral economy, and the universalisation of the market principles of monetary exchange based on supply and demand. As usual, both the actor-centred and the systemic perspective can be illuminating in understanding social process.

It would be too facile to draw the conclusion, on the basis of Bohannan's rendering of changes in the Tiv system of exchange, that the monetary principle (or 'general-purpose money') is inevitably 'morally bad'. Its spread has different consequences in different societies and for different persons, and an implication of Bourdieu's argument is that monetary exchange liberates the exchangers from the web of moral obligations, including hierarchy, entailed in reciprocity. Instead, monetary exchange creates new hierarchies. Social disruption is not necessarily undesirable and it may entail a liberation from feudal bonds. In several European societies, a change in domestic reciprocity relations has led to changes in the marriage institution since the 1960s. It is evident that the sharp increase in divorces is connected with the increased economic independence of women: they now earn their own money and are no longer forced into webs of reciprocity with male breadwinners. Many of the women concerned perceive this as an improvement. The same could be said of the challenges posed to the institution of arranged marriages in the Middle East, South Asia and among immigrants in Europe. In some segments of these populations, particularly in the middle classes, young men and women are no longer willing to be exchanged by their kin groups. Insofar as they are economically independent of their families because of participation in the capitalist labour market, they may actually marry on the basis of individual choice rather than being part of a family-based system of exchange. Although it may certainly be relevant to evaluate the moral and political aspects of a transition from a subsistence economy to capitalism – and the change has certainly been disastrous for many, not least Africans – the initial anthropo-logical task lies in mapping out the social and cultural consequences of the changes, not in grading them on a moral scale.

MONEY AS INFORMATION TECHNOLOGY

The collapse of the economic spheres, or the moral economy, of the Tiv entailed a wider comparability of values formerly regarded as incommensurable, as different in kind. The economy thereby lost its moral character and was gradually disengaged from the cultural values which had originally constituted it. Pure market principles of supply and demand replaced rules of right and wrong as well as distinctions between 'high' and 'low' values. Because of the introduction of general-purpose, universal money, however, the Tiv were also enabled to communicate economically through trade on a much larger scale than before. The brass rods, the former special-purpose money of the Tiv, had no value outside their tribal area, whereas pounds sterling (and later Nigerian nairas) had the same value over an enormous area. The sesame seeds grown by a Tiv after the introduction of general-purpose money could be sold to a wholesale retailer in the nearest city and might eventually end up on a breakfast table in Birmingham. For their own part, the Tiv could from now on buy, say, printed T-shirts and radios for money; goods which could not be bought for brass rods. With the introduction of general-purpose money, the Tiv thereby became integrated into a global system of production, distribution and consumption.

The economy of any society is always part of a wider social and cultural context, and the introduction of general-purpose money in any society, including Tiv society, has profound consequences. As noted, money challenged the traditional value hierarchy, altered the pattern of agricultural production and led to changes in marketing strategies and in consumption. Money was the medium enabling (or forcing) the Tiv to become economically integrated on a larger scale. In this way, money may be regarded as a form of information technology. The brass rods also had this function, but on a much more local scale. Money is impersonal and anonymous. It can be accumulated and invested. It makes communication and exchange on a vast scale possible: I can draw money from my bank account from a bank or ATM in any country in the world, and the money is a common denominator making it possible to compare a vast number of goods and services of the most diverse origins. Perhaps it could be said that the relationship between money and brass rods is comparable to the relationship between television and personal conversation? It is certainly no coincidence that the spread of the monetary economy has usually been concomitant with the spread of state institutions, literacy and quantified, linear time, all of which can be seen as standardising devices accompanying the transition from small-scale to large-scale integration.

Money is not a mere medium of exchange, a value standard and a means of payment; it also facilitates comparison across formerly separated domains and communication. As observed by Hart (2005, p. 172): 'Mauss was far-sighted when he sought to trace the foundations of the modern [monetary] economy back to its origin in the gift, rather than barter.'

THE MEANING OF ARTEFACTS

Clearly, as Appadurai (1986, p. 5) observes, 'things have no meaning apart from those that human transactions, attributions and motivations endow them with'. Their meaning thus varies cross-culturally and, moreover, 'abstract objects' such as words or services may take on the character of goods or commodities. In the Trobriand Islands, for example, magical incantations are inherited and sometimes purchased. There is no easy answer to the question of what turns an object (or non-material resource) into a commodity, but, as the earlier discussions on exchange, gifts and trade have shown, a study of the circulation of goods (in the wide sense, encompassing non-material valuables) can be highly illuminating. Since commodities are by definition scarce (Georg Simmel, quoted in Appadurai 1986, p. 3, says that 'we call those objects valuable that resist our desire to possess them'), the circulation of goods tells us about the cultural values dominant in a society. In the famous introductory chapters to *Capital*, Marx (1906 [1867]) describes how commodification entails the exchangeability and comparability of highly different objects, and several writers inspired by him, including György Lukács (1971 [1923]) and Jürgen Habermas (1967), have written about the spread of the commodity logic in modern society; how the market principle enters into a variety of social relationships formerly organised according to a different, more 'human' logic, and thereby contributes to social alienation and 'commodity fetishism'.

Contemporary anthropological perspectives on commodity circulation and consumption tend to differ from this line of thought, focusing not on alienation but rather on the ways in which commodities mediate and define social relationships and self-identity – in other words, their cultural meaning and social significance. Referring *inter alia* to Bohannan's study of economic spheres among the Tiv, Appadurai (1986) introduces the concept of regimes of value, which he defines as systems within which there are more or less consistently shared notions of value and exchangeability. Several such regimes may coexist within any society. Economic spheres clearly constitute such discrete regimes of value, but it is also obvious that many other distinct regimes exist in modern capitalist societies as well. Bourdieu (1988 [1984]) has analysed academia as an arena for the exchange of prestige and power, which thereby makes up a field in which only a minority of the population participate. Studying regimes of value can thus be a strategy for exploring diversity in a society, since the concept presupposes that there is no uniformity in the evaluation of commodities.

Although there is a calculative dimension present in all exchange, as both Appadurai (1986) and other anthropologists of consumption, such as Daniel Miller (1987, 2009), acknowledge, it cannot be divorced from its cultural content and social implications. On the one hand, objects and artefacts form part of the taken-for-granted part of our environment and thereby contribute to shaping our habitus – they 'order people' (Miller 1994, p. 404); on the other hand, they are consciously selected through consumption to create meaning and a particular self-identity. In a study of an English working-class housing estate, Miller (1988) shows how interior decorating conveys very specific messages about the people who live in each flat. The kitchens, which were initially identical, have been shaped self-consciously by their inhabitants, who, using standardised products available in shops, combine them in personal ways to express their individuality. Rather than seeing them as the alienated victims of 'commodity fetishism' (the orthodox Marxist view), Miller analyses the consumers as conscious actors who appropriate the material culture of their environment to strengthen their own sense of personhood and identity. Viewed in this way, things become important elements in cultural projects; they objectify social relationships and hierarchies, are used in the articulation of self-identity, are variously interpreted by different persons, and contribute to defining social relationships. Social and personal memory can also be embedded in artefacts; not just in tombstones and cathedrals, but also in mundane objects like 'old beer cans, matchbooks and comic books' (Kopytoff 1986, p. 80). In Miller's words (1994), 'commodities as well as gifts have the capacity to construct cultural projects wherein there is no simple dichotomy between things and persons'. In his later *A Theory of Shopping* (1998), Miller argues against what he sees as common, misleading views of consumption in modern society as an egotistic form of behaviour. Basing his argument largely on fieldwork among London housewives, he shows that their shopping expeditions are motivated by emotional concern for others; indeed, that shopping often satisfies the requirements of the Maussian total prestation. The longest chapter in his book is, tellingly, entitled 'Making Love in Supermarkets'.

CONSUMPTION AND GLOBALISATION

Far from being a mere matter of survival or maximisation, consumption can be seen as an integral dimension of what it means to be human. Whether mediated by a monetary economy or not, the exchange of goods and services, as Mauss saw so clearly, is fundamental for the development of trust, mutual obligations and myriad social relationships. While consumption creates differences and differentiation, it also creates solidarity and reinforces social ties as well as cultural meanings.

Anthropological research on consumption teases out the cultural meanings of what may appear hedonistic behaviour at a first glance, and it often arrives at surprising conclusions. Take, for example, the commonly held view that globalisation, in the world of goods, is a kind of Americanisation which threatens diversity and local cultural values; the global dissemination of American films, popular music, fast food and so on is seen as a – if not *the* – main form of cultural globalisation. However, the standardised American forms witnessed in the critiques of 'Disneyisation' and 'McDonaldisation' are not representative of the actual flow of commodities in the world. In fact, not even phenomena usually seen as typically American are necessarily American (Marling 2006). Fastfood restaurants are widespread worldwide, but rarely market-dominant, and not all the largest fastfood corporations are American; Compass, for example, is British. 7-Eleven is owned by Japanese. Volkswagen sells more cars in China than any American car maker, and Toyota is the third largest selling car make in the USA itself. Although American companies are market-dominant in some areas, such as computers and the media and entertainment world, this does not hold true as a general statement. Miller (2001) describes a family scene from somewhere in the Third World where the children are watching Pokémon on TV, their father has finally been able to afford a new Mercedes-Benz, and the adults celebrate with bottles of whisky. As a matter of fact, neither the car, the TV show nor the beverage have anything to do with the USA.

Although forms of consumption often described as 'Western' symbolise modern success in much of the world, the actual origins of the goods and services consumed varies hugely. Tracing the itinerary of Hindi films around the world, Brian Larkin shows not only how popular these films are among youths in Indonesia, Senegal, Nigeria and elsewhere, but also how local filmmakers, for example in northern Nigeria, 'borrow plots and styles from Bombay cinema' (2003: 171). In fact, Hindi ('Bollywood') films have been the most popular foreign films in northern Nigeria since the 1960s.

Even commodities that do have an American origin do not necessarily lead to 'Americanisation' in the sense of obliterating the local. Anthropologists have written about the *indigenisation of modernity*, arguing that foreign artefacts and practices are incorporated into pre-existing worlds of meaning, modifying these life-worlds somewhat, but not homogenising them (Sahlins 1994). Many of the dimensions of modernity seen as uniform worldwide, such as bureaucracies, markets, computer networks and human rights discourses, always take on a distinctly local character, not to mention consumption: a trip to McDonald's triggers an entirely different set of cultural connotations in Amsterdam from those triggered in Chicago, not to mention Beijing.

Or Moscow. As shown by Melissa Caldwell (2004), McDonald's restaurants became a familiar and popular fixture in the daily life of Russians with astonishing speed after the opening of the first outlet in 1990. Surprisingly, 'Muscovites have incorporated McDonald's into the more intimate and sentimental spaces of their personal lives: family celebrations, cuisine and discourses about what it means to be Russian today' (Caldwell 2004: 6). In her words, Russians have 'domesticated' the archetypal symbol of Americanness and made it a Russian one.

Examples of such appropriations of foreign goods and services are ubiquitous in the contemporary world. What may appear as dramatic cultural transformations, may not be perceived as such. Amazonian peoples who may have been contacted by the outside world only a decade ago, are perfectly at ease having swapped their body paint for Manchester United T-shirts, and do not see it as 'Westernisation' or even change. To them, change would mean a transformation of their relationship to each other, such as being forced to disperse, engage in migrant labour and so on. This would also be a valid perspective on the Pokémon-watching, whisky-drinking elite invoked above: insofar as their new patterns of consumption do not interfere with the fundamental structure of their relationships to each other, they do not lead to radical cultural change.

Similar points are made in Harold Wilhite's (2008) study of consumption in contemporary Kerala, but Wilhite takes the argument one step further to show that the uneven distribution of modern consumer goods has created new divisions in Keralan society based on the conflicting criteria of caste and wealth, and he also discusses the ways in which consumption is a controversial theme in Indian public life, where many argue that the ancient Hindu values of frugality and modesty are declining owing to the spread of mass consumption.

A RECONSIDERATION OF EXCHANGE

In the anthropological literature, it has been common to contrast 'the West' and 'the Rest' with regard to the logic of exchange (for a classic study, see Sahlins 1972). It should therefore be emphasised that the picture is less clear-cut than the previous discussion may suggest. Reciprocity and market exchange are not mutually exclusive, nor is it easy to draw a clear distinction between them. As Sahlins (1994) himself has noted in an essay on economic and cultural change in the Pacific, tribal peoples in highland New Guinea have by now become wageworkers, and money has bridged the boundaries between formerly discrete spheres. However, he adds, the highlanders do not invest the money chiefly in radios, cassette recorders and other paraphernalia of modernity, but in traditional institutions. The money may, for instance, enable them to sacrifice more pigs to the ancestors than they were formerly able to. We should not believe, therefore, that the introduction of a new economic system necessarily kills the old one, or that societies are either 'traditional' or 'modern'. Similarly, research on consumption in affluent societies also shows that there is no necessary opposition between consumption in a capitalist market economy and retention of valued social relationships, cultural values or personal identity.

A different, perhaps more fundamental critique of the classic dichotomy between reciprocity and market exchange is represented in an essay by John Davis (1992), who argues forcefully and elegantly against what he sees as an arbitrary distinction between gift-giving and market exchange. He is sympathetic to the project initiated by Mauss and developed further by Sahlins (1972), where the wider social and cultural contexts of exchange are revealed and where it is shown that non-industrial economies must be understood in cultural terms. However, Davis sees a shortcoming in that anthropologists, while showing the limitations of economic science when applied to non-industrial societies, have not developed similar cultural accounts of exchange in modern industrial ones. After discussing some of the forms of exchange made famous in Malinowski's studies of the Trobriands, he thus goes on to show that there are indeed at least as many distinct cultural categories of exchange in British culture (Figure 12.1), each of them associated with a particular, culturally based evaluation. Quite contrary to those who complain of the 'commercialisation of Christmas', Davis is 'rather pleased since it seems to me that it could be put the other way around: it could be an instance of the gifting of the market, and could be a demonstration of the instability of markets relative to the continuing strength of gift-giving' (1992, p. 53). Reciprocity is also an important part of everyday social interaction in any society, perhaps especially significant in the household. Davis's essay is a contribution to the ongoing anthropological project of deconstructing simplistic boundaries between 'us' and 'them', 'moderns' and 'traditionals', '*Gemeinschaft*' and '*Gesellschaft*'; in Appadurai's words, 'to restore the cultural dimension to societies that are too often represented simply as economies writ large, and to restore the calculative dimension to societies that are too often simply portrayed as solidarity writ small' (1986, p. 12).

alms-giving	expropriation	reciprocity
altruism	extortion	renting
arbitrage	futures trading	retailing
banking	giving	robbery
barter	huckstering	scrounging
bribery	insider dealing	shoplifting
burglary	insurance	shopping
buying/selling	marketing	simony
charity	money-lending	social wage
commodity-dealing	mortgaging	swapping
corruption	mugging	theft
donation	pawning	tipping
employment	profiteering	trading
exploitation	prostitution	wholesaling

Figure 12.1   Part of the British repertoire of exchange types
(Source: Davis 1992b, p. 29)

This does not mean that all systems of exchange are 'the same'. The breakdown of the 'economic spheres' among the Tiv and other peoples was an irreversible change with profound social implications. The generalisation of monetary exchange certainly does alter social relations and social scale, but its local importance needs to be studied empirically. In the next chapter, we consider social and cultural implications of changes in a different aspect of what we call economy, namely production.

SUGGESTIONS FOR FURTHER READING

Arjun Appadurai, ed.: *The Social Life of Things: Commodities in Cultural Perspective*. Cambridge: Cambridge University Press 1986.
John Davis: *Exchange*. Buckingham: Open University Press 1992.
Keith Hart: *The Memory Bank: Money in an Unequal World*. London: Profile 1999.
Daniel Miller: *Stuff*. Cambridge: Polity 2009.
Marshall D. Sahlins: *Stone Age Economics*. Chicago: Aldine 1972.

13   PRODUCTION, NATURE AND TECHNOLOGY

We live in a consumer society. I am quite sure that we will dispose of the 'natural peoples' when it becomes clear that they do not fulfil the intellectuals' demands for purity, that they do not incarnate Nature, but rather in many respects are more 'artificial' and 'civilised' than ourselves.

— *Hans Peter Duerr*

HUMANITY'S EXCHANGE WITH NATURE

The idea that there is an interrelationship between ecological conditions and ways of life can be traced back to the ancient Greeks, and it was also prevalent in Enlightenment thought in the mid eighteenth century (for instance in Montesquieu and in the Marquis de Sade's non-pornographic writings). Montesquieu, like many others, held that the main cause of Europe's technological and scientific advances was the harsh climate, which required the inhabitants to be inventive and sharp-witted to survive. Two centuries later, the human geographer Ellsworth Huntington (1945) argued for climatic determinism in an original study where he shows, among other things, the statistical correlation between rainy days and book lending at libraries in Boston. On sunny days, the inhabitants of Boston tended not to borrow books. (In other words, according to this simple model: too much sun appears to make people uninterested in intellectual pursuits.) Even today, many non-Africans assume that Africans never invented the combustion engine and the microchip because their material survival was so easy that they never 'had to use their brains'. Darwin, by contrast, argued already in the 1870s that even humans living in the 'state of nature' would need to be sharp-witted, inventive and intellectually alert to survive.

From a comparativist perspective, it is easy to argue against simple climatic determinism, the idea that one single causal factor (in this case ecological conditions) can account for the principal cultural variations in the world. For one thing, there are other regions in the world with climatic conditions comparable to those prevalent in Europe, in pre-conquest North America and south-eastern Australia, for example, which did not develop along the same lines. In Indonesia, under roughly the same ecological conditions, there are rice cultivators, horticulturalists and hunters and gatherers.

There is no simple causal link between ecological conditions and social organisation. However, there is no doubt that nature – in both senses of the

System Theory and Ecology

Ecological analyses were originally developed as a part of biological science, as a method for the description and analysis of processes and interrelationships in nature. However, ecological ways of thinking are also applied in other fields than biological nature. The Chicago sociologist Robert Park thus developed an 'urban ecology' in the 1920s, using ecological models to describe ethnic dynamics in Chicago. A couple of decades later, cybernetics and systems theory were developed as general, abstract theories about how systems work in general. A central idea in Gregory Bateson's work (1972, 1979) is the notion that very different kinds of systems function according to the same general principles. Writing on communication among dolphins, schizophrenia, biological evolution and initiation in New Guinea, Bateson consistently argues that very different phenomena are connected by an underlying pattern – which could be a metaphor, a kind of process, formal commonalities or something similar. He and other system theorists have struggled to depict culture and society as a continuous process.

Many anthropologists see system theory as an alternative to models focusing on form and classification, seeing it as a method for the conceptualisation of social life as something dynamic and continuously changing (e.g. Ingold 2002). Others criticise system theory for dealing inadequately with power and intentionality.

It is necessary to distinguish sharply between ecological analyses dealing with biological processes, and those applying ecological thinking to other domains. In the latter case, ecological models are used metaphorically as models, in about the same way as some structural-functionalists used biological models of the integration of organisms as metaphors for the integration of societies.

word (see Chapter 4) – limits the number of options available to humanity. If it is true that our inner nature is identical everywhere (this is the principle of the mental unity of humanity), that is certainly not the case with respect to external nature. If the climate is temperate, one cannot grow bananas; if it is sub-Arctic, one cannot even grow wheat. But there is no one-to-one relationship between ecological conditions and society: any ecosystem offers several different possibilities, although it also inevitably excludes some.

CULTURAL ECOLOGY

Cultural ecology is largely an American speciality in anthropology; it is associated with Julian Steward and Leslie White, who were particularly influential in the 1950s and 1960s. British anthropology has tended to stress the primacy of social organisation, while continental European anthropology, notably in France, has generally been more concerned with questions of cognition and symbolisation than with ecological determinants. As pointed out by Kuper (1994), cultural ecology can be traced back to Darwin and (to a lesser extent) to Marx, and is an entirely different research programme from both Boasian relativism (where culture is more or less *sui generis* or self-generating) and British social anthropology, which harks back to the sociological schools of Durkheim and Weber. White, who reacted against the culturalist and sometimes psychological bent of the Boasians, proposed ambitious theories of cultural evolution, where the level of development was seen as a function of the amount of energy harnessed by a society from its surroundings (White 1949). Although this view represents a rather crude view of cultural evolution, White at the same time regarded culture as an autonomous realm (an often neglected aspect of White's thought explored by one of his most famous students, namely Marshall Sahlins, in *Culture and Practical Reason* [1976]). In Steward's writings (e.g. 1955), cultural ecology is a doctrine about cultural evolution, seen as a result of the interaction between different kinds of material factors: demography, ecology and technology. Unlike the Marxists, Steward did not regard relations of production as decisive. In his general model of cultural evolution, he distinguishes between different levels of sociocultural integration, by which he means roughly the same thing as I have earlier described as small and large scale, namely varying size and complexity of societies. In Steward's scheme, however, material factors determine a society's level of sociocultural integration. The lowest level of integration, exemplified by the Shoshonean Indians in his own work, was that of the family. The highest level was that of the state. Steward, further, distinguished between a culture's *core* and 'the rest of culture'. The core elements pertained to the material processes of subsistence and determined important aspects of social organisation.

CULTURAL ECOLOGY AND MARXISM

In one of his most deterministic – and most famous – statements, Marx wrote that whereas the hand mill creates a society led by feudal landlords, the steam mill creates a society led by industrial capitalists. A cultural ecologist might, perhaps, retort that whereas a tropical savannah creates societies of pastoralists and millet-growers, a tropical rainforest creates societies of hunter-gatherers and horticulturalists.

There are several interesting parallels between cultural ecology and Marxism. Both schools emphasise the importance of material factors in social and cultural change, and both turn against sociobiology and would argue that 'human nature' can be moulded in an almost infinite number of different ways by interacting with the environment. Both emphasise the importance of factors located outside human consciousness.

The key difference between the two schools of thought concerns the role of human agency and social contradiction. In Marxism, the main contradictions in society are seen to lie in the social organisation of the relationship between technology and property, between labour and capital (in capitalist societies); and the chief driving force in history is class struggle. Cultural ecologists would rather focus on the interaction between demographic factors, ecological adaptation and technology in their accounts of historical change.

The Marxian criticism of Malthus may illustrate this important difference. In an early, hugely influential demographic study, Thomas Malthus (1982 [1798]) wished to show that population growth necessarily led to impoverishment. His fundamental idea was that whereas food production grew arithmetically (1, 2, 3, 4, etc.), the population grew geometrically or exponentially (1, 2, 4, 8, etc.). Marx and Engels accused Malthus of treating human beings as mere objects and societies as static. Instead of the Malthusian concept of overpopulation, Marx proposed the notion of 'relative overpopulation', which occurs when the productive forces (technology plus raw materials) are unable to satisfy human needs. The densely populated Japanese archipelago is poor in natural resources, but is nevertheless able to give its 130 million inhabitants one of the highest material standards of living in the world, thanks to the advanced forces of production there. Malthus's formula is misleading because, unlike Marxist and sociocultural analyses, it does not take technological innovations into account. The 'green revolution' beginning in the 1970s, for example, where new cereal breeds were introduced, led to a spectacular growth in Indian food production, enabling India to feed its growing population more successfully than anyone had expected during the famines of the 1950s and 1960s.

In this sense, the Marxists, who stress the primacy of the social over the environmental, have won over the cultural ecologists. On the other hand, the ecological crisis of the present time suggests that there are upper limits as to the size of the population the world is capable of supporting, certainly if most of them want a TV set and a motor vehicle, and in this respect, an ecological concept of absolute overpopulation can be helpful as a supplement to the sociological concept of relative overpopulation. Marx did not predict such a development; to him, natural resources were free, and there is a conspicuous lack of environmental concerns in his writings.

Both Marxism and cultural ecology raise ambitious and fascinating questions about the relationship between the factors that shape people's lives, and they propose very powerful explanatory schemes. I should therefore say a few words to explain why this book has not been written in the spirit of either Marxism or cultural ecology. First, both schools give marginal attention to factors associated with human consciousness. Partly for this reason, they tend towards functionalist explanations and also tend to leave out much of what is the very stuff of anthropology, namely cultural projects driven by human intentionality and shaped by the 'sedimented' social institutions and cultural norms of the past. Second, there is a tendency to the effect that grand theories of this kind reduce a multitude of cultural and social processes to dependent variables – to products of 'objective' factors. In this way, there is a real risk of losing the highly complex interplay between a variety of factors, which takes on specific and sometimes unique forms in different societies. It is quite clear that if we see cultural ecology and Marxism as general theories of society and culture, neither of the two is capable of accounting for all aspects of culture, society and cultural variation – including the phenomena that most anthropologists wish to explore. By embracing such powerful, all-encompassing theories wholesale, one runs the risk of using a bulldozer where a teaspoon might have been the appropriate tool.

A commonly invoked criticism of cultural ecology, moreover, is its tendency to apply a vocabulary borrowed from natural science to human societies. Peoples thereby become 'populations', human agency becomes 'behaviour' and the technical terms, while they look scientific, do not give a clear understanding of phenomena to do with consciousness, interaction and intentionality (Ardener 1989; Ingold 1994a). Of course, humans, like other organisms, are subject to natural laws, and many social and cultural anthropologists could benefit from learning more natural science, particularly ecology and evolutionary theory. But humans also place themselves outside these laws; they reflect, classify and theorise on the very laws that are believed to govern their lives, and this complicates matters seriously for someone who enters the study of human relations armed with a vocabulary developed for the study of insects and other non-verbal creatures. Perhaps, indeed, cultural ecology teaches us relatively little about ecology but rather more about culture? Consider this example.

THE WET AND THE DRY

'Whatever Morocco and Indonesia might have in common –' writes Geertz (1972, p. 24), 'Islam, poverty, nationalism, authoritarian rule, overpopulation, clean air, spectacular scenery, and a colonial past – the one thing they do not have in common is climate.'

Indonesia is wet, and Morocco is dry. With this contrast as a starting-point, Geertz discusses differences of social organisation in a Moroccan and an Indonesian (Balinese) locality. First, it is obvious that farmers in the two societies must grow different crops. The Moroccans studied by Geertz cultivate wheat and olives; the Balinese grow rice in irrigated paddies. Water is a scarce and costly resource in Morocco, while it is free and abundant in Bali. Southern Bali is criss-crossed with systems of irrigation canals, while such systems are scattered and clearly delineated in Morocco. What are the consequences of these simple differences for social organisation?

The Balinese irrigation systems are organised through *subaks*, irrigation cooperatives led by elected foremen. All owners of land automatically become members of the local *subak*, and are joint owners of the canal network. Although farmers each grow their rice independently, irrigation and maintenance of the canals has to be organised centrally. This is the role of the *subak*, which calls for coordination and cooperation. Geertz also argues that religion and ritual life are intimately linked with rice cultivation and the growth cycle of the plant. In an earlier study (Geertz 1963), he further argued that similar patterns appeared at a variety of levels in Javanese society (organised along similar lines as the Balinese), namely what he called 'involution' or the tendency to intensify and elaborate inwards instead of expanding outwards. This was necessary in the economy owing to the lack of available land combined with population growth; however, Geertz found the same kind of process in Javanese religion, poetry and music.

The Moroccans relate to water in a very different way from the Balinese. Not unexpectedly, the situation is one of stark competition over water rights between families. The wells are few and scattered, and the population is also much more scattered than in Bali.

In principle, water is individually owned, but since several families have to share the same well, ownership of water in practice means time-shares in the well; farmers each have a fixed time when they are allowed to use the well. The competition over water thus becomes a zero-sum game: what one family gains, the others lose. Unlike the Balinese system, where everyone has to cooperate, this system is based on competition.

Continuing his comparison of Morocco and Bali, Geertz finds a similar opposition between individualism and collectivism in many other social and cultural contexts as well. However, although he acknowledges his debt to Steward, he is careful to stress that he does not intimate that there are simple ecological or climatic causes for cultural phenomena:

This is not geographic determinism. It is an argument that the kind of sociocultural analysis that applies to kinship, village politics, child raising, or ritual drama applies equally, and not just in these two societies, to human transactions with the environment. (Geertz 1972: 38)

HUMAN MODIFICATIONS OF ECOSYSTEMS

Geertz, like many others writing on the nature–society relationship, did not propose a strong hypothesis regarding causal links. This kind of equation includes sociocultural factors as well as environmental ones – in other words, culture and society are not mere effects, but also part of the cause. Humans do not act mechanically on environmental factors, even if such factors affect their actions directly and indirectly. The opposition between sociocultural and natural dimensions, therefore, is a misleading one.

Some anthropologists writing on pastoralists have worked out accurate formulas which describe the exact interrelationship between the number of animals in a given area, viability limits for households and ecological sustainability. Among the Fulani (see Chapter 5), the lower limit for viability was set at 21 cows and a bull for a young household. There was also an upper limit to the size of herds; both due to social limitations (a household can only herd so many animals) and for ecological reasons, that is, because too large a herd would lead to the degradation of the grazing land and ultimately lead to desertification.

This way of reasoning makes it tempting to assume that societies are self-regulating in that they do not undermine the ecological conditions for their survival. The global environmental crisis of our time indicates that this is certainly not always the case. Moreover, environmental crises on a smaller scale have occurred earlier too; many pre-industrial societies altered their environment in irreversible ways. Large parts of the Arabian Peninsula have been desertified during past millennia, chiefly due to overgrazing and deforestation, and similar processes seem to be taking place in Australia and Southern Africa today, although these changes, when they take place today, are increasingly attributed to global climate change rather than local mismanagement (Oliver-Smith 2009).

Anthropology and Climate Change

There are two main ways in which anthropologists can explore issues concerning environmental crises and the possibility of dramatic climate change predicted by many leading climatologists.

On the one hand, anthropologists can study the spread of the crisis discourse. This would entail, following the lead of Douglas and Wildavsky (1980), studying the discourse formation, the public understandings of the crisis and bids to mitigate it without taking an explicit stance as to whether the crisis is 'real' or not. A research project along such lines could explore the emergence of consensus in large parts of the scientific community and the conviction of growing proportions of publics worldwide that we are indeed witnessing a situation of humanly induced climate change. It could also demonstrate how the discourses of climate change have a similar structure to several other popular narratives of the contemporary world – ethnic and religious conflicts, an ungovernable financial market and so on.

On the other hand, one can also carry out research on the empirical consequences of environmental crisis/climate change, looking at social realities rather than discursive constructions. This line of research might lead to an investigation of adaptation among transhumant reindeer herders in Siberia or Scandinavia, forced migration due to drought or flooding, perceptions of climate change among hunters and gatherers in Southern Africa, and so on (Crate and Nuttall 2009); in other words, reactions to environmental deterioration which has a tangible material dimension. Although these two kinds of perspectives can be complementary, they must be kept separate. In much of the sociological literature on risk, it is unclear whether the author is talking about actual risks or cultural discourses about alleged risks (see Furedi 2002), which makes it difficult to understand the analytical message.

The fact that it is possible, and historically not all that uncommon, for human societies to undermine the ecological conditions for their own survival proves beyond doubt that we are far from determined by, or perfectly adapted to, our ecosystem. However, this fact also serves as a reminder that there is a continuous, and necessary, mutual exchange between society and environment. Some societies have proven remarkably stable in that they have reproduced a technology which did not alter their environment irreversibly in ways requiring technical innovation or dramatic social change. The BaMbuti pygmies have been discussed in an earlier chapter (Chapter 4); another example might be the horticultural societies of highland New Guinea. Archaeological research indicates that horticulture was practised in the New Guinea highlands as early as 9000 to 10,000 years ago, probably using similar technology to what was common when anthropological research in the highlands began after the Second World War.

Provided the climate remains constant, two interrelated factors may dramatically speed up processes of change in the ecological environment: population growth and technological change. Technological changes tend to imply an intensified exploitation of natural resources and an increased use of energy. Population growth is often, but not always, a result of technological change. An area which is capable of sustaining perhaps 1000 hunters and gatherers, or 2000 horticulturalists, may perhaps be able to support 20,000 farmers with tractors and chemical fertiliser, but they will not be able to revert to horticulture, and in this sense have lost some of their flexibility (Bateson 1972).

TECHNOLOGY

Technology, in a very general meaning of the word, consists of the systematised acquired skills and man-made material implements humans reproduce and apply in their dealings with nature. However, it is a notoriously difficult term to define; in an article on the anthropological study of technology, Bryan Pfaffenberger (1988) notes that few of the anthropologists dealing with the topic have bothered to define it. One anthropologist who has done so is Tim Ingold, who describes technology as 'a corpus of culturally transmitted knowledge, expressed in manufacture and use' (1979, p. 202; see also Ingold 2002). He stresses its social and cultural character, and links technology to the superstructure in a Marxist sense, along with other kinds of culturally transmitted knowledge. It should also be kept in mind that technology literally means 'knowledge about technics', and therefore 'technology is to technics what ... linguistics is to language, for instance, or ethology to behaviour' (Sigaut 1994, p. 422). Technology is thus a theory about technics, or, as we might say, techniques.

Referring to the political scientist Langdon Winner, Pfaffenberger discerns two main pitfalls common among anthropologists in their dealings with technology. The first is technological somnambulism, which sees techniques as either trivial or irrelevant to social organisation and culture. Technical implements, according to this view, are simply made and put to use, and exert little influence on the way people think and act.

The second pitfall is technological determinism, which claims, often without substantial argument, that technology is of paramount importance for culture and social organisation, as 'a powerful and autonomous agent that dictates the patterns of human social and cultural life' (Pfaffenberger 1988, p. 239). Karl Wittfogel's famous 'Oriental despotism' thesis (1959) falls into this category. Wittfogel held that the structure of irrigation systems in rice-growing areas in Asia, which he called 'hydraulic societies', inevitably led to political centralisation and despotism since someone would have the power to turn the water on and off, and this person or kin group would accordingly be endowed with disproportionate power.

Pfaffenberger outlines a view of technology which, unlike the positions mentioned, does not 'gravely understate or disguise the social relations of technology' (1988, p. 241). Like artefacts, discussed in Chapter 12, technologies and techniques are cultural products which form part of ongoing processes in society and can therefore not be studied separately from those relationships. Techniques shape our relationships, but our relationships also shape techniques. The tractor makes sense as a means of production in very different kinds of society, even if it alters the concrete productive process in similar ways everywhere. It is nonetheless obvious that technology frequently does affect society and culture in profound ways. The introduction of the microcomputer in the rich countries from the late 1970s onwards has not, as anticipated, led to a decrease in the use of paper; but it has transformed parts of the labour market by creating new kinds of jobs and skills. Through the introduction of new information and communication technologies, ranging from email to electronic bookshelves, the microcomputer has enabled and encouraged millions of people to change the structure of their stream of social interaction in significant ways. What is interesting to anthropology is not the techniques in themselves, but which skills people employ and for what purposes, how they are transmitted and objectified, and how the distribution of skills is related to the production of cultural meanings and social organisation. Furthermore, as Pfaffenberger (1988) suggests, technology, seen as often-implicit doctrines about relevant techniques, can be studied as a form of ideology – he calls it 'a mystifying force of the first order' (p. 250). This is not least because technology tends to be regarded as 'natural'.

Techniques are embedded in the habitus and in knowledge systems, and technologies may be studied as ideology. However, the techniques result in the creation of material objects, which, unlike words and actions, 'have an enduring physical presence as components of the environment within which communicative events are framed' (Ingold 1994b; cf. Miller 1994). It was in this context that Sartre (1960), in his late neo-Marxist philosophy, introduced the concept of '*le champ pratico-inert*' – the practical-inert field (of action), the material field of building and artefacts which directs human action. Sartre argues that the sheer materiality of architecture and other 'inert material structures' inevitably shapes and freezes social relationships, restricting freedom and confirming hierarchies. At this point, he comes close to material determinism, and to argue against his view it would be sufficient to demonstrate how identical material structures can be used in significantly different ways. On the other hand, this also means that the relationship of humans to technologies embedded in durable artefacts – whether or not they are means of production – needs to be studied empirically.

SYSTEMS OF PRODUCTION

The world's systems of production may be classified according to various criteria. During the Cold War (1946–90), a major distinction in everyday language was between capitalist and socialist systems; those characterised by private ownership of means of production and those where the state owned the means of production, respectively. In Marxist scholarship, an important distinction is drawn between the capitalist mode of production and the various 'pre-capitalist' modes. Within this body of thought, the relations of production (property and the ability to control other people's labour power) and forces of production (raw materials, technology) make up a mode of production, and this is considered decisive for the organisation of society.

A different way of conceptualising the differences between economic systems classifies societies according to the dominant mode of subsistence. This, we should note, is not the same as a mode of production, but is related to dominant production techniques irrespective of property relations. A society of hunters and gatherers may well be capitalistic, provided its members sell their surplus individually in the marketplace and buy the bulk of their subsistence goods. Hunters and gatherers may thus, technically, have the same mode of production as industrial societies. Similarly, agricultural societies may well be based on collective as well as individual ownership. In other words, the same form of subsistence may be dominant under different modes of production.

The following typology aims at suggesting some interrelationships between modes of subsistence and other aspects of culture and society, including technology and the human relationship with the wider ecosystem.

Hunters and gatherers, or foraging peoples, generally have a division of labour based on gender and age, and a simple technology. Usually they are organised in small, family-based groups (or 'bands'); they are small-scale societies with (generally) an egalitarian political organisation. They tend to produce small surpluses and generally have limited opportunities for storage. Most such groups therefore have an economy based on immediate return, which does not encourage long-term planning. Until food cultivation began in some parts of the world around 10,000 years ago, all humans were hunters and gatherers; today they exist in scattered pockets in Australia, Southern Africa, the forests of Central Africa, South-East Asia, the Amazon basin and the circumpolar areas. Everywhere they are gradually being integrated into states and drawn into the social and cultural forms of modernity, and, because of loss of territory, their traditional mode of subsistence is becoming increasingly difficult to maintain.

Horticulturalists generally, but not invariably, have a more complex social organisation than hunters and gatherers, but they too tend to have a division of labour based on gender and age. Their productive technology includes simple cultivating tools (the most common one is the digging stick), while a widespread technique for manuring consists of burning off fields before planting them (swidden or slash-and-burn agriculture). The main source of nourishment is usually a starchy tuber (yams, manioc, taro, sweet potato), but it may also be dry rice, plantains or maize. Usually land rights are linked with lineages. Their economy, obviously, implies delayed return. Most horticultural peoples have limited possibilities for storage and produce a limited surplus. Today, most horticulturalists are found in the Amazon, in Melanesia, scattered throughout Africa, in South-East Asia and in Madagascar. They are confronted with some of the same problems and challenges as hunters and gatherers, and many are becoming proletarianised (see below).

Agriculturalists are, by conventional definition, distinguished from horticulturalists through the use of ploughs and draught animals. They are often organised at a higher level of scale than horticultural people, and produce enough surplus to have a differentiated division of labour which may include professional specialists such as priests, soldiers, scribes, blacksmiths and chiefs. Many cultural historians hold that the most important watershed in human history lay in the transition to agriculture, which made a hitherto unknown social complexity possible. Agriculturists' social organisation is frequently hierarchical, and land rights in such societies are usually based on kinship.

Pastoralists emerged after the agricultural revolution and not before it, as is often assumed. They always, or nearly always, live in some kind of symbiotic relationship with settled agriculturalists with whom they exchange products (raiding, also, is not unknown). The division of labour is usually based on gender and age, and the social organisation may be as simple as that of hunters and gatherers, a fact connected with the need for mobility and flexibility required by their economic system. The technology of production is flexible and mobile, and the main economic resource comprises animals (in contrast to agriculturalists, who see their chief resource as land, and to hunters and gatherers, as well as many horticulturalists, who see labour as their most important economic resource). Ownership of animals is frequently individual.

Peasants are a special case of agriculturalists. Perhaps the majority of the world's population today are peasants. The most commonly acknowledged definition (Wolf 1966) describes them as agriculturalists partly integrated into the world economy. Many of them have to pay rent for the land they cultivate: in peasant societies, land has become a commodity (it can be purchased), unlike the case in traditional agricultural societies. They produce food for subsistence, but also depend on selling and buying in a general-purpose money market.

Industrial societies are characterised by a very complex division of labour, specialisation of knowledge, separate political and economic institutions, a complex mechanical technology and social integration at a very high level of scale. Production is organised on the basis of individual labour contracts. Agriculture is industrialised. Nobody produces food first and foremost for subsistence (even farmers tend to be specialised and buy at least some of their food in shops), and the anonymous commodity market is a central institution in the economic life of any actor. Industrial societies have centralised states, anonymous labour markets, written legislations and systems of social control integrating an enormous number of people on the basis of principles other than kinship.

To this list one might add the information society, where the production of immaterial goods is the main economic activity. However, it is difficult to draw the line between industrial and information society, since many of the advanced information societies (such as Japan, the USA and Germany) also are leading industrial societies.

War and Protein

A long-lasting controversy has concerned the causes of war among Amazonian peoples. According to Marvin Harris, the main cause was the scarcity of protein; he argued that the groups were forced to expand their territory in order to get more food. Napoleon Chagnon, by contrast, held that the quest for women was more important. On the eve of Chagnon's departure for fieldwork among the Yanomamö, the two discussed the topic at a public meeting at Harvard. Harris argued that the Yanomamö probably ate less protein than a Big Mac equivalent per day (i.e. 30 grammes) and dared Chagnon to find out. If he was wrong, he said, he would eat his hat.

In this case, it turned out that there was no correlation between protein deficiency and war. The Yanomamö were well nourished, and as a matter of fact, the frequency of war was highest in areas particularly rich in protein. Confronted with Harris's view, the Yanomamö themselves admitted that they were fond of meat, but added that they were even more fond of women (Chagnon 1983, pp. 85–6). Chagnon does not say whether or not Harris actually ate his hat, and the debate nevertheless continues on a different tack, as other scholars working on the Yanomamö have raised serious criticisms against Chagnon's view of them as being particularly warlike. Marshall Sahlins, not particularly sympathetic to either of these approaches, once quipped, in an assessment of Harris's work, that the tendency to ask 'riddles of culture typical of Harris' work was amusing, but only until one discovered that protein was the answer to every single riddle ...'

Do typologies of this kind make sense? They are certainly simplistic, and in today's globalised capitalist world, there are scarcely any 'pure' forms left. However, such a breakdown into subsistence modes may nonetheless be useful in providing a list of ideal types which reveals the interrelationship between production technology, mode of subsistence and other aspects of culture and society. In real life, subsistence modes exist more often in mixed than in pure forms. Later chapters, indicating the relationship between subsistence forms and other aspects of society and culture, elaborate on the relationship between oral and written religions, between mechanical and 'concrete' time and between different modes of thought. If it can be agreed that it was not a complete coincidence that anthropology emerged in industrial society and not in a pastoralist society, for example, it is necessary to make clear distinctions between kinds of societies in order to understand how the diversity of humanity expresses itself in different, but not unconnected ways. When we do so, it is equally important to remember that these distinctions only exist at the level of the model to facilitate comparison, and that the world outside is always more complex than our models of it.

CAPITALISM AS A SYSTEM OF PRODUCTION

Throughout the twentieth century, and at an expanding rate since the Second World War, peoples all over the world have become participants in a global world economy. Although global systems certainly did exist earlier (Friedman 1994; Chase-Dunn and Hall 1997), the contemporary world system has a formal uniformity, reproduced chiefly by capitalism, the modern state and real-time communication technology, which lacks precedents. The shirt I am wearing as I write this was made in India and my trousers were produced in Portugal; the computer on which I write was assembled in China, and the grapes in front of me were grown in South Africa. The system of production, consumption and exchange is truly global, and few of the world's peoples are totally unaffected by it.

According to an influential theory about the capitalist world system (Wallerstein 1974–79), capitalism is not merely the dominant mode of production today, but it also sets the limits for – and constrains – other modes of production, whether they are 'pre-capitalist' or 'socialist'. The capitalist mode of production is ever expanding, according to Immanuel Wallerstein, who saw it as completely hegemonic in the 1970s. If anything, capitalism has become even more globally dominant in subsequent decades, although anthropologists have always demonstrated that many economic activities continue to take place outside of the formal monetary economy.

Wallerstein subdivides the capitalist world system into three distinct regions: the core, the semi-periphery and the periphery. In the periphery, economic development depends on the investments and needs of the core areas, and the economy in these areas is subjected to unpredictable fluctuations in market prices, low wages and low rates of investment. It has also been pointed out that the peripheral areas – notably Africa, Latin America and most of Asia – largely produce raw materials for the world market, at prices determined by the demand in the rich countries.

This kind of theory, much of it influenced by Marxist thought, is called dependency theory, since it assumes the fundamental dependence of the peripheral, poor countries on the rich ones and the exploitation of the former by the latter. Although it can be revealing, it is general and abstract and does not always fit the territory (Worsley 1984, 1990). Frequently, poverty and class differences in the countries sometimes spoken of collectively and simplistically as 'the Third World' can be explained by looking at local power disparities, as in the case of Congo (Chapter 11), and there are also today several examples of former producers of raw materials which have become industrial countries. On the other hand, there are doubtless very considerable power disparities between 'North' and 'South'. If wagework was uniformly remunerated on a global basis, Colombian plantation workers would earn about as much as apple pickers in the United States, while in fact most of them will never be able to afford a TV set. The underground railway that was opened in Kolkata (Calcutta) in 1984 had been largely dug out by hand. This tells us something about the price of labour in peripheral countries relative to the cost of machinery, and such disparities are a fundamental feature of the contemporary world economy even today.

The kind of theory represented in Wallerstein's and others' grand models of the world is nevertheless too sweeping in its generalisations to be immediately applicable to anthropological research. To anthropologists, it is necessary to study processes of change as they are expressed locally, taking as our point of departure aspects of local life. This implies an emphasis on local peculiarities that are generally neglected in world-system theory, which deals with social facts at a different level. In the case of economic activities, this would include an interest in the 'informal sector', a term coined by Keith Hart (1973) following observations in a local Ghanaian market, to refer to those aspects of the economy that cannot easily be identified, measured and governed – ranging from mutual favours to barter and semi-legal activities. General theory may supplement and inform ethnographic research, but it cannot replace it. Let us therefore turn to a couple of empirical cases revealing local contexts of integration into the capitalist system of production.

FROM PEASANTS TO PROLETARIANS

In many parts of the world, two or even several modes of production coexist side by side. Marx and others have assumed that one mode would always be dominant and that it ultimately would replace the 'earlier' (usually 'pre-capi-talist') one. But in many societies this has not happened, and nothing indicates that it will. In fact, it may be profitable for the formal capitalist economy to keep a non- or pre-capitalist mode of production going. If a labour migrant moving from the Rift Valley to Nairobi is to earn enough money for his own survival, his salary may have to be at least, say, 2000 shillings a week. However, if he has a *shamba* (farm) and a wife and children to work it in his tribal area, it may be sufficient to pay him 1000 shillings, as he will then be able to go home at the weekends, bringing food back to town with him. This is actually what many wageworkers in the South do, or – if they do not commute – the may supplement their income with a few chickens or a small plot of land, thereby becoming part-time peasants.

It may be said that capitalism, in this kind of context, is parasitic on other modes of production. In many parts of the world, capitalism and subsistence agriculture are combined in the way suggested above. Although many people have become involved in wagework, they still depend on producing food for subsistence. In other cases, the change may be more fundamental, more or less eradicating the subsistence sector. The following example indicates some of the changes induced by the transition from a peasant mode of production to capitalist wagework.

Ganadabamba was traditionally a typical local community in Peru (Miller 1965). Most of the 1000 inhabitants were Indian peasants and contract workers; the few inhabitants of European and mixed descent worked as administrators at the local hacienda (estate). The peasants generally controlled the land they rented from the hacienda; that is, the male head of household controlled it. His control of land was the basis for his local prestige, and although they had to pay rent for the land, land rights were inherited from father to son.

In the lower areas (under 2500 metres above sea level) maize was grown; in the higher areas, the potato was the main crop. There was wide-reaching exchange between the regions, and this functioned as a form of reciprocity in creating friendship and mutual obligations between the groups.

In connection with rites of passage, religious festivals and harvesting, large public feasts (*fiestas*) were organised. The entire village took part, and the feasts functioned as public rituals in the sense that they gave a visual, dramatised expression of both solidarity and local hierarchies.

From the beginning of the twentieth century, population pressure and scarcity of land forced a number of villagers to travel to the coast as plantation workers. In the early years, they regularly returned to Ganadabamba in the harvest season. They regarded the wagework at the coast as a temporary solution. Unlike the situation in the highlands, where the amount of work was regulated by the seasons, plantation work was constantly hard. Social life on the plantation was, moreover, unstable and unsatisfactory. There were no clubs or gathering places for the contract workers and there was no strong moral community. Individuals were left isolated; it was impossible to bring one's family along to the coast.

Eventually the Indian settlements on the coast became more permanent and the family structure was re-stabilised, largely through female co-migration. The social situation for the proletarianised Indians was nevertheless quite different from how it had been when they were peasants. They now had greater opportunities for social mobility; they could change their jobs, go on strike for wage increases and organise themselves in trade unions. Their children were offered schooling. Simultaneously, they became much more vulnerable than they had been earlier. When people were dismissed by the management, they now had no economic safety net. Other consequences were perhaps even more profound, and are related to the fundamental differences between the respective logics of peasant production and capitalist production.

This kind of transition is not unique to Ganadabamba, Peru or South America; it has been described in Africa, Asia and elsewhere as well. What is noteworthy, seen from a vantage-point more than a generation after Miller's analysis, is the fact that the apparently unstable situation where a peasant logic coexists with a capitalist one continues: there is no linear development or replacement of a peasant mode of production with wagework and capitalism. The 'informal sector' and subsistence agriculture continues. Labour migration and a mixed mode of production has become a permanent characteristic of many societies, from China to Southern Africa.

CAPITALISM AND PEASANTRY COMPARED

Capitalist production is split up: the individual worker carries out only a small part of the process of production. It is based on formal hierarchies and individual labour contracts, where the incumbents of the various statuses are replaceable. The production is mediated by money, and the value of the work is calculated as a function of money and measured labour time. The purpose of production is the accumulation of profits, and because of competition, technical innovations are necessary.

Peasant production is holistic: the individual worker takes part in all phases of the process. The organisation of work is based on kinship, local conventions and local hierarchies. The purpose of the production is first and foremost to satisfy the needs of the household. Peasants compete with others only to the extent that they sell products in the market, which is not a main activity. Labour time is not a scarce resource in a peasant economy and it is not measured.

Wageworkers take part in a global system of production, distribution and consumption; peasants are largely integrated locally. Wageworkers further become citizens in ways which peasants do not; as the Peruvian example shows, they may be organised in country-wide unions with an elected leadership and thousands of members who are unrelated and do not know each other except in an abstract way. The unions place demands on the state and the employers, usually in a written form. Peasants (and other 'traditional peoples') have no similar means of making demands towards others apart from their relatives and local powerholders; they usually master no information technology other than the spoken word. Wagework, further, has an individualising effect: the economic unit is now the individual instead of the household. Wageworkers can be replaced, and can change their jobs, while peasants are tied to their plot of land.

Wageworkers are integrated into several anonymous structures which contribute to shaping their lives. They can spend their salaries anywhere, buying anything from anybody. The literacy they (usually) acquire enables them to communicate on a very large scale, at least in principle. They pay taxes to the government, are committed to following the written laws of the country and may make certain demands of the state. Abstract time, which measures the value of their labour power, is another anonymous structure; it is not only valid for you and me but for everybody who follows it, and it serves to synchronise a very large number of persons in an anonymous way. A brief comparison with the mechanisms of social integration prevalent among, say, the Dogon, the Yanomamö or the Trobriand Islanders would indicate that capitalism and wagework entail not merely 'economic' changes, but also profound social and cultural changes. There is no simple determinism or a one-to-one relationship, but the capitalist system of production and exchange, once it has become an integral part of local society, inevitably creates new kinds of social relations as it contributes to defining premises for social relations far beyond the domain of production. Changes in the form of subsistence, or work, thus have far wider implications than cultural changes often commented upon by outsiders, such as the adoption of Western clothes or the introduction of pop music in a society. Such changes, insofar as they do not affect the social relations between family members and neighbours, are not necessarily perceived locally as change, while the individualising and often fragmenting effects of wagework are.

SUGGESTIONS FOR FURTHER READING

Susan A. Crate and Mark Nuttall, eds: *Anthropology and Climate Change: From Encounters to Actions*. Walnut Creek, CA: Left Coast Press 2009.

Philippe Descola and Gísli Pálsson, eds: *Nature and Society: Anthropological Perspectives*. London: Routledge 1996.

Eric Wolf: *Peasants*. Englewood Cliffs, NJ: Prentice Hall 1966.

14   RELIGION AND RITUAL

God is society, writ large.
— *Emile Durkheim*

Rituals always have a desperate and manic aspect.
— *Claude Lévi-Strauss*

In a study of the Basseri pastoralists of southern Iran, Barth (1961) expresses some surprise regarding their lack of religious interest (they describe themselves as 'slack Muslims'). His surprise is caused by the fact that religion seems to loom large in the lives of most of the peoples described in classic anthropological studies. This may be a major reason why religion has always been a central field of inquiry in anthropology, even if, as Evans-Pritchard (1962) once pointed out, social scientists have themselves often been indifferent or even hostile to religion.

In attempting to propose non-ethnocentric, comparatively useful definitions of politics, economy, nature, gender and other core concepts, anthropology is repeatedly confronted with problems usually related to the fact that these notions are in use, and have a specific meaning, in one's own society and in the anthropological vocabulary, but not necessarily in other societies. This makes them problematic as 'etic' concepts.

This problem of translation and conceptualisation is certainly valid where religion is concerned, and few concepts of social science have been defined, revised and criticised more often than this one.

Until the late nineteenth century, it was common in the professional literature to distinguish between religion and paganism, and between religion and superstition. The concept of paganism was associated with non-Christian religions, including their public rituals. The concept of superstition was largely reserved for descriptions of invisible interrelationships in the world which neither science, authorised religion nor 'common sense' could account for. From this kind of perspective, Islam and African ancestral cults would be located to the domain of paganism, while, say, the Trobriand Islanders' belief that they die because of witchcraft and the common notion, in the Mediterranean region and elsewhere, that some persons are possessed by the evil eye, would be expressions of superstition. In contemporary anthropology, this corresponds to a frequently invoked distinction between religion and knowledge. Religion may thereby be said to include forms of social belief in supernatural powers which are public and which are given public expression through rituals. Knowledge can be defined so as to include 'facts' of which people are reasonably certain and act upon.

Of course, knowledge can have a religious character, and the distinction is therefore debatable. In this chapter, we nevertheless concentrate on the notions associated with contact with the sacred and the hereafter, and its expressions through ritual; leaving other forms of knowledge to the next chapter.

Have I still not defined religion properly? If so, I join a large group of anthropologists in struggling with this concept. Ever since anthropologists began to study belief in traditional societies, there has been disagreement as to what religion is. One of the oldest definitions, suggested by Tylor, defines religion simply as the belief in supernatural beings. The question of what is supernatural immediately poses itself here, for does that not vary just like every other form of knowledge – is it not the case that what is natural to me is supernatural to you and vice versa? Is the garden magic of the Trobrianders, which is as necessary to them as manure is to a Western farmer, part of their religion or part of their production technology? Are ancestral spirits supernatural? Who says so and on what methodological grounds? As persons, we all hold views about such matters, but these views are not necessarily relevant in anthropological research, which does not set forth to find out whether others 'are right or wrong', but to elucidate, analyse and translate their life-world into a common professional language.

Is Understanding Religion Compatible with Believing?

This provocative question is the title of a much-discussed article by the philosopher Alasdair MacIntyre (1970). His answer is, briefly, no. According to MacIntyre, religion must be understood in sociological and logical terms, as stabilising and legitimising ideologies, and as systems of signification and action which provide a certain shape and meaning to the world and to human existence; which explains why we are here and what happens when we die. If one is to believe in religion, he continues, one has to move to a completely different mode of thought, which easily accepts contradiction and lack of coherence, appealing to concepts such as 'the absurd' (Kierkegaard), 'paradox' (Karl Barth) or 'mystery' (Marcel). The sceptic and the believer, he claims, have no shared conceptual world – the sceptic, who 'understands' religion, cannot conceptualise the reality of the believer. MacIntyre further seems to hold that the social context of modernity, which has created modern social science, is incompatible with religious faith since it is based on a wholly secular form of thought.

Many anthropologists would be inclined to disagree with MacIntyre (see Evans-Pritchard 1962). It seems likely, for example, that Catholics such as Victor Turner, Mary Douglas and E.E. Evans-Prichard have contributed somewhat to our understanding of religion.

Another possibility lies in following Durkheim, who assumed that a distinction is made between the profane and the sacred in every society, and who confined religion to the sacred domain. Durkheim also wanted to show how the function of religion in 'primitive societies' consisted of creating solidarity and integration through rituals and 'collective representations'. In his *Elementary Forms of the Religious Life* (Durkheim 2001 [1912]), he argued that religion at its most profound level entails society's worship of itself. This view has its problems (notably the problems of functionalist explanation), for example in not explaining why the inhabitants of one society believe in ancestral spirits whereas their neighbours believe in forest spirits, granted that both would be socially integrating beliefs.

A rather different approach to religion is represented in an influential essay by Geertz, 'Religion as a Cultural System' (in Geertz 1973). He defines religion like this:

(1) a system of symbols which acts to (2) establish powerful, pervasive, and long-lasting moods and motivations in men by (3) formulating conceptions of a general order of existence and (4) clothing these conceptions with such an aura of factuality that (5) the moods and motivations seem uniquely realistic. (1973, p. 90)

In other words, he argues that instead of looking at the social functions of religion, we ought to explore what religion means to people, how it helps to make sense of the world and how it gives a meaning and direction to human existence. We should study religion itself, not its social causes, and the ultimate aim of such an investigation ought to be how the world and human existence appear meaningful to the believer. Religion, in Geertz's view, is dual in that it simultaneously offers *models of* the world (ontology) and *models for* action (morality). A similar hermeneutical, or interpretive, procedure is evident in Evans-Pritchard's earlier work on Nuer religion (1956), which is a detailed ethnography aimed at translating emic Nuer beliefs into European (and Christian theological) concepts, thereby rendering them comparable to other religious phenomena, as well as relating religion to social organisation.

The approach advocated by Geertz and foreshadowed by Evans-Pritchard has been very influential in shaping the direction of current anthropological research on religion. This shift in perspective is a part of the general change in anthropological thinking mentioned earlier, whereby the main trends have swung from an interest in functions, structure and social integration, which was dominant roughly until the 1970s, to a concern with the interpretation of meaning, symbols and social processes. Several examples of this change have been noted in earlier chapters; in the study of religion, it has brought, among other things, a growing interest in relating meaning to experience and in understanding cosmologies.

A different perspective on religion, influenced by cognitive science and evolutionary theory, has been developed by another group of scholars (see Whitehouse 2001; Whitehouse and McCauley 2005) who argue that religions, as well as religiosity, are surprisingly similar phenomena worldwide and should therefore be analysed as outcomes of the evolutionary architecture of the mind. Harvey Whitehouse thus argues that much 'of what we have learned from ethnography, historiography, and archaeology (for instance) points to a massive amount of cross-cultural recurrence not only in the forms that religious systems take but even in relation to some aspects of doctrinal content' (2005: 207). This perspective, aiming to *explain* religion and not just to *understand* it, is not necessarily incompatible with the hermeneutical approach, but could be said to take the analysis a step further, beyond translation and interpretation towards a comparative analysis based on notions of human universals.

Yet another important perspective on religion sees it chiefly as a vehicle of social organisation, and studies in this vein, typically located in complex modern societies, tend to focus on the politics of identity. In Chapters 16–18, some of these studies will be dealt with.

In the first half of this chapter, the main concern is to understand religion and religiosity as such, but in the second half, dealing with rituals – religion as practice – we return to some of the problems first articulated by Durkheim, as well as identifying the ideological aspects of religion and ritual and making some connections to politics and power.

ORAL AND WRITTEN RELIGIONS

The distinction between oral and written religions is important and has a bearing on other aspects of culture and society as well. Written religions are based on a sacred text, are often described as 'religions of the book', are linked to a sacred text (like the Qu'ran) or a collection of sacred texts (like the Bible), and the believers are expected to have at least a rudimentary knowledge of the contents of the works. Such religions, including Judaism, Islam and Christianity, regard their content chiefly as being tied to the text and not to a particular cultural context. Since they are text-bound, these religions can be disseminated throughout the world to peoples who in other regards live very different kinds of lives. Islam, for example, is the main religion in societies as different as Java, Niger, Egypt and Iran; whereas Christianity dominates in countries like the Philippines, El Salvador and Germany. The written religions, and particularly the monotheistic ones with their origins in the Middle East, can also be described as religions of conversion – systems of belief to which one can be converted and in which one has to affirm one's faith. Unlike other religions, they tend to be exclusive and, at least in theory, not to accept 'syncretism'. Christian missionaries in Africa have often despaired at the sight of Africans cheerfully worshipping their God as well as water spirits and ancestral spirits.

Some written religions fulfil this pattern only partly; notably the Asian ones (of which Hinduism and Buddhism are the largest), which have a less fixed doctrine, more flexible practices and insist less on obedience to texts than the monotheistic script religions do.

However, the kinds of religion traditionally studied by anthropologists are markedly different from religions based on scriptures. First of all, they are locally confined. No Nuer or Kaguru in his right mind would expect the whole world's population to become 'disciples' of their revered spirits or even of their highest god, *thoth* (Nuer) or *mulungu* (Kaguru). The gods tend to be physically associated with revered places in the tribal area. For this reason, missionaries and others misguidedly held tribal peoples to be 'animists', holding the belief that trees, springs and rocks are imbued with divine powers ('*anima*' is Latin for spirit). Second, oral religions tend to be embedded in the social practices of society, whereas written ones are often more detached from other social institutions. This distinction, which is not absolute, corresponds to the previously discussed institutional differentiation in modern societies, which is largely lacking in small-scale traditional societies. However, it should be noted that one of the first specialised (non-food producing) occupations that develops as societies become more differentiated is the priestly one. Shamans, that is people who through the medium of the trance enter into communion with the spiritual realm, exist as a specialised profession even in acephalous and otherwise undifferentiated communities, such as traditional Inuit society.

A somewhat related distinction, which was introduced by Robert Redfield (1955), concerns 'little' and 'great' traditions. Redfield argues that qualitatively different forms of religion and knowledge exist side by side in many societies; they may be radically different, but are often interrelated. The Mediterranean belief in the evil eye, for example, clearly belongs to a 'little' tradition (neither Christianity nor Islam – the 'great' traditions of the region –supports the notion), as does the worship of saints in Muslim societies. In some coastal Portuguese communities, villagers believe in a wide range of healing rituals, sorcery, magic supposed to secure fishing luck and 'supernatural' explanations of misfortune (Brøgger 1990). These beliefs exist alongside the official doctrines of the Catholic Church, although they contradict the teachings of Christianity, and seem to have done so for centuries. The same individuals believe simultaneously in the 'great' and 'little' traditions. The currently widespread interest in 'new age' beliefs and practices in the North Atlantic societies, ranging from faith healing to clairvoyance and sacred crystals, can be seen as a similar 'little' tradition, although the 'great' tradition in this case may be science and not Christianity. In other societies, such as Indian ones, there may be a more clear-cut social distinction between the religious traditions. Brahmanic Hinduism is the official 'great' tradition, its beliefs and rituals sanctioned in the ancient Veda texts and centuries of monitored ritual practices. Low-caste Hindus nevertheless have their own rituals and beliefs, often more reminiscent of oral than written religions, which coexist with the 'high' or 'great' tradition but are socially segregated from it.

Oral religions are characterised by their local relevance, relative lack of dogma and tight integration with the 'non-religious' domains. An ethnographic example may illustrate these points.

AN ORAL RELIGION IN AFRICA

According to the Kaguru, God (*mulungu*) created the world, but they are uncertain as to when it happened (Beidelman 1971, p. 32). This God appears quite rarely in the lives of the Kaguru, however; usually they consult ancestral spirits instead of addressing the great *mulungu* when confronted with difficulties.

The ancestors (and ancestresses – the Kaguru are matrilineal) arrived from the north and the east in a mythical past, founded the present-day clans and divided the land between them. Each clan is assumed to have a 'mystical' connection (Beidelman's term) with its land. For the harvest to be good, the clan members must carry out annual rites so that the ancestral spirits will bless the land and secure its fertility. Notions and practices of this kind clearly go a long way to explain why land cannot be sold or bought in many traditional African societies.

When the Kaguru wish to consult an ancestor or a different spirit, they leave the village and enter a hillside or go into the bush. Usually, the consultations concern practical issues such as rites of passage and festivals intended to ensure the fertility of soil and women. The ancestral spirits are believed to wield real power over the living. A Kaguru woman who had lost several children thus blamed her deceased father, claiming that he was feeling lonely and had called her children to come and keep him company. Since the spirits are this powerful, it is important to pay them respect continuously and sacrifice to them regularly. They enter into every realm of life: birth, rites of passage, fertility and politics.

THE AFTERLIFE

The Kaguru, like most peoples in the world, are concerned with the afterlife. All religions deal with death and attempt to reconcile life and death. Most religions include notions about an afterlife, which frequently represents an idealised version of life here and now, devoid of the trivialities, problems and frustrations of this life. The Kaguru envision the afterlife as a mirror-image of life in Kaguruland, but marked by material abundance and lack of conflict. The Norse Vikings, for their part, assumed that people (or at least men), after an honourable death, came to Valhalla, a large hall where the fire burned day and night, there was plenty of fighting and an abundance of roasted meat. During fieldwork in Trinidad, incidentally, I once found a pamphlet from a North American missionary organisation in my mailbox. It painted, in vivid colours, the Christian paradise as a kind of amusement park reminiscent of Disneyworld, where people could fly, where there were video shows presenting highlights from biblical times and so on. The more intellectually oriented, and orthodox, versions of Christianity, like other written religions, rather depict the afterlife in more abstract terms. Oral religions tend to be more concrete on this point too. According to the traditional religion of the mountain Sami of northern Scandinavia, people are allowed to keep everything, including their reindeer herds, in the afterlife, the main difference being that pastures are abundant there. This kind of notion explains why the Sami (and many other peoples) were buried with their favourite clothes on, with their tools and, in the case of some hierarchical societies, their favourite slaves. Notions of the afterlife, be they abstract or concrete, obviously give an impression of continuity and serve to demystify death.

It should be added, though, that there are also peoples who do not believe in an afterlife; this unusual view seems to be particularly widespread in two of the most individualistic types of society of which we are aware, namely hunters and gatherers (Woodburn 1982) and modern industrial and post-industrial societies.

THE LOGIC OF ANCESTRAL CULTS

The great attention given to ancestors and ancestral spirits, which is found in most non-literate societies, also clearly deals with the problem of continuity – both in society and in the individual lifespan – when a life is suddenly stopped. In a much-discussed article on ancestral cults in Africa, Kopytoff (1971, see also Kopytoff 1981) observed that there is not necessarily a sharp termino-logical distinction between living humans and ancestral spirits. Living people become wiser, 'drier' and less mobile the older they become; the ancestors are thus perceived, he argues, merely as *extremely* wise, dry and immobile persons. There is no rigid boundary between life and death in this scheme, rather a gradual transition to another phase, which begins long before death.

As with other religious phenomena, the respect paid to ancestors also has a politically legitimating and socially stabilising effect. When age is a criterion of wisdom and a qualification for political office, which is nearly inevitable in kinship-based societies, politics becomes conservative. The ancestors showed the way, the elders are their intermediaries and their younger descendants have to listen and obey. As Robin Horton (1970) and others have pointed out, a great many rituals in African tribal societies are dramatic re-creations of the past intended to please the ancestral spirits by showing that the living are faithful to the values and practices taught by their elders.

The political aspects of ancestral cults are significant in practice, even if they cannot explain why people hold beliefs in ancestral spirits. In a general sense, one may perhaps state that any religion, like other kinds of ideology, must simultaneously legitimate a political order and provide a meaningful world view for its adherents, such as a reconciliation with one's own inevitable death. The death of a ruler, which signifies discontinuity, is always associated with crisis, and the belief in ancestral spirits may mitigate the effects of the rupture.

It should be remarked at this point that we have added a political dimension to Geertz's cultural definition of religion, which may lend some support to Marx's famous statement to the effect that religion is the opium of the people.

By this he meant that it functioned as a drug and diverted interest from the real political issues to silly fantasies about a happy afterlife for the pious and obedient. (Of course, a religious non-Marxist might retort that Marxism is the drug of preference for the Marxists.) We now turn to a closer look at the interrelationship between the cultural (ideational) aspects of religion and its social and political dimensions.

RITUAL: RELIGION IN PRACTICE

Most people in the world are faced with recurrent practical problems of an economic and social nature. Some of them can only be resolved with the help of specialists and, in many societies, such specialists are people with a privileged access to higher powers. Other kinds of problems are existential ones; they may deal with the mystery of birth or the fear of death, or simply the ultimate meaning of life. Rituals are largely directed towards problems of the latter kind, dramatising them and giving them articulation – if not necessarily resolving them.

Ritual has been defined as the social aspect of religion. If we may define religion as systems of notions about the supernatural and the sacred, about life after death and so on (with its obvious political implications), then rituals are the social processes which give a concrete expression to these notions. Very generally speaking, we may suggest that rituals are rule-bound public events which in some way or other thematise the relationship between the earthly and the spiritual realms.

The issue is somewhat more complex than this suggests, although it may be a fruitful beginning towards a useful definition. In fact, several of the greatest anthropologists of the twentieth century have devoted many years to trying to understand ritual. Since the early structural-functionalist accounts of rituals as manifestations of society's worship of itself, where the integrating functions of ritual were stressed, anthropology has developed complex theories about what ritual is and how it works. One influential perspective emphasises that rituals simultaneously legitimate power, and are thus important vehicles of ideology, *and* give the participants strong emotional experiences; another perspective focuses on the ability of rituals to give people an opportunity to reflect on their society and their own role in it. Victor Turner stresses the multivocality or ambiguity of ritual symbols (1969). One of the most famous analyses of rituals does not even deal with a religious ritual but a Balinese cockfight (Geertz 1973), while in the mid-1990s a team of Norwegian anthropologists carried out research on the 1994 Winter Olympics, which they saw as an enormous ritual celebrating and legitimating modernity (Klausen 1999).

This is, in other words, a very complex field, and it is important because the ritual can be seen as a synthesis of several important levels of social reality: the symbolic and the social, the individual and the collective; and it usually brings out, and tries to resolve – at a symbolic level – contradictions in society.

RITUALS AND INTEGRATION

Max Gluckman (1982 [1956]) has described a number of curious rituals from Southern Africa, whereby customary rules, conventions and hierarchies are turned upside down. One of them took place among the Swazi at the coronation of a new king. When this was about to happen, every citizen was expected to mock and criticise the king in public, making a grand spectacle of his inadequacy. Similarly, open social criticism was allowed at the medieval carnivals in parts of Europe, but not during the rest of the year. Actual social conflicts are allowed to play themselves out as theatrical performances. Gluckman describes several other 'rituals of rebellion' and concludes that 'by allowing people to behave in normally prohibited ways, [they] gave expression, in a reversed form, to the normal rightness of a particular kind of social order' (1982 [1956], p. 116; but see de Heusch 2000 for another interpretation).

Gluckman thus sees these rituals as functional in that they transform conflicts in a harmless direction, but he is also aware that strong experiences on the part of the participants are necessary for the rituals to be possible at all. In other words, he sees an interaction between individual motivations and societal 'functions'. In a famous study of ritual among the Tsembaga Maring in highland New Guinea, informed by demography and cultural ecology, Roy Rappaport (1968) looked almost exclusively at the functional aspect.

The Tsembaga Maring are horticulturalists and pig-raisers organised in local groups of 200 to 300 persons. Their political system is egalitarian, with the 'big man' and shaman the only formally recognised authorities. They are considered warlike and are frequently in feuds with neighbouring groups. Rappaport argues that there is an intrinsic functional link between war activities and the ritual cycle of the Tsembaga.

Every twelfth to fifteenth year, the Tsembaga organise the *kaiko* festival, which lasts for a full year and culminates in a declaration of war on the enemies of the local group. At the *kaiko* parties prior to this, large numbers of pigs are sacrificed to the ancestors and lavish ceremonial gift exchange takes place within the group. This year-long religious ritual begins when there are 'enough pigs', say the Tsembaga. Rappaport, however, holds that the *kaiko* festival begins when there are so many pigs in the village that they destroy more values (crops) than they produce (meat). The *kaiko* can thus be seen as a regulating response to the competition from and parasitism of the pigs. Moreover, when there are many pigs the population is less concentrated – the women, who are swineherds, have to move further and further away from the village during the day – and more vulnerable to military attacks.

The violent activity following the large-scale pig slaughter also serves to disperse the population, since the losers of the war have to move and raise new settlements, thus decreasing the pressure on the ecosystem.

The ecosystem, including the people in it, is analysed as a self-regulating system. Rappaport shows that the *kaiko* begins, and violence breaks out, when the number of pigs and humans in a given area has reached a critical level;

then, the ecosystem is near the limits of its sustainability. After the completion of the ritual cycle, the critical values decrease and the system is stabilised.

Rappaport's monograph was debated for years after its publication. The critics pointed out that a system cannot be 'rational' in this way – that an ecosystem cannot conceivably 'know' the limits of its sustainability and trigger rituals and war when the critical values appear. It was also stressed that humans are themselves the causes of their actions, that they take decisions within a cultural universe and that it is highly unlikely ecological fluctuations can 'create' rituals. What Rappaport succeeds in showing is, in the end, a statistical correlation between ecological pressure and ritual activity, where the pig–environment–social system relationship regularly reaches a threshold value where it is no longer viable, leading the humans to take action.

The problems inherent in Rappaport's analysis, which he addressed himself in a series of thoughtful responses to his critics (Rappaport 1984), are the classic problems of functionalist explanation. Although the rituals are 'functional' in the sense that they contribute to the long-term survival of Tsembaga society, this does not explain why they exist. Other institutions would also have taken care of that; besides, other societies change too. Functionalist accounts of rituals were perhaps first subjected to serious criticism from within in Edmund Leach's monograph on the Kachin (1954). In contrast to the conventional anthropological wisdom of the day, Leach discovered that the religious–ritual complex among the Kachin in no way functioned smoothly; instead, it spurred dissension and imbalance.

IDEOLOGICAL AND SOCIAL AMBIGUITIES

Unlike their neighbours the Shan, who are Buddhists, the Kachin worship their own gods and spirits (*nats*). The world of *nats* is conceived of as an extension of the earthly hierarchy, since the *nats* are ancestral spirits. They belong to lineages, and in a manner analogous to the distinctions of society, the Kachin distinguish between aristocratic *nats* and commoner *nats*.

Kachin society, Leach argues, is not stable either socially or ideologically, and there are two rival views regarding the values on which society should be based, called *gumlao* and *gumsa*. *Gumlao* refers to an egalitarian ideology with no ranking of lineages and conscious attempts to avoid the tendency towards hierarchy inherent in the *mayu–dama* relationships (see Chapter 8), while *gumsa* refers to a more hierarchical form. To some extent, Leach shows that Kachin societies oscillate between *gumlao* and *gumsa*. Now each local community has a patron saint, a *mung nat*, who is worshipped and sacrificed to during a ritual lasting for several days at a public place in the village. During hierarchical *gumsa* periods, the *mung nat* is regarded as a spiritual member of the chief's lineage; within the egalitarian *gumlao* system, he is considered the ancestor of all the lineages. The sky *nat* Madai, the ruler of the spiritual realm, is only recognised within the *gumsa* system.

Leach's argument is as follows. The spiritual world is construed as a mirror-image of society. Rituals – which largely consist of private and public sacrifices – are chiefly indirect and oblique ways of talking about society. Therefore it is understandable that one does not sacrifice to the 'king' of the spirits during the egalitarian *gumlao* phases.

Further, there is an intrinsic relationship between the myths (religion, or the cognitive aspect of religion) and the rituals, since the rituals dramatise the myths. However, Kachin myths are ambiguous and can be told in different ways. Some of these confirm the *gumsa* system; other, only slightly modified versions, confirm *gumlao* ideals. The different slants can be presented at the same time by different persons wishing to make different points. Leach shows that this fundamental ambiguity in myth and ritual practice in no way is a recipe for social stability. The inconsistencies in the Kachin ritual system are, in his view, fundamental and are therefore an eternal source of tension in society. Quite unlike what Durkheim, Malinowski and others had argued, Leach shows that the myths and rituals can positively encourage a lack of stability, since they offer themselves to conflicting interpretations. Kachin beliefs and rituals nevertheless always function ideologically in the sense of legitimating a particular power structure, but the ideology, reflecting instability in Kachin social organisation, is ambiguous.

In research on ritual, there has been considerable interest in one of the dimensions with which Leach deals, namely what he calls 'symbolic statements about the social order'. One interesting study in this vein is Bruce Kapferer's analysis of demon exorcism among the Sinhalese in Sri Lanka (1984). I shall not go into the details of the ritual; suffice it to say that these exorcisms are large, well-attended and heavily dramatised events which usually take place in the front yard of the home of the patient (the possessed person). In his analysis, Kapferer stresses that the rituals enable the participants to see the world more clearly than usual, and to reflect on their own position in it. For this to be possible, however, they must be able to move to and fro between the ritual, spiritual context and the everyday context: otherwise the two realms would remain separate. Paradoxically therefore, Kapferer writes, the part of the audience which is furthest away from the central stage is best able to carry out this kind of reflection. The patient, the relatives and the first rows of spectators are too immersed in the event to reflect on it, while the people at the back, sipping their tea and chatting together in low voices, are able to see the ritual at a distance and thereby use it consciously in their self-reflection. Here Kapferer finds a quite different pattern from Geertz (1973) in his famous analysis of the Balinese cockfight, where the latter argues that the only participants who fully understand all the symbolic nuances of the fight (which is saturated with several layers of cultural symbolism) are the central betters, who are placed at the inner circle near the fight itself. Only they engage in what Geertz calls 'deep play', which may be a euphemism for religious communion. In Kapferer's example, the opposite proved to be the case: the people of the inner circle understood little, because they were too deeply immersed in the drama to be able to reflect upon it.

It is likely that this difference in interpretation is caused by differences between the respective empirical settings. Such dissimilarities, of course, seem to complicate even further the matter of building a general theory of ritual. Nevertheless, we should be aware that from the system ecology of Rappaport, to the complex multi-level analysis of Leach, to the hermeneutic approach represented by Kapferer and Geertz, there is a clear continuity in that they all agree that ritual is an oblique, indirect way of making complex statements, with a noticeable ideological dimension, about society and the imponderabilities of life. Through a number of studies of the Ndembu of present-day Zambia, Victor Turner (1967, 1969, 1974) developed a sophisticated model of ritual symbolism, which introduced many of the concerns taken up by others later.

THE MULTIVOCALITY OF SYMBOLS

Symbols are central to rituals, and studies of ritual symbols must not merely investigate which symbols are being used, but must also look into their mutual relationship and their meanings (what they symbolise). In Christianity, white symbolises virtue and purity while black signifies evil and darkness; the number seven has sacred connotations, and the wafer consumed at communion has the paradoxical quality of being simultaneously an ordinary wafer and a part of Christ's body. The wafer can thus be seen as a liminal object forming a bridge between this world and the spiritual realm. In this way, it can truly be said that rituals both say something and do something. Moreover, many of the symbols of Christianity are ambiguous. In Turner's terminology, they are *multivocal*, which literally means that 'several voices can be heard'. Several meanings can be read into the number seven, and it is not universally agreed what the holy communion really means.

Turner sees the milk tree (*Diplorrhyncus mossambicensis*) as a central symbol at initiation rituals (Turner 1967). The tree is notable in that it secretes a thick, white, milkish fluid when its bark is cut. The Ndembu explain that it is important in the initiation of girls because the milk tree stands for human breast milk and for the breasts themselves. They also say that the tree 'belongs to mother and child'; that it symbolises the mother–child tie. In other words, the tree seems to have two main meanings: a biological and a social one. The Ndembu also emphasise that the milk tree expresses the continuity of the matrilineage and the cohesion of the tribe. 'The milk tree is our flag', said an educated Ndembu, invoking an apt analogy to an important multivocal symbol in nation-states.

Turner also notes that the milk tree can symbolise contradiction and fission. Especially at the girls' initiation rites, the tree forms the focus for the female spirit of community and their opposition to male dominance; the women dance around it, sing libellous songs against the men and so on. Further, says Turner, the tree represents the individual novice, as a young milk tree is being blessed at the same time that she enters the liminal phase. Thus, the tree represents the tension between individual and society. It can also represent a conflict between the mother of the novice and the other women: she loses her child who is becoming an adult, and is not allowed to join in the dance around the tree. Finally, the milk tree may represent the matrilineage of the novice and so serve as a reminder of the contradiction between the unity of the tribe and the separation of the lineages.

The milk tree is a dominant symbol, and Turner argues that all rituals are focused on similar symbols. Dominant symbols have the following characteristics. First, they are condensed, that is to say many different phenomena are given a common expression. Second, a dominant symbol amounts to a fusion of divergent meanings. In this way, otherwise different people can sense likeness and express solidarity through these symbols – such as flags in nation-states, which mean different things to different people and so are able to give people who are otherwise different a sense of shared identity. Third, dominant ritual symbols entail a polarisation of meaning. At one pole (the ideological), there is a set of meanings to do with the social and political order of society. At the other pole (the sensory), physiological and biological meanings are expressed. (To this, we would probably add emotional meanings today.) The milk tree thus represents, at one pole, matrilineality and the unity of Ndembu society (among other meanings); at the other pole it expresses breastmilk and the mother–child relationship.

A major insight in Turner's work is that symbols have to be multivocal, or ambiguous, to create solidarity: since persons are different, the symbols must be capable of meaning different things to different people. This could be said of rituals in general too, and Leach's Kachin study is a clear case in point. Another important insight from Turner, who belonged to a generation of British anthropologists concerned with bridging the gap between interpretation of meaning and accounting for social structure, is the idea that ritual symbols must speak both about politics (social structure, legitimation) and about existential or emotional cravings: they must be capable of fusing personal experiences with political legitimation if they are to be effective. In contemporary research on flags in ethnic and national identities, these concerns are no less relevant than they were in Turner's studies of the Ndembu (Bryan 2000; Eriksen and Jenkins 2007).

THE INHERENT COMPLEXITY OF RITUAL

In a study of the changing significance of circumcision rituals in Madagascar, Maurice Bloch (1986) has developed the points made here concerning ritual, social integration, ideology and power further.

The Merina (formerly known as Hovas), who live in the Malagasy highlands, are the most powerful ethnic group in the island. Having immigrated from what is now Indonesia about 2000 years ago, the Merina speak a Malayo-Polynesian language, have discernibly Austronesian physical features, and number about 3 million today. They subjected the other ethnic groups to Merina rule in the early nineteenth century, founding the Merina kingdom in 1824. Strongly hierarchically organised, the Merina succeeded in retaining some of their traditional power during French colonialism, even after formally surrendering to France in 1895. The Merina have a bilateral kinship organisation, and the fundamental unit of local organisation is the *deme* (Bloch 1971), consisting of a largely endogamous local group associated with a particular territory. The Merina are famous for their imposing tombs and their elaborate ancestral worship. In his principal study of Merina ritual, Bloch concentrates on male circumcision, which is the single most important public ritual.

Merina boys are circumcised at a very young age (between the ages of 1 and 2 years old), and this ritual involves practically the entire local group, as well as *deme* members living elsewhere. They give contributions to the child's family which are proportional to their kinship distance. During the ritual they sing and dance throughout the night, thereby dramatising the unity of the kin group. The circumcision itself usually takes place in the child's parents' house, but other *deme* members are appointed as the child's 'father' and 'mothers'. The child's 'father' is the circumciser, while the 'mothers' are young women who have a special responsibility for the child during the ritual, which can last for days. Other people also have special assignments; adolescent boys are expected to act mischievously and make practical jokes, while the men cook the food, which is usually a female task.

In a largely structuralist analysis of the symbolism of the ritual, Bloch describes how symbolic meanings are contrasted and inverted, and how both the social and the cosmic order are dramatised in suggestive, non-verbal ways. The unity represented in the ancestors' tombs and the division represented in the houses (inhabited by people from different lineages) are juxtaposed, while the male–female opposition is also expressed at a variety of levels. For example, the ritual always takes place during the cold season; in Bloch's view, this establishes a continuity between the life-giving ceremony of circumcision and the stone tombs of death and *deme* unity. The fact that the circumciser and 'mothers' are not close kin to the child, which negates biological kinship, also lends support to this view. During the very complex proceedings, objects and acts represent different forces and social relationships which interact in ambiguous ways; these include strong vital elements (which are 'wild' and include the *vazimba*, the mythical enemies of the Merina), intermediaries (which mediate and domesticate those vital forces, making them useful to the Merina), the tomb (unity and undifferentiated descent) and devalued entities (such as 'women on their own' and division; Bloch 1986, p. 99).

The central contradiction in the ritual is, in Bloch's multi-layered analysis, the symbolic association between blessing and its opposite, namely violence. Violence is enacted both symbolically and literally; the latter does not just occur in the act of removing the child's foreskin, but also in the killing of a bull to be consumed during the ritual. Each act of violence, however, is associated with a *tsodrano* or blessing ritual, where important men and women call on God and ancestors to give them their blessings. These elders then 'blow water' onto the child and the spectators, thereby mediating the blessings given by God and the ancestors. This contrast – between blessing and violence, life and death – is in Bloch's view a central contradiction in Merina ideology.

Drawing on historical sources enabling him to trace descriptions of the ritual back to the eighteenth century, Bloch shows how its central symbolic features have remained remarkably uniform despite important social and political upheavals – the growth of the centralised Merina statewhich at the height of its power nearly the entire island of Madagascar, colonialism and subsequently independence – and despite great variations in its size and social importance. During the period of the centralised state, the royal circumcision was the main state ritual, and was used to legitimate royalty, tax collection and centralised hierarchy at the expense of weakening the *demes*. For this purpose, the symbolic content of the ritual was altered slightly, although its key elements remained unchanged. During the French colonial period the ritual was a small-scale family undertaking, whereas since independence in 1960 it has increased in importance and taken on anti-elite connotations. Bloch's detailed analysis of both the symbolic and social elements of the ritual process and its changing historical significance shows that ritual is not determined by an easily intelligible set of factors.

Bloch expresses dissatisfaction with conventional anthropological approaches to ritual. On the one hand, various functionalist explanations (Marxist as well as non-Marxist) are inadequate for reasons discussed earlier in this chapter. On the other, what he calls intellectualist and symbolist views, including those of Geertz and Evans-Pritchard (in his 1956 book), which 'see religion as a speculation on nature and an intellectual accommodation of the beyond' (Bloch 1986, p. 8), fail to place the beliefs and rituals in a proper social context. In concluding his own historical analysis of the Merina circumcision ritual, Bloch concludes: 'Rituals are events that *combine the properties of statements and actions*. It is because of this combination that their analysis has proved endlessly elusive' (1986, p. 181). It should be noted, finally, that the ritual studied by Bloch is largely secular, in spite of discernible religious elements.

A fact which cannot be elaborated here, but which should be kept in mind, is that it is not always easy to distinguish clearly between theatrical and ritual performances. Schechner (1994, p. 622) proposes a continuum where the theatre represents entertainment and the ritual efficacy; the theatre stands for fun and appreciation, the ritual for results and beliefs. However, not least in contemporary Western dramatism, the object of a theatre performance may well be to make the audience reflect on the conditions of existence (consider, for example, the relationship between the Sinhalese exorcism ritual and Beckett's plays) or to act politically (as with Brecht). The close connection between dance, theatre and ritual, furthermore, is demonstrated through the ways in which anthropological studies of dance and theatre draw on analytical perspectives developed in the context of ritual and religion (Schechner 2002; Wulff 1998). In a study from the tiny Pacific atoll of Tokelau, moreover, Ingjerd Hoëm (2005) shows the potential of theatre anthropology to shed light on fundamental questions of the discipline.

Tokelauans distinguish between two forms of knowledge: private and shared; that which is a personal or collective possession has magical qualities and can be used strategically in zero-sum games – in other words, this is knowledge as a limited good; there is also knowledge that can be freely shared. The restricted form of knowledge may nevertheless be presented playfully in song. The book, taking the 'knowledge economy' of traditional Tokelau as its starting point, explores how communicative practices and identification are affected through new kinds of performance, the media and so on, in contemporary settings, thereby addressing questions to do with cultural change, symbolic power and indeed issues raised already by Malinowski concerning magical knowledge as a kind of property. Hoëm's monograph shows that it would be unwise for an anthropologist to regard religion and ritual as sectors of society which can be studied independently of the wider contexts of politics and change.

An Actor-centred Perspective on Ritual

In Chapters 11 and 12, actor-based definitions of politics and economy are presented. Rather than stating that politics, for example, is the social distribution of power, authority and rights, or that economy is society's routines for production, distribution and consumption, one may thus define politics and economy as aspects of action.

Leach has proposed a definition of the same kind regarding ritual (Leach 1968). Common anthropological definitions of ritual would locate them to ritual institutions – churches, mosques, sacrificial grounds, etc. – and focus on the systemic level. This would ultimately be misleading, Leach argues, and instead he calls attention to the ritual act, seeing rituals as an aspect of culturally standardised actions. The expressive, symbolic aspect of a conventional act – everything which is not obviously goal-directed – is ritual, says Leach, and points out that ritual acts do not necessarily take place in what we think of as 'ritual contexts'. This kind of definition, we should note, does not exclude the more 'substantivist' definition focusing on the ritual institutions, but complements it by focusing on the acts themselves and not merely the social framework.

POLITICAL RITUAL IN STATE SOCIETIES

Careful to avoid a simplistic reductionist explanation, Bloch analysed the ideological dimension of ritual perhaps more carefully than any earlier anthropologist. One of his main points, which he shares with many other anthropologists, is that rituals and ritual symbolism have to be ambiguous because they are representations of a social world that is contradiction-ridden. So: 'the message of ideology cannot be maintained simply as a statement ... because it is by its very nature in contradiction with human experience in the world' (Bloch 1986, p. 195). This is important. Ideology always simplifies the world and imposes hierarchy and a particular social order. In the case of the Merina, ideology as mediated by the circumcision ritual also served to justify state violence.

In modern state societies, the oblique ideological dimension of ritual is no less evident than in non-modern societies (see Handelman 1990). As noted earlier, national flags are sufficiently ambiguous (or multivocal) to be able to create a symbolic bond and a sense of community between persons who are very different and who represent contradicting interests. Insofar as they are able to interpret the flag in different ways, and thus identify with it on different grounds by relating it to different kinds of personal experiences, citizens can actualise themselves as a nation through such simple national symbols. In this way, state rituals may indeed function as charters for collective action.

In situations of social transformation, rituals belonging to the former social order may be reproduced, although their meaning may change, in order to give an impression of legitimacy. As Kertzer notes (1988, p. 46), New Year celebrations have been a constant feature of Russian society since pagan times. When the Russians became Christian, the church merged these festivities with Christmas, and after the 1917 Bolshevik Revolution, the new Soviet leaders actively sponsored the festival after a brief interlude of attempting to abolish it, but tried to re-codify it as a socialist ritual with minimal Christian content (see also Mach 1993, pp. 130ff.). During periods perceived as turbulent, for example, where a new political power structure tries to replace the old one, the new leaders may try to appropriate ritual symbols associated with the old, familiar order in order to create an impression of continuity and legitimacy. Such a use of familiar symbols in order to render an unfamiliar situation familiar, whether or not this is intentional, is characteristic of the legitimation of contemporary ethnic movements (A. Cohen 1974) and nationalism; this is dealt with in Chapter 18.

RITUALS OF MODERNITY: FOOTBALL

Although ritual is frequently seen as 'enacted religion', it must be kept in mind that the most famous analysis of a single ritual, namely Geertz's interpretation of the Balinese cockfight, concentrates on an entirely secular ritual; and, as noted above, dance and theatre may well be understood in a framework partly shared with the study of ritual. Other non-religious rituals certainly also merit attention. The affinities between rock concerts and religious rituals are obvious, but the most important rituals in the contemporary world are arguably those to do with sports. Estimates suggest that between a fourth and a third of the world's population followed the finals of the 2006 World Cup in football on television. Until the 1990s, anthropological studies of sports were marginal, but today, several important studies – particularly of football (soccer) – exist (including MacClancy 1994; Armstrong and Giulianotti 1997; Archetti 1999; Giulianotti and Robertson 2009). Already in 1982, however, Marc Augé suggested that the focus of anthropological football studies should be shifted from social history to religious anthropology.

Common to most studies of football is a concern with forms of social identity. Roberto DaMatta (1991) uses Turner's notion of the social drama to understand the dynamics of football fandom; Eduardo Archetti (1999) has analysed the game as a celebration of masculinity and the star players as religious icons; Hans Hognestad (2003) has studied long-distance fans such as Norwegian Liverpool supporters, while others have called attention to its class dimension (evident in many European countries and cities such as Liverpool), its pivotal role (at least at the operational level) in expressing national identity, and even its potential for bridging generation gaps (boys support the same teams as their fathers). As a multivocal symbolic realm, football can also be a vehicle for the expression of political views, as when people in Belfast support one of the Glasgow teams, the Catholic Celtic or the Protestant Rangers. Its unparalleled global character (witnessed through international tournaments, the transnational composition of teams, and the increasingly transnational character of supporter groups, leading to paradoxical situations whereby, for example, Manchester United, having transformed itself successfully into a global label relatively disconnected from the geographical site of Manchester, is virtually the home team of Singapore) needs further exploration. The unpredictability of the outcome of any given game, further, contributes to blurring the boundary between football, religion and witchcraft. A research question which cannot be answered straightforwardly and conclusively, concerns what exactly is the 'object of worship' in spectator sports such as professional football. It is all of the above and more.

* * *

It is perhaps nowhere more evident than in the study of religion, rituals and practical/cognitive systems of knowledge that anthropological research generates insights which would not have been available without fieldwork. For instance, contrary to much theoretical philosophy, anthropological research has shown how it is fully possible, in practice, to hold notions which are contradictory in theory. Different kinds of knowledge are used in different kinds of situations, and as long as they are not confronted in the same situation they may easily coexist in the mind of one person. In a study of medical systems in polyethnic Mauritius, Linda Sussman (1983) showed that Mauritians may well consult three or four different kinds of doctors – who in a sense work within totally different realities and have irreconcilable views on illness and healing – to be on the safe side. If they have a backache, they may see a Chinese herbal doctor, an Indian ayurvedic doctor, a European physiotherapist and an Afro-Creole traditional healer.

The general point here is that meaning is use: that religious as well as other knowledge becomes important to people only when it can be used for something, only when it is connected to their experience. Rituals, in this regard, dramatise the rather abstract tenets of religion, render the content of religion concrete and recognisable, link it to experience and legitimate the social and political order. Moreover, different kinds of knowledge are made relevant in different situations. Therefore it does not necessarily lead to a practical contradiction to believe in both the Bible and the scientific theory of evolution, as long as the two bodies of thought are kept in separate realms. Similarly, a Kachin may be favourable to both *gumlao* and *gumsa* values, but not simultaneously; just as a West Indian may well be favourable to the values of both respectability and reputation. Which of them is applicable, depends on the situation.

SUGGESTIONS FOR FURTHER READING

Clifford Geertz: Religion as a Cultural System, in Clifford Geertz, *The Interpretation of Cultures*. New York: Basic Books 1973.

Richard Schechner: *Performance Studies: An Introduction*. London: Routledge 2002.

Victor W. Turner: *The Forest of Symbols: Aspects of Ndembu Ritual*. Ithaca, NY: Cornell University Press 1967.

Harvey Whitehouse and Robert N. McCauley, eds: *Mind and Religion: Psychological and Cognitive Foundations of Religion*. Walnut Creek, CA: AltaMira Press 2005.

15 LANGUAGE AND COGNITION

Animals are divided into (a) belonging to the Emperor, (b) embalmed, (c) tame, (d) sucking pigs, (e) sirens, (f) fabulous, (g) stray dogs, (h) included in the present classification, (i) frenzied, (j) innumerable, (k) drawn with a very fine camelhair brush, (l) *et cetera*, (m) having just broken the water pitcher, (n) that from a long way off look like flies.

> *– Jorge Luis Borges (quoting from 'a certain Chinese encyclopedia')*

WHORF'S HYPOTHESIS AND THE PROBLEM OF TRANSLATION

Benjamin Lee Whorf was an insurance salesman in the US in the 1920s. A recurrent problem in his job concerned the interpretation of words; their precise meaning was often rather significant with regard to indemnity payments. What did it mean, for example, that a fire was 'self-inflicted'? And what did it mean that a drum of petrol was 'empty'? In some cases, it could be empty of petrol, but full of petrol gas and thus highly explosive. A fire which was caused by an empty petrol drum exploding could, however, not be defined as self-inflicted. Whorf's company lost some money on such cases.

Some years later, Whorf developed an hypothesis on the relationship between language and the non-linguistic world which has enjoyed great influence in anthropology. Whorf's mentor in linguistic anthropology, Edward Sapir, played a part in the development of the idea, and the hypothesis is sometimes named the Sapir–Whorf hypothesis, but I shall speak of it as Whorf's hypothesis (Whorf 1956). It postulates that there is an intimate connection between the categories and structure of a language and the ways in which humans are able to experience the world and express their world-view to others. Whorf paid special attention to the language of the Hopi, which was almost without nouns as we know them, and which also lacked the standard verb conjugations common to Indo-European languages. Since the language of the Hopi had these peculiar characteristics, Whorf argued, they would experience the world in a fundamentally different way from the descendants of European settlers in North America, who had brought their languages and grammars (mostly amalgamating into American English) to the continent. The language of the Hopi was process-oriented and focused on movement, whereas English and other European languages were oriented towards things and nouns in general.

Whorf believed that there was an intrinsic connection between the life-world of a people and its language; that every people will develop the linguistic tools it needs to solve tasks perceived as necessary, and that the language of a people will therefore be a significant source of knowledge about their mode of thought, their cosmology and their everyday life.

An immediate implication of Whorf's hypothesis is the problem of cross-cultural translation, one of the perennial problems of anthropology. Is it necessarily possible to translate, say, the life-world and culture of the Azande, a Central African people, into English? Or could it rather be the case that their form of life is so closely connected with the Zande language that such a project is doomed to fail – because we will always be forced to interpret them in our own terms, and not in theirs, when we try to describe them in a language other than their own? Whorf himself did not hesitate to describe the differences between the Hopi language and English in comparative, or 'etic', terms, and in practice he thus carried out cultural translation, even if such translations might be impossible if one were to take his hypothesis at face value. Such translations are, naturally, necessary for anthropology to be possible, but they are not unproblematic.

THE NOTION OF THE PRE-LOGICAL MIND

Such issues are fundamental to anthropology as a comparative social science. They do not concern research methodology only in the technical sense of translating between languages; they also deal with the question of whether all humans think in roughly the same way, or if there are culturally specific modes of thought which follow different logics and cannot be faithfully reproduced in a foreign language. When the great German explorer Karl von den Steinen reported, in the late nineteenth century, that the Bororo of Amazonas described themselves as red macaws, many – among them the philosopher Lucien Lévy-Bruhl – were to draw the conclusion that the Bororo were clearly unable to think logically. For how can it be possible to think that one is a parrot and a human being at the same time? The Bororo mode of thought thus had to be pre-logical; this people violated Aristotle's principle of contradiction, which states that an object cannot both have and not have one and the same property at the same time and in the same respect. One cannot, in other words, simultaneously believe and not believe that one is a parrot. (Later it became evident that the Bororo by no means contradicted themselves, but rather spoke metaphorically in a way incomprehensible to von den Steinen. He interpreted them too literally.)

The general problem of translation is still with us, although it has been reformulated many times since the early 1930s. The problem has three main aspects. First, do 'primitive', non-literate peoples think in a fundamentally different way from ourselves? Second, if this is the case, is it possible to understand their life-world and to translate it into a comparative anthropological terminology? Third, is the anthropological terminology inherently culturally embedded, or does it represent a kind of context-free, and therefore comparatively useful, kind of language? There are many ways to approach these issues, and the only answer on which nearly all anthropologists agree, is that any differences in modes of thought are not innate – they are not caused by 'racial' differences. We must, therefore, study and compare culture and social organisation, even when the topic is the relationship between abstract modes of thought among different peoples.

THE MENTAL UNITY OF HUMANITY

One of the central principles of anthropology is the principle of the mental unity of humanity. This refers to the belief that the innate characteristics of humanity are essentially the same everywhere – not in the sense that humans are identical, but rather in that inborn differences do not account for cultural variation. If, for example, one had believed that the 'races' had varying degrees of intelligence, one might have accepted that there were inherent genetic causes for the fact that Africans in colonial times were illiterate and engaged in ancestor worship whereas British gentlemen drank port and quoted Kipling. If this had been correct, the entire modern anthropological endeavour would have been superfluous, since it would have been futile to search in culture and social organisation, or even in ecological circumstances, for causes of human variation.

The scientific grounds for claiming that different human groups have systematically varying mental faculties have never been convincing. The variation *within* each group has frequently been shown to be greater than the variation *between* the groups. Within any random sample of individuals, there will be some 'smart' and some 'stupid' people, some 'enterprising' and some 'lazy' individuals, and so on; but one cannot say that, for example, the Sami are intelligent whereas the Mbuti are stupid. Human groups worldwide are endowed with roughly the same innate faculties and potentials, and cultural variation must be accounted for by referring to data other than DNA – which may well, in the final instance, be innate, but which do not vary between ethnic groups.

Many kinds of cultural variation have been accounted for in this way in previous chapters. Neither the *kula* exchange of the Trobriand islanders, the ancestor cults of the Kaguru nor the agricultural technology of the Dogon have been explained through reference to inborn characteristics of the 'races'. This chapter focuses on variations between different cultural modes of thought, which are some of the most difficult cultural differences both to understand and to account for in comparative terms. We begin by discussing whether it may be reasonable to believe in witches, and then move on to classification, cultural knowledge, literacy and the relationship between thought, power and social organisation.

WITCHCRAFT AND KNOWLEDGE AMONG THE AZANDE

The Azande are a patrilineal people of agriculturalists whose population of about 3 million is spread over a large area in the Democratic Republic of Congo, the Central African Republic and Sudan. In his influential monograph on their knowledge and belief system, Evans-Pritchard drew on fieldwork among Azande in Sudan (Evans-Pritchard 1983 [1937]). Their cosmology presumes (in the ethnographic present tense) the existence of a number of spirits of different kinds, including ancestral spirits. In addition, the institution of witchcraft is central to their daily life and world-view. It is seen as the individual ability to create misfortune for others in spiritual ways. Only some Azande possess this ability. Unlike magic, which involves medicines and magical formulas, witchcraft is a purely spiritual, generally involuntary activity: the witchcraft power frequently commits its acts while the carrier (the witch) is asleep.

Death and other unfortunate circumstances are usually seen as caused by witchcraft. Traditionally, witches were executed ritually, but by the time of Evans-Pritchard's fieldwork in the late 1920s this practice had been abandoned, although the belief in witchcraft continued; decades later, when many Azande had been proletarianised, witchcraft beliefs were still common (Reining 1966). Indeed, in many parts of Africa, there has been an upsurge in witchcraft accusations in recent years (Niehaus 2001; Haar 2007).

The witchcraft institution provides answers to important questions and explains why people suffer misfortunes. It cannot explain in general why one develops a fever after a snakebite, but it does offer an explanation for why a certain person was bitten by a certain snake on a certain day. The scientific doctrine about cause and effect cannot provide explanations of this kind: it cannot tell why the granary had to collapse just when several Azande were resting in its shade. Although the poles supporting the granary were destroyed by termites, the victims held that the accident was ultimately caused by witchcraft.

The notion of witchcraft is not incompatible with a belief in causality. A Zande might agree that certain diseases are caused by bacteria in the drinking water, but he would also want to know why he became ill when his neighbour did not. He would look for the cause in his enemies, whom he would suspect of witchcraft. The witchcraft institution answers questions of the 'why now?' and 'why me?' kind, which science cannot do.

Evans-Pritchard suggests that witchcraft is invoked as an explanatory principle 'whenever plain reason fails'. When somebody is accused of witchcraft, a prince or a witchdoctor consults an oracle to decide the matter. The most important is the poison oracle, which consists of a portion of poison and two fowls. The first fowl is served poison; if it survives, the accused is innocent, but if it dies, he or she is guilty. Then the validity of the verdict is double-checked by administering the poison to a second bird.

Evans-Pritchard took witches more seriously than any European scholar had done earlier, and was concerned to show how the belief in witches made sense and was perfectly rational within the Zande world. He was among the earliest to criticise and discard the idea, propagated by Lévy-Bruhl (but also present in Frazer's work), that there existed a specifically primitive, 'pre-logical' mentality. His aim was to explore the interrelationships between thought and social structure, but not to reduce the former to the latter.

However, at two important points Evans-Pritchard indicates that when all is said and done the Azande are wrong in assuming that witches exist. First, he introduces a sharp distinction between the witchcraft logic and the scientific logic, and frequently makes statements to the effect that 'obviously, witches do not exist'. He also distinguishes clearly between mystical notions, notions based on common sense and scientific notions. Since witchcraft is invisible and (in 'our' view) supernatural, a cosmology based on such beliefs falls squarely into the first category and must be less valid, on objective grounds, than scientific notions.

Second, Evans-Pritchard's monograph ends with a primarily structural-functionalist explanation of the witchcraft institution: the belief in witches and similar institutions exists, ultimately, because they contribute to social integration and check deviant behaviour – not because they produce valid insight and understanding.

WINCH'S CRITICISM

The philosopher Peter Winch, reacting against Evans-Pritchard's distinction between mystical and scientific notions, started a lengthy and heated debate on comparison, rationality and cultural translation when he wrote a paper in 1964 entitled 'Understanding a Primitive Society' (Winch 1970 [1964]).

Winch rejects the idea that there are universal standards available to compare witchcraft beliefs and science. To him, science is, just as much as witchcraft, based on unverifiable axioms. Winch also claims that Oxford professors are scarcely less superstitious than Azande; they too trust blindly in forces they do not fully understand. One of his examples is drawn from meteorology. How many of us really understand its principles? Yet we watch the weather forecasts and believe in them.

Winch agrees that ideas and notions must be tested in order for their validity to be justified. This, he argues, is done both in scientific experiments and in the Zande consultation of poison oracles, and there is no difference in principle between the two procedures.

Further, Winch claims that scientific experiments are meaningless to someone who is ignorant about the principles of science. For this reason, science – like witchcraft – is not inherently meaningful, but makes sense only within a particular, culturally created frame of reference. He compares the helplessness of an engineer deprived of his mathematics with the predicament of a Zande without access to his oracles.

To Winch, it is also important to note that the lives of the Azande seem to function well; that their relationship to witchcraft makes their existence meaningful, and that the system by and large is consistent.

The disagreement between Evans-Pritchard and Winch ultimately amounts to divergent views of science. Whereas Evans-Pritchard holds that the Azande are wrong, Winch argues that all knowledge is culturally constructed and that it can therefore only be deemed right or wrong within its own cultural context. Winch questions anthropology's assumption that its comparative concepts are culturally 'neutral' – when all is said and done, he suggests, even anthropology is a cultural practice.

He draws extensively on Ludwig Wittgenstein's theory of language games (1983 [1958]), where the latter argues that knowledge is socially created and that different systems of knowledge (language games, or in Winch's sense, cultures) are incommensurable and therefore cannot be ranked hierarchically or, strictly speaking, compared. This line of reasoning, which Winch applies not only to anthropological analysis but also to the anthropologists themselves, can be glossed as a strong version of Whorf's hypothesis, and it seems to render different cultural universes incommensurable for want of a neutral language of comparison.

Let us pose the question differently. Why is it that anthropology as an academic discipline developed in Western Europe and the USA, and not, say, in the Trobriand Islands or Azandeland? As an experiment in thinking, we may imagine a Zande anthropologist who arrives in Britain to look into the local cosmology and cultural perception of death. She would quickly discover that the witchcraft institution is absent in that country, something which clearly must be accounted for. If she is a faithful structural-functionalist, she might search for functional causes for the strange denial, among the British, of the existence of witches. Perhaps she would eventually draw the conclusion that the denial of witchcraft, the blind faith in 'natural causes of death', strengthened social integration in British society, since it prevented open conflict between families and lineages.

This kind of argument seems to lend support to Winch's relativist position. However, it is a matter of fact that social anthropology did not develop in Zandeland but in Britain and other northern countries, and this must also be taken into account. Perhaps the hypothetical example of the Zande anthropologist is best seen as a warning against simplistic functionalist explanations, but not as an argument against anthropology as a generalising, comparative discipline. Later in this chapter, some reasons are suggested as to why the Zande did not develop their own comparative science of society and culture. It must also be emphasised that there is no reason to discard Evans-Pritchard's pioneering analysis of an African knowledge system as bogus, notwithstanding Winch's critical points. Mary Douglas has forcefully argued that the book is primarily about knowledge, not about social integration (Douglas 1980), and the anarchist philosopher of science Paul Feyerabend (1975) mentions it as an outstanding example of non-ethnocentric science.

Winch's position is less radical than it might seem at a first glance. His view is that anthropologists studying other people's worlds are not obliged, or even entitled, to evaluate the validity of the informants' truth claims, since anthropology as an academic science does not contain criteria for such an evaluation. We anthropologists are neither physicists nor theologians. Rather, Winch calls for what scholars involved in the sociological study of science and technology (STS) later called the *symmetry principle* (Fuller 2006): that is the principle that any life-world, or scientific construction, should be described in neutral terms. If the scholar believes in nuclear physics but not in astrology, she should nevertheless describe the two belief systems in the same terminology, because – notwithstanding their variable relationship to an external reality – both are social constructions. This is not the same as relativising truth, but a way of saying what anthropology should be about: the study of other people's worlds, not a method for grading their achievements on a particular scale, ethnocentric or not.

HOW 'NATIVES' THINK

Just as many anthropologists had begun to believe that the rationality debate had been exhausted after a series of increasingly nuanced edited collections (B. Wilson 1970; Hollis and Lukes 1982; Overing 1985; Pálsson 1993), it reappeared at the very centre of American anthropology in the 1980s and 1990s. The antagonists were Gananath Obeyesekere and Marshall Sahlins, both highly respected anthropologists, who disagreed fundamentally about details concerning the death of Captain Cook at the hands of Hawaiians in 1779. Sahlins (1985) had originally argued that Cook was killed because the Hawaiians had initially perceived him as a god (Lono), but when he was forced to return at an inauspicious moment because of a broken mast, he spoiled the divine script into which he had been inscribed, and therefore had to be sacrificed as an imposter and a fraud. An examination of Sahlins' argument led Obeyesekere to write a book, *The Apotheosis of Captain Cook* (1992), where he accuses Sahlins of depicting the Hawaiians as irrational and primitive. Obeyesekere, an anthropologist influenced by Freudian psychoanalysis, claims that Hawaiians acted according to the same pragmatic, calculating rationality as anybody else would.

A few years later, Sahlins responded in kind, by offering a new book entitled *How 'Natives' Think: About Captain Cook, For Example* (1995). The title is a pun on Lévy-Bruhl's *How Natives Think*, which represents exactly the tradition of Western thinking about 'primitive peoples' that Obeyesekere tries to associate Sahlins with. While Obeyesekere accuses Sahlins of imperialist thinking (it is naturally pleasing, he intimates, for a white man to fancy that 'natives' used to believe that white men were gods), Sahlins turns the tables and argues that Obeyesekere is the imperialist, as he tries to impose a Western, utilitarian, rational-choice model of action on to the Hawaiians. Obeyesekere, in other words, emerges as the universalist, Sahlins as the relativist, and both doubt the other's ability to portray a non-European people on their own terms. Through the heated, learned debate between Sahlins and Obeyesekere (where Sahlins admittedly had the advantage of being the regional specialist), the issues of translation, interpretation, relativity and universality re-emerged – fresh, challenging and difficult to resolve in a conclusive manner.

CLASSIFICATION

Durkheim and Mauss were among the earliest to explore the interrelationship between social organisation and patterns of thought. The basic idea in their book *Primitive Classification* (1963 [1903]) was that thought is a social product and that different societies thereby produce different kinds of thought. (Unlike Winch, they did not question the privileged position of scientific thought.) A great portion of the book discusses primitive systems of classification; and since its publication, the study of classification has been a central concern in anthropology.

Classification, in the anthropological sense, entails dividing objects, people, animals and other phenomena according to socially pre-established categories or types. This is an important part of the knowledge system of any society, and knowledge is always related to social organisation and power. Arguments have just been presented against the notion that some kinds of knowledge are 'objectively and universally true', and in exploring systems of knowledge it is necessary to be aware of the interrelationship between knowledge and other parts of the social world; this includes one's own knowledge.

Just as witchcraft beliefs may seem 'irrational' to the ethnocentric observer, alien systems of classification may seem unsystematic to someone who takes the Western system for granted. Ethnographic studies have revealed great variations in the ways other people classify. One famous example is the Karam, a small people of highland New Guinea, who do not regard the cassowary as a bird (Bulmer 1967), although Linnaeus (the eighteenth-century founder of the scientific system of plant and animal classification) would definitely have done so. The cassowary resembles an ostrich: it has feathers and lays eggs, but does not fly. Therefore the Karam do not consider it a bird. On the other hand, they classify bats together with birds (as flying creatures), even though we 'know' that they are 'really' mammals.

For a long time, anthropologists tried to show that the logic of any system of classification was intrinsically connected to the usefulness of plants and animals; that it was simply a functional device for the material reproduction of society. This idea eventually had to be abandoned, and we now turn to showing why.

CLASSIFICATORY ANOMALIES

The Lele, a people today numbering about 80,000 in Kasai, central Congo (DRC), distinguish meticulously between different classes of animals (Douglas

Cannibalism

In which sub-field of anthropology does research on cannibalism properly belong? In the study of economic systems, politics, religion, cultural ecology, symbolism and modes of thought, classification – or in the autocritique of anthropology? Let me outline some highlights in research on cannibalism.

Some scholars, including Marvin Harris, held that the assumed widespread cannibalism among the Aztecs was caused by protein scarcity. Others, notably Sahlins, argued that there was enough protein available, and that the ritual consumption of human hearts was rather a deeply religious act.

According to Lévi-Strauss's theory of symbolic relationships between different kinds of food, boiled and roasted food constitute a binary pair of oppositions. In accordance with this model, Lévi-Strauss held that it was likely that endocannibals (who eat parts of deceased relatives) would boil them, while exocannibals (who eat enemies) would roast them. In a bid to test the 'hypothesis', the Harvard anthropologist Paul Shankman processed data from 60 societies assumed to practise cannibalism. He found that 17 boiled while 20 roasted; 6 did both. The rest used other techniques for preparation, including baking. Shankman found, further, that there was no correlation between the categorisation of the eaten and the mode of preparation (Harris 1979).

It must be said, in defence of Lévi-Strauss, that anthropological reports of cannibalism are uncertain and tend to be second-hand. Indeed, they are so uncertain that William Arens, in *The Man-Eating Myth* (1978), argues that cannibalism has probably never existed as a cultural custom. All the sources he has consulted suffer from weaknesses and inconsistencies. To the Spanish *conquistadors*, for example, it was useful to depict the Aztecs as bloodthirsty cannibals to justify the destruction of their highly advanced civilisation. Arens, referring to a mass of anthropological research, maintains he could not find a single reliable eye-witness account of cannibalism. He points out that many peoples tell stories to the effect that the neighbouring tribe are cannibals, which may explain why the belief in cannibalism is so widespread. Actually, he intimates that a rule against cannibalism may be as universal as the incest taboo.

If Arens is at least partly right, cannibalism has to do with classification, but not classification of food. Instead, it concerns the classification of people, and both anthropologists and other people have taken part in this kind of classification. However, he can hardly be entirely right. Too many reliable eye-witness accounts of cannibalism exist for this to be likely.

1966, 1975). For instance, birds are characterised by feathers, their ability to fly and the laying of eggs, and are thereby distinguished from other animals. However, there are certain animals that do not fit neatly into this logic. The monitor lizard and the tortoise are examples of such exceptions: they lay eggs, but walk on all fours and lack feathers. Douglas describes such 'deviant' creatures as anomalies; they fail to fit in. The anomaly, in a manner akin to the liminal phase in Turner's model of the ritual process (Chapter 9), is both outside and inside; it threatens the established order. Anomalous animals are subjected to certain rules; one can only eat them under specific circumstances, women are not allowed to touch them, and so on.

The most important anomalous creature among the Lele is the pangolin (*Manis tricuspis*). It has, the Lele explain, the tail and body of a fish and it is covered with scales, but it gives birth like a mammal. It has four small legs and climbs trees (Douglas 1975, p. 33). This animal occupies an important place in the mythology and ritual life of the Lele. There is a cult of fertility centred on it. The reason, argues Douglas, is that the pangolin is anomalous in a crucial way: in addition to everything else, it gives birth to only one offspring at a time. In this regard it resembles a human more than an animal. Just as the parents of twins and triplets (who are also anomalies on this score) are seen as mediators between the human and the spiritual worlds, the pangolin is seen as a mediator between humanity and the animal world.

Anomalies are usually associated with danger and pollution. One example, described by Douglas elsewhere (1966), is the pig in Middle Eastern religions: as a cloven-hoofed but not ruminant mammal, it was not classified as edible since edible animals ought to be either both cloven-hoofed and ruminant or neither – it was an anomaly. The rather more positive status of the pangolin is caused by the fact, Douglas argues, that the Lele have succeeded in turning a potential curse into a blessing, exploiting the ambiguous status of the animal to their advantage. The pangolin is not economically important, and yet it occupies a central place in Lele cosmology: it is a mediator.

TOTEMIC CLASSIFICATION

When the Bororo spoke of themselves as red macaws, to the bewilderment of von den Steinen, they referred to a system of classification known in the professional literature as 'totemism'. Totemism – the term is of Ojibwa origin – is a generic term for a kind of knowledge system whereby each subgroup in a society, usually a clan, has a special, ritual relationship to a class of natural phenomena, usually plants or animals. Totemism has traditionally been particularly widespread in Australia and the Pacific, the Americas and Africa. For example, the totems of the Algonquin in Quebec include the bear, the fish and thunder in a symbolic system whereby natural phenomena are seen to correspond to aspects of society. The question posed by many anthropologists, from Frazer onwards, was the exact nature of this correspondence.

Malinowski, writing on totemism in the Trobriand Islands, held, like Frazer before him, that totemic plants and animals were chosen because they were inherently useful to the maintenance of society (1974 [1948]). Radcliffe-Brown, who developed a more complex view of totemism, drew on Durkheim's notion that the attitude towards a totem was caused by a special relationship between it and the social order, and that the ultimate function of totemism was to maintain social integration (1952 [1929]). The totem is thus a tangible identity marker for a group; Durkheim himself, comparing with modern societies, mentions flags as a kind of totem.

Radcliffe-Brown then poses the question of why certain animals and plants are chosen as totems. Like Malinowski and others before him, he assumes that there must be a practical reason, so that, for example, experts in bear hunting take the bear as their totem. In this way, totemism could be seen as a symbolic expression of the division of labour in society.

In a later article, Radcliffe-Brown (1951) raises doubt about his earlier assumption that totemic animals are economically useful to society. At this point, he rather focuses on their symbolic meaning. However, he fails to draw a clear conclusion, and Lévi-Strauss is generally credited with resolving the enigma of totemism in anthropology (1963, 1966 [1962]). Drawing on an enormous mass of recorded ethnography, largely from North America and Australia, Lévi-Strauss shows that there is no inherent connection between the utilitarian value of a creature and its significance in the totemic system. Instead, he argues, certain animals are chosen because of their mutual relationship – that is, not because of their direct relationship to groups in a segmentary society. The differences between totemic animals (the way they are perceived by the people) correspond to the differences between groups in society (see Figure 15.1).

Totemic animals contribute to the creation of order; up to this point, Lévi-Strauss agrees with earlier theorists. However, as he puts it, they are not chosen because they are good to eat, but because they are 'good to think' (*bons à penser*).

Figure 15.1   Radcliffe-Brown's early view of the relationship between totemic animals and clans (left) and Lévi-Strauss's view (right)

The system of totems and the clans in society are further connected symbolically in two complementary ways, through metaphor and metonymy. A metaphor is a symbol which stands for something else, in the way the milk tree among the Ndembu stands for fertility among women (Chapter 14). A metonym is rather a part which symbolically expresses a whole. Metaphorically, the king may be represented by a lion, metonymically by the crown he wears on his head. The relationship between metaphor and metonymy can be said to correspond to the relationship between melody and harmony (see Leach 1976; Lakoff and Johnson 1980; Fernandez 1991). A metaphor acquires its meaning through its association with the object it represents, while metonymy consists of using a part to represent the whole.

In a totemic system therefore, each totemic animal stands metonymically for the whole chain of totems, just as each clan stands for the whole society (as a single word may represent the whole sentence). Simultaneously, of course, the totems are metaphors for each clan. The relationship between the bear and the eagle corresponds to the relationship between the bear clan and the eagle clan. Now, the totems themselves – say, the bear and the eagle – are arbitrary; what counts is the relationship between them.

UNDOMESTICATED THINKING

A major concern in Lévi-Strauss's work on totemism was to invalidate notions to the effect that there existed a 'pre-logical, primitive mode of thought' – although he follows a different path from Evans-Pritchard. The structuralism of Lévi-Strauss seeks to reveal not similarities in actual reasoning, but universal underlying principles for thought and symbolisation.

In *La Pensée sauvage*, 'Undomesticated thinking' (misleadingly rendered in English as *The Savage Mind*, 1966 [1962]), the fundamental cognitive processes among modern and non-modern peoples are seen as identical. People everywhere think in terms of metaphor and metonymy, and above all they think in contrasting pairs, so-called binary oppositions. This general model depicting organising principles of thought resembles Bateson's theory of information (1972, 1979), which famously argues that only differences that make a difference can create information. Both Lévi-Strauss and Bateson are concerned to show that what is essential are relationships rather than the objects themselves.

Lévi-Strauss argues that fundamental thought processes are identical everywhere, but he also indicates that people with different kinds of technology at their disposal will express their thought in very different ways. Those who depend on script and numbers clearly think along different lines than non-literates, he says. Lévi-Strauss compares the literate and non-literate styles of thinking, and describes the latter as the science of the concrete (*la science du concret*). When a non-literate person, living in a society with no script, is to think abstractly, he or she is forced to align his or her concepts with concrete, visible objects. Spirits, for example, are abstractions described in terms of their visible manifestations; this explains why many early explorers and missionaries erroneously thought that tribal peoples 'worshipped trees and rocks'. Original creativity, in this kind of society, is possible through novel juxtapositions of concepts referring to familiar objects. Lévi-Strauss describes this thought operation as *bricolage* (a *'bricoleur'* can be translated as a handyman, a jack-of-all-trades). This creative, associational and 'playful' mode of thought is contrasted with that of the 'engineer'; the abstract science dominant in Western societies, imprisoned and disciplined by writing and numbers (see also Liep 2000 on creativity).

However, *bricoleurs* have a limited repertory of symbols at their disposal. Engineers, who create abstractions from abstractions, may rather try to transcend the familiar. They are tied up – their thought is tamed or domesticated – by writing and numbers, but at the same time they are liberated from the direct communication with natural objects enforced on the 'untamed thought' of the *bricoleurs*.

The Social Construction of Emotions

Knowledge, belief systems and classification are social products, and a great deal of research has been carried out regarding their variations and relationship to power structures and other aspects of social organisation. Other aspects of culture have been studied less thoroughly until recent decades; one such aspect is emotions. Many anthropologists still take them more or less for granted and presume that they are inborn. The capacity for love, hatred, empathy, aggression and so on is thus seen as more or less uniformly distributed in the world, and it has also been tacitly assumed that emotions function roughly in the same way in different societies. This view has been challenged, especially since the late 1970s, by scholars who argue that emotions are socially constructed. For example, it has been shown that the European distinction between 'reason' and 'emotion' does not exist in societies such as the Ilongot of the Philippines (Rosaldo 1980), Ifaluk in the Pacific (Lutz 1988) and in Bali (Wikan 1992). It has also been argued that aggression, believed by many to be inborn, is a cultural product (Howell and Willis 1990), and that there exist societies where no concept comparable to our concept of aggression occurs (Howell 1989).

The distinction between *bricoleurs* and engineers should not be seen as absolute. Today most societies in the world are 'semi-literate', and Lévi-Strauss himself admits that some modes of thought reminiscent of *bricolage*, notably in music and poetry, exist even in thoroughly literate societies. Still, the distinction can be a useful starting-point for an exploration of the interrelationship between knowledge, technology and social organisation.

WRITING AS TECHNOLOGY

In *La Pensée sauvage*, Lévi-Strauss distinguishes between what he calls 'cold' and 'hot' societies. Cold societies see themselves as essentially unchanging, while hot societies are based on an ideology perceiving change as inevitable and potentially beneficial. This distinction corresponds not only to the *bricoleur*–engineer dichotomy, but also to the distinction between 'traditional' and 'modern' societies. For the sake of the argument, the contrast between these societal 'types' is overstated here, but the reader should keep in mind that 'modern' and 'traditional' are ideal types, and that real societies on the ground are more complex than this simple, analytical dichotomy implies.

The role of script as a form of technology has been discussed by generations of anthropologists (see for instance Goody 1968; Ong 1982; Finnegan 1988; Street and Besnier 1994). In a number of books, Jack Goody has argued that the introduction of writing may have fundamental implications for thought as well as social organisation, and his idea of a 'Great Divide' between non-literate and literate societies is close kin to Lévi-Strauss's studies of totemic versus historical thinking and the *bricoleur*–engineer contrast – characteristically, one of Goody's books on literacy is called, with a pun on Lévi-Strauss's book on totemic thinking, *The Domestication of the Savage Mind* (1977). It could be said that, just as Marx turned Hegel on his head (or on to his feet!), Goody tries to operationalise and sociologise Lévi-Strauss. Controversial among anthropologists who hold that this kind of distinction is simplistic (for example, Halverson 1992), Goody's main arguments nevertheless merit an outline here.

The introduction of writing, Goody argues, enables people to distinguish between concepts and their referents. Writing allows us to turn words into things, to freeze them in time and space. Speech, by contrast, is fleeting and transient and cannot be fixed for posterity. In this sense, writing entails a reduction of speech: the two are not 'the same', and the written version of a statement lacks its extra-linguistic context – facial expression, social situation, tone of voice, etc. Writing can indeed be seen as a kind of material culture; like artefacts, it is solid and enduring, and it can be analysed as objectified subjectivity; as 'frozen intentions'.

Writing arguably liberates thought from the necessity of mnemotechnics; we do not have to remember everything, but can look it up, today increasingly on the web. By implication, writing makes the accumulation of vast amounts of knowledge possible in ways orality is unable to. Writing also narrows the meanings of thoughts in the sense that it lends itself, Goody argues, to accurate critical examination in ways that oral statements do not. We may isolate a small bit of human discourse and subject it to thorough examination in ways that cannot be achieved in societies which lack writing. However – and this is a criticism that has repeatedly been levelled against this kind of theory – there are many examples of literate societies where criticism (in the scientific sense) is not encouraged. On the other hand, it may be retorted that writing is a necessary but not sufficient condition for science as we know it. This argument, one may agree, goes a long way towards explaining why the Azande did not develop their own comparative science of culture and society – but it does not alone explain why many literate peoples have not done so.

Writing also has great potential importance for social organisation. It has been noted that it was used at a very early stage (ancient Mesopotamia) for lists, inventories of the amount of grain in the granary, the number of slaves and animals in the city and so on. As witnessed in the Gospel of St Luke, censuses were also introduced early in the history of writing. Writing thus facilitates not only analytical thought, but also the surveillance of vast numbers of people. It can therefore be regarded as an important kind of technology in the political administration of complex societies. Recent research on censuses and collective identities, incidentally, emphasise the ways in which labelling and counting contribute to 'freezing' and reifying identities which were formerly fluid and less clearly bounded (Kertzer and Arel 2002).

Finally, a chief use of writing in most literate societies has lain in the building of archives, some of which eventually become history. Lévi-Strauss, commenting on the 'totemic void' in Europe and Asia (1966 [1962]), concludes that these societies have chosen history instead of totemic myths. He does not, in principle, see history as inherently 'truer' than myth, but rather as a special kind of myth.

The difference between literacy and orality should not be overemphasised: there is by no means a clear-cut distinction, and Goody's general theories have been modified and criticised by many anthropologists basing their argument on specifically local cases – indeed criticism of the literacy thesis was presented already in a book edited by Goody himself in 1968, where several anthropologists show that the general theory does not quite fit 'their people'. It is nevertheless difficult to deny that the uses of script form an important part of the technology of a society, although writing has more variable usage than initially supposed by Goody. An abstract ideology such as nationalism, for example (see Chapter 18), is unimaginable without the information technology of writing, which enables members of society to disseminate ideas over a vast area, thus creating cultural homogeneity and bonds of solidarity between millions of individuals who will never know each other personally.

TIME AND SCALE

Abstract time, that is the kind of time represented through clocks and calendars, may have effects analogous to those of writing. In the kind of society where most of the readers of this book were raised, it is generally believed that time is something one may have much or little of; something which can be saved, something which 'is money', something which can be measured independently of concrete events. Concepts like 'one hour' or 'one week' are meaningful even if we do not say what they contain by way of events. Time, in this kind of society, is conventionally conceptualised as a line with an arrow at the end, where a moving point called 'the present' separates past and future. This kind of abstraction is a cultural invention, neither more nor less. In a certain sense, clocks do not measure time, but create it.

Societies lacking clocks do not 'lack time', but rather tend to be organised according to what we may call concrete time (although, as usual, there are very important variations). In this kind of society – historically speaking, the vast majority of human societies – time exists only as embedded in action and process, not as something abstract and autonomous existing outside the events taking place. Rituals do not take place 'at 5 o'clock', but when all is ready – when the preparations are completed and the guests have arrived. In clockless societies, time is not a scarce resource, since it exists only as the events taking place. One cannot 'lose' or 'kill' time there.

Past and future take on a different meaning in societies with and without an abstract concept of time, respectively. Obviously, peoples without dates and calendars do not date previous events in the same way that we do. Bourdieu, further, has written of the Kabyles that they were shocked to learn of the way the French related to the future (Bourdieu 1963). 'The French see themselves as greater than God,' they said, 'for they believe that they can control the future. But the future belongs to God.' Many peoples, moreover, do not conjugate verbs in the future tense. One philosophically sound way of explaining this may be that events in the world create time, and since no events have yet taken place in the future, the future cannot constitute a time (Tempels 1959). Myths, Lévi-Strauss famously said, are 'machines to suppress the passage of time', and the time separating the present from the time of mythical origins is not mechanical; it cannot be measured accurately.

Linear, quantified, abstract time is not detached from social organisation, but it did not arise automatically in response to 'societal needs'. Just as writing, a tool for political control and the advancement of science, was first developed for ritual and mundane purposes, the first Europeans to use clocks were monks who needed them to coordinate prayers and work. Since medieval times, the significance of mechanical time as a means to coordinate and organise European (and eventually other) societies, has grown steadily. The cultural historian Lewis Mumford once wrote that the most tyrannical and authoritarian device developed in modern societies was neither the car nor the steam engine, but the clock. The philosopher Henri Bergson, writing in the late nineteenth and early twentieth centuries, was concerned to save the subjective experience of time, *la durée*, which he saw as being threatened by quantified, mechanical time in the era of technocratic rationality.

Why is it that people living in modern societies have become slaves of the clock, as it were, while others seem to manage perfectly well without it? The answer must be sought in the social organisation of society. If I wish to travel from Oslo to Prague, it would be extremely inconvenient to have to go to the airport and wait for a day or two until a sufficient number of passengers to Prague had found their way there. It seems more rational that the airline states that the departure will be at 11 a.m., that all of the passengers agree on the meaning of 11 a.m. and thus appear at the airport more or less simultaneously. In other words, the concept of abstract time and the omnipresence of clocks make it possible to coordinate the actions of a much larger number of people than is possible in a society with no shared, quantified notion of time. Thus, both script and abstract time make social integration at a very high level of scale possible. Money, dealt with previously, does roughly the same thing to exchange and wealth as clocks do to time, thermometers to temperature and writing to language: standardisation and, therefore, increased scale creates a society relying on ever more abstract relations, and capable of organising itself at a huge scale.

KNOWLEDGE AND POWER

Evans-Pritchard (1951) once wrote that he believed his studies of Zande witchcraft might contribute to the understanding of communist Russia. What he meant was that an understanding of the ideological underpinnings of the knowledge system of one society may give clues as to similar structures elsewhere. Undoubtedly, knowledge systems create a particular order in the world, and this does not only concern ideologies of gender, caste, class or ethnicity as dealt with in other chapters here, but also the very structuring of experience. In his celebrated novel *1984*, George Orwell (1984 [1949]) describes a society where the language has consciously been changed by the power elite, in order to prevent the citizens from undertaking critical thought. In 'Newspeak', the word 'freedom' has thus lost its meaning of 'individual freedom' and can only be used in sentences like 'the dog is free from lice'. Although such conscious manipulation of language may be rare, there can be no doubt that the kind of insight introduced by Whorf may profitably be used to study ideology and power structures. In our kind of society, the shift from 'chairman' to 'chairperson' (or simply 'chair') and similar changes in language use indicate a growing consciousness about the ideological character of language and concepts.

A different approach to the relationship between knowledge and power is exemplified in the study of so-called secret societies. Initiation into such societies, common in several parts of the world, is accompanied by the acquisition of esoteric, highly valued knowledge. In some societies, such as dynastic China, literacy was seen as esoteric knowledge and kept away from the masses. In *Homo Academicus*, Bourdieu (1988 [1984]) describes academic knowledge as a political resource of a similar kind. He describes the deliberately inaccessible language spoken by most academics, the pompous rituals and conventions surrounding academic life in France – allegedly necessary for the 'advance of science' – as expressions of symbolic power.

The relationship between knowledge and social organisation can be illuminated in many ways. For example, it is common to assume that culinary differentiation, particularly the development of *'haute cuisine'*, is connected with social differentiation and hierarchy. Virtually everything which is taken for granted has a social origin, be it totemic classification, dogmatic belief in the blessings of liberal democracy, belief in God or the idea that one should eat with a knife and a fork. Karl Marx was aware of this kind of relationship when he wrote, in the mid nineteenth century, that even the functioning of our five senses is a product of the whole of history up to this day.

Finally, we should be wary of empirical generalisations regarding the knowledge of this or that people. Knowledge is always socially distributed. Surveys indicate that less than half the adult population of Britain and the USA have any idea of what DNA is, and a survey cited by Worsley (1997, p. 6) suggests that a third of adult Britons believe that the sun goes around the earth. It should also be remarked, again, that it is not the business of the anthropologist to make value judgements about knowledge systems. Good studies of knowledge, ranging from Evans-Pritchard via Latour and Woolgar's (1979) study of the social production of scientific knowledge to Worsley's *Knowledges* (1997) and Barth's (2000) suggestions for a methodology facilitating comparison of different knowledge systems, chiefly try to make sense of the world following the native's point of view, whether the native is a nuclear physicist or an Australian Aborigine. Indeed, Mark Harris's *Ways of Knowing* (2007) is a collection of anthropological studies of anthropologists' knowledge of other societies, intended to improve self-reflection and sharpen methodological tools. This kind of perspective is not tantamount to postmodern relativism; it is simply the only viable method for developing and transmitting an understanding of the various life-worlds human beings create and maintain.

*   *   *

This chapter has discussed a number of simple contrasts frequently invoked by anthropologists (especially in the past), between witchcraft accounts and scientific accounts, between the *bricoleur* and the engineer, between literacy and orality, between abstract linear time and concrete time, and ultimately between large-scale, 'modern' and small-scale, 'traditional' societies. Such dichotomies, which have never provided a satisfactory empirical description of the world, have been maintained for generations, at least partly because they facilitate the classification of social and cultural phenomena – if not entire societies. In the remaining chapters, this kind of dichotomous modelling is subjected to critical scrutiny, and both its strengths and limitations are made clear.

SUGGESTIONS FOR FURTHER READING

E.E. Evans-Pritchard: *Witchcraft, Oracles and Magic among the Azande*, abridged edn. Oxford: Oxford University Press 1983 [1937].

Jack Goody: *The Domestication of the Savage Mind*. Cambridge: Cambridge University Press 1977.

George Lakoff and Mark Johnson: *Philosophy in the Flesh: The Embodied Mind and its Challenge to Western Thought*. New York: Basic Books 1999.

Peter Worsley: *Knowledges: What Different Peoples Make of the World*. London: Profile 1997.

16   COMPLEXITY AND CHANGE

Now that the Polynesian islands have been clad in concrete and transformed into hangar ships anchored in the Pacific Ocean, when all of Asia is beginning to look like a polluted suburb, when cities of cardboard and sheet metal spread all over Africa, when civilian and military airplanes violate the untouched innocence of American and Melanesian forests even before they take away their virginity – what can the so-called flight from reality entailed by travelling then result in, other than confronting us with the most unfortunate aspects of our own history?

— *Claude Lévi-Strauss*

Some of the previous chapters have examined different forms of political organisation, world-views and systems of economic production and distribution. It has been noted for decades that the ethnographic present, the tense conventionally used when anthropologists talk about different societies, is increasingly, and more and more rapidly, becoming a past tense. In Australia, 250 languages were spoken in the late eighteenth century. At the end of the twentieth century, there were about 30 left, and few of them seemed likely to survive for another generation in Australia. Virtually all inhabitants of the world live in states which define them as citizens (see Chapter 18), and a growing majority of the world's population depends on general-purpose money in their daily life. Nominally, well over half the world's adult population is literate.

URBAN ANTHROPOLOGY: CHANGE AND CONTINUITY

One of the most visible aspects of social and cultural change in the period since the Second World War has been urbanisation. While less than 5 per cent of Africa's population lived in cities in 1900, about 55 per cent did in 2005, and the numbers for Asia and Latin America are of a comparable order. For the first time in human history, a majority of the world's population is now urban. There are several related causes of urbanisation. Population growth in the countryside and transitions from subsistence agriculture to the production of cash crops lead to a general land shortage and greater vulnerability; simultaneously, new opportunities for wagework arise in and near the cities. Rural dwellers also lose their land and livelihood due to the 'development' of roads, industrialisation and industrial farming. Many are driven to the comparative safety of cities by war and unrest also. Most urban dwellers in non-industrial countries, however, are usually classified as poor, although their lot might not have been better if they had stayed in the countryside. The growth of urban slums has been spectacular in recent decades. The urban scholar and journalist Mike Davis (2007) describes a situation where the entire coastal area stretching from Benin City in Nigeria to Accra in Ghana could be designated a single continuous slum; where a similar development includes up to 50 million people along the coast from Rio de Janeiro to São Paolo; where African cities like Nouachott, with an infrastructure adapted to fill the requirements of 20,000 to 30,000 persons, have swelled into makeshift cities of 2 million, and so forth.

A series of early studies of urbanisation in Africa has been very influential both theoretically and methodologically. The group of researchers collectively known as the Manchester School undertook an ambitious exploration of urbanisation in Southern Africa under the leadership of Godfrey Wilson and later Max Gluckman from the late 1930s to the 1960s.

The development of the copper industry in Northern Rhodesia (today's Zambia) led to a great need for labour from the early decades of the twentieth century. The industry was concentrated in a 'belt' in the north-eastern region, known as the Copperbelt, and the miners often had to travel far to get to work. In the mining towns, they lived in barracks not intended for family life. Unlike many West African cities, such as Ibadan or Timbuktu, as well as older, coastal East African cities like Mombasa and Zanzibar Town, the towns in this part of the continent were founded and populated very quickly; they had no 'traditional sector' and no historical predecessors. There was thus a sharp social and cultural discontinuity between the towns and the outlying countryside. The mine-owners assumed that they could send the workers back to their villages in periods when their labour was not needed; this did not eventually come about, however. The labour migration, intended to be seasonal, led to a partial depopulation of the rural areas, and eventually entire families lived more or less permanently in the mining towns. A permanent proletarianisation of a former farmer population had taken place.

In the first anthropological study of urbanisation in the Copperbelt, Godfrey Wilson (1941–42) introduces the term de-tribalisation; in other words, he emphasises the qualitative change in social integration entailed by urbanisation. From being kinship-based subsistence producers, the workers become individual participants in the world economy, he writes, describing this society as:

... a community in which impersonal relations are all-important; where business, law and religion make men dependent on millions of other men whom they have never met; a community articulated into races, nations and classes; in which the tribes, no longer almost worlds in themselves, now take their place as small administrative units; a world of writing, of specialized knowledge and of elaborate technical skill. (G. Wilson 1941–42, p. 13; quoted in Hannerz 1980, p. 124)

Wilson also notes a change in the value-orientation of the proletarianised Africans, remarking that the Africans of Broken Hill are neither a cattle people nor a fishing people, but a 'dressed' people. In town, clothes became an object of investment, a kind of special-purpose money, an expression of individualism through conspicuous consumption and an expression of an emulation of a European lifestyle.

While Wilson in this early study concentrated on describing change, J. Clyde Mitchell later focused on the relationship between change and continuity in the small monograph *The Kalela Dance* (1956). The Kalela dance was performed every Sunday afternoon by labour migrants belonging to the Bisa people in the town of Luanshya. They were dressed in modern clothes and the dance did not form part of their traditional cultural repertoire. However, the dance and songs were definitely markers of 'tribal' group identity. Although the kin groups and tribal forms of organisation did not have a significant practical role in the towns, group identity was frequently overcommunicated; that is, it was given special emphasis in contexts of interaction. Moreover, the contrast with other groups became more visible here than it had been in the countryside. In towns, people categorised each other according to their place of origin (a criterion which had only rarely been relevant earlier), and many of the new forms of association made possible by the town – peer groups, clubs, etc. – were based on ethnic membership. Mitchell notes, significantly, that the notion of 'tribe' and group membership continues to be important after urbanisation, but that its significance changes in response to shifts in the overall social organisation. In this way, he – and other members of the group – foreshadows later developments in the study of ethnic symbolism (see Chapter 17). This body of work has nonetheless been criticised for taking a too facile view of social change, seeing the transition from village life to city life as an overly linear process (Ferguson 1990, 1999).

Many later studies of urbanisation and change have taken their cue from the studies carried out by the Manchester School. In a study of political organisation among Hausa in the Yoruba city of Ibadan, Abner Cohen (1969) shows how cultural symbols and traditional principles of social organisation change in meaning, but remain important, when they are moved from a traditional to a modern context. To mention a couple of further examples, David Lan (1985) has shown how traditional spirit mediums and old myths gained a new significance during the civil war in Zimbabwe (in the late 1970s) and provided legitimacy to entirely new political institutions, notably the guerrilla movement; whereas Richard Wilson (1991) has provided a similar kind of analysis of political mobilisation in marginal, Indian-populated highland Guatemala, where he shows that local political entrepreneurs may innovatively draw on both local and foreign symbols and sources of legitimacy in their bid to mobilise the local population in the initially alien modern political sphere.

In situations of change, there are certain aspects of culture and social organisation which alter, and certain aspects which do not. What changes and what does not is an empirical question: there is no general answer to it.

What is clear, however, is that change does not stop. In a re-study of the Copperbelt, carried out in the 1990s, James Ferguson (1999) describes a modernisation process which has been thwarted, rerouted and – in the opinion of many – stalled. Ferguson's elderly informants speak nostalgically about a time when they had 'owned a fine tuxedo or attended a concert by the Ink Spots or eaten T-bone steak at a restaurant' (1999, p. 238), the image that comes across is not so much one of 'expectations of modernity', as the book's title signals, but 'memories of modernity', a belief in progress which evaporated at some point along the route. The Zambian economy, Ferguson states, has been 'disconnected and excluded ... from the mainstream of the global economy' (1999, p. 238): it was a part of an incipient global modernity at the time of the initial Copperbelt studies, but no longer is.

CONCEPTUALISING COMPLEXITY

Urban anthropology in Southern Africa raised methodological issues which became increasingly relevant from the 1960s onwards, as fewer anthropologists now studied relatively isolated villages or local communities. In a city it is practically impossible for a researcher to develop an overview of the entire social universe. Many encounters with informants are brief, and there are thousands of members of the society under study whom one has no chance of ever meeting. Obviously, it is something quite different to study social relations in Luanshya or on Manhattan than it is to spend a year in a village in Kiriwina. Many contemporary anthropological studies are, moreover, multi-sited (Marcus 1998); to gain a full picture of the life-worlds of one's transnational informants, one has to do fieldwork in two or several locations. In order to solve some of the methodological problems raised in urban anthropology, the Manchester School developed a rigorous methodology to study social networks (see Chapter 6). They also proposed the extended case study as an alternative to the traditional, holistic style of inquiry. A case study would characteristically focus on an important public event, drawing conclusions about the wider social and cultural context on the basis of intensive exploration and interpretation of that event and its wider ramifications. *The Kalela Dance* (Clyde Mitchell 1956) was a typical case study along such lines.

Perspectives on Cultural Mixing

Commonly seen as 'Westernisation', processes of mutual cultural influence and mixing – the cultural dynamics of globalisation – must in fact be understood as a multidirectional and truly complex process (Amselle 2001; Appadurai 1996; Hannerz 1996). Moreover, it must be kept in mind that there is no such thing as a 'pure' culture. Mixing has always occurred, although its speed and intensity are greater in the contemporary world than before.

A number of terms are used by anthropologists and other social scientists to describe cultural mixing, and it may be useful to distinguish between the main forms (see also Stewart 2007).

Cultural pluralism directs attention towards the relative boundedness of the constituent groups or categories that make up a society. It is a close relative of *multiculturalism*. In the realm of consumption, pluralism would imply that different groups consume different kinds of goods systematically because of cultural differences.

- *Hybridity* directs attention towards individuals or cultural forms which are reflexively – self-consciously – mixed, that is syntheses of cultural forms or fragments of diverse origins. It is thus distinct from either *pluralism* or *multiculturalism*, where boundaries between groups remain intact.
- *Syncretism* directs attention towards the amalgamation of formerly discrete world views, cultural meaning and, in particular, religion.
- *Diasporic identity* directs attention towards an essentially social category consisting of people whose primary subjective belonging is in another country.
- *Transnationalism* directs attention, rather, to a social existence attaching individuals and groups not primarily to one particular place, but to several or none.
- *Diffusion* directs attention towards the flow of substances and meanings between societies, whether it is accompanied by actual social encounters or not.
- *Creolisation*, finally, directs the attention towards cultural phenomena which result from displacement and the ensuing social encounter and mutual influence between two or several groups, creating an ongoing dynamic interchange of symbols and practices, eventually leading to new forms with varying degrees of stability.

Hybridity is the most general concept used here, and it may refer to any obviously mixed cultural form. World music, various forms of contemporary 'crossover' cuisine and urban youth cultures borrowing elements from a variety of sources including minority cultures and TV, are typical examples of phenomena explored under the heading 'hybridity'. Hybrid cultural forms are often counteracted by quests for purity and 'authenticity, which may be, but are not necessarily, politicised in situations of increased ethnic diversity due to immigration.

In urban anthropology and, more generally, anthropology in modern societies, it is impossible to find out everything about everybody, due to the complexity and size of the societies concerned; in a word, their scale. Modern societies are large and highly differentiated.

There are several ways of approaching this problem. One possible solution is the case study. Another, related approach consists of focusing on a strictly delineated topic, such as the downward mobility of parts of the North American middle class in the 1980s (Newman 1988) or transnational adoption in Norway (Howell 2007). One may also choose to concentrate on a restricted topic *and* a delineated physical field, as in Marianne Gullestad's (1984) pioneering monograph on gender, material culture and everyday life in a suburb of Bergen, or Philippe Bourgois' (2003 [1995]) study of crack dealers in New York. A third strategy could be to single out a small group in a complex society, for example Gypsies in Britain (Okely 1983) or Iranian women in the Netherlands and California (Ghorashi 2003). Usually such studies have to give a great deal of attention to the relationship between the group and greater society, and may thereby shed light on a wider context in the same way as an extended case study does.

A study combining several of these approaches is David William Cohen's and E.S. Atieno Odhiambo's monograph on Siaya (1989). Siaya is an area in western Kenya, largely populated by Luo speakers, that is a classic labour power reservoir in the capitalist sector of the Kenyan economy. About 475,000 people lived in the region at the time of fieldwork; another 134,000 were born there but lived elsewhere, usually as migrant workers. Many households in Siaya are dependent on economic contributions from family members who work in Nairobi and elsewhere; the latter are, in return, dependent on food supplies from home. Daily life in Siaya is thus closely intertwined with the lives of migrants and the workings of large-scale Kenyan society and, at a further remove, the global economy. The example of Siaya thus shows how local life is interconnected with large-scale social and cultural processes.

First, labour migration has led to significant social and cultural changes locally. Second, the national educational system, the increasing scale of society and the new occupational opportunities have created a Luo middle class and new forms of internal social differentiation.

Third, urban Luos developed their own political organisations in Nairobi long ago (Parkin 1969), and there are parts of Nairobi, and certainly ethnic networks in Nairobi, which may be analytically included in Luoland. Fourth, as part of a national compromise between the largest ethnic groups of the country, Kenyan authorities reserved an area in the Rift Valley, away from the traditional tribal area of the Luo, for Luo settlement. This led to a further dispersal of the population and, doubtless, a stronger social integration into the Kenyan nation-state.

Fifth, the location of Siaya close to the Ugandan border has provided ample opportunities for local entrepreneurs. From the 1940s onwards, many people from Siaya took well-paid seasonal work in Uganda. During the 1970s, this changed. Under the rule of Idi Amin (1970–79), the Ugandan economy fared poorly and labour migration was no longer an option for Kenyans. Still, the flow of values across the border did continue, this time through smuggling. The Ugandan shilling was unstable, and Kenyan currency was highly valuable in Uganda. Tea, coffee, outboard motors, stereo equipment and other commodities were sold across the border in large quantities, and people in Siaya made large profits.

This border trade, most of it taking place in boats across Lake Victoria and much of it illegal, also had consequences for the larger system it was placed in. Among other things, it was said that the smuggling of petrol from Uganda to Kenya in the late 1970s was an important contributing factor to the downfall of Idi Amin.

Siaya is in many ways typical of the postcolonial world. Geographical and social mobility have increased, as has social differentiation. Ethnic self-consciousness has been strengthened due to the increased contact with the outside world (see Chapters 17–19), and the pattern of consumption has changed. The boundaries between Siaya and the external world are no longer unambiguous. In a certain sense, Cohen and Odhiambo (1989) write, Siaya exists in Nairobi too; while aspects of Kenya, and of the wider world, exist in Siaya. Siaya is what we could call a translocality.

THE INDIGENISATION OF MODERNITY

The encounter with global forces of modernity is worldwide, irreversible and ongoing. Some have argued that processes of modernisation leave few opportunities for local communities to choose their own direction of change. Doubtless, contact between traditional peoples and industrial society has frequently entailed some dramatic and frequently painful aspects. Historically, the encounter between traditional and modern societies has often taken place in the context of colonialism, and large-scale massacres of militarily weaker groups are part of this history. On the other hand, one would seriously underestimate the abilities of 'traditional peoples' if they were to be regarded merely as helpless victims of the avalanche of modernity. The encounter may take various forms and may be conceptualised in several ways.

The Trobriand Islanders are often mentioned as a 'traditional' people who have succeeded in incorporating elements of modernity such as general-purpose money without losing aspects of traditional culture and social organisation which they see as important. Back in the 1920s Malinowski wrote in *Argonauts* that it would probably only be a question of a few years before the *kula* trade and the ritual exchange of yams vanished, as missionaries and traders had already begun to arrive at Kiriwina in his time. Nearly a century on, it appears that important parts of Trobriand culture – including the *kula* trade and yam exchange – have survived, although the changes have been formidable. A famous expression of the Trobriander ability to incorporate new phenomena into pre-existing structures of meaning can be seen in the ethnographic film *Trobriand Cricket* (Leach and Kildea 1974), which shows that Trobrianders use cricket as a ritual way of communicating enmity and competition between matriclans, and that they have modified the rules to adapt it to local circumstances. Cricket is thereby used to strengthen traditional clan identity. On the other hand, it is clear that Trobriand culture is far from unchanged after its colonial encounter.

A different kind of reaction to modernisation is represented in the so-called cargo cults of Melanesia and Polynesia (Worsley 1968; see also Wagner 1981; Robbins 2004). These millenarian political or religious cults first emerged as a result of increased contact with the outside world after the First World War, and some are much more recent. They have a double aim: to re-establish traditional authority and to acquire some of the immense wealth of the foreigners (mostly Americans). In this, such movements represent, at the ideological level, a happy marriage, as it were, between the old and the new. For, as Roosens (1989) has remarked, indigenous peoples may wish to retain important aspects of their tradition, but they also tend to want modern commodities. Often, it must be added, neither aim is achieved.

One famous cargo cult is the John Frum movement in the New Hebrides (now Vanuatu), first analysed by Peter Worsley (1968, pp. 152–60). At the cultural level, it can be described as a mixture of Christianity, indigenous religion and consumerism. Many of the members of the movement were nominal Christians but were disappointed by the modest returns of Christianity, which chiefly offered prayers and songs with no material consequences. Early in the 1940s, therefore, Tanna men began organising meetings where they awaited messages from the prophet John Frum. He was expected to liberate them from the colonial domination of the British, re-establish the outlawed traditional customs, introduce a new currency 'with a coconut stamp' and ensure abundance of material goods (cargo). Among the magical paraphernalia used by the members of the cult was the Bible, which was assumed to have magical properties since it always seemed to accompany the cargo which arrived by ship and plane at the island. The movement was banned, and a man suspected of being John Frum was arrested. However, it continued to flourish, and celebrated its fiftieth anniversary at a solemn ceremony on John Frum Day in February, 2007.

How should such millenarian movements be understood? Are they merely functional techniques for re-establishing mental balance in periods characterised by uncertainty and turbulence? Worsley (1968) does not think so. He rather sees the cults as rational attempts to reform and adapt traditional society to new circumstances. It may be said, of course, that they do not provide the results called for, but on the other hand the reasoning of the John Frum movement is as logical as the Zande witchcraft institution, seen within the context of local knowledge and experience.

The widespread frustration which is a necessary condition for millenarian movements to arise, is generally based on a discrepancy between culturally defined aims and the available means: people want, for example, prosperity and political self-determination, but have no established methods for achieving these goals. There is a locally perceived gap between cultural lifestyle ideals and social reality, which is clearly a result of colonialism and increased contacts between 'the West' and indigenous peoples. In this context, it is often retorted that many peoples actually had shorter life expectations and suffered greater material hardships before colonialism. This is true, but on the other hand, the *perception* of scarcity is greater today, since people are taught – through school, advertising, mass media and direct encounters – to compare themselves with a European or North American middle-class way of life. Although many Melanesians are better off in absolute terms today than they were 100 years ago, they may be worse off in relative terms. They suffer *relative deprivation*. Poverty becomes a greater problem the moment wealth is perceived as a definite possibility.

WAYS OF CONCEPTUALISING ENCOUNTERS

In the social sciences, it has been common to regard encounters between rich, Northern and poor, Southern societies either in terms of modernisation or in terms of imperialism (see also Chapter 13). The former perspective, exemplified in the work of the development economist Walt Rostow (1965), presupposes a unilineal evolutionary view according to which the poor countries would eventually 'catch up with' the 'developed world'. Economic and political contact between North and South would then be beneficial, since it would lead to the 'development' of the Southern countries.

The other main view, which was influenced by Lenin's and Trotsky's analyses of imperialism, instead emphasised the ways in which the rich countries exploit the poor ones and that economic and political contact does not lead to the 'development' of the latter, but instead to their underdevelopment. Large state debts, low prices placed on the goods the poor countries sell (mostly raw materials) and the extraction of profits by multinational companies are symptoms of this situation of structural inequality (see, for instance, Frank 1979). Thus, the decolonisation of the post-war decades did not lead to the true independence and emancipation of poor countries, since they were tied up with a global capitalist system where they were bound to lose. At the level of culture, moreover, writers influenced by the theory of neo-imperialism argued that formerly colonised peoples become dependent on the models and knowledge systems of the former colonisers. This is the perspective predominant in research often called postcolonial, inspired by the works of Frantz Fanon (1956) and Edward Said (1978).

Anthropological perspectives on these processes differ, as we have seen, both from the models of global systems and from the normative judgements of postcolonialism. Although anthropologists may draw insights from the grand theories of development or underdevelopment, and are aware of the discrepancies of symbolic power bemoaned by postcolonial theorists, their main concern has been, and is, to show local variations in the encounters between different systems of knowledge and cultural practices. Detailed ethnographies describing colonial and postcolonial situations have indicated a need for a more nuanced understanding than that provided by general models of global relationships. Olivia Harris (1995), writing on cultural complexity in Latin America and particularly the Andean area, thus has proposed a typology depicting variations in the ways in which social encounters between knowledge systems can be conceptualised.

First, she describes the model of mixing or creolisation, sometimes described as syncretism, hybridity or, in Latin America, *mestizaje*. This model (see Chapter 19) shows how new meanings are generated from the mixing of diverse influences. What Harris sees as problematic about this is that it 'presupposes fixed points of origin for the cultures which then mix' rather than regarding the creation of meaning, in her view more accurately, as an ongoing process with no fixed starting-point or end-point.

The second model is the one of colonisation, which in the South American and Andean context implies European dominance, exploitation and violence towards Indians, including the enforced introduction of Christianity and the Spanish language. This model is strongly dualist and somewhat mechanical in its notion of power and, in Harris's view, draws a rather too strict line between European and Indian culture, reifying ('freezing') both in the act.

Third, an alternative to the rigid model of colonisation implies the attribution of 'more agency to the colonised' and a phrasing of 'the relationship in terms of borrowing'. The traditions remain discrete, but Indian elites (Harris refers particularly to Incas and Mayas) borrow knowledge from the Christians.

The fourth model is 'that of juxtaposition or alternation, where two radically different knowledge systems are both accepted without a direct attempt at integration'. Since, for example, Maya and Christian cosmologies entailed fundamentally different conceptualisations of time and of the past, they could not be mixed, but actors could draw situationally on either.

The fifth way of conceptualising the meeting is 'that of imitation, assimilation or direct identification', whereby persons self-consciously reject their own past and adopt a self-identity and knowledge system they perceive as better or more beneficial to themselves. A conversion from Indian to *mestizo* identity in the Andes, Harris notes, 'usually involves wholesale rejection of Indian identity, in favour of and identification with what is seen as white or Hispanic'.

The sixth and final mode discussed by Harris is that of 'innovation and creativity', where 'attention is firmly removed from contrasted knowledge systems and priority is given to autonomy and independent agency'. Unlike the five other models sketched, this kind of conceptualisation does not focus on origins.

If we look at Pacific cargo cults in relation to this typology, it becomes clear that several of the models may generate some understanding of them, and they are not mutually exclusive. In his classic study, Worsley (1968) emphasised the unequal power entailed by colonialism (the second model), the creativity of the Melanesians in coping with the new circumstances (the sixth model) and their self-conscious borrowing of cultural traits (such as the Bible) from the Europeans without altering their basic cultural identity (the fourth model).

MODERNITY AND THE BODY

Medical anthropology is a growing sub-discipline dealing with cultural knowledge and practices about the body, health and illness. Commonly, medical anthropologists distinguish between three 'bodies', the personal, the social and the political (Scheper-Hughes and Lock 1987; see also Singer and Baer 2007), all of which are socially constructed. Although the body, of course, does in an important sense exist biologically, it is imbued with cultural meanings.

Many medical anthropologists have concentrated their attention on the empirical relationship between 'Western medicine' and 'indigenous medical systems'. Although there has been a tendency to polemicise against Western medicine rather than studying it as a cultural system along with other cultural perspectives on health and disease, the most common perspective among medical anthropologists is probably expressed in Harris's fourth model, which indicates the presence of two (or several) mutually exclusive knowledge systems which remain discrete. As mentioned in the last chapter, Mauritians who suffer from some ailment draw pragmatically on the services of medical personnel who relate to radically different, and frequently contradictory, notions about health, illness and treatment. The 'Western' medical system recognises a distinction between body and mind, for example, which is not deemed relevant within the Indian ayurvedic school. In European societies, it is also clear that many inhabitants – immigrants as well as natives – relate to distinct knowledge systems pragmatically when faced with a practical problem such as a disease, without trying to mix them cognitively or in practice.

A different model, which could perhaps be classified as a creolisation model in Harris's scheme, is represented in Robert Welsh's (1983) work among the Ningerum of the New Guinea highlands. The Ningerum are described as a 'very traditional people' who nevertheless have accepted 'Western medicine' without much ado and integrated it into their pre-existing system of knowledge. Traditionally, the Ningerum had a wide repertoire of treatments for different ailments; some complaints could be cured by anyone, while others had to be treated by specialists. Since 1963, the Ningerum have had access to a dispensary staffed by nurses drawing on a Western medical system for diagnosis and treatment. The introduction of new knowledge and new skills was easily accepted, and actively appropriated, by the Ningerum, and moreover it did not seem to alter their traditional practices, which coexisted happily with the Western medical system. Two main factors account for this painless appropriation of new knowledge. First, Ningerum nurses were trained to staff the dispensary, so it was not run by outsiders for very long. Second, the new medical practices did not interfere with the indigenous knowledge system, which – contrary to Western medicine – held that the causes of disease were always external to the body (spirits and ghosts, bad food, etc.). Treatment, in their view, would either stop the external agent or strengthen the body. To the extent that the injections and pills offered by the dispensary had positive effects on the disease, they were easily accepted along with the other kinds of treatment the Ningerum had at their disposal.

The lesson from this example may be that 'meaning is use'. To the Ningerum, it made little difference that Western medicine presupposed a cosmology and knowledge system quite distinct from their own, as long as the treatment functioned satisfactorily. On the other hand, it could be argued that the assimilation of the alien knowledge might be more difficult if Ningerum were to become medical doctors. If so, the cosmologies and not merely the practices would be confronted directly.

Medical anthropology, and the anthropology of the body in a wider sense, has a considerable potential for dealing with several classic anthropological problems in novel ways. It can shed important light on cultural dynamics in polyethnic societies, not least among immigrants in rich countries; as the New Guinean example showed, it can give fresh perspectives on questions of relativism, including those in relation to development issues; and, moreover, medical anthropological research is at the forefront of cross-cultural research on concepts of personhood (Nichter and Lock 2002; see also Chapter 4).

We now turn to considering an encounter between cultural logics in the context of a development project. The following case adds to the complexity of cultural encounters, and additionally shows the importance of understanding culture and society when attempts are made to implement change through 'aid' or development programmes.

AN ANTHROPOLOGICAL PERSPECTIVE ON 'DEVELOPMENT'

Because of the methodological cultural relativism of the subject, it is difficult for anthropologists to see much intellectual value in a concept of 'development' which defines it, for example, as GDP per capita. Analytically, this kind of model is unacceptably evolutionist and reductionist, since it both ranks societies on an ethnocentrically defined ladder and disregards local, culturally specific value judgements. Among cattle nomads in East Africa, it may thus not be rational to produce as many animals as possible, slaughter them and make as big a profit as one can. For several of these groups, it is more highly valued to have a large herd than to have much money. Cattle with unusually large horns may have a special ritual value, and cattle are indispensable as bridewealth.

The cultural relativism inherent in anthropological methodology does not necessarily mean that anthropologists by default will be critical of development projects. It does imply, however, that an awareness of social and cultural variation is necessary for such projects to be meaningful. We have to take into account the fact that notions of 'quality of life', 'progress' and 'development' are locally constructed. The role of anthropologists in development projects has therefore tended to consist of providing a local context for the projects; explaining to the other professions involved (engineers, economists and others) what is unique about the locality in question.

A project in Ecuador, supported by the World Bank and led by the Ecuadorian Ministry of Agriculture, attempted to modernise and 'rationalise' the production of guinea-pigs in the rural highlands (Archetti 1992). Guinea-pigs had been raised and eaten for centuries, and it was held that an improvement of the techniques for production might improve the standard of living of the producers. The programme nevertheless failed at an early stage, and an anthropologist, Eduardo Archetti, was hired to explore what had gone wrong.

Traditionally, guinea-pigs were kept inside the local people's huts, more specifically in the kitchen. The feeding of the animals was unsystematic, there was widespread inbreeding and it was difficult to avoid the spread of disease. The development agents suggested that cages should be built, so that the guinea-pigs could be separated by gender, fed regularly and mated in such ways that degeneration could be avoided. In the beginning, the breeders were to receive the technical equipment free of charge. Nonetheless, very few villagers accepted the offer. The Ecuadorian Ministry of Agriculture was disappointed.

Archetti quickly discovered that guinea-pigs were not just perceived as any kind of food: they were a *special* kind of food, simultaneously pets and edible animals. They had an important symbolic place in the lives of the villagers. Guinea-pigs were not eaten at regular meals, but only at special occasions such as rites of passage, religious feasts and in connection with healing. The guinea-pig had special qualities (and may in this regard be compared to the pangolin among the Lele). It was also seen as an oracle which could divine the weather and interpret social events. For this reason, it was important to have one's guinea-pigs nearby. Animals which were mildly disfigured, for example because they had an extra toe (possibly as a result of inbreeding), were considered unusually wise creatures.

In addition, it is a fact that the new method of production entailed a considerable extra burden for the already overworked Quechua women. To the women, it was thus not rational to change their techniques of production, since the proposed changes ran contrary to established local values.

Are Europeans and North Americans more rational than the Quechua women? Analytically speaking, hardly. As Sahlins (1976) has pointed out in a critique of utilitarianism, North Americans consider themselves rational, but they rarely eat cats, dogs and horses, which would be a sensible thing to do from a nutritional perspective. The point is not, therefore, whether this or that person is 'rational' or not, but rather that there are different, culturally determined ways of delineating rationality or common sense.

IS ANTHROPOLOGY INHERENTLY CONSERVATIVE?

Upon completing his study of humans and guinea-pigs, Archetti did not draw the simple conclusion that 'cultures must be left alone' or that any attempt at tampering with long-established cultural values is either doomed to fail or is an expression of evil cultural imperialism. However, and this is his point, if such attempts are to be successful it is essential that the actors themselves must agree that the proposed changes serve their interests. Those interests, or aims, may of course change, but at this stage, he concludes, it is necessary to 'try to understand the guinea-pig in its social and symbolic totality' (Archetti 1992, p. 153).

Regarding questions of development and cultural change, anthropology may be regarded as an inherently conservative discipline. The reason is that both social and cultural anthropology have always (1) emphasised the study of interrelationships and sociocultural wholes, and (2) insisted on an attitude of cultural relativism, according to which any society or culture can, when all is said and done, only be understood in its own terms. From such a vantage-point, it seems only natural that changes instigated from the outside are potentially destructive.

This attitude is altering within the anthropological community. For what, really, are the 'own terms' of a society if women and men, young and old, urbanites and farmers in the same community disagree about the direction of change? In the study of guinea-pig breeding, Archetti points out that there is not just one Ecuadorian ideology about guinea-pigs, but several, and that the conflict between the Ministry of Agriculture and the rural women might well be understood as a conflict within Ecuadorian society. As a consequence, it becomes absolutely necessary to admit that societies or cultures are neither tightly integrated, nor unchanging and closed systems. They change and interact with the outside world. Nevertheless, no matter how 'global' the influences from the outside may be, the responses are always local, and we have seen several examples of local ways of handling imposed changes from the outside world (see also Chapter 19).

Change and cultural complexity also present peculiar methodological challenges to anthropology. Some of these problems are today part and parcel of many, if not most, anthropological research projects. This added complexity does not mean that earlier work has become obsolete, but rather that it must be supplemented by new perspectives in both theory and methodology.

DECOLONISING THE ANTHROPOLOGICAL MIND

With anthropological studies of minorities, labour migration, urbanisation, development issues and sociocultural processes in the context of nation-states and complex societies, it may seem as though anthropology is on its way home. The discipline began as the study of 'the Other'; it now increasingly includes the study of 'ourselves', or, to put it more accurately: the boundaries between 'us' and 'them' are becoming blurred.

Today anthropological research is increasingly becoming available to its 'objects' as they acquire literacy and as an educated middle class capable of reading anthropological studies develops. This forces researchers to take their 'objects of study' seriously in ways which were formerly unnecessary. This development has also led to a growing understanding of the peculiar historical and ideological circumstances which led to the growth of anthropology, perhaps particularly in Europe. There the discipline entered into new domains along with French and British colonial expansion. The anthropologist, in the view of many, was an accomplice of colonialism, and the professional interest developed in the subject – on both sides of the Atlantic – may be seen to reflect domestic concerns at least as much as it reflects the concerns of 'the Other' (Marcus and Fischer 1986; Kuper 2005). Anthropologists also contribute to the making of history: their perspectives and interpretations contribute to defining the world in a particular way. There are therefore several governments in the 'Third World' which tend to deny access to anthropological fieldworkers, not only because the anthropological emphasis on cultural variation is at odds with their development strategies but also because they see it as their own right to write their own contemporary history. By no means every government in 'the developing world' is content with depictions of their country insisting on the existence of headhunters, gift economies, traditional oral religions or unique initiation rituals among their citizens.

In his famous book *Orientalism*, the literary scholar Edward Said (1978) criticised classic European philological and historical scholarship about Asia for propagating an image of 'the Orient' as mystical and tantalising, but profoundly irrational. If the history of the Orient were to be written by Orientals themselves, the result would be quite different – not least because we speak of an area stretching at least from Turkey to Japan. Said argues that the Western researchers have reproduced stereotypes of 'the Oriental' in their production of myths about themselves, about the 'Western world' as the cradle of progress, rationality and science. The Bulgarian-French intellectual Tzvetan Todorov (1989) has demonstrated, in a similar vein, how French descriptions of 'primitives' have for centuries closely followed domestic discourse about politics and social philosophy, and he intimates that they indeed tell us more about France than about 'the Other'. This kind of criticism is taken very seriously by anthropologists, yet as Jean-Claude Galey (1992) argues, Orientalism and anthropology may have shared origins, but they have developed quite distinct methods and ways of conceptualising society and culture. Generally speaking, Orientalism may nevertheless be seen as a fundamental mode of misrepresenting others, to which anthropologists are no less prone than other commentators.

As regards India in particular, Ronald Inden (1990), writing from within 'Orientalism', has documented in great detail how conceptualisations of Indian society and culture have owed more to European preoccupations than to Indian society itself. Veena Das (1994), similarly, argues that India cannot be represented by foreign scholars as if the country itself were silent. Unlike their predecessors, she says, contemporary social scientists cannot lay claims to absolute truths, but 'can only insert their voices within a plurality of voices in which all kinds of statements – prescriptive, normative, descriptive, indicative – are waging a virtual battle about the nature of Indian society and the legitimate space for social sciences in this society' (Das 1994, p. 143; see also Chakrabarty et al. 2007).

South Africa and the Anthropologists

The policy of apartheid (Afrikaans for apartness or separation) was implemented in South Africa in 1948, and was officially abolished only in 1994. This policy entailed a strict separation of the 'races' in South African society, equipping each main 'race' with separate sets of legal, civil and political rights. Being implemented at exactly the same time as the European colonies in Africa and Asia began in earnest to demand independence, apartheid was, right from the beginning, out of kilter with the post-Second World War ideology in most of the world, denouncing racist policies as denigrating and objectionable.

What is perhaps not very well known is the fact that apartheid ideology was closely linked with South African anthropology (or *volkekunde*). Werner Eiselen, a professor of anthropology at the University of Stellenbosch, was in fact its main intellectual architect (Hammond-Tooke 1997). Drawing on German *Völkerkunde*, but also on early American cultural anthropology, Eiselen believed that cultures would be irredeemably harmed, losing their spirit and integrity in the process, if they were brought into overly close contact with each other. The perspective developed by Eiselen (which may not have been racist, strictly speaking, since he spoke mainly of 'cultures') was instrumental in shaping apartheid thought and policy. Moreover, this brand of anthropology, which was deeply embedded in the *Apartheid* state, was retained and cultivated at the Afrikaans-speaking universities throughout the period of apartheid, with P.J. Coertze at the University of Pretoria as Eiselen's intellectual heir.

In the English-speaking universities, the situation was very different (Sharp 1980). Perhaps especially at the University of Cape Town, in the department founded by Radcliffe-Brown, social anthropologists soon became vocal critics of the regime, many drawing on Marxist analyses as an alternative to the culturalism of the *volkekunde* school. As pointed out by Kuper (1999: xiii–xiv), already seven years before the implementation of apartheid, Radcliffe-Brown argued that the tribes and peoples of South Africa had already been integrated into a wider

▶

political and economic system, and that it would therefore be futile to see events as the interaction between cultures. Rather, what we see, according to Radcliffe-Brown, is 'the interaction of individuals and groups within an established social structure which is itself in process of change' (Kuper 1999: xiii–xiv).

Following the abolition of apartheid, the distinction between Afrikaans and English anthropology has become increasingly blurred, and no South African anthropology, or *volkekunde*, department is today based on the social outlook of apartheid. The story of South African anthropology, however, may serve as a reminder that the classic anthropological concept of culture is far from innocent. It may lend itself easily to abuse. And the end of apartheid did not, of course, signify the end of cultural group identities. Indeed, in a detailed study of the reconciliation work carried out in the years immediately following the abolition of apartheid, Richard A. Wilson (2001) shows the tension between the Truth and Reconciliation Commission, which based its work on a language of universal human rights, and the old culturalist way of thinking about group identities.

To be fair, it should be added that many 'metropolitan' anthropologists have in recent years begun to study native history from an insider's perspective. In his pathbreaking *Europe and the People without History*, Eric Wolf (1982) writes the history of the great 'discoveries' from the perspective of the 'discovered' peoples, and in *Islands of History* Sahlins (1985) compares Polynesian oral versions of history with written versions drawn up by foreigners, showing how they are all cultural interpretations of the same events and that the foreign histories are not necessarily more 'correct' than the native ones. Lévi-Strauss, in line with this mode of reasoning, has argued that history writing is the myth of our time because it, like oral myths, is based on an ideological interpretation of a very limited set of facts from the past (1966 [1962], chs 8–9). History writing, he argued in what was originally a polemic against Jean-Paul Sartre's ethnocentric views, is not a product of the past, but is rather created by the needs perceived by those who write history.

An analogous statement could be made about anthropology: it is not created by 'the Other', but by the interaction between anthropologists and 'the Other'. A consequence of processes of modernisation and decolonisation in the core areas of anthropology is the fact that our informants not only increasingly demand to be consulted on the content of our studies of them, but some of them also begin writing their own theoretical texts about their culture, history and society (Archetti 1994). This decentralisation (and some would say decolonisation) of the discipline, although admittedly still modest, has led to new challenges for anthropologists in bringing us closer to our objects of study and, in some cases, engaging in a theoretical dialogue with them. Another field of study partly turns the problem of Orientalism on its head, looking instead at non-Western images of the West, sometimes calling it Occidentalism (Carrier 1995). Notwithstanding the obvious power discrepancies, these ideas tend to be no less stereotypical and simplistic than Western notions of 'the Rest'.

*   *   *

There exists an enormous anthropological, sociological and philosophical literature about modernity and modern societies. Because of its attention to meticulous fieldwork, and because of its orientation towards non-European societies, anthropology has contributed important insights to the effect that 'modernity' and 'tradition' are not mutually exclusive, contrary to what Max Weber and other early sociologists of modernity believed. Modern politics, wagework and a modern state may well exist side by side with ancestral cults and a lineage organisation, although there are bound to be tensions and contradictions within such complex societies. It has also been shown that people who live in 'modern' societies can retain important 'traditional' characteristics, such as, for example, nepotism and moral particularism, social cohesion at the community level and a wide range of religious beliefs ranging from virgin birth to sorcery. At the same time, there is no doubt that modernisation entails irreversible social and cultural change.

One seemingly paradoxical result of modernisation in many parts of the world is the emergence of traditionalist movements praising the virtue of what they believe to be the ancestral culture. Like cargo cults, such movements may be understood as strategies to come to terms with new social and cultural circumstances; adapting to the new without letting go of the old entirely and thereby creating a sense of continuity with the past in a rapidly changing world. In the following two chapters, we look into some such movements and processes in some detail.

SUGGESTIONS FOR FURTHER READING

James Ferguson: *Expectations of Modernity: Myths and Meanings of Urban Life on the Zambian Copperbelt*. Berkeley: University of California Press 1999.

Anna Tsing: *Friction: An Ethnography of Global Connection*. Princeton, NJ: Princeton University Press.

Eric Wolf: *Europe and the People without History*. Berkeley: University of California Press 1982.

17   ETHNICITY

People become aware of their culture when they stand at its boundaries: when they encounter other cultures, or when they become aware of other ways of doing things, or merely of contradictions to their own culture.

— *Anthony P. Cohen*

A well-known musician from Finnmark, the Sami-dominated county in northern Norway, was once asked the following question by a journalist: 'Are you mostly a Sami or mostly a musician?' She tried to be accommodating and accordingly answered the meaningless question; if she had been an anthropologist, she would probably have discarded it as being absurd. This chapter, which outlines basic dimensions of ethnicity, explains why.

THE CONTEMPORARY UBIQUITY OF ETHNICITY

A systematic search through major anthropological journals and monographs from, say, 1950 to 2010, will quickly reveal a change in the language of the subject. The terminology has generally become more influenced by hermeneutics and literary theory than by natural science during this period. Words such as 'function' and 'social structure' have become less common. Those like 'class', 'infrastructure' and 'contradiction' had a brief spell of popularity in the 1970s, while terms such as 'discourse', 'resistance' and 'symbolic capital' have steadily grown more popular since the early 1980s. Such terminological changes reflect shifts in the dominant perspectives of the subject, but they may also reflect changes in the outside world. The very considerable interest in ethnicity which has developed since the late 1960s, the increased interest in nationalism since the early 1980s, and the enormous number of books titled something including the word 'global' since about 1990, indicate some such changes. For one thing, a term like 'ethnic group', which has largely replaced that of 'tribe', simultaneously expresses that tribal organisation is no longer common and that anthropology no longer works from a rigid boundary between 'us' and 'them'. For ethnic groups (and nations) are omnipresent and exist in the anthropologist's own society as well as elsewhere.

Looking at the political situation in the world in the early twenty-first century, the immediate impression is that most of the serious armed conflicts today have an ethnic and/or religious dimension. From Punjab to Congo, from Tibet to Quebec, from Sri Lanka to Central Asia, there is conflict and competition between different ethnic groups regarding political sovereignty and control over territories. There are also other kinds of conflicts where ethnic groups emerge as corporate groups. Indigenous peoples and immigrant groups may, for example, demand the right to cultural survival or the right to equality with the majority, usually without demanding their own state.

Other ethnic conflicts are not expressed through institutional politics. Clashes between natives and immigrants in Germany, or between blacks and whites in the US, are usually enacted in day-to-day situations. In other words, ethnicity may be articulated at many different levels in complex societies.

Ethnicity does not necessarily entail conflict: it may be expressed in quite undramatic ways through everyday definitions of situations, through impression management, in religious cults and other peaceful phenomena. It can be identified at all levels of scale – from dyadic interaction via civil society to civil war.

The phenomenon of ethnicity is, in other words, a multi-layered one. In everyday language, the concept 'ethnic group' is normally used to describe a minority group which is culturally and often visibly distinguishable from the majority, and as such the term encompasses groups in very different situations – ranging from New York Jews to the Yanomamö in Brazil. In anthropology, the expression 'ethnic group' may also be used to describe majority groups, and ethnicity concerns the relationship between groups whose members consider each other culturally distinctive.

This is still rather vague. Let us therefore be more specific.

COMMUNICATING CULTURAL DIFFERENCE

It is commonly held, not least among members of ethnic groups with a strong collective identity, that ethnicity has to do with 'objective cultural differences'. This would suggest that ethnicity becomes more important the greater the cultural differences are, and that the phenomenon is caused by the fact that different groups have lived in relative isolation from each other and have developed socioculturally in very different directions.

Anthropological research on ethnicity has shown this assumption to be false. In fact, ethnicity is frequently most important in contexts where groups are culturally close and enter into contact with each other regularly. Anthropology may therefore give an answer to a seeming paradox of our time, namely that whereas cultural differences in many regards become less apparent because of increased contact and the general processes of modernisation, ethnic identity and self-consciousness become increasingly important. The more similar people become, it seems, the more they are concerned with remaining distinctive.

Bateson (1979) has written that there must always be two 'somethings' to create a difference and thereby information. In line with this idea, we might say that the idea of an isolated ethnic group is meaningless. It is through contact with others that we discover who we are, and an 'isolated ethnic group' may therefore be compared with the sound of one hand clapping – an absurdity. The fact that two groups are culturally distinctive does not create ethnicity. There must be at least a minimum of contact between their respective members. We therefore have to draw the conclusion that the members of different ethnic groups must have something in common – some basis for interaction – in addition to being different.

Ethnicity occurs when cultural differences are made relevant through interaction. It thus concerns what is socially relevant, not which cultural differences are 'actually there'. In an early article on ethnic relations in Thailand, Michael Moerman (1965) showed that many of his informants mention cultural particulars which they presume are characteristic of themselves but which they in fact share with neighbouring peoples. Indeed, a variety of criteria can be used as markers of cultural difference in interethnic situations – phenotype (appearance or 'race'), language, religion or even clothes. If any such marker is socially recognised as an indicator of an ethnic contrast, it matters little if the 'objective cultural differences' are negligible.

In an influential essay on the social character of ethnicity, Fredrik Barth (1969) criticised a then influential view for being overly concerned with cultural content, or substance, instead of focusing on social processes in the study of ethnicity. Like Moerman (and Leach, Mitchell and others) before him, Barth emphasises that 'cultural traits' do not create ethnicity, and suggests that the focus of research ought to be the social boundaries between groups rather than the 'cultural stuff' they contain. In fact, he says, there may be a continuous flow of people and information across ethnic boundaries even though they are maintained as boundaries. If such divisions are maintained, this must be because they have some social relevance. In the relationship between the sedentary Fur and the nomadic Baggara in the Sudan, for example, there is an economic complementarity. They are mutually dependent on commodity exchange and occupy complementary ecological niches. As Gunnar Haaland (1969) showed in a contribution to the book edited by Barth, Fur may become Baggara by changing their way of life, just as Leach (1954) had showed that Kachin could become Shan; but the ethnic boundary separating the groups remains untouched in this process of individual mobility.

Barth stresses the social process in his model of ethnicity, which provides an image of interethnic relationships as dynamic and negotiable. Ethnicity must therefore be seen as an aspect of a relationship, not as a property of a person or a group. The existence of the ethnic group thus has to be affirmed socially and ideologically through the general recognition, among its members and outsiders, that it is culturally distinctive. In addition, this cultural distinctive-ness has to be related to social practices, such as religion, marriage (a rule of endogamy), language or work: for an ethnic identity to survive, it must be embedded in at least some of the social situations the actor goes through.

A further dimension of ethnicity, which was not dealt with in the volume edited by Barth but which has become politically important in many contemporary societies, is the appropriation of a shared history (Tonkin et al. 1989; see also Smith 1999) that simultaneously functions as an origin myth, justifies claims to a common culture and serves to depict the ethnic group as an extended kin group.

SOCIAL CLASSIFICATION AND STEREOTYPES

The studies of urbanisation in the Copperbelt (Chapter 16) are related to the line of reasoning developed by Barth. In *The Kalela Dance* (1956), Mitchell shows how ethnicity or 'tribalism' is expressed through a practical, everyday classification of persons. In the polyethnic situation of the mining towns of North Rhodesia, ethnicity did not have to be related to rank differences or an ethnically based division of labour. Rather, it expressed an internal cultural differentiation and emic concepts of relevant cultural differences, but it was ultimately based on social organisation in that the urbanites were still tied through kinship to their home village and traditional marriage rules. Ethnic classification, nonetheless, has something to do with the creation of order in the social environment by providing a division into 'kinds' of people. Such a classification may or may not be related to power disparities.

For a system of social classification to be effective, the actors have to experience its efficacy. They must be convinced that there are relevant differences which distinguish their group from members of the other groups. A classification of persons into *kinds* of persons which stresses the commonalities of each kind and undercommunicates their differences depends on stereotypes to be efficient. Stereotypes are simplistic descriptions of cultural traits in other groups which are conventionally believed to exist. One may have stereotypes about workers, women and royal families; for instance, a common stereotypical idea about male homosexuals amounts to their being 'effeminate'. Phrases like 'Jews are greedy' or 'the French are passionate' express stereotypes: they refuse to take individual variations into account. Ethnic stereotypes are often morally condemning (as in 'Hindus are selfish', 'Never trust an Arab'), and such images of others may strengthen group cohesion, boundaries and one's self-perception. In polyethnic societies, people also commonly hold stereotypes about themselves; an example could be the Creoles of Mauritius (Eriksen 1998), who tend to describe themselves collectively as honest, generous folk in implicit contrast to other ethnic groups.

It is impossible to make a general statement about the relationship of stereotypes to 'facts'. They can be exaggerated, overly generalising and ideologically charged descriptions of social facts. When the Creoles of Mauritius describe the Hindus as miserly, this stereotype corresponds to one that Hindus hold of themselves as hard-working and responsible people. Stereotypes may also function as self-fulfilling prophecies. A dominating group may, for example, turn a dominated group into under-achievers in the educational system by systematically bombarding them with statements to the effect that they are innately less intelligent than others.

Ethnic Anomalies

In the study of classification and cosmology, the term 'anomaly' is used to describe animals, plants or other phenomena which do not fit into the social system of classification. The pangolin is an anomaly among the Lele (Douglas 1975), and the duck-billed platypus was seen as an anomaly within the Linnaean system of classification when it was discovered in the nineteenth century: it was an egg-laying mammal with a duck bill.

Anomalies occur in social classification as well. An anomaly in an ethnic system of classification may be, for example, a poor Syrian in Trinidad, where wealth is seen as a defining characteristic of Syrians. A highly educated Gypsy would appear an anomaly in many European societies, where Gypsy identity is symbolically tied to low education. In many societies, moreover, children of ethnically mixed marriages are considered anomalies.

In certain polyethnic societies, entire categories of persons may be seen as anomalous. In Trinidad, the main contrasting pair of the ethnic system of classification is the Afro-Trinidadian/Indian contrast. The children of mixed African/Indian unions are locally known as *douglas* (which is Bhojpuri for bastard), and tend to be placed in an uncomfortable position oscillating between 'both–and' and 'neither–nor' in the system of classification. In Mauritius, a similar dilemma characterises the situation of the *gens de couleur* or 'mulattoes'; people of mixed African/European origin. They are not allowed to join the ethnic community of Mauritian whites, nor are they generally perceived as good Creoles by the black Creoles (of largely African descent). Frequently, they are described by black working-class Creoles as *kreol fer blan* – as Creoles who try to be white.

Seen from a systemic perspective, ethnic anomalies are helpless 'victims' of a hegemonic system of classification. Seen from an actor perspective, however, they may sometimes be regarded as ethnic entrepreneurs who succeed in being both, say, Indian and African and switching strategically between these identifications.

There are also many stereotypes with no clear relationship to social facts. Accusations about cannibalism in many societies are typical examples: they tend to be false (Arens 1978).

Stereotypes provide ideological legitimation of ethnic boundaries ('Don't marry one of those!') and strengthen group cohesion ('It's a good thing we're not like them'). When they are coupled with a rank system, stereotypes tend to support and strengthen it.

SITUATIONAL ETHNICITY

An important insight from the studies of the Copperbelt is the fact that ethnicity is relative and to some extent situational. As Mitchell (1966) expresses it, a man may behave as a tribal in some situations and as a wageworker in others. For a North Indian Brahmin in an English city, it would be deeply insulting if a native English person were to classify him in the same category as 'pitch-black' immigrants from Jamaica (in the broad category of 'non-white immigrants'). He might see himself as a white, 'clean' person, and would perhaps try to convince the native English person that he rightly belonged to a different category from the Jamaican. Such a negotiation over identity may be regarded as a struggle between different views of what the world looks like in ethnic terms, as competition between ideological descriptions of the world, or even as competition between world-views. Some groups, who may be the victims of damaging ethnic stereotypes, may try to argue the irrelevance of ethnic distinctions or to challenge the prevailing stereotypes, much in the manner of the Pan caste of Bisipara (Chapter 10), switching strategically from trying to exploit the system to their own advantage to rejecting the entire caste system.

The situational aspect of ethnicity has been explored by many anthropologists. In a study of ethnic relations on the sub-Arctic north Norwegian coast, Harald Eidheim (1971) has shown how ethnicity is made relevant in various ways, in various kinds of situations, between Norwegians and Sami. Here he introduces the concepts of dichotomisation and complementarisation to describe fundamental ethnic processes. Dichotomisation, or contrasting, refers to the articulation of ethnic relationships through mutual negations: the Sami define themselves in direct contrast to the non-Sami (usually the Norwegian). Complementarisation or matching, by contrast, gives an expression of ethnic relationships within a shared language where both groups appear as culturally distinctive and as structurally equivalent. Contrasting is expressed through stereotypes where the other group is seen as inferior ('the Sami are dirty', etc.), while matching is expressed through the school system, where both Norwegian and Sami history is taught. In matching, the members of one group will compare themselves directly with the other group, stating, for example, that *we* have our history, religion, folk music and arts; while they, too, have *their* history, religion, folk music and arts. In this way, ethnicity contributes to making cultural differences comparable. Eidheim also showed the essential falseness of widespread stereotypes about the Sami. Contrary to what many Norwegians held, they were, as a matter of fact, neither 'dirty', 'drunken' nor 'pagan'.

In the early 1960s, the coastal Sami were a culturally stigmatised group, meaning that they were looked down upon by the dominant Norwegians. For this reason, they undercommunicated their ethnic identity in public contexts, in the shop, on the local steamer and so on. They then presented themselves as Norwegians, and overcommunicated what they saw as Norwegian culture to escape from the stigma. In private 'backstage' situations, however, they always spoke Sami and expressed their common identity. In more recent years, Sami, like other indigenous groups, have found ways of using their cultural heritage to their advantage in a number of political contexts, although the stigma is not altogether gone.

A theoretical point from these studies is the fact that ethnicity is relational and processual: it is not a 'thing', but an aspect of a social process. This does not mean that the emotions and cultural heritage attaching individuals to ethnic groups are in some sense not 'real' (A.P. Cohen 1994; Jenkins 2008), but that they become operational only in relationships with others.

ETHNIC IDENTITY AND ORGANISATION

An important element in ethnic ideologies is the notion of the historical continuity of the group. By appealing to notions of shared tradition and history, such ideologies give the impression that the ethnic group is 'natural' and enjoys cultural continuity over a long period of time. In this way, every ethnic ideology offers a sense of cultural belongingness and security. Such ideologies also, naturally, have a political dimension. Both ethnic identity (group identification) and ethnic organisation (politics) are important, complementary expressions of ethnicity. How strong the we-feeling is, and what a possible ethnic organisation or corporation has to offer its members, varies greatly, however. The fact that ethnicity occurs in a society gives us no indication of its relative importance in the everyday life or politics of that society. Ethnic identity may vary both situationally and in absolute terms, in the sense that one's ethnic membership may be socially relevant in a negligible number of contexts, and that one's self-perception is made up by many other elements as well as the ethnic one. For example, all North Americans except the indigenous populations are descendants of people who arrived from other continents quite recently, but in most cases this origin has little social relevance. To the Swedish-Americans of South Dakota, it may be the case that their ethnic identity is made visible two or three times a year through public rituals; for the rest of the year, they are ordinary and not hyphenated Americans. By contrast, in everyday life in a highland village in Guatemala the dichotomisation between Ladinos (of mixed origin and Spanish-speaking) and Maya Indians is very powerful, and nearly everything an individual does – from dress to food to language to work to body language – can easily be read by the other villagers as an expression of his or her ethnic membership (Nash 1988). The local community is, as it were, saturated with ethnicity.

There is no agreement among specialists as to which is more fundamental, ethnic identity or organisation. Some assume that identity, as 'we-feeling', is the most basic aspect of ethnicity and that ethnically based politics consists of transferring this collective emotional attachment to a new field. Abner

Cohen, who studied ethnicity in Nigeria, Sierra Leone and London (1969, 1981, 1993), represents the opposite position. In his view, ethnic organisation – the pursuit of group interests – is the very *raison d'être* of ethnic identity; he holds that the identity would vanish if it had no organisational focus, and that the ethnic cohesion as well as the we-feeling are actually created through social and political processes, especially in contexts of competition for scarce resources.

Research on ethnicity indicates that there is variation in this area, although Cohen's view of ethnicity as an essentially political phenomenon is certainly valuable in the study of ethnicity in modern societies. Ethnicity, as it is being enacted, is clearly a combination of both dimensions – the symbolic and the social or political. Clearly, ethnic ideologies depend on a cultural 'raw material' as a point of departure, although this 'raw material' may be manipulated. Some aspects of the identity base of ethnicity cannot be manipulated, however. Obviously, Mauritian Hindu politicians who decide to exploit ethnicity in the quest for office will be unable to persuade a single voter that they are Hindus if they define themselves as Muslims. On the other hand, they may be able to persuade Hindus to vote along ethnic lines and may thus contribute to the formation of a corporate Hindu ideology.

It has also been argued that ethnic identities may continue to be important to their carriers even if they do not 'pay off'. The Creoles of Mauritius may provide an example: they are poorly organised politically, and define themselves in relation to ostensible cultural traits which make it difficult for them to compete with other groups in the labour market and in politics (Eriksen 1998, 2004; Boswell 2006). An important insight from Cohen and others who have studied ethnicity as a kind of political organisation is nevertheless that ethnicity attains its overall greatest importance when it is expressed as economic and political competition over scarce resources which both or all groups deem valuable.

There are thus degrees of ethnicity. Don Handelman (1977) once developed an influential typology of degrees of ethnic incorporation where he distinguishes between four levels; put in other terms, he classifies interethnic contexts as four distinctive degrees of social and cultural importance. His degrees of incorporation are as follows.

In the *ethnic category*, ethnicity as identity is reproduced over several generations through myths of origin and endogamy. Its social relevance outside the household and kinship levels of organisation is negligible.

The *ethnic network* is an interpersonal system of interaction, accompanied by a flow of value, which follows ethnic lines. For example, ethnic networks beyond the kinship level may be helpful in the search for a job, a house and a spouse.

The third level is the *ethnic association*, whose members are organised corporately in certain respects. It consists of a goal-directed collective organisation which pursues shared goals defined on behalf of the ethnic group as a whole.

Finally, Handelman speaks of the *ethnic community*. Here we have an ethnic group with a clear territorial base. At this, highest level of ethnic incorporation, group members have shared interests in their ethnic identity, their ethnic networks, their ethnic associations and their shared territorial estate. It is obvious that a society where virtually all scarce resources are held by ethnic groups in this way becomes much more 'ethnified' – ethnicity becomes a more pervasive dimension in politics and everyday life – than societies where neither politics nor the division of labour are strongly correlated with ethnic distinctions. There are thus important differences in degree as to the relative importance of ethnicity.

The apparent dualism between ethnic identity and ethnic organisation – personal fulfilment versus 'what's in it for me' – can be overcome, either by simply conceding that they are two sides of the same coin, or by conceptualising ethnicity as something akin to a total social phenomenon. Drawing on Weiner's concept of inalienable possessions (see Chapter 12), Simon Harrison (2000) does the latter. He discusses the symbols and markers of ethnic identity as core elements of selfhood, which cannot be bartered or traded. When one group tries to appropriate another's symbols, through piracy, or commercialisation (e.g. in the case of Aboriginal art), or in processes of social mobility (e.g. in Sanskritisation, cf. Chapter 10), the original group will try to protect its ethnic estate, which consists of the symbols, knowledge and artifacts that make them who they are. In such situations, identity and politics merge. A third option is the commercialisation of identity (Comaroff and Comaroff 2009), which may be used to good effect in cultural tourism, as well as – arguably – strengthening the self-esteem of those involved, provided commercialisation takes place on their own terms (Kasten 2004).

ETHNICITY AND RANK

In polyethnic societies, as in others, a variety of criteria is available for the classification of people, and ethnic status never gives sufficient information to describe a person's position in a system of social classification. Ethnic categories or groups are internally differentiated according to gender, age and (often) class, and there are also other independent criteria for differentiation which have no direct relationship to ethnicity. We can illustrate this with an example from Mauritius, that polyethnic island-state in the south-western Indian Ocean (Eriksen 1992, 1998).

Both Rajiv and Kumar are Hindus around 30 years of age. Their respective positions in Mauritian society are nevertheless very different, and one may almost say that all they have in common, apart from gender and age, is their ethnic identity.

Rajiv belongs to the Babojee caste, which makes him a Brahmin; in other words, he is a member of one of the highest castes. He is the son of a wealthy merchant in Vacoas and is eventually expected to take over his father's business, where he now works. Rajiv is also expected to travel to India to find a wife from his own caste within a couple of years. He has a BA degree from the University of Lucknow. He speaks English and French in addition to Creole (his vernacular) and takes evening classes in Hindi. He owns a car. Many of Rajiv's friends and acquaintances belong to other castes; some even belong to other ethnic groups.

Kumar belongs to the Ravi Ved caste, which is one of the lowest castes in Mauritius. Like his father, he is an agricultural worker on a sugar estate in Flacq, and the family lives in a small rented house on the estate. Kumar is hardly literate and can make himself understood only in Bhojpuri (a rural dialect of Hindi) and Creole, the low-status languages of Mauritius. He is married to a woman from the village and they have two children. Kumar's personal network largely consists of kinsmen, neighbours and colleagues from work, all of them low-caste Hindus like himself.

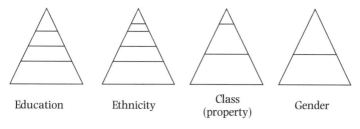

| Education | Ethnicity | Class (property) | Gender |

Figure 17.1   Four perspectives on rank in Mauritian society

According to a class analysis, Kumar belongs to the working class, while Rajiv belongs to the bourgeoisie. Their life-worlds are in many ways very different, and in this sense Kumar may have more in common with the Creoles who work in the sugar factory than with Rajiv. Nevertheless, they vote for the same party, the Hindu-dominated Labour Party.

There are political organisations and parties in Mauritius which argue that class differences and the rural–urban contrast are more fundamental than ethnic differences. Some of them have enjoyed some success in certain periods; for example, in the 1970s there were two general strikes where Creoles, Hindus and Muslims went on strike together against the state and the local capitalists, regardless of their ethnic membership. This illustrates the fact that the social relevance of ethnicity cannot be taken for granted, but is negotiable.

The example from Mauritius shows that ethnicity cuts across class. However, in many societies there is a strong correlation between ethnicity and class, so that some ethnic groups rank higher than others. Many Caribbean societies reveal such a pattern, where skin colour may frequently be read as an indication of class membership. In some places, moreover, it is possible to change one's ethnic membership as one changes one's class membership. In Peru, it may be *de facto* possible for Indians to become Ladinos if they acquire the way of life and external markers (dress, language) characteristic of the Ladinos (van den Berghe 1975; cf. Wade 1997). In Mauritius, Creoles may regard themselves as, and be regarded by others as, *gens de couleur* ('Coloured') if they acquire certain aspects of what is locally seen as a European way of life. Money and manners somehow makes the skin paler.

Both class and ethnicity are criteria for social differentiation and rank. As with the caste–class relationship discussed in Chapter 10, neither can be reduced to the other, but they do influence each other. For example, the Chinese of Trinidad, formerly a poor and somewhat despised group, have become one of the richest ethnic groups in the island over the years. As a result, people of mixed origin now tend to overcommunicate the 'Chinee' aspect of their identity. Although it is commonly assumed that ethnicity is ascribed while class is achieved, it may thus be possible to change one's ethnic membership in certain cases.

Gender is also a dimension of social differentiation which may influence the significance of ethnicity. Several anthropologists have pointed out how gender may create cross-cutting ties of loyalty, not least among women, who may develop female networks that cut across ethnic boundaries and thereby make them less rigid, frequently mitigating and preventing conflict (Little 1978; Schlee 2008).

If the relationship between class and ethnicity is difficult to grasp analytically, it is no easier to understand fully the relationship between class and ethnicity on the one hand and gender on the other. It is obvious that a Mauritian woman who belongs to the Franco-Mauritian upper class in many ways ranks higher than a man who is a low-caste Hindu and plantation worker. At the same time, there are conceivable situations where his rank – or power – may be higher than hers, by virtue of his gender. If the public spheres of society – politics, finance, journalism, etc. – are male dominated, the Hindu worker may be able to participate and compete there, while she will be more or less strictly confined to '*Kinder, Küche und Kirche*' (children, kitchen and church), namely the private sphere.

Ethnicity and class are to some extent comparable, since both phenomena are related to power discrepancies and competition in public space. Gender, on the contrary, cuts across both ethnicity and class and is not related to either of them in a simple way, yet it is important in a multitude of social situations. One cannot, therefore, easily decide which status is the most 'fundamental' out of class, gender and ethnicity. It is nevertheless a fact that the actors themselves in many societies regard ethnicity and gender as ascribed, and class as achieved. The ethnic status thereby appears as an imperative status, more compelling than other statuses. One can change one's class membership through social mobility; for most people, it is far more difficult (and sometimes impossible) to change one's ethnic membership.

SEGMENTARY IDENTITIES

Ethnic organisation can only be including if it is also excluding, and ethnic identity is largely defined by contrasts with others. It has been suggested above that ethnicity cannot by itself define the social identity of a person. This is caused, among other things, by the fact that every person is a member of several groups, and only some of them are formed on the basis of ethnicity. (For example, Cris Shore [1993] draws extensively on the theory of ethnic identification when he writes about communist identity construction in central Italy, a non-ethnic kind of identification which was nonetheless very important to the people involved and which resembled ethnicity in its functioning. In the recent scholarly literature on Muslims in Europe, where religion [and not ethnicity] is the main boundary marker, the theory of ethnicity is likewise used extensively in making sense of the social and cultural dynamics between majorities and minorities.)

First, we may imagine the social identities of an actor as a series of concentric circles, which includes an increasing number of people as we move from the small to the large scale. As in the segmentary organisation of the Nuer (Chapter 11), the concrete situation decides which group one participates in; or rather, which community is made relevant. To many of the inhabitants of Mauritius, their social identity as Mauritians became relevant only when the island began to attract large numbers of tourists, as well as becoming industrialised and starting to compete for market shares on a global scale. Simultaneously, kinship and ethnic membership continue to play a part in many situations, such as marriage and politics, but in other regards they have been replaced by the more encompassing phenomenon of Mauritian citizenship. In kinship-based societies, a societal level like the region or the state may be irrelevant to many of the inhabitants in most social situations, if their needs are by and large satisfied at lower levels of integration, such as those of the household, lineage or village.

Any person thus has many complementary social identities, and the context decides which of them is activated at any time. The model of segmentary identities serves as a reminder that identity is not fixed, is not 'innate', but is fashioned in the encounter between an individual and a social situation. The segmentary model may enable us to describe the social identities of a person as, say, citizen of the world, African, Kenyan, Kikuyu, someone from the Murang'a area, member of clan X, member of lineage A. However, as the discussion of segmentary identities in Chapter 11 indicated, individuals also have other identities which cut across a system of concentric circles. For example, a person may be 50 years old, a man, a spouse, a lawyer, a socialist, a stamp-collector and so on. He or she is a member of many groups with only partially overlapping membership. Which identity is assumed in a situation of conflict, when an individual must choose, say, between loyalty to the party and loyalty to the nation or ethnic group, is an empirical question.

IDEOLOGICAL USES OF THE PAST

As shown previously, myths of origin are powerful devices that have the potential to make sense of the present, legitimise the existing political order and offer group identity. In contemporary ethnic groups and nations, history is used in the same ways. Although written records and archives provide information of a different kind from oral transmissions, they too are ambiguous and open to 'tailoring' and varying interpretations. In a widely read and quoted volume entitled *The Invention of Tradition* (Hobsbawm and Ranger 1983), historians and anthropologists investigate how the past can be manipulated in order to justify a particular view of the present. As the title indicates, the focus is largely on consciously invented traditions; examples discussed include the Scottish highland tradition and rituals invented by colonial authorities to give the impression that the colonial empire was ancient and 'natural'.

However, there is no need to restrict oneself to 'traditions' that are recent creations that conceal political agendas. The past can be viewed in a multitude of ways, as any comparison of history textbooks from neighbouring countries will reveal. Obviously, the Napoleonic Wars are not described in identical ways to British and French schoolchildren, to mention one example. In many countries, there are vivid debates over the 'correct' depiction of past events, and official history has ideological and political implications. In Cyprus, divided between a Greek-speaking and a Turkish-speaking population, efforts have been made to rewrite history in order to reduce the conflict level between the groups (Papadakis 2005). As the present changes, so does the past – at least as it is portrayed in authoritative histories. The rise of ethnopolitics in many parts of the world has been an important factor in reassessments of the past, for example in Canadian and American depictions of native populations.

The analytical perspectives on ethnicity outlined here have focused on the social construction and maintenance of ethnic boundaries, the use of history as myth to justify boundaries, the communication of cultural differences (which may be 'real' or 'fictitious') and the situational character of social identification. Several readers may feel that these views on ethnicity, while no doubt analytically useful, are overly dispassionate tools for dealing with a world torn by brutal conflicts often described as ethnic. It is true that anthropological models of ethnic relationships have rarely presupposed power asymmetry, although they do not preclude it (Tambiah 1989; Tronvoll 2009). It is also true that the conceptualisation of ethnicity in this chapter has largely stressed the formal properties of ethnic relationships, rather than discussing, say, the civil war in Bosnia, racism in Western Europe or genocide in Guatemala. However, the standard anthropological perspectives on ethnic relationships *can* help us in understanding such conflicts, provided the analysis also takes the power relationships and the violent dimension into account.

It is characteristic of twenty-first-century politics that ethnic or religious identity is invoked in political discourse. In Bolivia, rural non-governmental organisations (NGOs) put forward their claims to be the representatives of an oppressed class in the 1970s; the same groups now use symbols which create a continuity with 'Pre-Columbian cultures' (Salman 2010). To the poor villagers, this shift makes little difference in practice. The shift from class analysis to the analysis of ethnic relationships mentioned at the outset of this chapter is symptomatic of an ongoing ethnification of politics and identification in many parts of the world, which will be analysed in further detail in the next chapter on nationalism and minority issues.

SUGGESTIONS FOR FURTHER READING

Fredrik Barth: Introduction, in Fredrik Barth, ed., *Ethnic Groups and Boundaries*. Oslo: Scandinavian University Press 1969.
Anthony P. Cohen: *The Symbolic Construction of Community*. London: Routledge 1985.
Thomas Hylland Eriksen: *Ethnicity and Nationalism: Anthropological Perspectives*, 3rd edn. London: Pluto 2010.
Richard Jenkins; *Rethinking Ethnicity*, 2nd edn. London: Routledge 2008.

18   NATIONALISM AND MINORITIES

People in different parts of the world still utter different sounds, but nowadays they say more or less the same things everywhere.

— *Ernest Gellner*

Scarcely anyone who has used the methods of ethnography to identify and describe ideologies anywhere in the world since the 1960s can have avoided encountering expressions of nationalist ideology. The growth of nationalism and nation-building has been, and still is, an important, spectacular and highly consequential dimension of the worldwide processes of change connected with colonialism and decolonisation. Nationalism is a kind of ideology which exists almost everywhere in the world, although it assumes very different forms and varies in significance. This does not mean that all the citizens of any state know about, or for that matter support, nationalist ideology – but it implies that nationalism is a cultural phenomenon of such importance that both anthropology and other social sciences have, since the 1980s, seen it as a main priority to try to come to grips with it analytically.

NATIONALISM AND MODERNITY

In anthropology, nationalism is usually defined as an ideology which holds that cultural boundaries should correspond to political boundaries; that is to say, that the state ought to contain only people 'of the same kind' (Gellner 1983). All nationalisms promote, in one way or the other, the congruence between state and the culture of citizens. While social theorists in the past might regard nationalism as an 'archaic survival' from a remote past, which would probably be superseded through modernisation and bureaucratisation (for instance, Weber 1978 [1919]), it soon become clear that it is actually a product of modernity. In fact, nationalism as we know it was developed in both France and Germany around the time of the French Revolution: it has a dual origin in the French Enlightenment and German Romanticism.

The parallel between the study of nationalism and that of ethnicity is obvious; most nationalisms – some would say all, but that is a matter of definition – are special cases of ethnic ideologies. Since most nationalist ideologies argue the ancient nature of their nation, it has been widely held that this was also the case with the ideology itself. This is not the case, and at this point it may be useful to distinguish between tradition and traditionalism. Nationalism tends to appear as a traditionalist ideology, glorifying a presumedly ancient cultural tradition. This does not entail that it is 'traditional' or 'ancient' itself. The example of Norwegian nationalism since the 1850s demonstrates this point. At that time, Norway was in an enforced union with Sweden as a result of the Napoleonic Wars, and a growing number of urban, educated Norwegians, inspired by similar movements elsewhere in Europe, felt that they ought to have their own state. Members of the cultural and political elite travelled to remote valleys where they found popular traditions which seemed peculiarly Norwegian; they brought them back to the cities, exhibited them and made them appear as an expression of the Norwegian people and its 'spirit'. Thus a national symbolism was gradually developed, stressing dimensions of Norwegian rural life that were seen as unique (not found in neighbouring Sweden and Denmark, with which Norwegian nationhood was contrasted), and this was used to establish the idea of the unique Norwegian nation. A national historiography was founded during the same period, stressing the continuity with the fearsome Vikings and the subsequent thirteenth century Norse empire based in Nidaros (now Trondheim) and, moreover, introducing a theory of migration making the Norwegian ethnic group appear unique, while a national literature, national art, national music and a new national language based on certain rural dialects – thereby markedly distinctive from Danish – were created. This concerted effort was intended to give the impression that Norway was really an old country with a unique cultural and ethnic identity, and therefore deserved political independence.

The rural culture of Norway, in a reinterpreted form, provided an efficient political weapon, not because it was statistically typical or because it was inherently more 'authentic' than urban culture, but because it could be used to express ethnic distinctiveness in relation to Danes and Swedes and because it embodied the rural–urban solidarity characteristic of nationalism. According to nationalist ideology, the important distinguishing lines between groups follow national boundaries, and internal differentiation is therefore under-communicated. Nationalism postulates that all members of society have a shared culture, which was a radical point of view in societies which had formerly been based on ascribed rank and feudal hierarchies.

The traditionalism which is expressed through nationalism is thus deeply modern in character, and this is a main paradox of nationalist ideology. The fact that the nationalists claim the Vikings were Norwegians does not mean that the nationalists are Vikings. We now need to examine more closely the relationship between nationalism and modernity, which has a strong bearing on earlier discussions of social scale, technology and forms of social integration.

NATIONALISM AND INDUSTRIAL SOCIETY

In Ernest Gellner's influential book about nationalism (1983), the author shows that European nationalism emerged as a response to industrialisation and people's disengagement from 'primordialities' like kin, religion and local communities. Industrialisation entailed a greater geographical mobility, and made people participate in social systems of a much larger scale than they had known earlier. Kin ideology, feudalism and religion were no longer capable of organising people efficiently. There was, in other words, a need for a cohesive ideology in the large-scale societies evolving in Europe in the nineteenth century, which both created social systems of enormous scale and inspired demands for individual equality and civil rights. Nationalism was able to meet such demands, and Gellner largely sees it as a functional replacement of older ideologies and principles of social organisation.

A fundamental difference between kinship ideology and nationalism is the fact that the latter postulates the existence of an abstract community; that is, as a nationalist or patriot, one is loyal to a legislative system and a state which ostensibly represents one's 'people', not to individuals one knows personally. The nation thus only exists if one is capable of imagining its existence – it cannot be observed directly – and it is in this sense that Benedict Anderson (2006 [1983]) has spoken of the nation as an imagined community. In his account of nationalism, he attributes great importance to the development of mass media, particularly the printed book. With print-capitalism, he argues, an immense number of people are able to appropriate the same knowledge, and this may take place without direct contact with the author. A standardisation of language and world-view on a huge scale thus becomes possible. (The similarity between Anderson's analysis of nationalism and Goody's view of literacy should be noted here.) The role of the state educational system in nation-states is immensely important here. All English schoolchildren have heard of Guy Fawkes, but few know why Pieter Stuyvesant is an important person in Dutch history. In the Netherlands, the situation is reversed.

At a cultural level, print media and standardised education imply a certain homogenisation of representations. At the level of social organisation, it facilitates geographical mobility over a large area, since it gives people in different areas roughly the same qualifications and thus makes them replaceable in the labour market. Large-scale communication and cultural standardisation or homogenisation are thus important features of nation-building, which contribute to explaining how it can be that people identify with such an abstract entity as a nation.

Both Gellner and Anderson emphasise the modern and abstract character of the nation. The nation and nationalism here appear as tools of state power in societies which would otherwise be threatened by fragmentation and anomie. Nationalism is a functional ideology for the state in that it creates loyalty and facilitates large-scale operations, and it is functional for the individual in that it replaces obsolete foci for identification and socialisation, notably the family. It is thus no mere cliché that the nation-state has taken over many of the former functions of the family and the local community in modern societies, as an institution representing, among other things, social control, socialisation and group belonging. The nation may, further, be seen as a metaphoric kin group.

Kinship is fundamental to human organisation everywhere, and nationalism tends to emerge in situations where kinship organisation has been weakened. From having been members of lineages or villages, people also, and perhaps more importantly, become citizens through processes of modernisation. The nation-state offers both a feeling of security and a cultural identity, as well as socialisation (through schooling) and career opportunities. It demands our loyalty in roughly the same way as the family: people are willing to kill and die for their relatives and their nation (if nationalism is a successful ideology), but for few other groups. The nation-state, in other words, is able to mobilise very strong passions among its members, and Anderson (2006) famously remarked that nationalism has more in common with phenomena such as religion and kinship than with ideologies like socialism and liberalism.

Some authors have argued that although nationalism is a modern phenomenon, it is rooted in earlier ethnic communities or '*ethnies*' (Smith 1986, 1991, 2008), but it would surely be misleading to claim that there is an unbroken continuity from pre-modern communities to national ones. As the Norwegian example shows, national dress and other symbols take on a very different meaning in the modern context from that which they had originally. Besides, it has been argued that the myths of origin giving nations their ideological legitimation need not be ethnic; non-ethnic nations, not least in the Americas, appear capable of creating a sense of patriotism without referring to an imputed common ethnic origin (Eriksen 2004).

THE NATION-STATE

For a nation-state to exist, its leaders must simultaneously be able to legitimate a particular power structure and sustain a popular belief in the ability of the nation to satisfy certain basic needs in the population. A successful nationalism implies, in most cases, an intrinsic connection between an ethnic ideology of shared descent and a state apparatus. Let us briefly consider some of the characteristics of the nation-state, seen as a mode of social organisation. It may be relevant to compare it with other forms of social organisation described earlier in this book: there are both similarities and differences between, say, the French nation and the Dogon village.

Above all, the nation-state is based on nationalist ideology; that is the doctrine that state boundaries should correspond with cultural boundaries. Further, the nation-state has a monopoly on the legitimate use of violence, the enforcement of law and order, and the collection of taxes. It has a bureaucratic administration and written legislation which covers all citizens, and it has – at least ideally – a uniform educational system and a shared labour market for its people. Most nation-states have an official national language; some have even banned the public use of minority languages.

In other societies too, the political authorities have monopolies on violence and taxation. What is peculiar to the nation-state in this regard is the enormous concentration of power it represents. If we compare a modern war with a feud among the Yanomamö, we see the difference clearly. In the same way as the abstract community of nationalism encompasses an incredible number of people (usually many millions) compared to societies integrated on the basis of kinship (among the Yanomamö, there is an upper limit of a few hundred people), the modern state may in many cases be seen as an enormous enlargement of other forms of social organisation. This does not mean that the nation-state is 'just like other kinds of society', only bigger, but we ought to be aware of the similarities between state and non-state forms of organisation, not merely the differences. A distinction between contemporary states and earlier ones may also be relevant, not least in the context of this chapter. In *Pluralism and the Politics of Difference* (1998), Ralph Grillo shows that ethnic plurality was generally seen as less problematic in earlier state formations – from the Alur (Uganda) to the Aztecs and the Ottomans – than it is in most contemporary nation-states. 'Minority issues' are therefore the trueborn child of the modern state, where the ambitions to standardise and unify, and the demands of participation, are greater than in other large-scale political entities. Of course, not all citizens are complacent, loyal or even directly affected by the state's demands: it is an empirical question how and to what extent state policies are being felt. Moreover, a paradox studied in depth by Michael Herzfeld (2005) is the fact that people who criticise and resist state intervention into their lives may at the same time, albeit in different situations, be fervent nationalists: a distinction between informal nationalism (from below) and formal nationalism (from above) might be clarifying here (see Eriksen 1993b). The point is nevertheless that the state, with varying degrees of efficiency, now takes on many of the tasks typically performed by kin groups and village leaderships in traditional societies.

Multiculturalism and Anthropology

The growing importance of self-conscious constructions of cultural identities, which is a global phenomenon, is evident in consumption patterns, politics and the arts. In many countries, perhaps particularly the rich ones with substantial immigrant populations, debates about 'multiculturalism' have highlighted several of these dimensions. Is it meaningful, for example, to talk of 'ethnic art', and should it be evaluated according to culturally specific criteria? Many feel that this approach can lead to the justification of mediocre work in the name of cultural pluralism, but ultimately not to the benefit of the artists and their 'communities', because of the patronising attitude. On the other hand, as Charles Taylor (1992, p. 67) remarks, to 'approach, say, a raga with the presumptions of value implicit in the well-tempered clavier would be forever to miss the point'. An important debate in recent social philosophy, which is relevant for this issue, opposes communitarianism to liberalism. Communitarians like Michael Sandel

▶

and Alasdair MacIntyre (1981) hold that the community is prior to the individual and favour a certain degree of relativism in value judgements, while liberals like Richard Rorty (1991) warn against the pitfalls of communitarianism (including fundamentalism) and defends the undiluted rights of the individual. A 'middle ground' has been defined by Will Kymlicka, who argues for cultural rights on individualist grounds (Kymlicka 1995).

In the political field, related issues have brought about a focus on the relationship between human rights and minority rights. Multi-culturalism could be defined as a doctrine which holds that discrete ethnic groups are entitled to the right to be culturally different from the majority, just as the majority is entitled to its culture. However, as many critics have pointed out, this kind of doctrine may serve to justify systematic differential treatment of ethnic groups (as in apartheid), and may indeed, even in its more benevolent forms, be at odds with individual rights. On the one hand, then, every citizen is in theory entitled to equal treatment from the state and greater society; on the other hand, persons with different cultural backgrounds may also claim the right to retain their cultural identity. When this cultural identity entails, for example, corporeal punishment in child-raising and this is unlawful, the conflict between the right to equality and the right to difference becomes clear. Should groups have rights and not just individuals, and if so, how can one prevent oppression and abuse owing to internal power discrepancies in the group? Although anthropologists would be expected to play an important part in these discourses, they have in general been reluctant to do so. Perhaps multiculturalism is too close for comfort; after all, the very notion of multiculturalism draws on a concept of culture developed in anthropology, but which has today been abandoned by most anthropologists for being too rigid and bounded (Clifford and Marcus 1986; James et al. 1997; Kuper 1999; T. Turner 1993).

The 1999 GDAT debate, an annual debate in anthropological theory (see box in Chapter 6 for details), incidentally concerned the motion 'The Right to Difference is a Fundamental Human Right' (Wade 2000). The motion was eventually defeated by 43 votes against 30 (15 abstentions).

NATIONALISM AND ETHNICITY

The difference between nationalism and ethnicity is simple if we stick to the level of commonly used definitions. A nationalist ideology may, following common usage, be defined as an ethnic ideology which demands the right to its own state on behalf of the ethnic group. In practice, the distinction is less clear-cut.

First, groups or categories of persons may be located analytically to a grey zone between nationhood and ethnic identity. It is simply not true that ethnic groups 'have a shared will'. If some of their members wish independence, while others are content to have linguistic and other rights within an existing state, and yet others want to assimilate into the majority, the category in question may appear both as a nation, as an ethnic group and as a category of individuals, depending on who is speaking. A person may also switch situationally between being a member of an ethnic minority and a member of a nation. An Argentine migrant to France belongs to an ethnic minority while in France, but belongs to a nation the moment she returns to her country of birth.

Second, nationalism may sometimes express an ideology which represents, and is supported by, a majority of ethnic groups. This is the case in Mauritius, where no ethnic group openly wishes to make nation-building an ethnic project on its own behalf. Nationalist ideology in such countries may be seen as polyethnic or supra-ethnic in that it tries to reconcile ethnic differences, but not abolish them, within a shared framework of a nation.

Third, we should keep in mind that everyday language and mass media continuously mix up the concepts of nation and ethnic group; when, for example, people speak of the '104 nations' of the former Soviet Union, they clearly refer to ethnic groups, a few of which are nations in the sense that their leaders want to have states where they are dominant.

Nationalism and ethnicity are related phenomena, but there are many ethnic groups which are not nations, and there are also nations which are not ethnic groups – that is, polyethnic nations or countries which are not founded on an ethnic principle. Naturally, most of the world's countries are as a matter of fact polyethnic, but many of them are dominated by one ethnic group; the French in France, the English in Great Britain and so on. The model of nationalism presented above, as well as models endorsed by nationalists, rarely fits the territory. Notably, there is rarely, if ever, a perfect correspondence between the state and the 'cultural group'. This simple fact is the cause of what, in the contemporary world, is spoken of as minority issues.

MINORITY AND MAJORITY

Two kinds of ethnicity studies which have placed a great emphasis on power and power discrepancies are studies of labour migrants from poor to rich countries, and studies of indigenous peoples. Both are concerned with the relationship between minorities and majorities, where the majority – usually a national group represented in a nation-state – is in several ways more powerful than the minority.

An ethnic minority may be defined as a group which is politically non-dominant, and which exists as an ethnic category. Although the term 'minority' usually refers to inferior numbers, in the professional literature it denotes political submission. A great number of peoples in the world may therefore be seen as minorities. Their relationship to the nation-state nevertheless varies, as do the strategies of the nation-state towards these minorities.

The term 'minority' is relative to both the scale and the form of organisation in the total social system. As has been shown earlier, any delineation of a social system is relative. This means that (1) minorities are created when the compass of the social system increases, as when formerly tribal peoples become integrated into nation-states (the Yanomamö were no minority before they entered into a relationship with the state); (ii) minorities may often become majorities if they are able to delimit the system in new ways (for example, by setting up a new state, or by creating a looser political union); and (iii) ethnic groups which are minorities in one place may become majorities in another.

The Sikhs make up less than 2 per cent of the total population of India; in Indian Punjab, however, they comprise 65 per cent of the population. In accordance with (2) above, some of their leaders are struggling to set up an independent Sikh state, thereby transforming the group collectively from minority to majority status. On the other hand, Hungarians in Transylvania (Romania) and Jamaicans in Britain exemplify (3): they are a minority, but their group is a majority elsewhere.

POWER ASYMMETRIES

So far in the discussion of ethnicity and nationalism, we have not emphasised uneven or asymmetrical power relations between ethnic groups. Many classic studies of ethnicity concentrate on the maintenance of ethnic boundaries and negotiations over identity, without looking more closely at the ways in which power disparities may be decisive for interethnic relationships. The famous studies of ethnicity (or 'tribalism') in the Copperbelt, to mention one example, rarely mentioned the wider context of colonial mining society, which defined Africans as second-class citizens in relation to Europeans.

Stanley Tambiah (1989) has proposed a typology of contemporary societies that differentiates them according to their ethnic composition (see Eriksen 2010 and Horowitz 1985 for alternative typologies of minority–majority relationships):

1. Countries which are almost ethnically homogeneous (where the dominant group has more than 90 per cent of the total population), such as Japan, Iceland and Bangladesh.
2. Countries with a large ethnic majority (75–89 per cent of the population), including Bhutan, Vietnam and Turkey.
3. Countries where the largest ethnic group makes up 50–75 per cent of the population and where there are several minorities, for instance Sri Lanka, Iran, Pakistan and Singapore.
4. Countries with two groups of roughly the same size, such as Guyana, Trinidad & Tobago and Malaysia.

5. Truly plural countries composed of many ethnic groups where no one of them is dominant; for example India, Mauritius, Nigeria and the Philippines.

A problem with this kind of typology is that it lumps together countries which are politically and culturally very different. Within each category there are stable and unstable countries, parliamentary democracies and military dictatorships, countries with good as well as bad records regarding human rights and so on. Ethnically homogeneous Somalia was plunged into a protracted civil war in the 1990s, while there is no threat to the territorial integrity of neighbouring multi-ethnic Kenya. Eritrea's secession from Ethiopia in the early 1990s, moreover, was not an ethnic issue, as Eritrea's population is composed of about 12 ethnic groups, including both Christian and Muslim groups. The 1998–2000 war between Eritrea and Ethiopia largely involved Tigrinya speakers on both side of the border, many of them related

---

Non-ethnic Nations

Theories of nationalism have often been Eurocentric (Handler and Segal 1993; Gladney 1998) and, unsurprisingly, non-European countries have often failed to fit the model. If by nationalism we mean the doctrine of congruence between state and ethnic group, even the USA does not seem to be a nation. In Central and South America, few see their own country as essentially ethnically homogeneous; in Mexico, for example, the notion of *mestizaje* (cultural and racial mixing) has become a symbol of the Mexican nation. Africa presents a no less complex picture, with scarcely a single ethnically homogeneous country, and large parts of Asia are also ethnically very complex – not only in fact, but also at the level of ideology (unlike in Europe, where the societies are often polyethnic but the ideology of nationalism mono-ethnic). If the nation of Tanzania is to be imagined by its citizens, therefore, it cannot be imagined as a Chagga, Swahili or Nyakyusa nation (Tanzania has more than 120 ethnolinguistic groups), but as a symbolic community which exists at a higher segmentary level than the ethnic groups that make it up. In such countries, national ideology must therefore be associated with equal rights and civil society rather than with any particular ethnic group. When it works, it may still have the ability to stir patriotic emotions and create loyalty to the state.

Would these polyethnic imagined communities still be nations in an analytical sense? That is a matter of definition. In my view, they would (Eriksen 2004). It is certain, however, that if the concept of nationalism is going to be cross-culturally valid, it cannot be restricted to the European nations only: it will have to be refined to fit the global territory better.

through kinship (Tronvoll 2009). Mauritius, a truly ethnically plural society, is one of the most stable parliamentary democracies in the Third World. Ethnic plurality as such cannot, in other words, account for violence and political instability (Turton 1997; Schlee 2008).

However, if we add a distinction between ranked and unranked polyethnic systems, it may be easier to understand why some such societies are unstable and others are not. Typically, ethnic groups which are systematically deprived of civil rights and career opportunities will tend to perceive the political order as unjust. This applies only in societies where rights are in practice unevenly distributed on the basis of ethnic membership, but this kind of situation is far from uncommon. For now, we will restrict ourselves to considering asymmetrical relationships between dominant ethnic groups which control the state, and minorities.

SEGREGATION, ASSIMILATION AND INTEGRATION

Short of physical extermination (which has actually been quite common), states may use one or several of three principal strategies in their dealings with minorities. First, the state or the majority may opt for segregation. This means that the minority group becomes physically separated from the majority, often accompanied by the notion that the members of the minority are inferior. The former South African ideology of apartheid promoted segregation, and many North American cities are *de facto* segregated along ethnic lines.

Assimilation is also a possible outcome of contact between majority and minority. If it happens on a large scale, it eventually leads to the disappearance of the minority, which melts into the majority. In England, this happened to the Norman upper class which ruled the country after the invasion in 1066. After a few generations, the descendants of this group became English.

Assimilation may be enforced or chosen. In some cases, it is practically impossible, if ethnic identity has a strong phenotypical component. In the US, most immigrant groups have historically become assimilated; usually they lost their mother-tongue after two generations and retained only a vague memory of their country of origin. But this did not happen with the descendants of the black slaves, since skin colour is an important criterion for social classification. Notwithstanding the election of Barack Obama in 2008, a black American cannot become a 'typical', that is white, American in the same way as the grandchild of a German immigrant may do. In these situations, where assimilation becomes impossible, it may be useful to speak of entropy-resistant traits (Gellner 1983): the distinguishing marks of the minority cannot be removed, whether or not its members wish to do so.

Integration is the third 'type' of relationship between majority and minority. It usually refers to participation in the shared institutions of society, combined with the maintenance of group identity and some degree of cultural distinctiveness. It represents a compromise between the two other main options.

An ethnically based division of labour is compatible with segregation as well as integration, but only assimilation and certain forms of integration are compatible with full political participation in greater society. Chosen segregation may form the rationale for a nationalist movement, or it may be an elite option chosen to keep valuable resources within the ethnic group, but most segregated minorities are 'second-class citizens', whether they are indigenous peoples or recent arrivals.

Most empirical cases of majority–minority relationships display a combination of segregation, assimilation and integration. Assimilation may well take place at an individual level, even if the chief tendency might be segregation or ethnic incorporation. Despite the fact that the Sami of northern Scandinavia have moved towards a stronger ethnic incorporation and chosen segregation in recent decades, there are still individuals who are being assimilated to a majority ethnic identity (Norwegian, Finnish or Swedish, as the case may be).

In studies of majority–minority relationships, it is difficult to escape from an analysis of power and power discrepancies. The majority not only possesses the political power; it usually controls important parts of the economy and, perhaps most importantly, defines the terms of discourse in society. Language, codes of conduct and relevant skills are defined, and mastered, by the majority. The majority defines the cultural framework relevant for life careers, and thus has a surplus of symbolic capital over the minorities. For this reason, many minority members may be disqualified in the labour market and other contexts where their skills are not valued. A Somalian refugee in Germany may be highly skilled if he speaks four languages, but he has no chance in the German labour market if those languages happen to be Somali, Swahili, Italian and Arabic.

MIGRATION

Migrants are a special kind of minority. They often lack citizenship in the host country, and they often have their origin in a country where they belong to a majority. In many cases, migrants are only temporarily settled in the host country. Sociological and anthropological research on migration from poor to rich countries has mainly concentrated on three topics: aspects of discrimination and disqualification on the part of the host population; strategies for the maintenance of group identity; and the relationship between immigrant culture and majority culture. Increasingly, this research has to account for the transnational relationships between the community of origin and the sociocultural environment in the host country, since most migrants maintain significant ties to their place of origin (Georges 1990; Olwig 2007).

In a comparative study of two polyethnic neighbourhoods in London, Sandra Wallman (1986) discovered important differences in the relationships between majority and minorities. Bow in East London was characterised by a strong polarisation and dichotomisation between people born in Britain and immigrants, whereas ethnic relationships in Battersea, south London, were much more relaxed and less socially important. Both areas were largely populated by manual and lower white-collar workers, and they included roughly the same proportions of immigrants from roughly the same places of origin (Africa, Pakistan, India, the West Indies).

Wallman shows that the social networks of the two areas were constituted in significantly different ways. In Bow, the same people interacted in many different types of situation, and the different groups of which each individual was a member overlapped a good deal. In Battersea, on the contrary, each individual was a member of many different groups with different criteria for membership. In Bow people worked and lived in the same area; in Battersea, people tended to work in other parts of London. The British-born population in Bow was extremely stable, while Battersea was characterised by a greater flux.

These and related factors, Wallman argues, have contributed to creating fundamentally different types of ethnic relationships in the two areas. She describes Bow as a closed homogeneous system and Battersea as an open heterogeneous system (see Figure 18.1). In Battersea, unlike in Bow, there were a great number of 'gates' and 'gatekeepers': there are, in other words, many ways in which one may cross group boundaries as an immigrant. One becomes a member of the local community the moment one moves in. But in the closed environment of Bow, people have to have lived their entire lives there in order to be accepted. In Bow, the ethnic boundaries are sharper than in Battersea because the different social networks are so strongly overlapping that an immigrant will have to cross several 'gates' or fences *simultaneously* in order to become an accepted member of the locality. In practice, this is impossible.

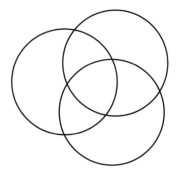

Heterogeneous/open type
(Battersea)

Homogeneous/closed type
(Bow)

Figure 18.1   Degrees of overlap between social sub-systems in Battersea and
Bow (Source: Wallman 1986, p. 241)

Wallman's study strengthens the idea, discussed elsewhere in this book, that cross-cutting ties may have a mitigating effect on conflict. Other researchers, rather than choosing a sociological approach, have focused on the personal identity of migrants. Here, a common perspective amounts to the view that migrants often 'live in two worlds', that they switch between different cultural codes when they move between contexts. Whereas ethnic identity may be undercommunicated in relationships with the host population, it may be overcommunicated internally.

A different, more dynamic perspective would rather focus on social and cultural change, indicating that a Pakistani identity in England necessarily means something different from a Pakistani identity in Pakistan. In some respects, such migrants are 'Anglified'; in other respects, they may self-consciously work to strengthen their cultural identity; in yet other respects, there may be strong cultural values in the midst of the community which are difficult to change even if some members of the group may want to – regarding, for example, the tradition of arranged marriages. The field of migration may in this way prove to be an interesting area for the study of cultural dynamics and change (see also Chapter 19). It also highlights issues to do with the negotiation of identity, discussed in the context of gender in Chapter 9.

'THE FOURTH WORLD'

The term 'indigenous peoples' refers, in everyday language, to a non-dominant population associated with a non-industrial mode of production. This does not mean that members of indigenous peoples never take part in national politics or work in factories, but merely that they are associated with a way of life that renders them particularly vulnerable when faced with the trappings of modernity and the nation-state. It can therefore be instructive to distinguish indigenous peoples from migrants, who are fully integrated into the capitalist system of production and consumption, and who make no territorial claims.

One cannot speak of 'indigenous peoples' in a value-free way. Technically speaking, all inhabitants of the world are indigenous peoples of the planet. The term is always used in a political context, usually in order to make specific political claims.

Indigenous peoples all over the world are placed in a potentially conflictual relationship to the nation-state – not just to one particular nation-state, but to the state as an institution. Their political project frequently consists of securing their survival as a culture-bearing group, but they rarely if ever wish to found their own state. Many indigenous peoples have too few members, and are insufficiently differentiated, for such an option to seem realistic.

The most common conflict between indigenous peoples and nation-states concerns land rights. For this reason, issues regarding these groups and their rights have become increasingly relevant – both in politics and in anthropological research – as nation-states have progressively expanded their territories and spheres of influence. As a reaction against this development, the indigenous peoples of Greenland, Australia, New Zealand, Amazonas, Southern Africa, the Andes, northern Scandinavia, North America and elsewhere have organised themselves through global associations and networks to protect their rights to their ancestral land and cultural traditions. In other parts of the world, including Borneo, New Guinea and large parts of Africa, such forms of organisation are still embryonic, partly because the coming of the modern nation-state has taken place at a later stage.

Perhaps paradoxically, the cultural survival of indigenous peoples necessitates important changes in their culture and social organisation. The Sami of northern Norway provide a good example of this. Only after having acquired literacy and a certain mastery of modern mass media and the national political system was it possible for them to present their political case in effective – and ultimately successful – ways. Generally, the global 'Fourth World' movement is 'Western' and modern in every respect insofar as it is based on human rights ideology, draws on modern mass media and is oriented towards political bodies such as the United Nations. Peoples who retain their traditions unaltered to a greater extent than, for instance, the pragmatic and resourceful Sami stand a much smaller chance of survival in the long run, since they have no effective strategy for handling their encounter with the hegemonic, modern state. This odd paradox of indigenous politics relates to a more general paradox of ethnicity and nationalism, namely that there is no one-to-one relationship between culture and cultural identity, although the two are connected. The distinction between tradition and traditionalism may help to clarify this relationship.

ETHNIC REVITALISATION

That 'reawakening' of traditional culture in a modern context, which seems necessary for indigenous peoples to survive, is often spoken of in more general terms as 'ethnic revitalisation'. The discovery, or invention, of the Norwegian past described earlier is a classic example. The concept of revitalisation literally means that cultural symbols and practices which have lain dormant for a while regain their lost relevance. However, we have to be aware that a revitalised culture is always very different from the original. Revitalisation movements are traditionalist in that they seek to make tradition relevant in a context which is not itself traditional, but modern. An instance of this kind of process is the revitalisation of Hinduism in Trinidad (Klass 1991; Vertovec 1992; Khan 2004).

Several hundred thousand Indians arrived in Trinidad and other plantation colonies following the abolition of slavery in 1839. Most of them never returned to India, and in Trinidad people of Indian origin today make up about 40 per cent of the total population of 1.2 million. For generations, the Indians (or 'East Indians') were the poorest and in many ways most marginal part of the population: they were illiterate, rural and culturally stigmatised by the dominant European and Afro-Trinidadian groups. Since the Second World War, they have increasingly taken part in the institutions of the Trinidadian state: they slowly acquired adequate schooling, trade unions and political representation; they became occupationally differentiated and experienced a general rise in their standard of living. Since the 1970s, Hindu symbolism and the Indian cultural heritage have played an increasingly important part in the Indo-Trinidadian community. In the 1980s a Hindu weekly paper was founded, and during the same period it became common for Indo-Trinidadians to go to India on vacation. Religious attendance was increasing, and political organisations aiming to strengthen the Indian identity were formed. Later, Trinidadian Hindus pioneered the use of Internet resources to strengthen their ties not only to India, but also to the larger Hindu diaspora.

This revitalisation may seem paradoxical. In many ways, the Indians have been assimilated into Trinidadian society. All Indo-Trinidadians now speak Trinidad English or Trinidadian Creole as their vernacular; the caste system has lost most of its functions and categories, and research indicates that the 'East Indians' have the same dreams and aspirations as the rest of the population. Nevertheless, many of them are determined to retain and strengthen their ethnic identity and Indian heritage.

This process is actually very common in ethnopolitical movements. Before 1960 the Indo-Trinidadians were socially and politically fragmented, many were illiterate and they lacked a strong group identity. Only when they were integrated into the modern institutions were they able to mobilise political resources enabling them to function as a corporate group (or an 'imagined community'). Moreover, the concerted presentation of ethnic symbols – itself dependent on a modern infrastructure – gives a meaningful focus to the movement, in creating cohesion at the same time as responding to the individual quest for dignity.

Cultural homogenisation within the modern nation-state may contribute to explaining ethnic revitalisation in other ways as well. Since the Second World War, Indo-Trinidadians have entered into more intensive relationships with the rest of the Trinidadian population, which has led to the erasure or challenging of ethnic boundaries in a number of fields. Many Indians have therefore felt that their identity is threatened, and speak of 'creolisation' as a danger to the integrity of the Indian 'way of life'. A response to perceived creolisation (or enforced dilution of cultural tradition) has been conscious contrasting and overcommunication of distinctiveness. In general, we might say that an ethnic identity becomes important the moment its carriers feel that it is being threatened, or that one is being discriminated against on ethnic grounds. Evidently, this is connected to the fact that ethnicity is created by contact, not by isolation. It also adds substance to the claim that nationalism, and identity politics more generally, are enhanced if not created by modernity, since contacts between groups are intensified in modern settings with their huge labour markets and rapid communication technologies.

It would not be correct to state that ethnicity occurs exclusively within the framework of a modern state, but the ethnic dimension can be expressed in unusually powerful ways there. Although ethnicity does not necessarily relate to processes of modernisation, most ethnic studies deal with social and cultural change. In Norway, there were not necessarily fewer Sami in 1940 than in 1990, but they were less visible, less culturally self-conscious and lacked both a corporate organisation and an 'imagined' collective identity. They did not deal directly with the state and had no minority status; Sami–Norwegian ethnicity was still at the interpersonal level.

As for labour migrants and refugees, their very migration is a tangible expression of modernisation, of links mediated by the state and capitalist modes of production and consumption. Villages in Jamaica and Ghana are becoming economically tied to cities in Britain, and in certain towns in Pakistani Punjab, the labour market in Oslo is generally better known than the labour market in Lahore.

Indigenous populations find themselves in a precarious position. In a certain sense, they are wedged between the reservation and cultural genocide. On the one hand, they may try to opt for isolation and build solid boundaries about their customs and traditions. Such strategies have nearly always been unsuccessful. On the other hand, they may try to promote their political interests through established channels, and for this to be possible they – or some of them – must go through a process of modernisation in order to learn the rules of the relevant political game. This strategy may nevertheless be successful, and in the next chapter it will be clear in what way.

THE GRAMMAR OF IDENTITY POLITICS

Whether nationalist, ethnic, religious or regional in nature, identity politics is a *glocal* phenomenon: it is confined to a territory and a particular in-group, yet it depends on a global discourse about culture and rights in order to succeed. It can indeed be argued that identity politics in very different settings, in spite of important differences, share a number of formal traits (Eriksen 2001) making comparison viable. The late twentieth-century phenomenon of Hindu nationalism (van der Veer 1994) can be invoked to illustrate this.

Although Hinduism is an old religion, politicised Hinduism is recent. The idea of *hindutva*, or Hindu-ness, first appeared in the 1930s, but became a mass phenomenon only in the late 1980s. In the 1990s, the Hindu nationalist BJP (Bharatiya Janata Party or 'the Party of the Indian People') emerged as the most influential party in India, amidst heated controversy over the nature of the Indian state. Its many critics (among them Indian sociologists and anthropologists) pointed out that India had from its inception been a secular state, and that the idea of a Hindu state (which the BJP promoted) was disruptive and harmful in a country with large Muslim, Christian and other minorities.

Also, the idea of a shared collective identity encompassing all Hindus is far from obvious to most Indians; both caste and important linguistic distinctions have divided Hindus as much as uniting them. Unlike egalitarian European societies, Indian society has thrived on hierarchy and difference. *Hindutva* nevertheless emphasises similarity.

Ideologically, *hindutva* is reminiscent of both European nationalisms and identity politics elsewhere. Some of its features, which can be identified in many other settings as well – from Fiji to Yugoslavia – are as follows. The examples in brackets are largely illustrations.

- The external boundary is overcommunicated; internal differences are undercommunicated. (In the case of *hindutva*, the significant others are Muslims – both Indian and Pakistani.)
- History is interpreted in such a way as to make the in-group appear as innocent victims. (The Mughal period, when India was ruled by Muslims, is described as oppressive and humiliating for Hindus.)
- Cultural continuity and purity are overcommunicated. (Sanskrit epics have been commercialised and popularised.)
- Mixing, change and foreign influence are undercommunicated. (This is evident in the clothing, food and language – generally Hindi rather than English – preferred by *hindutva* leaders.)
- Non-members of the in-group are demonised when it is deemed necessary in order to strengthen internal cohesion. (The Ayodhya affair and subsequent riots in 1992–93, when thousands of Muslims were killed, showed this.)
- Conflicting loyalties and cross-cutting ties are strongly discouraged. (At the interpersonal level, relationships between Muslims and Hindus have become more strained.)
- Cultural heroes of the past (from poets to warriors) are reconceptualised as modern nationalists. (The great poet Rabindranath Tagore, to mention one example, is invoked virtually as a *hindutva* ideologist.)

These and related dimensions indicate that identity politics serves to magnify certain social differences perceived as major, thereby minimising other distinctions – in a sense, it could be said that it tries to transform a world consisting of many small differences into a world consisting of a few large ones, namely those pertaining to nationhood, ethnic identity, religion or territorial belonging. Yet, as Frøystad (2005) and others have pointed out, caste appears to be a social institution which is more deeply embedded in Indian daily life than the Muslim/Hindu contrast. Even attempts to simplify the world thus have to compete with rivalling simplifications!

IDENTITY THROUGH CONTRASTING

In the preceding discussion, nationalism and minority issues have been discussed as modern phenomena. I have nevertheless pointed out that there are parallels with other ideologies and forms of organisation, which are more typical of the societies traditionally studied by anthropologists. One parallel with non-modern societies which deserves to be mentioned concerns the production of identification through contrast. The Iatmul of coastal New Guinea, studied by Bateson (1958 [1936]), recounted a myth of origin which expresses a line of reasoning reminiscent of the white North American stigmatisation of black and Indian citizens, and which suggests that ethnicity is not a mere tool of dominance but expresses a need for order, classification and boundaries. In the earliest of times, according to the myth, there was on the shore an enormous crocodile, Kavwokmali, which flapped its huge tail, front legs and hind legs so that soil and water were continuously muddled together in an unpalatable mixture. Everything was mud: there existed neither land nor water. The great culture hero Kevembuangga then came along, killing the crocodile with his spear. The mud sank, and the distinction between land and water was a reality. Boundaries, outlines, clear distinctions appeared for the first time.

This myth, not dissimilar to the Judeo-Christian myth of origin described on the first pages of Genesis, exemplifies the social production of distinctions and classification – differences that make a difference. The production of ethnic distinctions may be regarded as a special case of this general phenomenon, which has been discussed in Chapter 15. Perhaps the fact of ethnic conflict and ethnic discrimination is better analysed not as a result of ethnicity but rather of unjust social arrangements. Perhaps when we speak of the tragedy of nationalist war, the problem is war and not nationalism.

Finally, we should keep in mind that neither ethnic groups nor nations are eternal. They appear, they flourish, are transformed, and eventually vanish. Since history is always written by the victors, it is easy to forget that for every successful nationalism there are perhaps ten or more unsuccessful ones. The members of such potential nations, or their descendants, were either exterminated or assimilated in the long run.

SUGGESTIONS FOR FURTHER READING

Benedict Anderson: *Imagined Communities: An Inquiry into the Origins and Spread of Nationalism*, 2nd edn. London: Verso 1991.

Ernest Gellner: *Nations and Nationalism*. Oxford: Blackwell 1983.

A.D. Smith: *The Cultural Foundations of Nations: Hierarchy, Covenant and Republic*. Oxford: Blackwell 2008.

19   ANTHROPOLOGY AND THE PARADOXES OF GLOBALISATION

Every culture must liberate its creative potential by finding the correct equilibrium between isolation and contact with others.

— *Claude Lévi-Strauss*

One reason why anthropologists have so often approached globalization through the formula of 'the global and the local' is precisely that 'the local' often turns out to be quite resilient, even as it changes, and that a grasp of its earlier forms is thus very valuable in understanding the present.

— *Ulf Hannerz*

An anecdote is told about a tribe of transhumant camel nomads in North Africa, whose annual migration had taken place in March since the dawn of time. Recently their migration was several months delayed. The reason was that they did not want to miss the final episodes of *Dallas*.

The point is not whether or not this tale is true. What it may tell us is that the world is no longer what it used to be – or rather, perhaps, what anthropologists and everybody else used to imagine it to be. For it is easy to find evidence that changes in the world have been dramatic in earlier times too, that there has been extensive and regular communication and contact between societies, and that truly cosmopolitan cities like Byzantium and Timbuktu existed already in medieval times. The opening words of the first classic of twentieth-century British social anthropology, Malinowski's *Argonauts of the Western Pacific*, reads as follows:

Ethnology is in the sadly ludicrous, not to say tragic, position, that at the very moment when it begins to put its workshop in order, to forge its proper tools, to start ready for work on its appointed task, the material of its study melts away with hopeless rapidity. Just now, when the methods and aims of scientific field ethnology have taken shape, when men fully trained for the work have begun to travel into savage countries and study their inhabitants – these die away under our very eyes. (1984 [1922], p. xv)

Malinowski's worries concern phenomena which are today sometimes described as imperialism, or cultural imperialism, and sometimes as the globalisation of culture; that is, the worldwide dissemination of certain cultural forms and social institutions because of colonialism, trade, missionary activity, technological change, mobility and the incorporation of tribal peoples into states and large-scale systems of exchange. When the first American anthropologists began to return from Bali in the 1920s, they described, in a concerned tone of voice, how Balinese culture was about to be completely destroyed by mass tourism (which still, in the early twenty-first century, does not seem to have come about; see Wikan 1992; Howe 2005) – and similar grim predictions have been made on behalf of many of the peoples who have been explored anthropologically. Ever since the feeble beginnings of modern comparative anthropology, practitioners have been worried about the disappearance of the cultural variation which it is our aim to explore. In the 1960s and 1970s many spoke of the importance of 'urgent anthropology', which entailed recording the culture and social organisation of the peoples still living in a traditional way before they disappeared from the face of the earth. In recent years, new concerns have to some extent replaced these, and anthropologists now investigate, in different ways, the new complexities engendered by the increased contact between societies.

WHERE ARE THEY NOW?

What has become of the peoples first explored by anthropologists during colonialism? Nearly all of them are, to varying degrees, integrated into larger – in the final instance global – economic, cultural and political systems. To some, such as the Tsembaga Maring of Papua New Guinea, this integration is still of relatively minor importance in their everyday life. Although wagework and a monetary economy have entered their society, they still get their livelihood from pig-raising and horticulture. Because of the increasingly efficient state monopoly of violence, it has nevertheless become difficult to go to war in the highlands. Missionary activity and labour migration, however, has made an impact on the lives of many peoples in the New Guinea highlands for years, and organisations aiming to preserve and disseminate local cultural forms have been set up.

For many of the other peoples dealt within earlier chapters of this book, the changes have been more radical. Among the Azande of Central Africa, proletarianisation has been widespread – many found wagework in cotton and peanut plantations – and yet, the basic social institutions, including that of witchcraft, still function. The Yanomamö in Brazil and Venezuela have reluctantly been drawn into the global economy too – notably, gold has been found in their territory – and, simultaneously, they now have professional spokesmen travelling around the world to promote their interests as an indigenous population. A majority of Yanomamö still chiefly live off subsistence horticulture, although the monetary sector is becoming increasingly important. A more tragic part of recent Yanomamö history has been the spread of diseases such as measles, relatively harmless to Europeans but deadly to isolated, formerly unexposed groups. As for the Mundurucú further south in Brazil, as early as the 1950s they were being drawn into a capitalist economic system. Several of the villages depended on wagework on rubber plantations, and in this setting their pattern of settlement was changed: the men's house was gone, and men lived with their wives and children in nuclear families. In general, the Murphys report (1985), the women were happy with the changes, which meant that men contributed more to the household; whereas the men spoke in nostalgic terms about a largely mythical past, when they fought heroic battles and game was abundant.

One of the most important changes among the Dogon since the period of French colonisation in Mali has been the fact of peace. Their old enemies, the Fulani, have been prevented from attacking them and thus the Dogon have been able to expand their territory. Like the Fur, the Fulani, the Hausa and many other peoples, however, the Dogon have been severely hit by the combination of recurrent droughts in the Sahel region and population growth. The Dogon are today in many ways integrated into the nation-state of Mali; the children go to school, are vaccinated and learn French as a foreign language. The monetary economy has become more widespread and certain industrial products, such as factory-made clothes, transistor radios and bicycles, have become common. As with many other African peoples, Islam has been an important factor in cultural change among the Dogon. In this respect, the increased peaceful contact with the Fulani, who are Muslims and active missionaries, has been particularly important.

Turning to the Nuer and Fur, their greatest problem apart from devastating droughts has been the long-lasting civil war in the Sudan (1983–2005), which made trade difficult, apart from draining off both economic and human resources from their societies. Many Nuer fought and died on the south Sudanese side in the war against the Islamic north; in accordance with Evans-Pritchard's model of segmentary oppositions, they were occasionally integrated at a higher level of segmentation than they used to be, fighting side by side with the more numerous Dinka. In Darfur, as in many other local communities in the Sudan, large numbers of refugees from politically unstable Ethiopia led, particularly in the 1980s, to a further strain on already very scarce resources. Darfur has also been a region where war and unrest did not end with the signing of the peace treaty in 2005. Unrest between some of the ethnic groups of the region (including the Fur and Baggara) was corroborated by the intrusion of Arab militias known as the Janjawid, who were believed to have been responsible for massacres, arson and rapes around 2003. Fighting, raiding and massacres have nevertheless continued since then, and hundreds of thousands of Darfurians have been displaced. At the time of writing, the entrenched conflicts surrounding Darfur, involving both ethnic conflict within Sudan and border disputes with Chad, are presently (2010) unresolved, although an important peace treaty was signed in 2007.

As mentioned in an earlier chapter, the Trobriand Islanders largely seem to have adapted to processes of modernisation on their own terms (Malnic and Kasaipwalova 1998). Modernisation has led to changes in political organisation, in the economy and in the politics of identity, but both the kinship system and the system of ceremonial exchange still function, even if they do not have the same overall significance as before

The kind of diachronic perspective implied in these snapshots of change provides a starting-point for anthropological studies of local life which alters and which is connected with systems of enormous scale. The main task of anthropology can no longer be to explore and describe alien ways of life for the first time, but rather to account for processes taking place at various points and various levels in the global system.

A GLOBAL CULTURE?

As the quotation above from Malinowski indicates, since the early days of twentieth-century ethnography, anthropologists have been aware of tendencies towards what we may call cultural entropy – that historical process which is sometimes described as 'cultural globalisation', as 'creolisation' or 'hybridisation', or again, rather inaccurately, as 'Westernisation'. However, one may still wonder if we are not presently at the threshold of a new era in the history of humanity, the era of the global information society. The previous three chapters have dealt exclusively with phenomena belonging to modern contexts; in some cases, as with nationalism and minority issues, these topics have only been relevant for a few decades in large parts of the world. In these final pages, we investigate in what sense it may be reasonable to consider our time a 'global age' and, above all, look into the relationships between the global and the local. First of all, we need to look more closely at the currently fashionable term 'globalisation'. For this word does not mean that we are all becoming identical, but rather that we express our differences in new ways.

If by the word 'modernity' one refers to everything that capitalism, the modern state and individualism mean to human existence, modernity has been hegemonic in the world at least since the First World War; that is to say, it has dominated. The dissemination of modernity has nevertheless accelerated since the Second World War. During the last few decades, there has been an intensified flow of people, commodities, ideas and images on a global scale. Since the appearance of the jet plane, and after satellite television became common in many parts of the world, and even more recently, since the phenomenal rise of the Internet from the early 1990s, the limitations on cultural flow represented in space and time have been significantly reduced. We have witnessed a formidable time-space compression, to use the words of the geographer David Harvey (1989).

Modern communication technology contributes in two ways to the disembedding of certain cultural phenomena from space. First, a multitude of phenomena – including aspects of 'youth culture', prestige commodities from Coca-Cola cans to pop CDs and jeans, popular films, and transnational political issues such as the environmental crisis – exist both globally (everywhere) and locally (in particular places) simultaneously. Second, the jet plane has made it possible for a growing number of people to move rapidly and comfortably all over the world, while telephones, fax machines, the Internet and satellite video telephony make it feasible, in principle, to communicate with people anywhere in the world at any time. Space can no longer be said to create a buffer between 'cultures'.

To anthropology, which has historically concentrated on the study of local communities, or at least more or less clearly delineated sociocultural systems, these changes have implied new and complex challenges, both at the level of theory and at the level of methodology.

MODERNITY AND GLOBALISATION

Although modern societies differ in marked ways, modernity has certain shared dimensions everywhere. These commonalities, or parallels, can be observed both at the level of institutions and at the level of cultural representations.

The state and citizenship are today nearly universal principles of social organisation, although they exist in many variants. Their meaning should not be exaggerated – it is still possible, in some parts of the world, to live an entire life without regular contact with the state. It is nevertheless becoming increasingly difficult. Virtually nobody in today's world can escape citizenship completely, and the state's power over its citizens is reflected in its double monopoly on taxation and legitimate violence. If agents other than the state collect taxes or commit violent acts, they are now guilty of crimes.

Wagework and capitalism are also important dimensions of globalised modernity. Capital is increasingly disembedded from territory, which means that companies and capitalists may invest virtually anywhere. If it is cheaper to produce computer chips in Malaysia than in Scotland, the microchip producer may easily move the assembly plant there. Such moves correctly presuppose that there is a globally available workforce prepared to enter into labour contracts.

Within modernity, consumption is by and large mediated by money. This simply means that people buy the goods they need in a market where general-purpose money is the dominant medium of exchange. Subsistence production and barter are becoming less important.

From this, it follows that both politics and economies are integrated in an abstract, anonymous and globally connected network of investments, exchange and migration. No single person can affect this system in decisive ways, and events taking place at one point in the system can have ramifications – frequently unforeseen – in other parts of it. If the Taiwanese exports of personal computers increase one year, a fashion shop in a middle-class area in California may go bankrupt. The reason is, simply, that many of the shop's former customers have lost their jobs in the Silicon valley computer industry. These processes cannot be described satisfactorily in simple causal or intentional accounts. They take place at the abstract level of the system and can be likened to what are sometimes spoken of as 'butterfly effects': a butterfly flaps its wings in Rio de Janeiro and creates a small wind, triggering a long chain of events of growing magnitude, which eventually create a storm in New York.

One consequence of increasing systemic integration at a global level is the fact that certain political issues affect the entire planet. The environmental crisis is an obvious example. If the rainforests of Amazonia, Indonesia and Central Africa disappear, there is likely to be a climatic change perceptible everywhere. And when the Chernobyl nuclear reactor suffered a meltdown in 1986, newspapers in Venezuela, Japan and Mauritius carried daily, worried reports about the catastrophe.

The creation of agencies and NGOs with a worldwide scope also indicates the importance of globalisation. The UN and organisations such as the Red Cross and Amnesty International, as well as Fourth World networks, have contributed to the development of a global discourse about morality and politics, although the system of sanctions is still weak. In an earlier chapter it was argued that it is difficult to find universal criteria for human rights; because of the globalisation of culture, politics and economic and military power, it seems that such criteria are about to be developed – at least in theory (Wilson 1997; Mitchell and Wilson 2003).

The worldwide dissemination of AIDS is another instructive – if grotesque – example indicating that globalisation is not limited to contact mediated by abstract structures such as the mass media; contact across national and regional boundaries can be physical and direct.

DIMENSIONS OF GLOBALISATION

Although it is neither true that globalisation leads to global cultural uniformity nor that global connections were unknown before the late twentieth century, there are sound reasons to concede that the interconnectedness of the contemporary world signifies a new situation regarding social and cultural dynamics. Some of the key dimensions of globalisation are the following (taken from Eriksen 2007b).

- *Disembedding*, including de-localisation. Globalisation entails that distance is becoming irrelevant, relative or at the very least less important. Ideas, songs, books, investment capital, labour and fashions travel faster than ever, and even if they stay put, their location is frequently less important than it would have been formerly. This aspect of globalisation is driven by technological and economic changes, but it has cultural and political implications. Disembedding, however, also includes all the ways through which social life becomes abstracted from its local, spatially fixed context.
- *Acceleration*. The speed of transport and communication has increased throughout the twentieth century, and this acceleration continues. It has been said that there are 'no delays any more' in an era of

instantaneous communication over cellphones, Internet servers and television satellites. Although this is surely an exaggeration – delays exist, even if only as unintended consequences – speed is an important feature of globalisation. Anything from inexpensive plane tickets to cheap calls contribute to integrating the world, and the exponential growth in the numbers of Internet users since 1990 indicates that distance, for a great number of persons, no longer means separation.

- *Standardisation.* Continuing the processes of standardisation begun by nationalism and national economies, globalisation entails comparability and shared standards where formerly there were none. The rapid increase in the use of English as a foreign language is suggestive of this development, as is the worldwide spread of, for example, similar hotels and shopping centres, as well as the growing web of international agreements.
- *Interconnectedness.* The networks connecting people across continents are becoming denser, faster and wider every year. Mutual dependence and transnational connections lead to a need for more international agreements and a refashioning of foreign policies, and create both fields of opportunities, constraints and forms of oppression.
- *Mobility.* The entire world is on the move, or so it might sometimes seem. Migration, business travel, international conferences and, not least, tourism have been growing steadily for decades, with various important implications for local communities, politics and economies.
- *Mixing.* Although 'cultural crossroads' where people of different origins met are as ancient as urban life, their number, size and diversity is growing every day. Both frictions and mutual influence result. Additionally, at the level of culture, the instantaneous exchange of messages characteristic of the information era leads to probably more cultural mixing than ever before in human history.
- *Vulnerability.* Globalisation entails the weakening, and sometimes obliteration, of boundaries. Flows of anything from money to refugees are intensified in this era. This means that territorial polities have difficulties protecting themselves against unwanted flows. Typical globalised risks include AIDS and other contagious diseases, most recently swine flu, transnational terrorism and climate change. None can effectively be combated by single nation-states, and it has often been pointed out that the planet as a whole lacks efficient political instruments able to deal with and govern the technology- and economy-driven processes of globalisation.
- *Re-embedding.* A very widespread family of responses to the disembedding tendencies of globalisation can be described as re-embedding. In fact, all of the seven key features of globalisation mentioned above have their countervailing forces opposing them and positing alternatives. The fragmented, fleeting social world made possible through disembedding processes is counteracted through networks of moral commitment,

concerns with local power and community integration, national and sub-national identity politics, cultural 'authenticity' and rooted identities. New social movements based on dissatisfaction with global capitalism also fit into this picture (Maeckelbergh 2009).

Moreover, acceleration is counteracted through social movements promoting slowness in many guises, standardisation is counteracted by 'one-of-a-kind' goods and services, transnational interconnectedness through localism and nationalism, movement through quests for stability and continuity, mixing through concerns with cultural purity, vulnerability through attempts at self-determination and relative isolation. Globalisation is thus a dialectical process, where, for example, processes leading to the weakening of boundaries are met with bids to strengthen them again; where the wealth generated by transnational trade also results in a growth in poverty (witnessed in the spread of urban slums); and where transnational migration is often accompanied by cultural revitalisation and a strengthening of ideologies emphasising rootedness and origins.

World Music

Processes of cultural mixing do not imply that 'everything is becoming the same' or that all kinds of cultural flow are equally susceptible to mixing. Many forms of knowledge and practice remain local, and many are more influenced by others than they themselves influence others.

An area of signification which is often mentioned as a happy breeding-ground for the exchange of diverse influences is contemporary rhythmic music. Blues, jazz and rock are thus often described as 'creolised' forms developed by the descendants of African slaves in North America. More recently, and particularly since the mid-1980s, a new trend in rhythmic music has been showcased as an expression of the creative intermingling of discrete traditions; known as 'World Music' or 'World Beat', it features non-European musicians in a European environment, using modern studio equipment and electrical instruments to convey, for example, 'the spirit of Africa'.

There are conflicting views on the nature of world music. Some argue that it represents a commodification and commercialisation of authentic tribal music; that the Western record companies have merely adapted African and Asian music to cater to the jaded palates of Western consumers, and have destroyed it in the act. On the other hand, it could be pointed out that 'Westernised' artists such as Youssou N'Dour are also incredibly popular in Africa itself – so how could their recordings be regarded as adulterated and 'inauthentic'? In most cases, the domestic popularity of artists is actually boosted by their recognition abroad. Steven Feld (1994) sees the trend of world beat

▶

largely as a reinvigorating force for rhythmic music in general, where Fela Anikulapo Kuti may just as well borrow from James Brown as Peter Gabriel may hire a group of African drummers. The 'Africanization of world pop music and the Americanization of African pop', Feld writes (1994, p. 245), 'are complexly intertwined', although he also discusses issues of copyright and power inequalities between the metropolitan artists and record companies, and the non-European artists.

In a later article, Feld is less sanguine about world music. In 'A Sweet Lullaby for World Music', he describes how 'any and every hybrid or traditional style could ... be lumped together by the single market label world music' (2003, p. 195), adding that this signified not only the triumph of the commercial, but also a disquieting banalisation of difference. Taking as an example a song, 'Rorogwela', composed by Afunakwa, a Baegu woman from the Solomon Islands, Feld goes on to show how oral and indigenous music is being transformed and re-created by Western musicians, and describes the difficulties involved in giving the original composers recognition and their rightful part of the revenues generated. In discussing this topic, Feld touches upon a much larger family of issues, namely those to do with intellectual property rights (IPRs). In an era where the cultural production of traditional peoples is being repackaged as commercially palatable 'exotic' products, it has become a question of key importance to many, especially indigenous peoples themselves, to be able to defend their legal rights to their music, literature and handicrafts (see Kasten 2004).

The flows of musical influences often have paradoxical effects. Lewellen (2002) describes the development of the Congolese rhumba from the 1920s to the 1940s, a guitar-based style borrowing from Cuban music. By the 1970s, the influence from soul was also apparent: partly African in origin, Cuban music and American soul returned to Africa to be merged with locally developed styles. Later, a variant of Congolese popular music, the *soukouss*, became popular in Europe, where it was regarded as '*la vraie musique africaine*'. However, *soukouss* was hardly listened to in Africa itself, where the lyrics sung in local languages, often strongly political, were as important as melody and rhythm.

Musical discourses are fields where identities are shaped, and for this reason, the global flow of popular music can be a fruitful field for studying contemporary cultural dynamics as well as the political economy of meaning. The debate about authenticity is in itself interesting, as it reveals conflicting views of culture: as unbroken tradition, or as flux and process. These issues are not merely aesthetic ones, but are inevitably politicised and have a bearing on personal identity.

LOCAL APPROPRIATIONS OF GLOBAL PROCESSES

At the level of interaction, global processes are expressed in a many areas. The 2001 terrorist attack on the USA was discussed instantaneously in Chinese villages and Iranian towns; the election of Obama for the presidency of the USA was commented upon by newspaper columnists in every country; Michael Jackson's death in the summer of 2009 filled headlines from Argentina to Uzbekistan and so on. A majority of the world's population has probably been exposed to these events. Occasionally, moreover, political events affecting every corner of the globe, such as the climate crisis and transnational terrorism, engage people everywhere although they are not directly affected. There are, in other words, situations where a large proportion of the world's population take on an identity as 'citizens of the world' in the sense that they are concerned with problems relevant for all the world's inhabitants.

The fact that a cultural phenomenon is 'global' does not, however, imply that it is known to everybody or concerns every individual on the face of the earth. Even the Coca-Cola logo, possibly the single most famous image in the world, is not familiar to everybody. The point, however, is that such phenomena are disembedded from particular places. An event like the Winter Olympics has a truly global dimension (Klausen 1999), even if the majority of the world's population is ignorant of it. Whether one happens to be in Montreal, Milan or Birmingham, one can follow such a sports event simultaneously, thanks to webcasts and television. This does not, we should note, imply that everyone who relates to these cultural forms perceives them in identical ways: global symbols and globalised information are interpreted from a local vantage-point (and contribute to shaping that vantage-point). In this way, a fashion magazine like *Vogue* is read differently in a tropical island such as Mauritius compared with Paris; and a soap opera like *The Young and the Restless* takes on a different meaning in Trinidad compared with the USA. These and many other cultural phenomena are global in the sense that they are not located in a particular place; at the same time, they are local in that they are always perceived and interpreted locally.

Cultural flows do not simply take place from North to South. Food, literature and music may just as well move in the opposite direction. Events taking place in a remote location may be interpreted into a situation of local struggles, so that, for example, the Israeli attack on the Gaza Strip in 2009 led to violent demonstrations among minority youths in European cities protesting just as much against the discrimination they experienced from greater society, as against the Israelis.

TOURISM AND MIGRATION

One perspective on globalisation consists in investigating how people, wherever they are, can participate in a shared production of meaning, appropriate the same information and yet interpret it into widely different life-worlds. A complementary perspective may be an exploration of the ways in which people move physically from place to place. Tourism and business travel are widespread forms of movement, which so far have not received significant attention from anthropologists (but see Hannerz 1992; Appadurai 1996; Löfgren 1999; Yamashita 2003; Hitchcock et al. 2008). Is it, for example, the case that place, in the meaning of locality, is entirely irrelevant to tourists and business travellers; that international business hotels are 'the same' everywhere, that a shared 'business culture' exists and that there is a shared, global 'leisure' culture – identical in Cancun (Mexico) and the Canary Islands? Further, could these cultural forms, evident in hotels, airports, boardrooms and beach clubs, profitably be seen as 'third cultures' mediating between different local cultures? In a historically oriented study, Orvar Löfgren (1999) charts the rise of tourism from the nineteenth century to the present, indicating how the phenomenon has shifted in meaning as new groups (from middle class to working class) have increasingly come to replace the elite travellers. Among other things, he is fascinated by the sheer growth of the tourism sector. If one goes to the northern shores of the Mediterranean on holiday, one might as well get used to staying at a permanent building site; such is the growth rate. According to forecasts from the WTO (here: World Tourism Organization), the number of tourists going abroad will be 1.6 billion by the year 2020. In 2000, it was already about 1 billion.

Moving a step further, Comaroff and Comaroff (2009) have investigated ways in which a number of ethnic groups in Southern Africa have developed 'corporate strategies' to profit economically from their cultural identities, largely through the sale of commodities and cultural tourism. In opting for a commercialisation of identity rather than its politicisation, some of these groups have enjoyed considerable success without posing a political threat to the nation-state.

A related field of interest, which has been researched much more thoroughly, is migration – immigration or emigration, depending on which country one sees it from, or simply transnationalism, which covers both countries and especially the ambiguous, or liminal, cultural space between them (Vertovec 2009).

Labour migrants move within the parameters of modernity. They carry passports and are citizens; a precondition for their movement is their willingness to take part in wagework. For labour migration to be possible, the migrants must already be, at least partially, integrated into the cultural logic of capitalism.

Several possible analytical perspectives may shed light on their situation. One approach is to focus on the relationship between majority and minority in the host country; another is to compare the situation, culture and social organisation of migrants in the home country and in the country of destination. A third approach might be to compare different perspectives on migration. For example, Kuwait and other Gulf states attract many thousands of immigrants or 'guest workers'. From the dominant perspective of the

Kuwaiti, these migrants are a 'necessary evil'; they are necessary because they carry out manual work, and they are an evil because they are seen to constitute a potentially threatening foreign element in a country where only around 20 per cent of the population are of Kuwaiti origin. From a humanist European perspective, frequently invoked in sociological studies of migration, the situation of the migrants can be described as a case of severe exploitation; they are underpaid, overworked and lack certain rights which – thanks to the globalisation of culture – are regarded as universal. From a third perspective, namely that of the migrants themselves, the position may appear to be different. Thousands of Malaylees from Kerala, south India, eagerly await their chance to work in the Gulf. When they return to their hometown they bring money and gifts, and they frequently return to the Gulf given the chance (Wilhite 2008). The Indian minister of finance praises them publicly for bringing hard currency to the country.

Where you stand depends on where you sit. Every social and cultural phenomenon can be interpreted in a multitude of different ways, according to the perspective from which one sees it. Where interaction within the global system is concerned, ambiguities of this kind are typical, and they may remind us that people do not become 'the same' just because they engage in increased contact with each other. People's lives are neither wholly global nor wholly local – they are *glocal*.

Additionally, it becomes increasingly clear that the term 'Western culture' is notoriously inaccurate. Depending on definition and delineation, 'the West' contains between 700 million and 1 billion inhabitants. It is not, in other words, 'a culture', but a very large number of societies and a large number of strikingly different cultural environments. Besides, the emerging patterns of cultural variation due to migration and cultural globalisation imply that 'the West' exists just as much in a middle-class suburb of Nairobi as in Melbourne, and that Buenos Aires may be seen as a more typical 'Western' city than Bradford, where a large proportion of the population are Muslims of South Asian origin. 'The West' cannot meaningfully be conceptualised as a kind of society: it must rather be regarded as an aspect of culture and social organisation not localised in a particular 'cultural area', namely what has here been called 'modernity'.

MIGRATION AND CULTURAL IDENTITY

A salient feature of the world at the beginning of the third millennium is mobility, displacement and exile. More than 200 million people lived outside their country of birth in 2008, and the number is growing fast. In addition, many descendants of migrants (who are born in their present country of residence) tend to form, whether voluntarily or not, minorities (Chapter 18). An area which has a turbulent past and present in this respect is the Caribbean, and some of the most important anthropological studies of migration have been carried out here.

Karen Fog Olwig's studies of Caribbean culture and history (1993, 2003, 2007) reveal clearly why so much contemporary anthropological research can neither have a community focus nor be synchronous 'snapshots'. In her analyses of Nevisian society (Olwig 1993; Nevis forms part of St Kitt's and Nevis, and has about 10,000 inhabitants), she shows that this society has never been self-sufficient politically, culturally or economically – or indeed demographically. The ancestors of the present inhabitants arrived there as slaves and planters, and the Afro-Caribbean culture and social organisation in the island have developed in the interface between local factors and global processes. As part of a worldwide capitalist system, Nevisians are dependent on external forces; but Olwig also shows how they have actively shaped their own way of life. The high level of out-migration in the decades after the Second World War – few Nevisians do not have relatives living in metropolitan cities such as London, New York or Toronto – could similarly be seen as an expression of extreme dependence; but it can equally well be studied as a result of entrepreneurship and remarkable cultural adaptability.

Studying Nevisian migrants in Britain, Olwig shows that the codification and indeed creation of a distinct Nevisian identity takes place there, in intense contact with alien culture, as a counterforce to the local British identity. Further, perhaps more surprisingly, she argues that the annual Caribbean carnival in Notting Hill, West London (see also Abner Cohen 1993) can be seen not just as a construction of a Caribbean cultural identity, but also as a revitalisation of a lost English carnival tradition. Migration, far from severing ties with their island of birth, strengthens the local identifications of Nevisians, who talk of Nevis with compassion and nostalgia. They regularly send remittances to their families and many even invest in real estate in Nevis. The migrants and their children thus become important actors in both cultural and economic projects in Nevis, even if they live on the other side of the Atlantic.

Cultural identity is a major issue among many migrant or diasporic populations. Calls for purity and 'authenticity' are met – within and outside the minority – by pleas for individual rights, change and choice. In the societies described as post-traditional by Giddens (1991), tradition does not go away, but it has to be chosen self-consciously and defended against its alternatives. As described by Gerd Baumann (1996) in a study of a multi-ethnic English neighbourhood, the options available are as numerous as they can be controversial.

EXILE AND DE-TERRITORIALISATION

The Satanic Verses (Rushdie 1988), the novel which earned its author a *fatwa*, or death penalty, from Shi'ite imams in Tehran, is not primarily a book about Islam. Rather, it is about the condition of exile; about being on Air India's Flight 420 halfway between Bombay and London – permanently. In the book, Rushdie shows how the shift in perspective entailed by exile creates doubt and uncertainty, because the person in exile discovers that the world, the past and (ultimately) even the truth appear differently when viewed from different positions. Ethnic revitalisation among migrant groups may be understood within this perspective. Drawing on nostalgia and a sense of alienation, such movements contrive to re-instil a sense of continuity with the past, ontological security and personal security.

Although it has received intense attention from anthropologists and sociologists, ethnic and religious revitalisation represents only one side of the coin. Clearly, the processes which sometimes inspire revitalisation, but which may also lead to the opposite (namely uncertainty, ambivalence and individualism), merit attention. These are the processes of globalisation, whereby people become embedded in shifting social and cultural networks of sometimes staggering scale, where society, in Zygmunt Bauman's view, 'proclaims all restrictions on freedom illegal, at the same time doing away with social certainty and legalizing ethical uncertainty' (1992, p. xxiv).

From an anthropological point of view, this needs to be studied empirically (see Eriksen et al. 2010). Some years ago, Appadurai (1990) proposed a framework for exploring cultural flow in the contemporary world, which is drawn upon (and often modified slightly) in much contemporary research on cultural complexity. He distinguishes between five dimensions in global cultural flow, which have different ways of functioning.

The *ethnoscape* refers to 'the landscape of persons who constitute the shifting world in which we live'; in other words, the demographic attributes of the world – tourism, migration, exile, business travel, but also stable communities.

The *technoscape* means the 'global configuration ... of technology', which in important ways shapes the flow of cultural meaning, and also includes the uneven global distribution of technology.

The *finanscape* is the flow of capital, which has increasingly become disembedded from territories. Together, these three dimensions form a global infrastructure of sorts, but it is by no means predictable, since each 'is subject to its own constraints and incentives'.

The final two dimensions, which are ideational, are the *ideoscape* and the *mediascape*; referring, respectively, to ideological messages and mass media constructions.

A major point in Appadurai's article, and one that later writers on globalisation have also made, is that de-territorialisation – which does not merely amount to large scale, but also to the reduced importance of the spatial dimension as such – necessitates new conceptualisations of the social and cultural world. Ideas, technologies, people and money can be, and are, moved about more frequently, quickly and easily across the globe in the contemporary age than ever before. One result, often described in terms of displacement, is the growth of populations on the move or living in exile. Another consequence is the self-conscious construction of place, since place, as a space imbued with cultural meaning, can for many people no longer be taken for granted. One's place of residence may change dramatically, or one may move somewhere else; and places are also multivocal like symbols in the sense that they mean different things to different people or in different situations (Rodman 1992). All this does not mean that people are becoming de-territorialised, but that the construction of place becomes a project in its own right – like that of cultural identity – whereas formerly it could be taken for granted. It also means that 'place' becomes a fluid term, so that 'Nevis' becomes a network with nodal points in London, Nevis and elsewhere. The fact of migration in an era of fast communications thus also paves the way for *long-distance nationalism* (Anderson 1992), whereby the political scene in a given territory may be partly shaped by the agency of migrants. In an account of Tamil immigrants to Norway, Øivind Fuglerud (1999) shows that the overarching concern for many of the migrants does not consist in integrating into a European society, but supporting the separatist movement in Sri Lanka. Ideological differences and tensions among the migrants reflect differences in Sri Lanka, not in Norway. The Rushdie affair, in other words, was just a spectacular instance of a more general process whereby territorial boundaries do not vanish, but are challenged by telecommunications and diasporic populations.

Some walls are torn down and others appear. The idea of an unbounded world has not been realised through the contemporary processes of globalisation; rather, old tensions are rephrased, and new tensions occur. A growing number of persons find themselves in a culturally complex situation, where their cultural identity, values and practices cannot be taken for granted, do not go without saying and have to be defended actively.

We now move on to a few further consequences of globalisation (or 'glocalisation') for anthropological research.

SOME CONSEQUENCES FOR ANTHROPOLOGY

The globalisation of culture does not entail that groups and individuals become culturally identical; rather it engenders the growth of new kinds of cultural difference in the interface between the global and the local. Before moving on to some empirical examples, I should like to sum up the discussion so far regarding the consequences of globalisation for anthropological thought and research.

- It is becoming increasingly clear that the concepts 'tradition' and 'modernity' refer to a purely analytical distinction; that is to say, it is untenable to speak of traditional and modern societies in an empirical sense.
- The concepts of society and culture have become more problematic than ever before. The networks of communication, migration, trade, capital investments and politics cross virtually every boundary; with a few exceptions, neither states nor local communities are really clearly delineable in every regard. 'Cultures' are neither closed nor internally uniform.

- Since it has become impossible, in many cases, to delineate clearly the system being investigated, it has become increasingly interesting to explore specified groups or specified cultural phenomena (such as the football World Cup, tourism, migration) which do not make up autonomous systems in a social or cultural sense, but which can nevertheless be isolated for analytical purposes.
- Classic fieldwork has become quite insufficient as the sole method of collecting the data and insights required to understand social and cultural life on the planet. Fieldwork, which is now often translocal or multi-sited, must generally be supplemented with additional sources giving access to the wider context of the phenomena being explored through participant observation – statistics, mass media, locally produced texts and so on.

THE 'INDIGENISATION OF MODERNITY'?

As early as the 1960s, the media theorist Marshall McLuhan introduced the concept of 'the global village' (McLuhan 1962). This notion was intended to account for the new cultural situation in the world, following the spread of modern mass media, notably television. The world had become one place, McLuhan argued, and he called this place a global village. He did not, incidentally, view it as a harmonious place, but one characterised by friction, conflict and insecurity. (Like, an anthropologist might add, many real villages.)

An essential point in anthropological research on globalisation lies in the necessity to account for the relationship between the global on the one hand, and the village, or the localised environment, on the other. To an anthropologist, McLuhan's term therefore implies an unhealthy mix of two levels, the level of interaction and the anonymous level: micro and macro.

The central paradox of globalisation is, perhaps, that it has made the world both larger and smaller at the same time. It has become smaller in the sense that it is possible to travel anywhere in less than 24 hours, and that it is practically possible to have the same lifestyle anywhere in the world. On the other hand, it has become larger in the sense that we thereby know more about remote and 'exotic' places, and thus more easily recognise our mutual differences. Jonathan Friedman once phrased it like this: 'Ethnic and cultural fragmentation and modernist homogenisation are not two arguments, two opposing views on what is happening in the world today, but two constituent trends in global reality' (1990, p. 311). There is, in other words, a movement towards integration into ever larger systems – where a growing majority of the world's population takes part in a perfectly unlimited system of exchange – and, at the same time, a localising emphasis on cultural uniqueness. What needs to be studied ethnographically, Sahlins argues, is 'the indigenization of modernity' (1994). This, as noted in Chapters 17 and 18, frequently takes the form of 'traditionalist' movements, often presented as ethnic or nationalist ones. Remarking on the modernist, reflexive conception of culture and its global dissemination, Sahlins writes:

'Culture' – the word itself, or some local equivalent – is on everyone's lips. Tibetans and Hawaiians, Ojibway, Kwakiutl and Eskimo, Kazakhs and Mongols, native Australians, Balinese, Kashmiris and New Zealand Maoris: all now discover that they have a 'culture'. For centuries they may hardly have noticed it. But today, as the New Guinean said to the anthropologist, 'If we didn't have *kastom*, we would be just like white men.' (1994, p. 378)

On a more specific note, Edvard Hviding (1994) has showed how Solomon Islanders, whose kinship concepts and practices have strong cognatic leanings, have in recent years begun to emphasise patrilineal descent, which proves more efficient in the formation of corporations and for making land claims. Whether this should be labelled 'indigenisation of modernity' or 'modernisation of indigenity' is an open question, but it is clear that the shift in kinship practices and concepts is related to sociocultural change and the spread of the idea of culture as a political resource.

TWO LOCALISING STRATEGIES

Paris is one of the most important 'African' cities in the world, and it attracts thousands of musicians, students, labour migrants and refugees from the Francophone parts of Africa. Many Parisians have West African parents and a personal identity partly connected to Senegal, Cameroon or the Ivory Coast, and many West Africans travel to and fro between the city and the home country.

Friedman (1990; see also Gandoulou 1989) has described a particular category of labour migrants to Paris. They originate in Brazzaville (Congo), where they are collectively known as *les sapeurs* (literally, 'the underminers'). Most of them are of humble origins, but they manage to travel to Paris, where they work very hard and consume as little as possible, in order to buy expensive fashion clothes to display publicly in the streets of Brazzaville at a later stage. This kind of consumption strategy falls squarely into the general category described earlier as conspicuous consumption: it expresses rank and prestige. What is interesting about '*les sapeurs*' is not only the fact that they are much poorer than they look, but also that most of them belong to an ethnic group no longer in power. Friedman thus interprets their conspicuous consumption as a local political strategy: as a way of challenging power by overcommunicating one's own superiority and success. '*La sape*' thus appears as a local counter-cultural strategy drawing on local evaluations of prestige and power, which in turn draw on what is globally prestigious; that is, expensive fashion clothes. It would not have been possible to understand this phenomenon in its full context without knowledge of both the local and the non-local levels.

An example of a rather different kind is Katarina Sjöberg's (1993) study of the Ainu, a Japanese minority. Officially, the Ainu have no status as an ethnic minority, since the Japanese government does not recognise the existence of minorities. Instead, they are categorised as an 'underdeveloped group'. Like indigenous people elsewhere, the Ainu have been subjected to systematic discrimination (they resemble Europeans and have historically been considered pale, hairy, unattractive people); they lost their traditional right to land generations ago and suffer from high rates of alcoholism and unemployment. Until the 1970s, it seemed as though Ainu identity was about to disappear completely. The language was nearly extinct, and the Ainu seemed to be about to become a Japanese underclass instead of an ethnic group. Then an ethnic revitalisation movement emerged – as with many other indigenous peoples during the same period. In the 1970s and 1980s an active revitalisation movement developed, its aim being to make the Japanese state recognise the Ainu as an ethnic group with a right to its own customs and its own language. The strategy, however, largely consisted of presenting Ainu culture as a commodity. Old rituals, traditional dress, handicrafts and culinary specialities were revitalised and presented in a commercialised, 'touristified' way. In this way, Japanese tourists to the Ainu north might discover that the Ainu 'had a culture' worthy of their respect, but the language of that 'culture' first had to be translated into the global language of commodity exchange, so to speak. In 2008, the Ainu were finally recognised as an ethnic minority by the Japanese state.

Commenting on Sjöberg's work and his own, Friedman (1990) notes that the strategies of both '*les sapeurs*' and the Ainu may look like recipes for cultural suicide, since they are based on cultural premises which are not indigenous. The Congolese express prestige and individuality through the appropriation of foreign symbols; the Ainu express (and create) their ethnic identity by turning it into a commodity; they adapt it to a commercial market. The anthropological point in this respect is nevertheless not whether the 'cultures' expressed 'as a matter of fact' are local, 'authentic', etc., but whether they are efficient in promoting the experience of identity and political interests among the groups in question.

A SEAMLESS WORLD: HOMOGENISATION AND DIFFERENTIATION

As the last chapters have shown, cultural identity and 'uniqueness' have become, since the 1960s, coveted political resources in large parts of the world. A growing number of groups 'discover' their cultural uniqueness and exploit it for political purposes. Why does this happen?

A simple explanation might be that social identities become important only from the moment they feel threatened, and that tendencies towards the globalisation of culture, appearing to eradicate cultural distinctiveness, more or less automatically trigger counter-reactions in the shape of ethnic or traditionalist movements.

A related, but probably more accurate explanation – which is also consistent with the account of ethnicity and nationalism in the two previous chapters

– would be that the demarcation of boundaries about social identities (1) is perceived by many as necessary as a result of intensified contact between groups, and (2) becomes practically possible because of technological and cultural changes resulting from modernisation.

Concerning the cultural consequences of globalisation, a strong case could be made for both homogenisation and differentiation, depending on one's point of view. Indeed, as the examples of the Ainu and the Congolese '*sapeurs*' indicate, people may in fact favour both at the same time, in the sense that localising strategies are framed in 'global' terms – in the languages of commodity exchange and individual rights.

One important point to be made here is that the interrelationship between culture and identity is subjective and intersubjective, not objective. A social identity, whether ethnic, national or something else, can be created in a variety of ways. Anthropologists, for example, have a shared identity wherever they are; they form a community of sorts, however loosely incorporated. As with ethnicity, the double criterion for a social identity to be socially valid is 'self-ascription and ascription by others' (see Chapter 17).

Another important point concerns power. Economic dependence in poor countries and poor localities has largely been studied through a focus on underpaid labour, unequal exchange and unequal relations of production. A stronger focus on, and a critical view of, the notion of cultural dependence, coupled with analyses of economic dependence, would certainly give increased depth to studies of the globalisation of culture. For even if people may choose their strategies, they do not do so under circumstances of their own choosing – and these circumstances differ greatly, not only with respect to differential access to, say, CNN on TV, but also regarding personal autonomy and the right to define who they are.

* * *

In an interview, Lévi-Strauss related the following anecdote. He was visiting South Korea, and his hosts eagerly took him around to show him the great advances made by this much publicised NIC (newly industrialised country). They showed him sports stadia, freeways, skyscrapers and factories. Lévi-Strauss was not particularly interested, and wandered off as often as he could to museums where he could study old masks. 'Professor Lévi-Strauss!', his hosts eventually exclaimed, 'you are only interested in things that no longer exist!' – 'Yes,' he replied sullenly, 'I am only interested in things that no longer exist.'

To Lévi-Strauss, the cultural variation within modernity was not sufficient to call for his attention; to him, Seoul appeared more or less identical with Paris. To another anthropologist, keen to explore diversity within modernity, Seoul would definitely not appear similar to Paris.

Seen from this kind of perspective, it is clear that the cultural variation of the world has been radically narrowed. Fewer and fewer anthropologists today encounter radical otherness of the kind described by Lévi-Strauss in *Tristes tropiques* (1976 [1955]). In this beautiful, melancholy book, he describes a field trip to Amazonia, where he met natives who were so close that he could touch them, and yet they seemed infinitely far away: he could not understand them.

A little less than a year before his death in 2009, Lévi-Strauss celebrated his hundredth birthday, and was duly visited by President Sarkozy, France being a country where politicians can still build prestige by associating with intellectuals. Lévi-Strauss told the president that the world, in his view, was now too full. *Le monde est trop plein.* Presumably he meant that it was overfilled by humans and the products of their activities. At the time of his birth in 1908, the planet was inhabited by a grand total of 1.7 billion persons; the global population now stands at more than 6.5 billion, and the percentage with their own Internet accounts and mobile telephones increases every year. No matter how one goes about measuring degrees of connectedness in the contemporary world, the only possible conclusion is that many more people today are much more connected than ever before in history. There are more of us, and each of us has, on average, more links to the outside world than our predecessors, through business travel, information, communication, migration, vacations, political engagement, trade, development assistance, exchange programmes and so on.

From a certain point of view, the world is becoming progressively disenchanted, to use Max Weber's expression about modernity (*Entzauberung*): it seems to hide fewer and fewer secrets. The white spots on the map are gone, and there are probably no peoples left who have not, to a greater or lesser degree, been in contact with the modern world. Halfway through the twenty-first century, there may be no matrilineal peoples left. A sense of loss is apparent not only among anthropologists, but among very many of the peoples of the world. Yet – and that has been the perspective of this chapter – new cultural forms and social projects are continuously being developed in local settings all over the world, and the processes of change take place in unpredictable and frequently surprising ways. There will, in other words, always remain variations in world-views, ways of life, power relations and life-projects that are certain to provide ample challenges to anyone who is committed to trying to understand the differences and similarities between humans in societies. Precisely the very fullness of the world, which Lévi-Strauss so regretted, could indeed justify another century of anthropological research into human diversity.

SUGGESTIONS FOR FURTHER READING

Arjun Appadurai: *Modernity at Large: Cultural Dimensions of Globalization.* Minneapolis: University of Minnesota Press 1996.

John L. Comaroff and Jean Comaroff: *Ethnicity, Inc.* Chicago: University of Chicago Press 2009.

Ulf Hannerz: *Anthropology's World: Life in a Twenty-first-century Discipline.* London: Pluto 2010.

EPILOGUE: MAKING ANTHROPOLOGY MATTER

So what might anthropology become in the twenty-first century? My guess is that the general premise of universal movement will lead people to seek stable order in the least and most inclusive levels of human existence, that is the self as an identity and the world as a unity; and especially in the construction of a meaningful relationship between the two.

— *Keith Hart*

[W]e may be faced with a world in which there simply aren't any more headhunters, matrilinealists, or people who predict the weather from the entrails of a pig. Difference will doubtless remain – the French will never eat salted butter. But the good old days of widow burning and cannibalism are gone forever.

— *Clifford Geertz*

What is the ultimate point of social anthropology? One may, obviously, use the subject to collect academic distinctions and eventually get a job in research or teaching. On the other hand, in most cases there are faster and more rewarding methods, at least in a pecuniary sense, of acquiring a livelihood. Fortunately, there are also other reasons for becoming involved in the subject.

The single most important human insight to be gained from this way of studying and comparing societies is perhaps the realisation that everything could have been different in our own society – that the way we live is only one among innumerable ways of life which humans have adopted. If we glance sideways and backwards, we will quickly discover that modern society, with its many possibilities and diversity in life-projects, its dizzying complexity and its impressive technological advances, is a way of life which has not been tried out for very long. Perhaps, psychologically speaking, we have just left the cave: in terms of the history of our species, we have spent but a moment in modern societies.

As well as offering knowledge, insight and perhaps a drop of wisdom, anthropology has its problematic side too – at least if we try to turn it into a moral philosophy. Although cultural relativism is a research method and not a world-view, there is an inherent tendency among students of anthropology to invest it with a moral dimension: as long as one can justify some notion or other as 'cultural', one feels committed to defending it. The result, of course, is that one becomes unable to pass moral judgement on anything at all. It must therefore be said that it is possible to understand without liking, 'You don't have to be one to know one', as Geertz once put it. It is possible to understand

327

the mass worship of private cars and the death penalty as expressions of a particular cultural universe dominant in North America without approving of them; and it is possible to understand the principles for the exchange of women among the Kachin, or the principles of political organisation among the Nuer, without feeling obliged to regard them as 'superior' or 'inferior' to our own.

It is also perfectly feasible to admire New Guinean garden magic without being against the industrial mass production of iPods and potato chips. It is not even certain that one is doing a favour to one's chosen people by trying to protect them against the impact of modernity. On the other hand, as the world is shrinking due to the forces of globalisation, anthropologists – like everybody else – are often forced to take a moral stance when different value systems are being confronted in their own society, or in the society they study. This kind of situation, where the informants are not only 'talking back' but also form part of an increasingly seamless world of which you and I are also members, calls for new forms of engagement among anthropologists and raises some difficult questions: if one comes across practices that one considers deeply objectionable (or illegal) during fieldwork, is one obliged to report them to the outside world (or the police)? Should anthropologists take a clear moral stance regarding say, child abuse or female circumcision? My answer is that we should indeed, but not necessarily in academic texts, which do not serve an explicit normative purpose.

Related to the dilemmas of participant-observation in societies where one is simultaneously a participant and an observer is a syndrome that we might choose to call 'sociologism'. This is the tendency to interpret absolutely everything about human existence within a sociological or anthropological frame of understanding. Art and literature, love and aesthetic experiences may thus be understood purely as social products. If one prefers Beethoven to pop, this is allegedly due to one's upbringing and the need to maintain symbolic fences vis-à-vis the lower classes, not to the fact that Beethoven's music may happen to possess artistic qualities which most pop lacks. When the attitude of sociologism is profoundly embedded in one's personality, the whole world may appear as a set of 'phenomena', possibly classified into 'interesting' and 'uninteresting' ones. One ends by turning everything into 'empirical material', ultimately one's own life.

Anthropology deals with 'the others', but it also in crucial ways concerns ourselves. Anthropological studies may provide us with a mirror, a window, a contrast which makes it possible to reflect on our own existence in new ways. Descriptions of life in the Trobriand Islands remind us that our own society is not the only conceivable one. The Ndembu, the Inuit and the Dogon may tell us that our whole life could have been very different and, thanks to anthropological analyses of their societies, they may even tell us *how* it might have been different. They force us to ask fundamental questions about ourselves and our own society. Sometimes they may even force us to act accordingly.

Anthropology also teaches us something about the complexity of culture and social life. Sometimes, as in the analysis of rituals, it may indeed seem that there is no easy question to the answers provided by anthropological research. Our job, faced with ideological simplifications, prejudice, ignorance and bigotry, must be to make the world more complex rather than simplifying it.

Anthropology may not provide the answer to the question of the meaning of life, but at least it can tell us that there are many ways in which to make a life meaningful. If it does not provide final answers, anthropology may at least give us the feeling of being very near the big questions.

BIBLIOGRAPHY

Alford, Richard D. 1988. *Naming and Identity: A Cross-cultural Study of Personal Naming Practices*. New York: Harper & Row.

Amselle, Jean-Loup. 2001. *Branchements: Anthropologie de l'universalité des cultures*. Paris: Flammarion.

Anderson, Benedict. 1992. *Long-distance Nationalism: World Capitalism and the Rise of Identity Politics*. Amsterdam: Centre for Asian Studies.

—— 2006 [1983]. *Imagined Communities: An Inquiry into the Origins and Spread of Nationalism*, 3rd edn. London: Verso.

Anthias, Floya and Nira Yuval-Davies, eds. 1989. *Woman – Nation – State*. London: Macmillan.

Appadurai, Arjun. 1986. Introduction: Commodities and the Politics of Value. In Arjun Appadurai, ed., *The Social Life of Things: Commodities in Cultural Perspective*, pp. 3–63. Cambridge: Cambridge University Press.

—— 1990. Disjuncture and Difference in the Global Cultural Economy. In Mike Featherstone, ed., *Global Culture: Nationalism, Globalization, and Modernity*, pp. 295–310. London: SAGE.

—— 1996. *Modernity at Large: Cultural Dimensions of Globalization*. Minneapolis: University of Minnesota Press.

Archetti, Eduardo P. 1991 [1984]. De l'idéologie du pouvoir: analyse culturelle comparative. In Arne Martin Klausen, ed., *Le Savoir-être norvégien: regards anthropologiques sur la culture norvégienne*, pp. 243–62, trans. Marina-Christine Coidan and Evelyne Nomme. Paris: L'Harmattan.

—— 1992. *El mundo social y simbólico del cuy*. Quito: CEPLAES. (English version: *Guinea-Pigs*. Oxford: Berg 1997.)

—— 1994. Introduction. In Eduardo P. Archetti, ed., *Exploring the Written: Anthropology and the Multiplicity of Writing*, pp. 11–30. Oslo: Universitetsforlaget.

—— 1999. *Masculinities: Football, Polo and the Tango in Argentina*. Oxford: Berg.

Ardener, Edwin. 1977. Belief and the Problem of Women. In Shirley Ardener, ed., *Perceiving Women*, pp. 1–17. London: J.M. Dent & Sons.

—— 1989. *The Voice of Prophecy and Other Essays*, ed. Malcolm Chapman. Oxford: Blackwell.

Arens, William. 1978. *The Man-eating Myth: Anthropology and Anthropophagy*. Oxford: Oxford University Press.

Armstrong, Gary and Richard Giulianotti, eds. 1997. *Entering the Field: New Perspectives on World Football*. Oxford: Berg.

Asad, Talal. 1972. Market Model, Class Structure and Consent: A Reconsideration of Swat Political Organisation. *Man* (n.s.) **7**: 74–94.

Atkinson, Paul, Sara Delamont, Amanda Jane Coffey, John Lofland and Lyn H. Lofland, eds. 2007. *A Handbook of Ethnography*. London: SAGE.

Augé, Marc. 1982. Football: de l'histoire sociale à anthropologie réligieuse. *Le Débat* **19**:59–67.

Bailey, F.G. 1968. Parapolitical Systems. In M.J. Swartz, ed., *Local-level Politics: Social and Cultural Perspectives*, pp. 281–93. Chicago: Aldine.

—— 1969. *Stratagems and Spoils: A Social Anthropology of Politics*. Oxford: Blackwell.

—— 1971. *Gifts and Poison*. Oxford: Blackwell.

Bamberger, Joan. 1974. The Myth of Matriarchy: Why Men Rule in Primitive Society. In Michelle Z. Rosaldo and Louise Lamphere, eds, *Woman, Culture, Society*, pp. 263–80. Stanford, CA: Stanford University Press.

Barkow, Jerome, Leda Cosmides and John Tooby, eds. 1992. *The Adapted Mind: Evolutionary Psychology and the Generation of Culture*. Oxford: Oxford University Press.

Barnard, Alan. 2000. *History and Theory in Anthropology*. Cambridge: Cambridge University Press.

—— . 2007 *Anthropology and the Bushman*. Oxford: Berg.

—— and Anthony Good. 1984. *Research Practices in the Study of Kinship*. London: Academic Press.

Barnes, John A. 1962. African Models in New Guinea Highlands. *Man* **62**(1): 5–9.

—— 1990 [1954]. *Models and Interpretations: Selected Essays*. Cambridge: Cambridge University Press.

Barth, Fredrik. 1959. *Political Leadership among Swat Pathans*. London: Athlone Press.

—— 1961. *Nomads of South Persia: The Basseri Tribe of the Khamseh Confederacy*. Oslo: Universitetsforlaget.

—— 1966. *Models of Social Organization*. London: Royal Anthropological Institute, Occasional Papers **23**.

—— 1967. Economic Spheres in Darfur. In Raymond Firth, ed., *Themes in Economic Anthropology*, pp. 149–74. London: Tavistock

—— ed. 1969. *Ethnic Groups and Boundaries: The Social Organization of Culture Difference*. Oslo: Universitetsforlaget.

—— 1975. *Ritual and Knowledge among the Baktaman*. Oslo: Universitetsforlaget.

—— ed. 1978. *Scale and Social Organization*. Oslo: Universitetsforlaget.

—— 1981. *Features of Person and Society in Swat: Selected Essays of Fredrik Barth*, vol. 2. London: Routledge & Kegan Paul.

—— 1993. *Balinese Worlds*. Chicago: University of Chicago Press.

—— 2000. An Anthropology of Knowledge. *Current Anthropology* **43** (1): 1–18.

—— Andre Gingrich, Robert Parkin and Sydel Silverman. 2005. *One Discipline, Four Ways: British, German, French, and American Anthropology*. Chicago: University of Chicago Press.

Bateson, Gregory. 1958 [1936]. *Naven*. Stanford, CA: Stanford University Press.

—— 1972. *Steps to an Ecology of Mind*. New York: Chandler.

—— 1979. *Mind and Nature*. Glasgow: Fontana.

—— and Mary Catherine Bateson. 1988. *Angels Fear: Towards an Epistemology of the Sacred*. Chicago: University of Chicago Press.

Bauman, Zygmunt. 1992. *Intimations of Postmodernity*. London: Routledge.

Baumann, Gerd. 1996. *Contesting Culture*. Cambridge: Cambridge University Press.

Beaudoin, Gérard. 1984. *Les Dogons du Mali*. Paris: Armand Colin.

Beidelman, T.O. 1971. *The Kaguru: A Matrilineal People of East Africa*. New York: Holt, Rinehart & Winston.

Benedict, Ruth. 1970 [1934]. *Patterns of Culture*. Boston, MA: Houghton Mifflin.

—— 1974 [1946]. *The Chrysanthemum and the Sword*. Boston, MA: Houghton Mifflin.

Berger, Peter and Thomas Luckmann. 1967. *The Social Construction of Reality*. Harmondsworth: Penguin.

Berger, Peter, Birgitte Berger and Hansfried Kellner. 1973. *The Homeless Mind*. Harmondsworth: Penguin.

Bernstein, Basil. 1972. Social Class, Language and Socialization. In Pier Paolo Giglioli, ed., *Language and Social Context*, pp. 157–78. Harmondsworth: Penguin.

Berreman, Gerald. 1962. *Behind Many Masks: Ethnography and Impression Management in a Himalayan Village*. Monograph no. **4**. Indianapolis, IN: Society for Applied Anthropology.

—— 1979. *Caste and Other Inequalities: Essays on Inequality*. Meerut: Folklore Institute.

Bloch, Maurice. 1971. *Placing the Dead: Tombs, Ancestral Villages and Kinship Organization in Madagascar*. London: Seminar.

—— ed. 1975. *Marxist Analyses and Social Anthropology*. London: Malaby.

—— 1986. *From Blessing to Violence*. Cambridge: Cambridge University Press.

—— 1991. Language, Anthropology and Cognitive Science. *Man* **26**: 183–98.

—— 2005. *Essays on Cultural Transmission*. Oxford: Berg.

Boas, Franz. 1897. The Social Organization and the Secret Societies of the Kwakiutl Indians. In *Report of the U.S. National Museum for 1895*, pp. 311–738. Washington, DC: US National Museum.

Boellstorff, Tom. 2007. Queer Studies in the House of Anthropology. *Annual Review of Anthropology* **36**: 17–35.

Bohannan, Laura. 1952. A Genealogical Charter. *Africa* **22**: 301–15.

—— and Paul Bohannan. 1953. *The Tiv of Central Nigeria*. London: Oxford University Press.

Bohannan, Paul. 1959. The Impact of Money on an African Subsistence Economy. *Journal of Economic History* **19**: 491–503.

Borofsky, Robert. 1994. On the Knowledge and Knowing of Cultural Activities. In Robert Borofsky, ed., *Assessing Cultural Anthropology*, pp. 331–47. New York: McGraw-Hill.

—— 2005. *Yanomami: The Fierce Controversy and What We Can Learn from It*. Berkeley: University of California Press.

Boserup, Ester. 1970. *Women's Role in Economic Development*. London: Allen & Unwin.

Boskovic, Aleksandar, ed. 2008. *Other People's Anthropologies*. Oxford: Berghahn.

Boswell, Rosabelle. 2006. *Le Malaise Créole: Ethnic Identity in Mauritius*. Oxford: Berghahn.

Bourdieu, Pierre. 1963. The Algerian Peasant's Attitude towards Time. In Julian Pitt-Rivers, ed., *Mediterranean Countrymen*, pp. 55–72. Paris: Mouton.

—— 1977 [1972]. *Outline of a Theory of Practice*, trans. Richard Nice. Cambridge: Cambridge University Press.

—— 1982. *Ce que parler veut dire*. Paris: Fayard.

—— 1984 [1979]. *Distinction*, trans. Richard Nice. London: Routledge.

—— 1988 [1984]. *Homo Academicus*, trans. Peter Collier. Cambridge: Polity.

Bourgois, Philippe. 2003 [1995] *In Search of Respect: Selling Crack in El Barrio*, 2nd edn. Cambridge: Cambridge University Press.

Brøgger, Jan. 1990. *Pre-bureaucratic Europeans*. Oslo: Universitetsforlaget.

Brown, Donald. 1991. *Human Universals*. New York: McGraw-Hill.

Bryan, Dominic. 2000. *Orange Parades: The Politics of Ritual, Tradition and Control*. London: Pluto.

Bulmer, Ralph. 1967. Why Is the Cassowary Not a Bird? A Problem of Zoological Taxonomy among the Karam of New Guinea. *Man* (n.s.) **2**: 5–25.

Burghart, Richard. 1990. Ethnographers and their Local Counterparts in India. In Richard Fardon, ed., *Localizing Strategies*, pp. 260–79. Edinburgh: Scottish Academic Press.

Buss, David M. 2004. *Evolutionary Psychology: The New Science of the Mind*. Boston, MA: Pearson.

Caldwell, Melissa. 2004. Domesticating the French Fry: McDonald's and Consumerism in Moscow. *Journal of Consumer Culture* **4**(1): 5–26.

Carrier, James, ed. 1995. *Occidentalism: Images of the West*. Oxford: Oxford University Press.

—— ed. 2005. *A Handbook of Economic Anthropology*. Cheltenham: Edward Elgar.

Carrithers, Michael. 1992. *Why Humans Have Cultures: Explaining Anthropology and Social Diversity*. Oxford: Oxford University Press.

Carsten, Janet. 1997. *The Heat and the Hearth: The Process of Kinship in a Malay Fishing Community*. Oxford: Oxford University Press.

—— 2004. *After Kinship*. Cambridge: Cambridge University Press.

Castells, Manuel. 2009. *The Rise of the Network Society*, 2nd edn. London: Blackwell.

Castles, Stephen and Mark J. Miller 2003. *The Age of Migration: International Population Movements in the Modern World*, 3rd edn. Basingstoke: Palgrave Macmillan.

Cavalli-Sforza, Luca, Paolo Menozzi and Alberto Piazza, eds. 1994. *The History and Geography of Human Genes*. Princeton, NJ: Princeton University Press.

Chagnon, Napoleon A. 1983. *Yanomamö: The Fierce People*, 3rd edn. New York: Holt, Rinehart & Winston.

Chakrabarty, Dipesh, Rochona Majumbar and Andrew Sartori, eds. 2007. *From the Colonial to the Postcolonial: India and Pakistan in Transition*. Oxord: Oxford University Press.

Chase-Dunn, Christopher and Thomas Hall. 1997. *Rise and Demise: Comparing World-Systems*. Boulder: Westview Press.

Claessen, H.J. and Peter Skálnik, eds. 1978. *The Early State*. The Hague: Mouton.

Classen, Constance. 1993. *Worlds of Sense: Exploring the Senses in History and Across Cultures*. London: Routledge.

—— ed. 2005. *The Book of Touch*. Oxford: Berg.

Clastres, Pierre. 1977. *Society Against the State*. Oxford: Mole.

Clifford, James and George Marcus, eds. 1986. *Writing Culture: The Poetics and Politics of Ethnography*. Berkeley: University of California Press.

Cohen, Abner. 1969. *Custom and Politics in Urban Africa*. London: Routledge.

—— 1974. *Two-dimensional Man*. London: Tavistock.

—— 1981. *The Politics of Elite Culture*. Berkeley: University of California Press.

—— 1993. *Masquerade Politics: Explorations in the Structure of Urban Cultural Movements*. Berkeley: University of California Press.

Cohen, Anthony P. 1985. *The Symbolic Construction of Community*. London: Routledge.

—— 1994. *Self Consciousness*. London: Routledge.

Cohen, David William and E.S. Atieno Odhiambo. 1989. *Siaya: The Historical Anthropology of a Landscape*. London: James Currey.

Collier, Jane and Sylvia Yanagisako. 1987. *Gender and Kinship: Essays toward a Unified Analysis*. Stanford, CA: Stanford University Press.

Comaroff, John L. and Jean Comaroff. 2009. *Ethnicity, Inc*. Chicago: University of Chicago Press.

Connerton, Paul. 1989. *How Societies Remember*. Cambridge: Cambridge University Press.

Cowan, Jane, Marie-Bénédicte Dembour and Richard A. Wilson, eds. 2001. *Culture and Rights: Anthropological Perspectives*. Cambridge: Cambridge University Press.

Crate, Susan A. and Mark Nuttall, eds. 2009. *Anthropology and Climate Change: From Encounters to Actions*. Walnut Creek, CA: Left Coast Press.

Csordas, Thomas J. 1999. The Body's Career in Anthropology. In Henrietta Moore, ed., *Anthropological Theory Today*, pp. 172–205. Cambridge: Polity.

Daly, Martin and Margo Wilson. 1988. *Homicide*. New York: Aldine de Gruyter.

—— 1998. *The Truth about Cinderella: A Darwinian View of Parental Love*. London: Weidenfeld & Nicolson.

DaMatta, Roberto. 1991. *Carnivals, Rogues and Heroes: An Interpretation of the Brazilian Dilemma*. London: University of Notre Dame Press.

D'Andrade, Roy. 1995. *The Rise of Cognitive Anthropology*. Cambridge: Cambridge University Press.

Das, Veena. 1994. The Anthropological Discourse on India. In Robert Borofsky, ed., *Assessing Cultural Anthropology*, pp. 133–44. New York: McGraw-Hill.

Davidoff, Leonore. 1998. Gender and the Great Divide: Public and Private in British Gender History. *Journal of Women's History* **15**(1): 11–27.

Davis, John. 1992. *Exchange*. Buckingham: Open University Press.

Davis, Mike. 2007. *Planet of Slums*. London: Verso.

Dawkins, Richard. 1976. *The Selfish Gene*. Oxford: Oxford University Press.

Descola, Philippe and Michel Izard. 1992. Guerre. In Pierre Bonté and Michel Izard, eds, *Dictionnaire de l'ethnologie et de l'anthropologie*, pp. 313–16. Paris: Presses Universitaires de France.

—— and Gisli Pálsson, eds. 1996. *Nature and Society: Anthropological Approaches*. London: Routledge.

Despres, Leo, ed. 1975. *Ethnicity and Resource Competition in Plural Societies*. The Hague: Mouton.

Douglas, Mary. 1966. *Purity and Danger*. London: Routledge & Kegan Paul.

—— 1970. *Natural Symbols*. London: Barrie & Rockliff.

—— 1975. *Implicit Meanings*. London: Routledge & Kegan Paul.

—— 1978. *Cultural Bias*. London: Royal Anthropological Institute.

—— 1980. *Evans-Pritchard*. Glasgow: Fontana.

—— 1987. *How Institutions Think*. London: Routledge.

—— and Baron Isherwood. 1978. *The World of Goods: Towards an Anthropology of Consumption*. New York: Basic Books.

—— and Aaron Wildavsky. 1980. *Risk and Culture: An Essay on the Selection of Technical and Environmental Dangers*. Berkeley: University of California Press.

Dumont, Louis. 1969 [1961]. Caste, Racism and 'Stratification': Reflections of a Social Anthropologist. In André Béteille, ed., *Inequality*, pp. 337–61. Harmondsworth: Penguin.

—— 1980 [1969]. *Homo Hierarchicus: The Caste System and its Implications*, 2nd edn, trans. Mark Sainsbury, Louis Dumont and Basia Gulati. Chicago: University of Chicago Press.

—— 1986. *Essays on Individualism: Modern Ideology in Anthropological Perspective*. Chicago: University of Chicago Press.

Dunbar, Robin. 1999. Culture, Honesty and the Freerider Problem. In Robin Dunbar, Chris Knight and Camilla Powers, eds., *The Evolution of Culture*, pp. 194–213. Edinburgh: Edinburgh University Press.

—— Chris Knight and Camilla Power, eds. 1999. *The Evolution of Culture*. Edinburgh: Edinburgh University Press.

Durham, William H. 1991. *Coevolution: Genes, Culture, and Human Diversity*. Stanford, CA: Stanford University Press.

Durkheim, Émile. 1951 [1897]. *Suicide: A Study in Sociology*, trans. John A. Spaulding and George Simpson. New York: Free Press.

—— 2001 [1912]. *The Elementary Forms of the Religious Life*, trans. Carol Cosman. Oxford: Oxford University Press.

—— and Marcel Mauss. 1963 [1903]. *Primitive Classification*, trans. Rodney Needham. London: Cohen & West.

Edwards, Jeanette, Sarah Franklin, Eric Hirsch, Frances Price and Marilyn Strathern. 1993. *Technologies of Procreation: Kinship in the Age of Assisted Conception*. Manchester: Manchester University Press.

Eidheim, Harald. 1971. *Aspects of the Lappish Minority Situation*. Oslo: Universitetsforlaget.

Ellen, Roy F., ed. 1984. *Ethnographic Research*. London: Academic Press.

Epstein, A.L. 1978. *Ethos and Identity*. London: Tavistock.

Eriksen, Thomas Hylland. 1990. Liming in Trinidad: The Art of Doing Nothing. *Folk* **32**: 23–43.

—— 1992. *Us and Them in Modern Societies: Ethnicity and Nationalism in Mauritius, Trinidad and Beyond*. Oslo: Universitetsforlaget.

—— 1993a. *Typisk norsk: Essays om kulturen i Norge* ('Typically Norwegian: Essays about Culture in Norway'). Oslo: Huitfeldt.

—— 1993b. Formal and Informal Nationalism. *Ethnic and Racial Studies* **16**(1): 1–25.

—— 1998. *Common Denominators: Ethnicity, Nation-building and Compromise in Mauritius*. Oxford: Berg.

—— 2001. Ethnic Identity, National Identity and Intergroup Conflict: The Significance of Personal Experiences. In Richard D. Ashmore, Lee Jussim and David Wilder, eds, *Social Identity, Intergroup Conflict, and Conflict Reduction*, pp. 42–70. Oxford: Oxford University Press.

—— 2004. The Case for Non-ethnic Nations. *Nations and Nationalism* **10**(1–2): 49–62.

—— 2006. *Engaging Anthropology: The Case for a Public Presence*. Oxford: Berg.

—— 2007a. Complexity in Social and Cultural Integration: Some Analytical Dimensions. *Ethnic and Racial Studies* **30**(6): 1055–69.

—— 2007b. *Globalization: The Key Concepts*. Oxford: Berg.

—— 2010. *Ethnicity and Nationalism: Anthropological Perspectives*, 3rd edn. London: Pluto.

—— and Richard Jenkins, eds. 2007. *Flag, Nation and Symbolism in Europe and America*. London: Routledge.

—— and Finn Sivert Nielsen. 2001. *A History of Anthropology*. London: Pluto.

—— Ellen Bal and Oscar Salemink, eds. 2010. *A World of Insecurity: Anthropological Perspectives on Human Security*. London: Pluto.

Evans-Pritchard, E.E. 1940. *The Nuer*. Oxford: Clarendon.

—— 1951. *Social Anthropology*. Glencoe, IL: Free Press.

—— 1956. *Nuer Religion*. Oxford: Clarendon.

—— 1962. *Social Anthropology and Other Essays*. New York: Free Press.

—— 1983 [1937]. *Witchcraft, Magic and Oracles among the Azande*, ed. Eva Gillies. Oxford: Oxford University Press.

Fanon, Frantz (1956) *Peau noire, masques blancs*. Paris: Seuil.

Feld, Steven. 1982. *Sound and Sentiment: Birds, Weeping, Politics and Song in Kaluli Expression*. Philadelphia: University of Pennsylvania Press.

—— 1994. Notes on 'World Beat'. In Charles Keil and Steven Feld, *Music Grooves*, pp. 238–46. Chicago: University of Chicago Press.

—— 2003. A Sweet Lullaby for World Music. In Arjun Appadurai, ed., *Globalization*, pp. 189–216. Durham, NC: Duke University Press.

Feldman, Allen. 1991. *Formations of Violence: The Narrative of the Body and Political Terror in Northern Ireland*. Chicago: University of Chicago Press.

Ferguson, James. 1990. Mobile Worker, Modernist Narratives: A Critique of the Historiography of Transition on the Zambian Copperbelt. *Journal of Southern African Studies* **16**(3–4): 385–412 and 603–21.

—— 1999. *Expectations of Modernity: Myths and Meanings of Urban Life on the Zambian Copperbelt*. Berkeley: University of California Press.

Fernandez, James W., ed. 1991. *Beyond Metaphor: The Theory of Tropes in Anthropology*. Stanford, CA: Stanford University Press.

Feyerabend, Paul K. 1975. *Against Method*. London: Verso.

Finnegan, Ruth. 1988. *Literacy and Orality: Studies in the Technology of Communication*. Oxford: Blackwell.

Firth, Raymond. 1951. *Elements of Social Organization*. London: Watts.

—— 1989. The Future of Social Anthropology. Lecture given at the University of Oslo, November.

Fison, Lorimer and William A. Howitt. 1991 [1880]. *Kamilaroi and Kurnai: Group-marriage and Relationship, and Marriage by Elopement Drawn Chiefly from the Usage of the Australian Aborigines*. Canberra: Aboriginal Studies Press.

Fitzgerald, Thomas K. (1993) *Metaphors of Identity: A Culture_Communication Dialogue*. New York: SUNY Press.

Fortes, Meyer. 1945. *The Dynamics of Clanship among the Tallensi*. London: Oxford University Press.

Foucault, Michel. 1979. *Discipline and Punish: The Birth of the Prison*, trans. Alan Sheridan. New York: Vintage.

Fox, Robin. 1967. *Kinship and Marriage*. Harmondsworth: Penguin.

Frank, Andre Gunder. 1979. *Dependent Accumulation and Underdevelopment*. New York: Monthly Review Press.

Frazer, James. 1974 [1922]. *The Golden Bough* (abridged edn). London: Macmillan.

Freeman, Derek. 1983. *Margaret Mead and Samoa: The Making and Unmaking of an Anthropological Myth*. Cambridge, MA: Harvard University Press.

Friedman, Jonathan. 1990. Being in the World: Globalization and Localization. In Mike Featherstone, ed., *Global Culture: Nationalism, Globalization, and Modernity*, pp. 311–28. London: SAGE.

—— 1994. *Cultural Identity and Global Process*. London: SAGE.

Friedman, Kajsa Ekholm. 1991. *Catastrophe and Creation: The Formation of an African Culture*. London: Harwood.

—— 1994. *Den magiska världsbilden: Om statens frigörelse från folket i Folkrepubliken Kongo*. Stockholm: Carlssons.

Frøystad, Kathinka. 2005. *Blended Boundaries: Caste, Class, and Shifting Faces of 'Hinduness' in a North Indian City*. New Delhi: Oxford University Press.

Fuglerud, Øivind. 1999. *Life on the Outside: The Tamil Diaspora and Long-distance Nationalism*. London: Pluto.

Fuller, Steve. 2006. *The Philosophy of Science and Technology Studies*. London: Routledge.

Furedi, Frank (2002) *Culture of Fear*, 2nd edn. London: Continuum.

Galey, Jean-Claude. 1992. Orientalisme et anthropologie. In Pierre Bonté and Michel Izard, eds, *Dictionnaire de l'ethnologie et de l'anthropologie*, pp. 529–32. Paris: Presses Universitaires de France.

Gandoulou, J.-D. 1989. *Dandies à Bacongo: le culte de l'élégance dans la société congolaise contemporaine*. Paris: L'Harmattan.

Geertz, Clifford. 1963. *Agricultural Involution: The Processes of Ecological Change in Indonesia*. Berkeley: University of California Press.

—— 1972. The Wet and the Dry: Traditional Irrigation in Bali and Morocco. *Human Ecology* **1**(1): 23–29.

—— 1973. *The Interpretation of Cultures*. New York: Basic Books.

—— 1983. *Local Knowledge: Further Essays in Interpretive Anthropology*. New York: Basic Books.

—— 1988. *Works and Lives: The Anthropologist as Author*. Cambridge: Polity.

—— 2000. *Available Light: Anthropological Reflections on Philosophical Topics*. Princeton, NJ: Princeton University Press.

Gellner, Ernest. 1983. *Nations and Nationalism*. Oxford: Blackwell.

Georges, Eugenia. 1990. *The Making of a Transnational Community: Migration, Development and Cultural Change in the Dominican Republic*. New York: Columbia University Press.

Ghorashi, Halleh. 2003. *Ways to Survive, Battles to Win: Iranian Women Exiles in the Netherlands and United States*. New York: Nova.

Giddens, Anthony. 1979. *Central Problems in Social Theory*. London: Macmillan.

—— 1984. *The Constitution of Society*. Cambridge: Polity.

—— 1985. *The Nation-state and Violence*. Cambridge: Polity.

—— 1991. *Modernity and Self-Identity*. Cambridge: Polity.

Gilmore, David D. 1989. *Manhood in the Making: Cultural Conceptions of Masculinity*. New Haven, CT: Yale University Press.

Gingrich, Andre. 2005. The German-speaking Countries. In Fredrik Barth, Andre Gingrich, Robert Parkin and Sydel Silverman, *One Discipline, Four Ways: British, German, French, and American Anthropology*, pp. 61–156. Chicago: University of Chicago Press.

Giulianotti, Richard and Roland Robertson. 2009. *Globalization and Football*. London: SAGE.

Gladney, Dru C., ed. 1998. *Making Majorities: Constituting the Nation in Japan, Korea, China, Malaysia, Fiji, Turkey, and the United States*. Stanford, CA: Stanford University Press.

Gledhill, John. 2000. *Power and its Disguises: Perspectives on Political Anthropology*, 2nd edn. London: Pluto.

Gluckman, Max. 1982 [1956]. *Custom and Conflict in Africa*. Oxford: Blackwell.

Godelier, Maurice. 1975. Infrastructures, Societies and History. *Current Anthropology* **19**(4): 763–71.

—— 2004. *Métamorphoses de la parenté*. Paris: Fayard.

—— 2009. *In and Out of the West: Reconstructing Anthropology*. London: Verso.

Goffman, Erving. 1978 [1959]. *The Presentation of Self in Everyday Life*. Harmondsworth: Penguin.

Goodale, Mark, ed. 2009. *Human Rights: An Anthropological Reader*. Oxford: Blackwell.

—— and Sally Engle Merry, eds. 2007. *The Practice of Human Rights: Tracking Law between the Global and the Local*. Cambridge: Cambridge University Press.

Goody, Jack, ed. 1968. *Literacy in Traditional Societies*. Cambridge: Cambridge University Press.

—— 1977. *The Domestication of the Savage Mind*. Cambridge: Cambridge University Press.

—— 1982. *Cooking, Cuisine and Class*. Cambridge: Cambridge University Press.

—— 1995. *The Expansive Moment: The Rise of Anthropology in Britain and Africa, 1918–1970*. Cambridge: Cambridge University Press.

Gough, E. Kathleen. 1959. The Nayars and the Definition of Marriage. *Journal of the Royal Anthropological Institute* **89**: 23–34.

Gould, Stephen Jay. 2002. *The Structure of Evolutionary Theory*. Cambridge, MA: Belknap Press.

Graeber, David. 2004. *Fragments of an Anarchist Anthropology*. Chicago: Prickly Paradigm Press.

—— 2005. Value: Anthropological Theories of Value. In James Carrier, ed., *A Handbook of Economic Anthropology*, pp. 439–54.Cheltenham: Edward Elgar.

Gray, J. Patrick. 1998. Ethnographic Atlas Codebook. *World Cultures* **10**(1): 86–136.

Grillo, Ralph. 1998. *Pluralism and the Politics of Difference: State, Culture and Ethnicity in Comparative Perspective*. Oxford: Oxford University Press.

Guha, Ranajit and Gayatri Chakravorty Spivak, eds. 1988. *Selected Subaltern Studies*. New Delhi: Oxford University Press.

Gullestad, Marianne. 1984. *Kitchen-table Society*. Oslo: Universitetsforlaget.

—— 1992. *The Art of Social Relations*. Oslo: Universitetsforlaget.

—— 2006. *Plausible Prejudice*. Oslo: Universitetsforlaget.

Gupta, Akhil and James Ferguson, eds. 1997. *Anthropological Locations: Boundaries and Grounds of a Field Science*. Berkeley: University of California Press.

Haaland, Gunnar. 1969. Economic Determinants in Ethnic Processes. In Fredrik Barth, ed., *Ethnic Groups and Boundaries: The Social Organization of Culture Difference*, pp. 58–74. Oslo: Universitetsforlaget.

Haar, Gerrie ter, ed. 2007. *Imagining Evil: Witchcraft Beliefs and Accusations in Contemporary Africa*. Trenton, NJ: Africa World Press.

Habermas, Jürgen. 1967. *Wissenschaft und Technik als 'Ideologie'*. Frankfurt-am-Main: Suhrkamp.

Halbwachs, Maurice. 1999 [1925]. *On Collective Memory*. Chicago: University of Chicago Press.

Halverson, John. 1992. Goody and the Implosion of the Literacy Thesis. *Man* **27**(2): 300–17.

Hammond-Tooke, W. David. 1997. *Imperfect Interpreters: South Africa's Anthropologists, 1920–1990*. Johannesburg: Wits University Press.

Handelman, Don. 1977. The Organization of Ethnicity. *Ethnic Groups* **1**: 269–74.

—— 1990. *Models and Mirrors. Towards an Anthropology of Public Events*. Cambridge: Cambridge University Press.

Handler, Richard and Daniel Segal. 1993. How European is Nationalism? *Social Analysis* **32**(1): 1–15.

Hannerz, Ulf. 1980. *Exploring the City: Inquiries toward an Urban Anthropology*. New York: Columbia University Press.

—— 1992. *Cultural Complexity*. New York: Columbia University Press.

—— 1996. *Transnational Connections*. London: Routledge.

—— 2010. *Anthropology's World: Life in a Twenty-first-century Discipline*. London: Pluto.

Haraway, Donna. 1991. *Simians, Cyborgs, and Women: The Reinvention of Nature*. London: Routledge.

Harris, Mark, ed. 2007. *Ways of Knowing: New Approaches in the Anthropology of Knowledge and Learning*. Oxford: Berghahn.

Harris, Marvin. 1964. *The Nature of Cultural Things*. New York: Random House.

—— 1979. *Cultural Materialism: The Struggle for a Science of Culture*. New York: Random House.

Harris, Olivia. 1995. Knowing the Past: The Antinomies of Loss in Highland Bolivia. In Richard Fardon, ed., *Counterwork: Managing Diverse Knowledges*, pp. 105–23. London: Routledge.

Harrison, Simon. 2000. Identity as a Scarce Resource. *Social Anthropology* **7**(3): 239–52.

Hart, Keith. 1973. Informal Income Opportunities and Urban Employment in Ghana. *Journal of Modern African Studies* **11**(1): 61–89.

—— 1999. *The Memory Bank: Money in an Unequal World*. London: Profile.

—— 2005. Money: One Anthropologist's View. In James Carrier, ed., *A Handbook of Economic Anthropology*, pp. 160–75. Cheltenham: Edward Elgar.

Harvey, David. 1989. *The Condition of Postmodernity*. Oxford: Blackwell.

Hastrup, Kirsten. 1992. Writing Ethnography: State of the Art. In Helen Calloway and Judith Okely, eds, *Anthropology and Autobiography*, pp. 116–33. London: Routledge.

Headland, Thomas N., Kenneth L. Pike and Marvin Harris, eds. 1990. *Emics and Etics: The Insider/Outsider Debate*. London: SAGE.

Hellman, Hal. 1998. *Great Feuds in Science: Ten of the Liveliest Disputes Ever*. New York: Wiley.

Herdt, Gilbert. 1987. *The Zambia: Ritual and Gender in New Guinea*. New York: Holt, Rinehart & Winston.

Herzfeld, Michael. 1992. *The Social Production of Indifference: Exploring the Symbolic Roots of Western Bureaucracy*. Oxford: Berg.

—— 2005. *Cultural Intimacy: Social Poetics in the Nation-state*, 2nd edn. London: Routledge.

Heusch, Luc de. 2000. L'Ethnie: Vicissitudes of a Concept. *Social Anthropology* **8**(2): 99–115.

Hitchcock, Michael, Victor T. King and Michael Parnwell, eds. 2008. *Tourism in Southeast Asia: Challenges and New Directions*. Copenhagen: NIAS Press.

Hobsbawm, Eric and Terence Ranger, eds. 1983. *The Invention of Tradition*. Cambridge: Cambridge University Press.

Hoëm, Ingjerd. 2005. *Theatre and Political Processes: Staging Identities in Tokelau and New Zealand*. Oxford: Berghahn.

Hognestad, Hans Kristian. 2003. Long-distance Football Support and Liminal Identities among Norwegian Fans. In Noel Dyck and Eduardo Archetti, eds, *Sport, Dance and Embodied Identities*, pp. 97–114. Oxford: Berg.

Hollis, Martin and Steven Lukes, eds. 1982. *Rationality and Relativism*. Oxford: Blackwell.

Holmes, Lowell D. 1987. *Quest for the Real Samoa: The Mead/Freeman Controversy and Beyond*. South Hadley, MA: Bergin & Garvey.

Holy, Ladislav. 1990. Strategies for Old Age among the Berti of the Sudan. In Paul Spencer, ed., *Anthropology and the Riddle of the Sphinx*, pp. 167–82. London: Routledge.

—— 1996. *Anthropological Perspectives on Kinship*. London: Pluto.

—— and Milan Stuchlik. 1983. *Actions, Norms and Representations*. Cambridge: Cambridge University Press.

Horowitz, Donald. 1985. *Ethnic Groups in Conflict*. Berkeley: University of California Press.

Horton, Robin. 1970. African Traditional Thought and Western Science. In Bryan R. Wilson, ed., *Rationality*, pp. 131–71. Oxford: Blackwell.

Howe, Leo. 2005. *The Changing World of Bali: Religion, Society and Tourism*. London: Routledge.

Howell, Signe. 1989. 'To Be Angry Is Not to Be Human, but to Be Fearful Is': Chewong Concepts of Human Nature. In Signe Howell and Roy Willis, eds, *Societies at Peace: Anthropological Perspectives*, pp. 45–59. London: Routledge.

—— 2007. *The Kinning of Foreigners: Transnational Adoption in a Global Perspective*. Oxford: Berghahn.

—— and Marit Melhuus. 1993. The Study of Kinship; the Study of Person; a Study of Gender? In Teresa del Valle, ed., *Gendered Anthropology*, pp. 38–53. London: Routledge.

—— and Marit Melhuus. 2007. Race, Biology and Culture in Contemporary Norway: Identity and Belonging in Adoption, Donor Gametes and Immigration. In Peter Wade, ed., *Race, Ethnicity and Nation: Perspectives from Kinship and Genetics*, pp. 53–72. Oxford: Berghahn.

—— and Roy Willis, eds. 1989. *Societies at Peace: Anthropological Perspectives*. London: Routledge.

Howes, David. 2003. *Sensual Relations: Engaging the Senses in Culture and Social Theory*. Ann Arbor: University of Michigan Press.

—— ed. 2004. *Empire of the Senses. The Sensual Culture Reader*. Oxford: Berg.

Hubert, Henri and Marcel Mauss. 1964 [1898] *Sacrifice: Its Nature and Functions*. Chicago: University of Chicago Press.

Huntington, Ellsworth. 1945. *Mainsprings of Civilization*. London: Wiley.

Hviding, Edvard. 1994. Indigenous Essentialism? 'Simplifying' Customary Land Ownership in New Georgia, Solomon Islands. *Bijdragen* **149**: 802–24.

—— 1996. *Guardians of Marovo Lagoon: Practice, Place and Politics in Maritime Melanesia*. Honolulu: University of Hawai'i Press.

—— 2006. Knowing and Managing Biodiversity in the Pacific Islands: Challenges of Environmentalism in Marovo Lagoon. *International Social Science Journal* **58**(1): 69–85.

Inden, Ronald. 1990. *Imagining India*. Oxford: Blackwell.

Ingold, Tim. 1979. The Social and Ecological Relations of Culture-bearing Organisms: An Essay in Evolutionary Dynamics. In Philip C. Burnham and Roy F. Ellen, eds, *Social and Ecological Systems*, pp. 271–92. London: Academic Press.

—— 1986. *Evolution and Social Life*. Cambridge: Cambridge University Press.

—— 1994a. Humanity and Animality. In Tim Ingold, ed., *Companion Encyclopedia of Anthropology: Humanity, Culture and Social Life*, pp. 14–32. London: Routledge.

—— 1994b. Introduction to Social Life. In Tim Ingold, ed., *Companion Encyclopedia of Anthropology: Humanity, Culture and Social Life*, pp. 735–37. London: Routledge.

—— ed. 1996. *Key Debates in Anthropology*. London: Routledge.

—— 2002. *The Perception of the Environment: Essays on Livelihood, Dwelling and Skill*. London: Routledge.

James, Allison. 1993. *Childhood Identities: Self and Social Relationships in the Experience of the Child*. Edinburgh: Edinburgh University Press.

—— and Adrian L. James. 2004. *Constructing Childhoood: Theory, Policy and Social Practice*. Basingstoke: Palgrave Macmillan.

—— Jenny Hockey and Andrew Dawson, eds. 1997. *After Writing Culture: Epistemology and Praxis in Contemporary Anthropology*. London: Routledge.

Jarvie, Ian C. 1968. Limits to the Functionalism and Alternatives to it in Anthropology. In Robert A. Manners and David Kaplan, eds, *Theory in Anthropology – A Source Book*, pp. 196–203. Chicago: University of Chicago Press.

Jenkins, Richard. 1993. *Pierre Bourdieu*. Cambridge: Polity.

—— 2008. *Rethinking Ethnicity*, 2nd edn. London: SAGE.

Jiménez, Alberto Corsín, ed. 2008. *Culture and Well-being: Anthropological Approaches to Freedom and Political Ethics*. London: Pluto.

Kapferer, Bruce. 1984. The Ritual Process and the Problem of Reflexivity in Sinhalese Demon Exorcism. In John MacAloon, ed., *Rite, Drama, Festival, Spectacle*, pp. 179–207. Ithaca, NY: Cornell University Press.

—— 1988. *Legends of People, Myths of State*. Baltimore, MD: Smithsonian Institution Press.

Kasten, Erich, ed. 2004. *Properties of Culture – Culture as Property*. Berlin: Dietrich Reimer Verlag.

Keesing, Roger M. 1981. *Cultural Anthropology – Contemporary Perspectives*. New York: Holt, Rinehart & Winston.

—— 1994. Theories of Culture Revisited. In Robert Borofsky, ed., *Assessing Cultural Anthropology*, pp. 301–9. New York: McGraw-Hill.

Kertzer, David I. 1988. *Ritual, Politics and Power*. New Haven, CT: Yale University Press.

—— and Dominique Arel, eds. 2002. *Census and Identity: The Politics of Race, Ethnicity and Language in National Censuses*. Cambridge: Cambridge University Press.

Khan, Aisha. 2004. *Callaloo Nation: Metaphors of Race and Ethnic Identity among South Asians in Trinidad*. Durham, NC: Duke University Press.

Klass, Morton. 1991. *Singing with Sai Baba: The Politics of Revitalization in Trinidad*. Boulder, CO: Westview Press.

Klausen, Arne Martin, ed. 1999. *The Olympic Games as Performance and Public Event*. Oxford: Berghahn.

Kluckhohn, Clyde and Alfred E. Kroeber. 1952. *Culture: A Critical Review of Concepts and Definitions*. Cambridge, MA: Harvard University Press.

Knauft, Bruce M. 1990. Melanesian Warfare: A Theoretical History. *Oceania* **60**: 250–311.

—— 1996. *Genealogies for the Present in Cultural Anthropology*. London and New York: Routledge.

—— 1999. *From Primitive to Postcolonial in Melanesia and Anthropology*. Ann Arbor: University of Michigan Press.

Knudsen, Anne. 1987. Silent Bodies and Singing Minds. *Folk* **29**: 239–56.

—— 1992. Dual Histories. In Kirsten Hastrup, ed., *Other Histories*, pp. 82–102. London: Routledge.

Kolenda, Pauline. 1985. *Caste in Modern India: Beyond Organic Solidarity*. Prospect Heights, IL: Waveland.

Kopytoff, Igor. 1971. Ancestors as Elders in Africa. *Africa* **41**: 129–41.

—— 1981. The Authority of Ancestors. *Man* **16**(1): 135–38.

—— 1986. The Cultural Biography of Things: Commoditization as Process. In Arjun Appadurai, ed., *The Social Life of Things: Commodities in Cultural Perspective*, pp. 64–94. Cambridge: Cambridge University Press.

Kroeber, Alfred L. 1952 [1917]. *The Nature of Culture*. Chicago: University of Chicago Press.

Krohn-Hansen, Christian. 1994. The Anthropology of Violent Interaction. *Journal of Anthropological Research* **50**(4): 367–81.

—— 2009. *Political Authoritarianism in the Dominican Republic*. New York: Palgrave Macmillan.

—— and Knut Nustad, eds. 2005. *State Formation: Anthropological Perspectives*. London: Pluto.

Kuhn, Thomas. 1962. *The Structure of Scientific Revolutions*. Chicago: University of Chicago Press.

Kuklick, Henrietta. 1991. *The Savage Within: A Social History of British Anthropology, 1885–1945*. Cambridge: Cambridge University Press.

Kulick, Don. 1998. *Travesti: Sex, Gender and Culture among Brazilian Transsexual Prostitutes*. Chicago: University of Chicago Press.

—— and Margaret Wilson, eds. 1995. *Taboo: Sex, Identity and Erotic Subjectivity in Anthropological Fieldwork*. London: Routledge.

Kuper, Adam. 1994. Anthropological Futures. In Robert Borofsky, ed., *Assessing Cultural Anthropology*, pp. 113–18. New York: McGraw-Hill.

—— 1996. *Anthropology and Anthropologists: The Modern British School*, 3rd edn. London: Routledge & Kegan Paul.

—— 1999. *Culture: The Anthropologists' Account*. Cambridge, MA: Harvard University Press.

—— 2005. *The Reinvention of Primitive Society: Transformations of a Myth*. London: Routledge.

Kuznetsov, Anatoly M. 2008. Russian Anthropology: Old Traditions and New Tendencies. In Aleksandar Boskovic, ed., *Other People's Anthropologies*, pp. 20–43. Oxford: Berghahn.

Kymlicka, Will. 1995. *Multicultural Citizenship: A Theory of Liberal Rights*. Oxford: Clarendon.

Labov, William. 1972. The Logic of Nonstandard English. In Pier Paolo Giglioli, ed., *Language and Social Context*, pp. 179–216. Harmondsworth: Penguin.

Lakoff, George and Mark Johnson. 1980. *Metaphors We Live By*. Chicago: University of Chicago Press.

—— 1999. *Philosophy in the Flesh: The Embodied Mind and its Challenge to Western Thought*. New York: Basic Books.

Lan, David. 1985. *Guns and Rain: Guerrillas and Spirit Mediums in Zimbabwe*. London: James Currey.

Larkin, Brian (2003) Itineraries of Indian Cinema: African videos, Bollywood and Global media. In Ella Shohat and Robert Stam, ed., *Multiculturalism, Postcolonialism and Transnational Media*, pp. 170–92. New Brunswick, NJ: Rutgers University Press.

Latour, Bruno and Steve Woolgar. 1979. *Laboratory Life: The Social Construction of Scientific Facts*. London: SAGE.

Leach, Edmund R. 1954. *Political Systems of Highland Burma*. London: Athlone.

—— 1967. An Anthropologist's Reflections on a Social Survey. In D.G. Jongmans and Peter Gutkind, eds, *Anthropologists in the Field*. Assen: van Gorcum.

—— 1968. Ritual. *Encyclopedia of the Social Sciences*. New York: Free Press.

—— 1976. *Culture and Communication: The Logic by which Symbols Are Connected*. Cambridge: Cambridge University Press.

—— 1982. *Social Anthropology*. Glasgow: Fontana.

Leach, Jerry W. and G. Kildea. 1974. *Trobriand Cricket: An Ingenious Response to Colonialism* (documentary film). Berkeley: University of California Extension Media Center.

Lee, Richard. 1968. What Hunters Do for a Living, or How to Make out on Scarce Resources. In Richard Lee and Irven deVore, eds, *Man the Hunter*, pp. 30–48. Chicago: Aldine.

Leenhardt, Maurice. 1947. *Do kamo: la personne et le mythe dans le monde mélanésien*. Paris: Gallimard.

Lévi-Strauss, Claude. 1963. *Totemism*, trans. Rodney Needham. Boston, MA: Beacon Press.

—— 1966 [1962]. *The Savage Mind*. Chicago: University of Chicago Press.

—— 1969 [1949]. *The Elementary Structures of Kinship*, trans. Rodney Needham. London: Tavistock.

—— 1976 [1955]. *Tristes tropiques*, trans. John Weightman and Doreen Weightman. Harmondsworth: Penguin.

—— 1983. *Le Regard éloigné*. Paris: Plon. (English edn.: *The View from Afar*. New York: Basic Books 1985.)

Lewellen, Ted C. 2002. *The Anthropology of Globalization*. Westport, CT: Bergin & Garvey.

Lewis, Gordon K. 1983. *Main Currents in Caribbean Thought*. Kingston: Heinemann.

Lieberman, Philip. 1994. The Origins and Evolution of Language. In Tim Ingold, ed., *Companion Encyclopedia of Anthropology: Humanity, Culture and Social Life*, pp. 108–32. London: Routledge.

Lien, Marianne. 1988. *Fra boknafesk til pizza* (From Boknafesk [dried and salted cod] to Pizza). Occasional papers no. 18. Department of Social Anthropology, Oslo University.

Lienhardt, Godfrey. 1985. From Study to Field, and Back. *Times Literary Supplement* 7 June.

—— 1987. Self, Public, Private: Some African Representations. In Michael Carrithers, Steven Collins and Steven Lukes, eds, *The Category of the Person: Anthropology, Philosophy, History*, pp. 141–45. Cambridge: Cambridge University Press.

Liep, John, ed. 2000. *Locating Cultural Creativity*. London: Pluto.

Linton, Ralph. 1937. *The Study of Man: An Introduction*. New York: Appleton-Century-Crofts.

Little, Kenneth. 1978. Countervailing Influences in African Ethnicity: A Less Apparent Factor. In Brian du Toit, ed., *Ethnicity in Modern Africa*, pp. 175–89. Boulder, CO: SAGE.

Lizot, Jacques. 1984. *Les Yanōmami Centraux*. Paris: Editions de l'EHESS.

—— 1994. On Warfare: An Answer to N.A. Chagnon. *American Ethnologist* **21**: 841–58.

Löfgren, Orvar. 1999. *On Holiday: A History of Vacationing*. Berkeley: University of California Press.

Lukács, György. 1971 [1923]. History and Class Consciousness: Studies in Marxist Dialectics, trans. Rodney Livingstone. London: Merlin.

Lukes, Steven. 2004. *Power: A Radical View*, 2nd edn. London: Macmillan.

Lutz, Catherine. 1988. *Unnatural Emotions*. Chicago: University of Chicago Press.

Maanen, John van. 1988. *Tales of the Field: On Writing Ethnography*. Chicago: University of Chicago Press.

MacClancy, Jeremy, ed. 1994. *Sport, Identity and Ethnicity*. Oxford: Berg.

—— 1996. Popularizing Anthropology, in Jeremy MacClancy and Chris McDonaugh, eds, *Popularizing Anthropology*, pp. 1–57. London: Routledge.

McLuhan, Marshall. 1962. *The Gutenberg Galaxy: The Making of Typographic Man*. Toronto: Toronto University Press.

Mach, Zdzislav. 1993. *Symbols, Conflict, and Identity: Essays in Political Anthropology*. New York: SUNY Press.

MacIntyre, Alasdair. 1970. Is Understanding Religion Compatible with Believing? In Bryan R. Wilson, ed., *Rationality*, pp. 62–77. Oxford: Blackwell.

—— 1981. *After Virtue: A Study in Moral Theory*. London: Duckworth.

Maeckelbergh, Marianne. 2009. *The Will of the Many: How the Alterglobalisation Movement is Changing the Face of Democracy*. London: Pluto.

Malinowski, Bronislaw. 1967. *A Diary in the Strict Sense of the Term*. London: Routledge & Kegan Paul.

—— 1974 [1948]. *Magic, Science and Religion and Other Essays*. London: Souvenir.

—— 1984 [1922]. *Argonauts of the Western Pacific*. Prospect Heights, IL: Waveland.

Malkki, Liisa H. 1995. *Purity and Exile: Violence, Memory and National Cosmology among Hutu Refugees in Tanzania*. Chicago: University of Chicago Press.

Malnic, Jutta and John Kasaipwalova. 1998. *Kula: Myth and Magic in the Trobriand Islands*. Halstead: Cowrie Press.

Malthus, Thomas. 1982 [1798]. *An Essay on the Principle of Population*. Harmondsworth: Penguin.

Mandelbaum, David G. 1988. *Women's Seclusion and Men's Honour: Sex Roles in North India, Bangladesh, and Pakistan*. Tucson: University of Arizona Press.

Manganaro, Marc, ed. 1990. *Modernist Anthropology: From Fieldwork to Text*. Princeton, NJ: Princeton University Press.

Marcus, George. 1998. *Ethnography Through Thick and Thin*. Princeton, NJ: Princeton University Press.

—— and Michael Fischer. 1986. *Anthropology as a Cultural Critique: An Experimental Moment in the Human Sciences*. Chicago: University of Chicago Press.

Marling, William H. (2006) *How 'American' is Globalization?* Baltimore, MD: Johns Hopkins University Press.

Martin, Emily. 2001. *The Woman in the Body: A Cultural Analysis of Reproduction*. Boston, MA: Beacon Press.

Marx, Karl. 1906 [1867–94]. *Capital: A Critique of Political Economy*. New York: Modern Library.

—— and Friedrich Engels. 1968 [1848]. *The Communist Manifesto*. New York: The Modern Reader.

Mathews, Gordon and Carolina Izquierdo, eds. 2008. *Pursuits of Happiness: Well-being in Anthropological Perspective*. Oxford: Berghahn.

Mauss, Marcel. 1954 [1924] *The Gift*, trans. Ian Cunnison. London: Cohen & West.

—— 1985 [1938]. A Category of the Human Mind: The Notion of the Self. In Michael Carrithers, Steven Collins and Steven Lukes, eds, *The Category of the Person. Anthropology, Philosophy, History*, pp. 1–26. Cambridge: Cambridge University Press.

Mead, Margaret. 1978 [1928]. *Coming of Age in Samoa*. Harmondsworth: Penguin.

Meillassoux, Claude. 1967. Recherche d'un niveau de détermination dans la société cynégetique. *L'Homme et la société* **6**: 95–105.

Merleau-Ponty, Maurice. 1962 [1945] *Phenomenology of Perception*, trans. James Edie. Evanston, IL: Northwestern University Press.

Miller, Daniel. 1987. *Material Culture and Mass Consumption*. Oxford: Blackwell.

—— 1988. Appropriating the State on a Council Estate. *Man* **26**: 323–41.

—— 1994. Artefacts and the Meaning of Things. In Tim Ingold, ed., *Companion Encyclopedia of Anthropology: Humanity, Culture and Social Life*, pp. 396–419. London: Routledge.

—— 1998. *A Theory of Shopping*. Cambridge: Polity.

—— 2001. The Poverty of Morality. *Journal of Consumer Culture* **1**(2): 225–43.

—— 2009. *Stuff*. Cambridge: Polity.

—— and Don Slater. 2000. *The Internet: An Ethnographic Approach*. Oxford: Berg.

—— 2003. Ethnography and the Extreme Internet. In Thomas Hylland Eriksen, ed., *Globalisation – Studies in Anthropology*, pp. 38–58. London: Pluto.

Miller, Solomon. 1965. Proletarianization of Indian Peasants in Northern Peru. In Dwight B. Heath, ed., *Contemporary Cultures and Societies of Latin America*, pp. 135–42. Prospect Heights, IL: Waveland.

Mills, David. 2003. Professionalizing or popularizing anthropology? *Anthropology Today*, **19**(5): 8–13.

Mintz, Sidney. 1974. *Caribbean Transformations*. Chicago: Aldine.

Mitchell, J. Clyde. 1956. *The Kalela Dance: Aspects of Social Relationships among Urban Africans in Northern Rhodesia*. Livingstone: Rhodes-Livingstone Papers **27**.

—— 1966. Theoretical Orientations in African Urban Studies. In Michael Banton, ed., *The Social Anthropology of Complex Societies*, pp. 37–68. London: Tavistock.

Mitchell, Jon P. and Richard A. Wilson, eds. 2003. *Human Rights in Global Perspective: Anthropological Studies of Rights, Claims and Entitlements*. London: Routledge.

Moerman, Michael. 1965. Who Are the Lue? Ethnic Identification in a Complex Civilization. *American Anthropologist* **67**: 1215–29.

Moore, Henrietta L. 1993. The Differences Within and the Differences Between. In Teresa del Valle, ed., *Gendered Anthropology*, pp. 193–204. London: Routledge.

—— 1994. *A Passion for Difference*. Cambridge: Polity.

—— 1999. Gender and Other Crises in Anthropology. In Henrietta L. Moore, ed., *Anthropological Theory Today*, pp. 151–71. Cambridge: Polity.

Morris, Brian. 1994. *Anthropology of the Self: The Individual in Cultural Perspective*. London: Pluto.

Mukenge, Tsilemalea. 2002. *Culture and Customs of the Congo*. Westport, CT: Greenwood Press.

Murdock, George P. 1945. The Common Denominator of Cultures. In Ralph Linton, ed., *The Science of Man in the World Crisis*, pp. 123–42. New York: Columbia University Press.

Murphy, Yolanda and Robert Murphy. 1985. *Women of the Forest*. New York: Columbia University Press.

Nash, Manning. 1988. *The Cauldron of Ethnicity in the Modern World*. Chicago: University of Chicago Press.

Needham, Rodney. 1962. *Structure and Sentiment*. Chicago: University of Chicago Press.

—— 1971a. Incest. In Rodney Needham, ed., *Rethinking Kinship and Marriage*, pp. 24–34. London: Tavistock.

—— ed. 1971b. *Rethinking Kinship and Marriage*. London: Tavistock.

Newcomer, Peter J. 1972. The Nuer are Dinka. *Man* **7**(1): 5–11.

Newman, Katherine. 1988. *Falling from Grace: The Experience of Downward Mobility in the American Middle Class*. New York: Vintage.

Nichter, Mark and Margaret Lock, eds. 2002. *New Horizons in Medical Anthropology*. London: Routledge.

Niehaus, Isak, with Eliazaar Mohlala and Kally Shokane. 2001. *Witchcraft, Power and Politics: Exploring the Occult in the South African Lowveld*. London: Pluto.

Obeyesekere, Gananath. 1981. *Medusa's Hair: An Essay on Personal Symbols and Religious Experience*. Chicago: University of Chicago Press.

—— 1992. *The Apotheosis of Captain Cook: European Mythmaking in the Pacific*. Princeton, NJ: Princeton University Press.

Okely, Judith. 1983. *The Traveller-gypsies*. Cambridge: Cambridge University Press.

—— and Helen Calloway, eds. 1992. *Anthropology and Autobiography*. London: Routledge.

Oliver-Smith, Anthony. 2009. Climate Change and Population Displacement: Disasters and Diasporas in the Twenty-first Century. In Susan A. Crate and Mark Nuttall, eds, *Anthropology and Climate Change: From Encounters to Actions*, pp. 116–38. Walnut Creek, CA: Left Coast Press.

Olwig, Karen Fog. 1993. *Global Culture, Island Identity*. Chur, Switzerland: Harwood Academic Publishers.

—— 2003. Global Places and Place-identities – Lessons from Caribbean Research. In Thomas Hylland Eriksen, ed., *Globalisation – Studies in Anthropology*, pp. 58–77. London: Pluto.

—— 2007. *Caribbean Journeys: An Ethnography of Migration and Home in Three Family Networks*. Durham, NC: Duke University Press.

Ong, Walter J. 1969. World as View and World as Event. *American Anthropologist* **71**(4): 634–47.

—— 1982. *Orality and Literacy: The Technologizing of the Word*. London: Methuen.

Oppong, Yaa P.A. 2002. *Moving Through and Passing On: Fulani Mobility, Survival, and Identity in Ghana*. London: Transaction.

Ortner, Sherry B. 1974. Is Female to Male as Nature Is to Culture? In Michelle Z. Rosaldo and Louise Lamphere, eds, *Woman, Culture and Society*, pp. 67–87. Stanford, CA: Stanford University Press.

—— 1984. Theory in Anthropology Since the Sixties. *Comparative Studies in Society and History* **26**: 126–66.

—— 1997. *Making Gender: Politics and Erotics of Culture*. Boston, MA: Beacon Press.

—— ed. 1999. *The Fate of 'Culture': Geertz and Beyond*. Berkeley: University of California Press.

—— and Harriet Whitehead. 1981. Accounting for Sexual Meanings. In Sherry B. Ortner and Harriet Whitehead, eds, *Sexual Meanings*, pp. 1–27. Cambridge: Cambridge University Press.

Orwell, George. 1984 [1949]. *1984*. Oxford: Clarendon.

Overing, Joanna, ed. 1985. *Reason and Morality*. London: Tavistock.

Pace, David. 1983. *Lévi-Strauss: The Bearer of Ashes*. London: Routledge.

Paine, Robert. 1994. *Herds of the Tundra: A Portrait of Saami Reindeer Pastoralism*. Washington, DC: Smithsonian Institute.

Pálsson, Gisli, ed. 1993. *Beyond Boundaries: Understanding, Translation and Anthropological Discourse*. Oxford: Berg.

Papadakis, Yiannis. 2005. *Echoes from the Dead Zone: Across the Cyprus Divide*. London: I.B. Tauris.

Parkin, David. 1969. *Neighbours and Nationals in an African City Ward*. London: Routledge & Kegan Paul.

Parkin, Robert. 2005. The French-speaking Countries. In Fredrik Barth, Andre Gingrich, Robert Parkin and Sydel Silverman, *One Discipline, Four Ways: British, German, French, and American Anthropology*, pp. 157–255. Chicago: University of Chicago Press.

Parsons, Talcott. 1977. *The Evolution of Societies*. Englewood Cliffs, NJ: Prentice-Hall.

Pehrson, Robert N. 1964. *The Bilateral Networks of Social Relations in Könkämä Lapp District*. Oslo: Ethnographic Museum.

Pfaffenberger, Bryan. 1988. Fetishised Objects and Humanised Nature: Towards an Anthropology of Technology. *Man* (n.s.) **23**: 236–52.

Pinker, Steven. 1993. *The Language Instinct*. New York: Morrow.

Polanyi, Karl. 1957 [1944]. *The Great Transformation: The Political and Economic Origins of our Time*. Boston, MA: Beacon Press.

Popper, Karl. 1968 [1959]. *The Logic of Scientific Discovery*. New York: Harper & Row.

Porqueres i Gené, Enric. 2007. Kinship Language and the Dynamics of Race: The Basque Case. In Peter Wade, ed., *Race, Ethnicity and Nation: Perspectives from Kinship and Genetics*, pp. 125–44. Oxford: Berghahn.

Pratt, Mary Louise. 1986. Fieldwork in Common Places. In James Clifford and George E. Marcus, eds, *Writing Culture: The Poetics and Politics of Ethnography*, pp. 27–50. Berkeley: University of California Press.

Quigley, Declan. 1993. *The Interpretation of Caste*. Oxford: Clarendon.

Radcliffe-Brown, A.R. 1951 [1929]. The Comparative Method in Social Anthropology. *Journal of the Royal Anthropological Institute* **81**: 15–22.

—— 1952. *Structure and Function in Primitive Society*. London: Cohen & West.

Rappaport, Roy A. 1968. *Pigs for the Ancestors: Ritual in the Ecology of a New Guinea People*. New Haven, CT: Yale University Press.

—— 1984. Epilogue, 1984. In Roy A. Rappaport: *Pigs for the Ancestors*, 2nd edn. New Haven, CT: Yale University Press.

Redfield, Robert. 1955. *The Little Community: Viewpoints for the Study of a Human Whole*. Chicago: University of Chicago Press.

Reining, Conrad C. 1966. *The Zande Scheme: An Anthropological Case Study of Economic Development in Africa*. Evanston, IL: Northwestern University Press.

Renteln, Alison Dundes. 1990. *International Human Rights*. London: SAGE.

Richards, Audrey. 1956. *Chisungu: A Girls' Initiation Ceremony among the Bemba of Northern Rhodesia*. London: Faber & Faber.

Riegelhaupt, Joyce. 1967. Saloio Women: An Analysis of Informal and Formal Political and Economic Roles of Portuguese Peasant Women. *Anthropological Quarterly* **40**: 109–36.

Riesman, Paul, 1998. *Freedom in Fulani Social Life: An Introspective Ethnography*. Chicago: University of Chicago Press.

Rivers, W.H.R. 1924. *Social Organization*. London: Kegan Paul.

Robbins, Joel. 2004. On the Critique in Cargo and the Cargo in Critique. In Holger Jebens, ed., *Cargo, Cult, and Culture Critique*, pp. 243–60. Honolulu: University of Hawai'i Press.

Robin, Ron (2004) *Scandals and Scoundrels: Seven Cases that Shook the Academy*. Berkeley: University of California Press.

Robinson, Victoria. 2008. *Everyday Masculinities and Extreme Sport: Male Identity and Rock Climbing*. Oxford: Berg.

Rodman, Margaret C. 1992. Empowering Place: Multilocality and Multivocality. *American Anthropologist* **94**: 640–56.

Roosens, Eugeen E. 1989. *Creating Ethnicity: The Process of Ethnogenesis*. London: SAGE.

Rorty, Richard. 1991. *Contingency, Irony and Solidarity*. Cambridge: Cambridge University Press.

Rosaldo, Michelle Z. 1974. Woman, Culture and Society: A Theoretical Overview. In Michelle Z. Rosaldo and Louise Lamphere, eds, *Woman, Culture and Society*, pp. 17–43. Stanford, CA: Stanford University Press.

—— 1980. *Knowledge and Passion: Ilongot Notions of Self and Social Life*. Cambridge: Cambridge University Press.

—— 1984. Toward an Anthropology of Self and Feeling. In Richard Shweder and Robert A. LeVine, eds, *Culture Theory*, pp. 137–54. Cambridge: Cambridge University Press.

—— and Louise Lamphere, eds. 1974. *Woman, Culture and Society*. Stanford, CA: Stanford University Press.

Rose, Hilary and Steven Rose, eds. 2001. *Alas Poor Darwin: Arguments against Evolutionary Psychology*. London: Jonathan Cape.

Rostow, Walt W. 1965. *The Stages of Economic Growth: A Non-Communist Manifesto*. Cambridge: Cambridge University Press.

Rushdie, Salman. 1988. *The Satanic Verses*. London: Viking.

Sahlins, Marshall D. 1963. Poor Man, Rich Man, Big Man, Chief: Political Types in Melanesia and Polynesia. *Comparative Studies in Society and History* **5**: 285–303.

—— 1968. *Tribesmen*. New York: Prentice-Hall.

—— 1972. *Stone Age Economics*. Chicago: Aldine.

—— 1976. *Culture and Practical Reason*. Chicago: Aldine.

—— 1977. *The Use and Abuse of Biology*. Chicago: University of Chicago Press.

—— 1985. *Islands of History*. Chicago: University of Chicago Press.

—— 1994. Goodbye to Tristes Tropes: Ethnography in the Context of Modern World History. In Robert Borofsky, ed., *Assessing Cultural Anthropology*, pp. 377–94. New York: McGraw-Hill.

—— 1995. *How 'Natives' Think: About Captain Cook, For Example*. Chicago: University of Chicago Press.

—— 2000. Jungle Fever. *Washington Post Book World* 10 December.

Said, Edward. 1978. *Orientalism*. New York: Pantheon.

Salemink, Oscar. 1991. *Mois* and *Maquis*: The Invention and Appropriation of Vietnam's Montagnards from Sabatier to the CIA. In George W. Stocking, ed., *Colonial Situations: Essays on the Contextualization of Ethnographic Knowledge*, pp. 243–84. Madison: University of Wisconsin Press.

—— 2002. *The Ethnography of Vietnam's Central Highlanders: A Historical Contextualization 1850–1990*. London: Routledge.

—— 2010. Ritual Efficacy, Spiritual Security and Human Security: Spirit Mediumship in Contemporary Vietnam. In Thomas Hylland Eriksen, Ellen Bal and Oscar Salemink, eds, *A World of Insecurity: Anthropological Perspectives on Human Security*. London: Pluto.

Salman, Ton. 2010. Taking Risks for Security's Sake: Bolivians Resisting Their State and Its Economic Policies. In Thomas Hylland Eriksen, Ellen Bal and Oscar Salemink, eds, *A World of Insecurity: Anthropological Perspectives on Human Security*. London: Pluto.

Salmond, Anne. 1982. Theoretical Landscapes: On a Cross-cultural Conception of Knowledge. In David Parkin, ed., *SemanticAnthropology*, pp. 65–87. London: Academic Press.

Sand, Christophe. 2002. Melanesian Tribes vs. Polynesian Chiefdoms: Recent Archaeological Assessment of a Classical Model of Sociopolitical Types in Oceania. *Asian Perspectives* **41**(2): 284–96.

Sartre, Jean-Paul. 1957 [1943]. *Being and Nothingness: An Essay on Phenomenological Ontology*. London: Methuen.

—— 1960. *Critique de la raison dialectique*. Paris: Gallimard.

Saussure, Ferdinand de. 1965 [1916]. *Course in General Linguistics*. New York: McGraw-Hill.

Schechner, Richard. 1994. Ritual and Performance. In Tim Ingold, ed., *Companion Encyclopedia of Anthropology: Humanity, Culture and Social Life*, pp. 613–47. London: Routledge.

—— 2002. *Performance Studies: An Introduction*. London: Routledge.

Scheper-Hughes, Nancy. 2004. Parts Unknown: Undercover Ethnography of the Organs-trafficking Underworld. *Ethnography* **5**: 29–73.

—— and Philippe Bourgois, eds. 2003. *Violence in War and Peace: An Anthology*. Oxford: Blackwell.

—— and Margaret Lock (1987) The Mindful Body: A Prolegomenon to Future Work in Medical Anthropology. *Medical Anthropology Quarterly* **1**: 6–41.

Schlee, Günther. 2008. *How Enemies are Made: Towards a Theory of Ethnic and Religious Conflicts*. Oxford: Berghahn.

Schlegel, Alice. 1977. Male and Female in Hopi Thought and Action. In Alice Schlegel, ed., *Sexual Stratification*, pp. 186–210. New York: Columbia University Press.

Schneider, David M. 1984. *A Critique of the Study of Kinship*. Ann Arbor: University of Michigan Press.

Scott, James C. 1985. *Weapons of the Weak: Everyday Forms of Peasant Resistance*. New Haven, CT: Yale University Press.

—— 1999. *Seeing Like a State: How Certain Schemes to Improve the Human Condition have Failed*. New Haven, CT: Yale University Press.

Shandy, Dianna J. 2007. *Nuer-American Passages: Globalizing Sudanese Migration*. Gainesville: Florida University Press.

Sharp, John. 1980. Two Separate Developments: Anthropology in South Africa. *RAINews* **36**: 4–6.

Shore, Cris. 1993. Ethnicity as Revolutionary Strategy: Communist Identity Construction in Italy. In Sharon Macdonald, ed., *Inside European Identities*, pp. 27–53. Oxford: Berg.

—— and Stephen Nugent, eds. 2002. *Elite Cultures: Anthropological Perspectives*. London: Routledge.

Sigaut, François. 1994. Technology. In Tim Ingold, ed., *Companion Encyclopedia of Anthropology: Humanity, Culture and Social Life*, pp. 420–59. London: Routledge.

Singer, Merrill and Hans A. Baer. 2007. *Introducing Medical Anthropology: A Discipline in Action*. Boston, MA: Rowman & Littlefield.

Sjöberg, Katarina. 1993. *The Return of the Ainu: Cultural Mobilization and the Practice of Ethnicity in Japan*. London: Harwood.

Skálnik, Peter. 1992. Etat. In Pierre Bonté and Michel Izard, eds, *Dictionnaire de l'ethnologie et de l'anthropologie*, pp. 239–42. Paris: Presses Universitaires de France.

Smith, Anthony D. 1986. *The Ethnic Origins of Nations*. Oxford: Blackwell.

—— 1991. *National Identity*. Harmondsworth: Penguin.

—— 1999. *Myths and Memories of the Nation*. Oxford: Oxford University Press.

—— 2008. *The Cultural Foundations of Nations: Hierarchy, Covenant and Republic*. Oxford: Blackwell.

Smith, Raymond T. 1956. *The Negro Family of British Guiana*. London: Routledge & Kegan Paul.

Sokolovsky, Jay. 2004. Aging. In Carol A. Ember and Melvyn Ember, eds. *Encyclopedia of Medical Anthropology*, vol. 1, pp. 217–23. New York: Kluwer.

Southall, Aidan. 1976. Nuer and Dinka are People: Economy, Ecology and Logical Possibility. *Man* **11**(4): 463–91.

Spencer, Jonathan. 1989. Anthropology as a Kind of Writing. *Man* **24**(2): 145–64.

Sperber, Dan. 1989. L'Etude anthropologique des réprésentations: problèmes et perspectives. In Denise Jodelet, ed., *Les Représentations sociales*, pp. 115–30. Paris: Presses Universitaires de France.

—— 1996. *Explaining Culture: A Naturalistic Approach*. Oxford: Blackwell.

Spiro, Melford E. 1986. Cultural Relativism and the Future of Anthropology. *Cultural Anthropology* **1**(3): 259–86.

Srinivas, M.N. 1952. *Religion and Society among the Coorgs of South India*. Oxford: Clarendon.

Stenning, Derrick J. 1962. Household Viability among the Pastoral Fulani. In Jack Goody, ed., *The Developmental Cycle of Domestic Groups*, pp. 92–119. Cambridge: Cambridge University Press.

Steward, Julian. 1955. *The Theory of Culture Change: The Methodology of Multilinear Evolution*. Urbana: University of Illinois Press.

Stewart, Charles, ed. 2007. *Creolization: History, Ethnography, Theory*. Walnut Creek, CA: Left Coast Press.

Stoller, Paul. 1989. *The Taste of Ethnographic Things: The Senses in Anthropology*. Philadelphia: University of Pennsylvania Press.

—— 1997. *Sensuous Scholarship*. Philadelphia: Pennsylvania University Press.

Stone, Linda S. 2009. *Kinship and Gender: An Introduction*, 4th edn. Boulder, CO: Westview Press.

Strathern, Andrew and Pamela J. Stewart. 2005. Ceremonial Exchange. In James Carrier, ed., *A Handbook of Economic Anthropology*, pp. 230–45. Cheltenham: Edward Elgar.

Strathern, Marilyn. 1988. *The Gender of the Gift: Problems with Women and Problems with Society in Melanesia*. Berkeley: University of California Press.

—— 1992. *After Nature: English Kinship in the Late Twentieth Century*. Cambridge: Cambridge University Press.

Street, Brian W. and Niko Besnier. 1994. Aspects of Literacy. In Tim Ingold, ed., *Companion Encyclopedia of Anthropology: Humanity, Culture and Social Life*, pp. 503–26. London: Routledge.

Sussman, Linda K. 1983. *Medical Pluralism on Mauritius: A Study of Medical Beliefs and Practices in a Polyethnic Society*. Ann Arbor, MI: University Microfilms.

Talle, Aud. 1988. *Women at a Loss: Changes in Maasai Pastoralism and their Effects on Gender Relations*. Stockholm: Stockholm Studies in Social Anthropology **19**.

Tambiah, Stanley J. 1989. The Politics of Ethnicity. *American Ethnologist* **16**(2): 335–49.

Taussig, Michael. 1984. Culture of Terror – Space of Death. Roger Casement's Putamayo Report and the Explanation of Torture. *Comparative Studies in Society and History* **26**(3): 467–97.

Taylor, Charles. 1992. *Multiculturalism and the Politics of Recognition*, ed. Amy Gutmann. Princeton, NJ: Princeton University Press.

Tempels, Placide. 1959. *Bantu Philosophy*. Paris: Présence Africaine.

Thin, Neil. 2005. Happiness and the Sad Topics of Anthropology. WED Working Paper **10**. Bath: Wellbeing in Developing Countries ESRC Research Group.

—— 2008. Why Anthropology Can Ill Afford to Ignore Well-being. In Gordon Mathews and Carolina Izquierdo, eds. 2008. *Pursuits of Happiness: Well-being in Anthropological Perspective*, pp. 23–44. Oxford: Berghahn.

Tierney, Patrick. 2000. *Darkness in El Dorado: How Scientists and Journalists Devastated the Amazon*. New York: Norton.

Tinker, Hugh. 1974. *A New System of Slavery: The Export of Indian Labour Overseas, 1830–1920*. Oxford: Oxford University Press.

Todd, Emmanuel. 1989. *The Explanation of Ideology: Family Structures and Social Systems*. Oxford: Blackwell.

Todorov, Tzvetan. 1989. *Nous et les autres: la réflexion française sur la diversité humaine*. Paris: Seuil.

Tonkin, Elizabeth, Maryon Mcdonald and Malcolm Chapman, eds. 1989. *History and Ethnicity*. London: Routledge.

Tönnies, Ferdinand. 1963 [1889]. *Community and Society*. New York: Harper & Row.

Tooby, John and Leda Cosmides. 1992. The Psychological Foundations of Culture. In Jerome Barkow, Leda Cosmides and John Tooby, eds, *The Adapted Mind: Evolutionary Psychology and the Generation of Culture*, pp. 19–136. Oxford: Oxford University Press.

Tronvoll, Kjetil. 2009. *War and the Politics of Identity in Ethiopia: The Making of Enemies and Allies in the Horn of Africa*. London: James Currey.

Tsing, Anna. 2004. *Friction: An Ethnography of Global Connection*. Princeton, NJ: Princeton University Press.

Turnbull, Colin. 1979 [1961]. *The Forest People*. London: Picador.

—— 1983. *The Mbuti Pygmies: Adaptation and Change*. New York: Holt, Rinehart & Winston.

—— 1985. *The Human Cycle*. New York: Simon & Schuster.

Turner, Terence. 1993. Anthropology and Multiculturalism: What is Anthropology that Multiculturalists Should be Mindful of it? *Cultural Anthropology* **8**(4):411–29.

Turner, Victor. 1967. *The Forest of Symbols: Aspects of Ndembu Ritual*. Ithaca, NY: Cornell University Press.

—— 1969. *The Ritual Process*. Chicago: Aldine.

—— 1974. *Dramas, Fields, and Metaphors*. Ithaca, NY: Cornell University Press.

Turton, David, ed. 1997. *War and Ethnicity: Global Connections and Local Violence*. Woodbridge, Suffolk: University of Rochester Press

Tylor, Edward B. 1968 [1871]. The Science of Culture. In Morton Fried, ed., *Readings in Anthropology*, vol. II: *Cultural Anthropology*. New York: Crowell.

Van den Berghe, Pierre. 1975. Ethnicity and Class in Highland Peru. In Leo Despres, ed., *Ethnicity and Resource Competition in Plural Societies*. The Hague: Mouton.

Van der Veer, Peter. 1994. *Religious Nationalism: Hindus and Muslims in India*. Berkeley: University of California Press.

Van Gennep, Arnold. 1909. *Les Rites de passage*. Paris: Emile Nourry.

—— 1960. *The Rites of Passage*, trans. Monika B. Vizedom and Gabrielle L. Caffee, Introduction by Solon T. Kimball. London: Routledge.

Veblen, Thorstein. 1953 [1899]. *The Theory of the Leisure Class: An Economic Study of Institutions*. New York: Mentor Books.

Vermeulen, Han F. 2008. Anthropology in the Netherlands: Past, Present, and Future. In Aleksandar Boskovic, ed., *Other People's Anthropologies*, pp. 44–70. Oxford: Berghahn.

—— and Arturo Alvarez Roldán, eds. 1995. *Fieldwork and Footnotes: Studies in the History of European Anthropology*. London: Routledge.

Vertovec, Steven. 1992. *Hindu Trinidad*. London: Macmillan.

—— 2009. *Transnationalism*. London: Routledge.

Wade, Peter. 1997. *Race and Ethnicity in Latin America*. London: Pluto.

—— ed. 2000. *The Right to Difference is a Fundamental Human Right*, 10th annual GDAT debate. Manchester: Group for Debates in Anthropological Theory.

—— 2002. *Race, Nature and Culture: An Anthropological Perspective*. London: Pluto.

—— ed. 2007. *Race, Ethnicity and Nation: Perspectives from Kinship and Genetics*. Oxford: Berghahn.

Wagner, Roy. 1981. *The Invention of Culture*. Chicago: University of Chicago Press.

Wallerstein, Immanuel. 1974–79. *The Modern World-System* (3 vols). New York: Academic Press.

Wallman, Sandra. 1986. Ethnicity and the Boundary Process in Context. In David Mason and John Rex, eds, *Theories of Race and Ethnic Relations*. London: Macmillan.

Watson, C.W., ed. 1999. *Being There: Fieldwork in Anthropology*. London: Pluto.

Weber, Max. 1978 [1919] *Economy and Society: An Outline of Interpretive Sociology*, ed. Günther Roth and Claus Wittich. Berkeley: University of California Press.

Weiner, Annette B. 1988. *The Trobrianders of Papua New Guinea*. New York: Holt, Rinehart & Winston.

—— 1992. *Inalienable Possessions. The Paradox of Keeping-while-giving*. Berkeley: University of California Press.

Welsh, Robert L. 1983. Traditional Medicine and Western Medical Options among the Ningerum of Papua New Guinea. In Lola Romanucci-Ross, Daniel E. Moerman and Laurence R. Tancredi, eds, *The Anthropology of Medicine*, pp. 32–51. New York: Praeger.

White, Leslie. 1949. *The Science of Culture: A Study of Man and Civilization*. New York: Grove Press.

Whitehouse, Harvey. 2005. The Cognitive Foundations of Religiosity. In Harvey Whitehouse and Robert N. McCauley, eds, *Mind and Religion: Psychological and Cognitive Foundations of Religiosity*, pp. 207–232. Walnut Creek, CA: AltaMira Press.

—— ed. 2001. *The Debated Mind: Evolutionary Psychology versus Ethnography*. Oxford: Berg.

—— and Robert N. McCauley, eds. 2005. *Mind and Religion: Psychological and Cognitive Foundations of Religiosity*. Walnut Creek, CA: AltaMira Press.

Whorf, Benjamin Lee. 1956. *Language, Thought, and Reality*. New York: Wiley.

Wikan, Unni. 1992. *Managing Turbulent Hearts*. Chicago: University of Chicago Press.

Wilhite, Harold. 2008. *Consumption and the Transformation of Everyday Life: A View from South India*. Houndmills: Palgrave Macmillan.

Williams, Raymond. 1981. *Keywords*. London: Flamingo.

Wilson, Bryan, ed. 1970. *Rationality*. Oxford: Blackwell.

Wilson, Edward O. 1975. *Sociobiology: The New Synthesis*. Cambridge, MA: Harvard University Press.

—— 1978. *On Human Nature*. Cambridge, MA: Harvard University Press.

—— 1998. *Consilience: The Unity of Knowledge*. New York: Knopf.

Wilson, Godfrey. 1941–42. *An Essay on the Economics of Detribalization in Northern Rhodesia, Parts I–II*. Livingstone: Rhodes-Livingstone Institute.

Wilson, Peter J. 1978. *Crab Antics*, 2nd edn. New Haven, CT: Yale University Press.

Wilson, Richard Ashby. 1991. Machine Guns and Mountain Spirits: The Cultural Effects of State Repression among the Q'eqchi' of Guatemala. *Critique of Anthropology* **11**(1): 33–61.

—— ed. 1997. *Human Rights, Culture and Context*. London: Pluto.

—— 2001. *The Politics of Truth and Reconciliation in South Africa: Legitimizing the Post-Apartheid State*. Cambridge: Cambridge University Press.

Winch, Peter. 1970 [1964]. Understanding a Primitive Society. In Bryan Wilson, ed., *Rationality*, pp. 1–18. Oxford: Blackwell.

Wittfogel, Karl. 1959. *Oriental Despotism: A Comparative Study of Total Power*. New Haven, CT: Yale University Press.

Wittgenstein, Ludwig. 1983 [1958]. *Philosophical Investigations*, trans. G.E.M. Anscombe. Oxford: Blackwell.

Wolf, Eric. 1964. *Anthropology*. Englewood Cliffs, NJ: Prentice-Hall.

—— 1966. *Peasants*. Englewood Cliffs, NJ: Prentice-Hall.

—— 1969 [1956]. The Hacienda System and Agricultural Classes in San José, Puerto Rico. In André Béteille, ed., *Inequality*, pp. 172–92. Harmondsworth: Penguin.

—— 1982. *Europe and the People without History*. Berkeley: University of California Press.

—— 1999. *Envisioning Power: Ideologies of Dominance and Crisis*. Berkeley: University of California Press.

Woodburn, James. 1982. Social Dimensions of Death in Four African Hunting and Gathering Societies. In Maurice Bloch and Jonathan Parry, eds, *Death and the Regeneration of Life*, pp. 187–210. Cambridge: Cambridge University Press.

Worsley, Peter. 1968. *The Trumpet Shall Sound*, 2nd edn. New York: Schocken.

—— 1984. *The Three Worlds: Culture and World Development*. London: Weidenfeld & Nicolson.

—— 1990. Models of the Modern World-system. In Mike Featherstone, ed., *Global Culture. Nationalism, Globalization and Modernity*, pp. 83–96. London: SAGE.

—— 1997. *Knowledges: What Different Peoples Make of the World*. London: Profile.

Wulff, Helena. 1998. *Ballet across Borders: Career and Culture in the World of Dancers*. Oxford: Berg.

Yamashita, Shinji. 2003. *Bali and Beyond: Explorations in the Anthropology of Tourism*, trans. J.S. Eade. Oxford: Berghahn.

INDEX

Compiled by Sue Carlton